Library of
Davidson College

Employment, Income, and Welfare in the Rural South

Brian Rungeling
Lewis H. Smith
Vernon M. Briggs, Jr.
John F. Adams

The Praeger Special Studies program—utilizing the most modern and efficient book production techniques and a selective worldwide distribution network—makes available to the academic, government, and business communities significant, timely research in U.S. and international economic, social, and political development.

Employment, Income, and Welfare in the Rural South

PRAEGER SPECIAL STUDIES IN U.S. ECONOMIC, SOCIAL, AND POLITICAL ISSUES

Praeger Publishers New York London

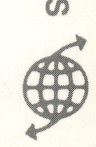

Library of Congress Cataloging in Publication Data

Main entry under title:

Employment, income, and welfare in the rural South.

(Praeger special studies in U.S. economic, social, and political issues)
Bibliography: p.
Includes index.
1. Rural poor—Southern States. 2. Economic assistance, Domestic—Southern States. 3. Discrimination in employment—Southern States. 4. Southern States—Rural conditions. I. Rungeling, Brian S.
HC107.A13E64   1977   301.44'1'0975   77-10612
ISBN 0-03-023041-1

This study was prepared for the Employment and Training Administration, U.S. Department of Labor, under Grant No. 51-13-72-10. Since grantees preparing research under government sponsorship are encouraged to express their own judgments freely, this study does not necessarily represent the Employment and Training Administration's official opinion or policy. Moreover, the authors are solely responsible for the factual accuracy of all material developed in the study.

Reproduction in whole or in part permitted for any purposes of the United States Government.

PRAEGER SPECIAL STUDIES
200 Park Avenue, New York, N.Y., 10017, U.S.A.

Published in the United States of America in 1977
by Praeger Publishers,
A Division of Holt, Rinehart and Winston, CBS, Inc.

789   038   987654321

© 1977 by Praeger Publishers

All rights reserved

Printed in the United States of America

PREFACE

The impetus for this book is found in the proposed welfare reform that seemed imminent in 1971. The impact of federal welfare reform on the people and the economy of the South would have been greater than in any other area of the nation and most dramatic in the rural South. With the contemplation of the impact of welfare reform on the institutions and the economy of the rural South, in particular on the labor market, came the realization that little is known and even less is documented by primary data about the structure, operation, and behavior of Southern rural labor markets.

Perhaps simpler in operation than complex urban labor markets, with larger populations and diversities of occupations, rural labor markets have been relatively understudied. Consequently, rural labor markets and their problems have tended to be "invisible" to the public at large. Specific problems of the rural population and labor force seldom receive or attract attention that is often a prerequisite for formulation of public policy.

As events were to unfold, the proposal to federalize the Aid for Families with Dependent Children as well as to broaden its coverage to include the working poor was not enacted, but this did not alter the basic need for information relating to the nature and operations of rural Southern labor markets. Most of the accumulated wisdom is based exclusively upon urban labor market studies or national studies that are heavily biased by urban results. The studies that have focused upon rural labor markets and related policy matters have usually dealt only with agricultural workers. To fill this perceived void, the project that led to this book was launched.

Funding for the initial research that preceded this book was provided by a grant from the Employment and Training Administration of the U.S. Department of Labor. Additional support was provided by the Center for Manpower Studies and the Computer Center of the University of Mississippi, as well as the Center for Insurance Research at Georgia State University.

We also wish to recognize the contribution of Roosevelt Steptoe and Maurice E. McDonald who were original members of the research consortium. Professor Steptoe was precluded from participation in many of the discussions and of the actual writing of the manuscript by appointment during the early stages of the project as President of the Baton Rouge campus of Southern University. Professor McDonald passed away suddenly before the analysis and preparation of the report began. The extensive computer programming assistance of James O. Smith, Jr., was of significant importance to the completion of the project.

To Barbara Badre, Rhonda Willemoes, and Maria Otto, the authors owe a special debt for their patient typing of the numerous drafts that preceded the final copy. The comments offered by Ellen Sehgal, Robert Fairweather, and Howard Rosen of the U.S. Department of Labor of the earlier research report are also acknowledged. The interpretations drawn, the views expressed, and the accuracy of the contents are, however, solely the responsibility of authors.

To all of the abovementioned persons and organizations, we express our most sincere and long-lasting gratitude.

CONTENTS

	Page
PREFACE	v
LIST OF TABLES	xii

Chapter

1 INTRODUCTION ... 1

    Definition of Study Area ... 2
    General Population Characteristics ... 3
    A Brief Historical Perspective ... 7
    Issues to be Examined ... 8
    Notes ... 10

2 STUDY DESIGN ... 11

    Selection of Counties ... 11
    Household Survey Design ... 12
        Sample Selection ... 12
        Sample Size ... 13
        Reference Period ... 13
        Nature of the Data ... 14
        Verification and Validation of Results ... 14
    Bias and Nonresponse ... 16
    Representativeness of the Sample ... 16
    County Business and Institutions Survey ... 18
    Comparability of the Household Sample with
        the Rural South ... 20
    Note ... 22

3 DEMAND IN RURAL SOUTHERN LABOR MARKETS ... 23

    Employment Trends and Industrial Structure ... 23
        Employment by Industry ... 25
        Potential for Increases in Labor Demand ... 27
    Occupational Labor Demand ... 29
    Nature and Aspects of Current Labor Demand ... 31

Chapter		Page
	Recruitment and Selection Procedures in Rural Labor Markets	37
	Sources of Skill Training	39
	Seasonal Labor Demand	39
	Absenteeism and Turnover	41
	Concluding Observations	42
	Notes	42
4	LABOR SUPPLY: CHARACTERISTICS AND DETERMINANTS	44
	Human Capital Endowment	46
	Labor Force Participation in Rural Labor Markets	48
	The Labor Force Status Model	51
	Demographic Characteristics of Job Seekers in Rural Labor Markets	58
	Job-Search Methods	62
	Search Method Most Used	64
	Search Method by Which Job Obtained	66
	Job-Search Effectiveness	69
	Two Measures of Effectiveness	70
	A New Measure of Effectiveness	71
	Occupational Structure and Status	76
	Occupational Variation by Worker Characteristics	76
	Occupational Movements	80
	Occupational Status	80
	Geographic Mobility	84
	Concluding Observations	87
	Notes	89
5	INCOME AND EARNINGS	92
	Distribution of Current Income	92
	Sources of Income	95
	County Distributions of Sources	96
	Sources of Earned Income	98
	Determinants of Earnings	104
	Wages in the Rural South	104
	Time Worked in Rural Labor Markets	115
	Income from Other than Current Earnings	127
	Private Sources	128
	Government Transfers	128

Chapter		Page
	Discrimination in Southern Rural Labor Markets	130
	Wage Discrimination: Race	131
	Occupational Discrimination	133
	Wage Discrimination: Sex	133
	Observations on Discrimination	135
	Health Problems and Income	135
	Subemployment in Rural Areas	141
	Concluding Observations	144
	Notes	146
6	POVERTY	150
	Definition of Poverty	150
	Incidence of Poverty	151
	Characteristics of Poverty	152
	Economic Characteristics of the Poor	154
	Household Size of the Poor	158
	Related Dimensions of Poverty	158
	The Working Poor	161
	The Near Poor	162
	Special Case of the Elderly	164
	Correlates of Poverty	164
	Notes	168
7	THE WELFARE SYSTEM IN THE RURAL SOUTH	171
	The Categorical Programs	172
	Personal Characteristics of Recipients	174
	Economic Characteristics of Recipients	178
	Assessment of the Existing Categorical Welfare	181
	Food-Stamp Program in the Rural South	184
	Characteristics of Food-Stamp Participants	187
	Changes in Food-Stamp Participation	190
	Eligible Nonparticipants	191
	Causes of Nonparticipation	193
	Food Stamps and the Elderly	197
	Perceptions of the Welfare System in the Rural South	199
	Concluding Observations	202
	Notes	204
8	MANPOWER DEVELOPMENT AND TRAINING	207

Chapter		Page
	Training-Program Participation	209
	Effects of Training on Participants	216
	Relevance of Training	216
	Wage Rates and Training	219
	Job Tenure	220
	Attitudes toward Training Programs	221
	Limitations of Past Federal Manpower Training Efforts	223
	Potential for Manpower Programs in Rural Areas	226
	Potential for Improvement under CETA in Rural Areas	229
	Concluding Observations	231
	Notes	232
9	ECONOMIC DEVELOPMENT	234
	Measures of Economic Development	234
	Industrial Measures	235
	Human-Resource Measures	235
	The Economic Development Process	242
	Impediments to Economic Development	243
	Efforts to Attract Industry	244
	Federal Legislative Efforts to Encourage Regional Economic Development	247
	The Rural South: Potential for Development	251
	Notes	256
10	SPECIAL ISSUES	259
	Chicanos: Migrants and Nonmigrants	259
	The Rural Labor Market of South Texas	260
	Proximity of Mexican Border	270
	Migrant Farm Workers	273
	Water and Land-Ownership Restrictions	274
	The Dilemma of Public Policy in South Texas	275
	Concluding Observations	280
	Agricultural Workers in the Rural South	281
	Characteristics of Agricultural Workers	282
	Opportunities for Unionization	286
	Prospects for Improvement	287
	Notes	288

Chapter		Page
11	WELFARE REFORM IN THE RURAL SOUTH: A SPECULATIVE VIEW	291
	Relevant Sections of H.R. 1	292
	Estimated Impact of H.R. 1 on the South	293
	Primary Impact in Sample Counties	297
	Employment and Income of Eligible Families	299
	Income Effect of Welfare Reform	301
	Impact on Entire Rural South	303
	Multiplier Effects	303
	Effects of Family Assistance on Work Incentives	304
	Welfare Reform and Food Stamps	305
	Concluding Observations	306
	Notes	306
12	CONCLUSIONS AND POLICY IMPLICATIONS	309
	Findings and Conclusions	311
	Inability to Obtain an Adequate Level of Income	311
	Poor Health and Educational Deficiencies	318
	The Need for Welfare Reform	321
	Discrimination by Race and Sex	324
	Policy and Program Needs in the Rural South	325
	Current Program Priorities for Rural Areas	328
BIBLIOGRAPHY		333
ABOUT THE AUTHORS		356

LIST OF TABLES

Table		Page
1.1	United States and Southern Region, Various Population Components, 1970	4
1.2	Selected Employment and Income Data, Rural South, South, and United States, 1970	5
1.3	Occupational Data for All over Age 16, Rural South, South, and United States, 1970	6
2.1	Number of Households, Estimated Sample Size Needed for Each County to Achieve 800 Completed Interviews, and Number of Interviews Completed and Used	13
2.2	Number of Completed Interviews and Number and Percentage Verified, Field Contact and Mail, 1974	15
2.3	Number of Completed Interviews and Number and Percentage Validated, 1974	15
2.4	Distribution of Population, Labor Force, Employment and Unemployment, Sex and Race, Four Sample Counties, 1970, and the Survey Sample, 1974	17
2.5	Total Population, by Age and Education Level, Four Sample Counties, 1970, and the Sample, 1974	19
2.6	Total and Rural Population, Selected Characteristics, South and Rural South, 1970, and the Sample, 1974	21
3.1	County Employment Data, Total and Four Counties, 1950 and 1970	24
3.2	Selected Rural Employment Data, 1950 and 1970	24
3.3	Industry of People Employed: 1970 Percentage Distribution of Total Employed, Selected Areas	26

Table		Page
3.4	Industry of People Employed: Percentage Change of Total Employed, 1950-70, Selected Areas	28
3.5	Total Employment, by Major Occupational Groups, Selected Areas, 1970	30
3.6	Total Employment, by Major Occupational Groups, Selected Areas—Percentage Change, 1950-70	32
3.7	Number of Firms, by County and by Employment Size, 1973	34
3.8	Industrial Indexes for Rural Study Counties	35
3.9	Employee-Recruitment Methods Used by Employers	38
3.10	Sources of Employee Training, as Cited by Employers	40
3.11	Specific Training Methods Cited by Employers	40
4.1	Characteristics of the Potential Labor-Force-Age Population and the Actual Labor Force in the Four Counties	45
4.2	Characteristics of the Population of Labor Force Age, by Race, for Survey Counties	46
4.3	Labor Force Participation Rates of Survey Respondents 16 Years of Age and Older, by Race	49
4.4	Labor Force Status and Labor Force Participation Rates, by Race and Sex, Rural versus National Population, 1973	50
4.5	Regression Coefficients for the EWAGE Equation	54
4.6	Regression Results: Labor Force Status Equations	55
4.7	Sex of Job Seekers	59
4.8	Race of Job Seekers	59

Table		Page
4.9	Age Distribution of Job Seekers	60
4.10	Industry of Head-of-Household Job Seekers	61
4.11	Occupational Preference of Head-of-Household Job Seekers	62
4.12	Comparison of Job-Search Methods Used by Job Seekers	63
4.13	Search Methods Used by Household Heads	64
4.14	Search Methods Most Used	65
4.15	Search Methods Most Used, by Race and Sex	65
4.16	Comparisons of Methods of Search by Which Job Was Found: Percent of Sample Using Each Method	67
4.17	Search Method by Which Job Was Obtained, by County	68
4.18	Search Method by Which Job Was Obtained, by Sex	69
4.19	Search Method by Which Job Was Obtained, by Race	70
4.20	Effectiveness of Job-Search Methods: Method I	72
4.21	Effectiveness of Job-Search Methods: Method II	72
4.22	Job-Search-Effectiveness Equations	75
4.23	Occupational Distribution of Employed Household Heads, by Race, 1974	77
4.24	Occupational Distribution of Employed Household Heads, by Sex and Race, 1974	78
4.25	Occupational Distribution of Employed Household Heads, by Age, 1974	79

Table		Page
4.26	Occupational Distribution of Employed Household Heads for First Job Held, by Race, as Reported in 1974	81
4.27	Current Occupational Status of Employed Household Heads, by Race	82
4.28	Current Occupational Status of Employed Household Heads, by Sex	83
4.29	Upward Occupational Movement of Employed Household Heads as Percentage of Total in Occupation, by Race	83
4.30	Regression Results: Occupational Status of Household Heads	85
4.31	Willingness to Move of Household Heads in Rural Survey, by Race, Sex, and Age	86
5.1	Mean Incomes of Households, by Race, Sex, Age, and County, 1973	93
5.2	Total Income of Sample Households, by Race and Sex, 1973	94
5.3	Total Household Income, by Age, 1973	95
5.4	Source of Income of Households Receiving, by County, 1973	96
5.5	Source of Household Income, by Race, 1973	97
5.6	Earned Income as a Percentage of Total Income, by Income Category, 1973	100
5.7	Earnings of Household Head as a Percentage of Total Household Income, 1973	101
5.8	Mean Earnings of Household Heads, by Selected Characteristics, 1973	102
5.9	Wives' Earnings as a Percentage of Total Household Income, by County, 1973	103

Table		Page
5.10	Mean Wage Rate, by County, Race, and Sex	106
5.11	Mean Hourly Wage Rate, by Years of Education, by County	107
5.12	Regression Results: Relation between the Wage Rate of Employed Heads of Households in Rural Areas to Selected Individual Characteristics	111
5.13	Regression Results: Relation between the Wage Rate of Employed Individuals (16 Years and Over) in Rural Areas and Selected Individual Characteristics	114
5.14	Distribution of Hours Worked, by Sex and Race, Rural Household Heads, 1973	117
5.15	Hours Worked by Household Heads, by Occupation, 1973	118
5.16	Hours Worked by Household Heads, by Industry, 1973	119
5.17	Regression Coefficients for Hours-Worked Equation	122
5.18	Distribution of Weeks Worked within Occupations, Household Heads	125
5.19	Regression Coefficients for Weeks-Worked Equation	127
5.20	Households Receiving Private Income, by Race, 1973	128
5.21	Households Receiving Government-Transfers Income, by Race, 1973	129
5.22	Anglo-Black Estimates of Employment Probabilities	134
5.23	Household Heads under Age 65 with Health Problems, by Race and Sex, 1973	137
5.24	Work Activity by Household Heads, by Health Status, Race, and Sex, 1973	138

Table		Page
5.25	A Comparison of SI Components for the United States and the Rural Sample	144
6.1	Federal Poverty Income Guidelines, 1973	151
6.2	Personal Characteristics of Poverty Households Heads in the Survey Counties, 1974	152
6.3	Selected Characteristics of Poverty Household Heads in the Survey Counties, 1974	153
6.4	Distribution of Poverty Households by Income, by County, 1973	155
6.5	Distribution of Households by Sources of Income, by County, 1973	156
6.6	Sources of Income of the Poor and Nonpoor Households, by Race, 1973	157
6.7	Mean Household Income for the Poor, by Household Size, 1973	158
6.8	Total Income of the Poor, by Household Size, 1973	159
6.9	Characteristics of Working and Nonworking Poor, 1974	162
7.1	Participation in Categorical Welfare Programs in the Four Counties, 1973 and 1974	173
7.2	Recipients of AFDC, by Race, by County and Total, 1973	175
7.3	Recipients of OAA, by Race, by County and Total, 1973	175
7.4	Recipients of AB and APTD, by Race, by County and Total, 1973	176
7.5	Recipients of Categorical Welfare Assistance, by Sex and County, 1973	176

Table		Page
7.6	Average Age of Recipient Household Head of Categorical Welfare Assistance, by County, 1973	177
7.7	Mean Family Size of Recipients of Categorical Welfare Assistance, by County, 1973	177
7.8	Mean Values of Educational Attainment for Household-Head Recipients of Categorical Welfare Assistance, by Program and by County, 1973	178
7.9	Labor Force Status of Recipients of Categorical Welfare Assistance, by County, 1973	179
7.10	Occupational Employment History of Household Heads Who Are Recipients of AFDC Payments, All Counties Combined, 1973	180
7.11	Mean Dollar Value of Annual Benefits Received from Categorical Welfare Assistance Programs, by County, 1973	181
7.12	Mean Value of Total Income of All Families That Were Recipients of Welfare Assistance, by Category of Assistance, by County, 1973	182
7.13	Difference between Welfare Payments and Poverty Level for AFDC and OAA Recipients, Distribution by County, 1973	183
7.14	Receipt of Food Stamps by Recipients of Categorical Welfare Assistance, by County, 1973	185
7.15	Food-Stamp Purchase Schedule for Four-Person Household, February 1, 1974	186
7.16	Current Food-Stamp Recipients in Sample, Selected Characteristics, by County, Spring 1974	187
7.17	Household Size, Income, and Employment of Head for Food-Stamp Households in Sample, by County, Spring 1974	189

Table		Page
7.18	Number of Months Food Stamps Purchased During 1973, by County	191
7.19	Households Eligible for and Percent Receiving Food Stamps, by County and by Race	192
7.20	Eligible Nonparticipants Subsample, Selected Characteristics of Household Heads	194
7.21	Primary Reasons for Not Applying for Food Stamps, Spring 1974	195
7.22	Secondary Reasons for Nonparticipation in Food-Stamp Program	197
8.1	Participation in Training Programs, 1974	210
8.2	Type of Training Program Taken by All Adults	212
8.3	Adult Training-Program Participants and Nonparticipants, by Race, Sex, and County, 1974	213
8.4	Regression Analyses for Adult Participation in Any Training Program, and Any Program Exclusive of Military and "Other"	214
8.5	Frequency of Participation and Completion Rates, by Types of Training Programs, 1974	217
8.6	Regression Analysis of "Ever Used" Training in Any Job for Those Who Completed Their Training Programs	218
8.7	Wage Rates of Participants and Nonparticipants among Employed Heads of Households, 1974	219
8.8	Regression Equation for Wage Rates of All Persons 16 Years and Older, Military and "Other" Trainees Excluded	220
8.9	Job Tenure for Heads of Households Classified by Participation of Nonparticipation in Training Programs, as Reported in 1974	222

Table		Page
8.10	Characteristics of Potential CETA Title I Participants, Household Heads, Ages 16 to 65, 1975	228
9.1	Value Added by Manufacture and Number of Establishments Employing More than 20 Employees, Selected Areas, 1972	236
9.2	Industrial Index for the Study Counties, 1973	236
9.3	Employment in Agricultural and Manufacturing Industries, by County and the United States, 1970	237
9.4	Real per Capita Income, by County and Nonmetropolitan United States: 1950, 1959, 1969, 1972	238
9.5	Median Household Income, by County and for Nonmetropolitan Areas of the United States, 1973	239
9.6	Households with Total Income Less Than $3000, by County and Nonmetropolitan Areas of the United States, 1973	239
9.7	Labor Force Participation Rates, by Age for Survey Respondents and the United States, 1973	240
9.8	Percentage Distribution of the Adult Population, by Years of School Completed of Survey Respondents and Persons in the United States, 1973	241
10.1	Age Distribution of Household Heads, by Major Segments, 1974	261
10.2	Employment Status of Starr County Labor Force, by Migrant and Nonmigrant Household Heads, 1974	262
10.3	Years of Residency in Starr County, by Major Labor Market Segments, 1973	263
10.4	Distribution of Hourly Wage Rates for Employed Migrant and Nonmigrant Workers in Starr County, 1974	264

Table		Page
10.5	Mean Incomes of Household Heads, by Counties and by Race, 1973	265
10.6	Income of Household Heads for Major Labor Market Segments in Starr County, 1974	266
10.7	Total Family Income, by Major Labor Market Segments for Starr County, 1974	267
10.8	Educational-Attainment Distribution of Household Heads, by Major Segments in Starr County, 1974	269
10.9	Agricultural Employment for Four Survey Counties, 1950 and 1970	282
10.10	Selected Characteristics of Agricultural and All Workers 16 Years of Age and Older	283
10.11	Selected Characteristics of Household Heads Employed During 1973, by Farm Work and No Farm Work	284
10.12	Household Income in 1973 for Farm and Nonfarm Workers	285
10.13	Weeks Worked in 1973 for Farm and Nonfarm Workers	286
11.1	Estimates of Coverage of H.R. 1 in the South, FY 1973	294
11.2	Estimates of Racial and Sex Characteristics of Family Heads in the South Eligible for Coverage under H.R. 1, FY 1973	295
11.3	Total Number of Families in the South, 1970	296
11.4	Potential Impact of H.R. 1 on Various Population Groups in the Four Sample Counties	298
11.5	1973 Income for Eligible Families, Selected Sources	299
11.6	Weeks Worked in 1973: Eligible Families, by Current Employment Status of Household Head	300

Table		Page
11.7	Mean Income of Eligible Families, by Selected Characteristics, 1973 Income and H.R. 1 Income	302
11.8	Total Number of Families and Total Number of Eligible Familes in the Rural South, 1973	303

Employment, Income, and Welfare in the Rural South

CHAPTER

1

INTRODUCTION

Since the end of World War II the United States has sustained unparalleled growth in its aggregate economic well-being. Yet despite these laudable quantitative accomplishments, the period has also witnessed a growing recognition that certain geographic regions and population subgroups have benefitted little from this period of general prosperity and material expansion. In any such comparative appraisal, the South in general and the rural South in particular are lagging regions. The population contains the largest number of impoverished and economically disadvantaged people of any geographic region of the nation. Despite the considerable economic progress that the South has sustained during the postwar era, the low base from which it started has kept it below the non-South as judged by most economic indicators.

More relevant for this study than South and non-South comparisons are the contrasts of the urban South and the rural South. The latter has remained a largely depressed region while much of the urban South has advanced markedly in economic terms. Vast portions of the South—for example, most of Appalachia and all of the Mississippi Delta, the Ozark Plateau, the South Texas border region, the Black Belt of the Old South, and the Atlantic Coastal Plains—are (with the possible exception of some isolated Indian reservations of the West) the most economically deprived areas of the nation. It is precisely these vast Southern land areas, of course, that encompass most of the rural South.

In 1970 the population of the South accounted for almost 30.9 percent of the nation's total population and, more importantly, 41.3 percent of the nation's rural population. Over half of the black and almost one-third of the Chicano population of the nation resided in the region. By most indexes of human welfare, however, many

Southerners are not well off. Over 45 percent of the persons in the nation who lived below the federal poverty threshold in 1970 were in the South. In addition to pervasive low-income patterns, the Southern population is also characterized by high rates of dependency, ill health, malnutrition, and low educational attainment. In each category the highest proportions are to be found in the rural areas.

The economy of the rural South has traditionally been based on an industrial mix geared disproportionately toward either low wages (for example, agriculture, textile manufacturing, wood products, and personal services) or resource exports that are highly capitalized but low generators of local employment opportunities (that is, coal mining or oil and gas extraction). The labor force of the rural South is virtually nonunionized. Typically, local governments are either unable or unwilling to address issues pertaining to human needs. Accordingly, the secular decline of employment opportunities in the rural South has caused an exodus of persons to the urban areas of both the South and the non-South. Hence, the resolution of the economic problems of this region is of both regional and national consequence. It is to this goal that this work is addressed.

DEFINITION OF STUDY AREA

Before embarking upon the study it was necessary to set forth a statistical definition of both the South and the rural South. Traditionalists tend to define the South as the 11 states of the Confederacy. The Bureau of the Census, however, uses a different alignment of states in its reports. Because of the periodic use of Census data in the study, it was necessary to define the "Census South." It is the composite region of the Atlantic, East South Central, and West South Central statistical areas of the Census. This configuration, therefore, contains the 11 states of the Confederacy in addition to Delaware, Kentucky, Maryland, Oklahoma, West Virginia, and the District of Columbia.

The next step was to obtain a working definition for rural South. The decision was complicated by the fact that various government agencies define the term "rural" in different ways. The Bureau of the Census defines the rural population as those persons who live in "places" with fewer than 2500 persons. The U.S. Department of Labor, however, defines as rural counties those in which a majority of the people live in places with populations below 2500. Since the latter definition includes people living in places larger than 2500, if those places were in counties where a majority of the people lived in places with populations of less than 2500, the U.S. Department of Labor definition is more inclusive than is that of the Census Bureau.

INTRODUCTION

Other data were collected on metropolitan and nonmetropolitan bases, the difference being whether the county (or group of counties) contains one city (or group of cities) with 50,000 or more and is designated as a Standard Metropolitan Statistical Area (SMSA) by the federal government. "Rural" and "nonmetropolitan" are sometimes used interchangeably. This is an error because land areas classified as nonmetropolitan greatly exceed areas classified as rural by the U.S. Bureau of the Census.

The definition of rural that was used to select the counties that were intensively surveyed in this study is set forth in Chapter 2. The selected counties are compatible with the U.S. Department of Labor definition of rural. The Census definition was used to compile data on the overall rural South. Because of the use of the Census definition to delineate the rural South this work is compatible both with Census data and with other studies.

GENERAL POPULATION CHARACTERISTICS

In 1970 the Southern states of the United States had a total population of 62.8 million persons (30.9 percent of the U.S. population). As shown in Table 1.1, the South had 50.3 million whites (28.3 percent of the U.S. white total). At the same time 12.1 million of the Southern and 22.7 million of the U.S. populations were black, giving the South 53.2 percent of the total U.S. black population. For the United States 2.9 million, as compared with 0.4 million in the South, represent "other races," giving the South 14 percent of this group's total. Of the Spanish-surnamed population of 4.6 million persons in 1970, 1.6 million resided in the South (or 34.9 percent of the U.S. Spanish-surname total).*

With respect to location of residence of the population, 149.3 million (73.5 percent) of the U.S. total were classified as urban; 40.5 million (64.6 percent) of the South's population were so classified. At the same time, 53.9 million of the U.S. population and 22.3 million of the Southern population (26.5 percent and 35.4 percent, respectively) were classified as rural.

---

*The Spanish-surname data are collected for only one state (Texas), in which the Spanish-surname population is almost exclusively of Mexican ancestry. In Census publications, data on Chicanos are included in all figures labeled as being for "whites." In this study, the inclusion of one county that was predominantly Chicano gave rise to the need to separate the Chicano data from that of "whites." Hence, the term "Anglo" was used to categorize all white persons who did not have Spanish surnames.

TABLE 1.1

United States and Southern Region, Various
Population Components, 1970
(thousands)

	United States	Percent of Total U.S.	South	Percent of Total South	South as Percent of U.S.
Total population	203,212	100.0	62,795	100.0	30.9
White	177,656	87.4	50,327	80.1	28.3
Black	22,675	11.2	12,064	19.2	53.2
Other	2,822	1.4	403	0.6	14.0
Location					
Urban	143,323	73.5	40,538	64.6	27.1
Rural	53,889	26.5	22,257	35.4	41.3
Age distribution					
Under 5	57,915	28.5	18,148	28.9	31.3
15-64	125,179	61.6	38,619	61.5	30.9
65 and over	20,117	9.9	6,028	9.6	30.0

Source: Everett S. Lee, Martin R. L. Levin, William Pendleton, and Patricia D. Postma, Demographic Profiles of the United States, the South Atlantic States, Oak Ridge National Laboratory–U.S. Department of Housing and Urban Development Joint Publication 24, 5: 26-27.

Of the 22.3 million persons in the rural South, 80.5 percent are Anglos, 17.6 percent are black, and 1.9 percent are of Spanish surname. The rural South accounts for 35.4 percent of the South's total population; 38.2 percent of the South's Anglo population; 33.6 percent of its black population; and 10.8 percent of the Spanish-surname population.

Labor force participation rates are significantly lower in the rural South than in the South and the United States as a whole (see Table 1.2). This is, in part, a reflection of the small number of jobs available in rural areas.

The unemployment rate for the rural South is slightly higher than those for the South and for the nation as a whole. However, if anything, the urban bias of the sample data collection process and data definitions utilized in constructing unemployment statistics

INTRODUCTION

probably underestimate the actual number of people available for employment.

The occupational distribution of the working-age population for the rural South indicates that many residents of the area are found in the lower wage-paying occupations. For example, operatives and general laborers are overrepresented in the rural South relative to the rest of the South and the nation (see Table 1.3).

Income data for poverty families in Table 1.2 reveal that the rural South is the most poverty-stricken region of the nation. Almost one-quarter of the families living in the rural South are below the poverty level. The percentage of families below the poverty level in the rural South is twice the rate for the entire nation.

TABLE 1.2

Selected Employment and Income Data, Rural South, South and United States, 1970

	Rural South	South	United States
Adults (16 years and over)	15,016,523	43,320,525	144,087,220
Labor force			
Males	5,218,306	15,483,150	51,502,114
Labor force participation rate	71.2	74.9	76.6
Unemployment	3.5	3.3	3.9
Females	2,745,346	9,228,028	30,546,667
Labor force participation rate	35.7	40.7	41.4
Unemployment	5.6	5.0	5.2
Percent families below the poverty level	22.2	16.2	10.7
Percent families with income less than 125 percent of poverty level	29.5	22.1	15.0

Source: U.S. Department of Commerce, Bureau of the Census, United States Census of Population: 1970, General Social and Economic Characteristics, Final Report PC(1)-C1 United States Summary, Table 90, p. 390; Table 95, p. 400; Table 161, pp. 500-501; Table 182, pp. 543-48.

TABLE 1.3

Occupational Data for All over Age 16, Rural South, South and United States, 1970

Category	Number	Percent	Number	Percent	Number	Percent
Professional, technical and kindred	674,942	9.0	3,109,526	13.6	11,348,814	14.8
Managers and administrators	505,193	6.7	1,913,692	8.4	6,371,149	8.3
Sales workers	359,911	4.9	1,583,496	6.9	5,443,318	7.1
Clerical and kindred	841,154	11.2	3,744,119	16.4	13,745,144	18.0
Craftsmen	1,238,957	16.5	3,257,329	14.3	10,608,010	13.9
Operatives, except transportation	1,494,780	19.1	3,233,343	14.2	10,496,050	13.7
Transportation operatives	367,037	4.9	946,733	4.2	2,957,935	3.7
Laborers, except farm	467,210	6.2	1,165,928	5.1	3,426,546	4.5
Farmers and farm managers	395,672	5.3	433,431	1.9	1,426,044	1.9
Farm laborers and foremen	328,718	4.4	413,870	1.8	953,501	1.2
Service workers	671,647	8.9	2,424,122	10.6	8,624,993	11.3
Private household	176,650	2.3	571,888	2.5	1,152,095	1.5
Total	7,521,871	100.0	22,797,427	100.0	76,553,599	100.0

Source: U.S. Department of Commerce, Bureau of the Census, United States Census of Population: 1970, General Social and Economic Characteristics, Final Report PC(1)-C1 United States Summary, Table 91, p. 392; Table 165, pp. 506-11.

INTRODUCTION

A BRIEF HISTORICAL PERSPECTIVE

Underdevelopment has been the historic characteristic of the economy of the South. Some of the explanatory factors stem from a deficiency of certain essential physical resources, a shortage of money capital, a low level of technological development, and an absence of a class of innovators and entrepreneurs.[1]

The South has added to its own economic woes by fostering certain institutional practices that restrict development. A long tradition of segregation and discrimination as well as the evolving of powerful and conservative elite groups have impaired industrialization and the growth of per capita income in the South. W. W. Rostow claims that the South differs from the rest of the nation in that it was not "born free" but, rather, it has had a traditional society to overcome before industrialization could take place. Specifically, he observed: ". . . the long, slow disengagement of the South from its peculiar version of a traditional society belongs to the general (European) and not to the special (American) case."[2] As a result of these institutional factors, the South has long been the most poverty-stricken and economically backward part of the United States.

The advent of the Industrial Revolution in the mid-1700s in other parts of the world directed attention to this region that was to become "the South," for it was a source of food, fiber, and wood products. The establishment of a slave-based plantation system and the need for imports of industrial raw materials encouraged agricultural production. The legacy of this bygone era remains in the rural South to the present.

Abolition of slavery had little effect on the nature of production activities in the South. It soon became evident, however, that a large surplus of unskilled and uneducated cheap labor had been "released" for dependency on the market system. Agriculture became all important; cotton was to be "king." All this was made possible by an abundant supply of cheap labor.

The productivity of Southern agriculture, in spite of the good climate and the rich soils, has traditionally been low. Consequently the South lagged behind the Northeast in terms of per capita income.[3] In fact, beginning in 1840, per capita income started to decline in the South relative to the United States. It was not until around 1900 that this trend was reversed. Between 1900 and 1920 the prices paid for farm goods and the demand for timber products increased. This was, in part, the result of World War I. In addition, almost 5 percent of the South's population emigrated from the region during this period. Therefore, per capita income increased. Nevertheless, in the South in 1920 it was only 53 percent of that in the non-South.[4]

Beginning in the 1920s, technological change associated with agriculture as well as the destructive invasion of the boll weevil sharply curtailed the demand for labor in the rural South. Most of the displaced workers had few skills and little education. Released from the agricultural sector, many moved out, and a number of them left not only the rural South but the entire region. Thus, part of the South's problem became that of other regions of the nation. Often those who remained either were the least productive or had the least potential.

Since 1930 real per capita income in the South has increased at a faster rate than that of the nation as a whole.[5] This change in the South's development has resulted from the increased federal expenditures in the region as well as from the increased amounts of income and earnings generated by manufacturing, construction, and mining in the South.

Prompted by technological change and the evaporation of many agricultural jobs, the rural South has experienced a secular population decline. Despite high birth rates in rural areas, out-migration has increased to the point that, since World War II, absolute declines in rural county populations have become quite common.

The out-migration during the World War II era was encouraged by the "pull factors" of job opportunities in the war-production industries of the North and West. Many of those out-migrants were low-income black families. Nevertheless, those who left tended to be younger and to have higher skills than those who remained.

Between 1940 and 1960 agricultural employment in the South decreased by 60 percent. The trend has extended into the 1970s. At the same time manufacturing employment has been increasing. It has been estimated that nonfarm employment in the South between 1960 and 1970 grew at a rate of 21.6 percent, for a gain of over 415,900 jobs. Although this was largely offset by a decline of farm jobs, overall employment grew at a rate of 8.2 percent, for a net gain of almost 189,500 jobs.[6] It should be noted that, significantly, this employment expansion was not as rapid as the natural rate of population increase of 14.4 percent in the region.

ISSUES TO BE EXAMINED

The thrust of the present work is to analyze the economics of Southern rural labor markets. Answers to both general and specific propositions are sought. The applicability of prevailing analytic concepts as well as the viability of existing public policy to the rural economy are assessed. New proposals and the alteration of existing approaches are suggested.

INTRODUCTION

The overriding theme of this work is an inquiry about the factors that inhibit the adjustment of the labor market of the rural South to economic change. Attention is directed, however, toward a series of specific problems and issues. Among the topics and the questions that are examined are the following:

1. <u>Labor Market Operations</u>. To what degree is the legacy of past racial discrimination in the region still a factor in determining occupational outcomes? To what degree is sex discrimination a factor? How satisfactory are formal and informal labor market information systems? What factors contribute or inhibit occupational, industrial, and geographic mobility of labor? What is the structure of the market for full-time, part-time, and seasonal employment opportunities?

2. <u>Labor Force Characteristics</u>. What are the characteristics of the rural population with respect to health, training, housing, and education, and to what extent have decades of insufficient attention to these human needs handicapped present-day efforts to achieve economic well-being? Are there significant group variations by race, sex, and age that affect labor market experience? If so, of what policy consequences are these differences? How large is the pool of persons who could benefit from occupational training or retraining activities either within their local communities or, if they were to move, elsewhere? What is the level of training that currently exists in rural areas, and of what benefit has it been to participants?

3. <u>Labor Market Data and Concepts</u>. How adequate are contemporary labor market descriptors of rural labor conditions? What other factors, if any, should be considered? Do rural labor markets require different sets of performance criteria from urban areas?

4. <u>Labor Market Policy Issues</u>. How willing are rural workers to move to partake of training and/or job opportunities that exist elsewhere? How responsive and how capable are prevailing human resource delivery systems in rural areas? What are the respective roles of the private and public sectors in providing training? How adequate are supportive services—such as child care, health services, and job counseling—in rural areas? Should public programs in rural areas be funded by formulas different from those in urban areas? Is it in the national interest to perpetuate the past patterns of out-migration of rural workers to urban areas due to the lack of any meaningful alternatives in rural areas?

5. <u>Employment Policy Issues</u>. What are the prospects of stimulating the demand for labor through economic development efforts? What is the appropriate role, if any, of private versus public efforts to increase job opportunities in rural areas? If there is a public responsibility, what is the appropriate role of each of

the various layers of government? How supportive are local vested-interest groups likely to be of efforts to increase the level of employment and to alter the composition of present employment patterns? How important is the level and coverage of the federal minimum wage to rural workers? How significant is the exclusion of agricultural workers from major social legislation, such as the National Labor Standards Act, as a contributory factor to low-income patterns? What is the need for job creation in the way of public-service employment?

6. <u>Income Policy Issues</u>. Of what magnitude and of what consequence are present income supplement programs—such as Aid to Families with Dependent Children, Social Security, and Food Stamps—in the rural South? Are all eligible recipients for existing programs actually participating? If not, why not? What income needs are not presently being met either because of ineligibility under existing programs or because of inadequacy of present programs?

NOTES

1. See, for example, James G. Maddox et al., <u>The Advancing South</u> (New York: The Twentieth Century Fund, 1967); Ray Marshall, <u>Labor in the South</u> (Cambridge, Mass.: Harvard University Press, 1967).

2. W. W. Rostow, <u>The Stages of Economic Growth</u> (Cambridge: Cambridge University Press, 1960), p. 18.

3. Maddox, <u>The Advancing South</u>, p. 10.

4. Ibid., pp. 38-39.

5. Ibid., p. 41.

6. James L. Walker, <u>Economic Growth, Poverty and Race in the Nonmetropolitan South</u> (Austin: Center for Economic Development of The University of Texas at Austin, 1973), p. 10.

CHAPTER 2
STUDY DESIGN

Basic influences on labor market behavior come from experiences and attitudes of members of the economic decision-making unit. For analytical purposes, the household is normally treated as the basic unit with regard to economic decisions. Since most of these decisions, particularly with respect to labor-market behavior, concern the activities of the household head, a substantial portion of the analysis in this study is focused on the household head. Decisions concerning the activities of other household members are assumed to be conditional on those of the head.

Other factors important to the structure of this analysis include the social and political environment of the communities and other such forces that may influence personal and employer decisions. These provide the framework in which the household decision process takes place.

Two surveys were carried out to collect the necessary information for this work. One, an extensive survey of households, was designed to obtain economic, social, demographic, and behavioral information concerning the populations in the areas chosen for study. The second was a survey of county institutions designed to obtain specific information concerning business activities, as well as insights into the economic and social structure and organization of the community.

SELECTION OF COUNTIES

Economic and physical limitations imposed by study objectives made it necessary to select a well-defined universe that could be studied reasonably at the micro level. Therefore, the methodology chosen for this study led to the selection of four counties, each roughly representative of large segments of the rural South. The principal criteria used in the selection of the counties were as follows:

1. Each of the counties was to be rural, that is, nonmetropolitan, with evidence of an historical economic domination by agriculture, as well as a continued importance of agriculture.
2. Each of the counties was to have a substantial poverty population.
3. There was to be a diversity of racial groups.

Each of the counties selected varied in the degree to which it reflected these criteria, but each is sufficiently representative of the rural South to permit in-depth analysis. The following four counties were chosen:

1. <u>Dodge County</u>. Located in central Georgia, two-thirds of its population was Anglo and one-third was black; one-third of the combined population was below the poverty level in 1970.
2. <u>Natchitoches Parish</u>. Located in central Louisiana, about 37 percent of the population was black, and about 45 percent of the total population was below the poverty level in 1970.
3. <u>Starr County</u>. Located in South Texas (a border county), 98.5 percent of its population was Chicano and over half of the total population was below the poverty level in 1970.
4. <u>Sunflower County</u>. Located in the Delta area of Mississippi, over 60 percent of its population was black and about 46 percent of the total population was below the poverty level in 1970.

HOUSEHOLD SURVEY DESIGN

A list containing addresses or locations of all dwelling units in each of the four counties was updated from the 1970 Census records, using aerial photographs and local authorities, such as tax assessors, registrars and postal officials. The resulting list of households constitutes the sampling frame. An address was selected from the sampling frame, and all persons living at that address constituted the household. The sampling unit for this study was the household, rather than the family, because of the difficulty of segregating individual data for subunits.

Sample Selection

A simple random sample was drawn from the list of households in each of the counties by the use of random numbers. Numbers were

STUDY DESIGN

drawn without replacement until an appropriate size was obtained. After selection was completed, addresses were arranged by area and given to the interviewers.

Sample Size

A pilot survey using the proposed questionnaire was carried out in two rural counties in Georgia to estimate the nonresponse rate due to vacancies, respondent's being not at home on initial contact, and refusals to be interviewed. From this pilot survey, estimates of expected response rates were made to determine the sample size needed to achieve 800 or more completed interviews per county, and to produce reasonable statistical precision in results. The numbers selected for the original sample, the interviews completed, and the numbers of usable interviews obtained are shown in Table 2.1.

Reference Period

Although the interviews of households were conducted during the period from January 25 to April 30, 1974, the reference period for most of the survey data collected is the calendar year 1973. Certain data, however, such as "currently receiving welfare benefits," age,

TABLE 2.1

Number of Households, Estimated Sample Size Needed for Each County to Achieve 800 Completed Interviews, and Number of Interviews Completed and Used

County	Number of Households	Number of Households Selected	Number of Interviews Completed	Completion Rate	Number of Responses Used
Dodge County	4,767	1,366	894	65.4	878
Natchitoches Parish	10,072	1,235	851	68.9	838
Starr County	5,447	1,384	851	61.5	810
Sunflower County	10,396	1,230	826	67.2	831
Total	30,682	5,215	3,422	65.6	3,357

Source: Primary data generated by study.

present employment status, and wages "last week," relate to the actual time of the interview.

Nature of the Data

Information sought may be broadly classified into several types: demographic information; labor force information, both historical and current; economic information, including income and earnings and physical assets; welfare program information; and behavioral and attitudinal information. A special schedule was developed and added to the questionnaire for households in Starr County, Texas, to obtain particular information pertaining only to Chicanos. All data were classified and arranged to permit tabulation for heads of household and for all adult household members.

All data in the household survey were collected by personal interviews with the head of household. The interviewing procedure required two call-backs in each case, if necessary, to obtain an interview with the head of the household. Subsequently, as a cleanup measure, a third call-back was made in each case. A field edit of each questionnaire was completed, including isolation of inconsistencies or data gaps. If such problems were found, the questionnaire was returned to the field to obtain the missing or correct information before final editing and coding.

Verification and Validation of Results

Following the completion of the questionnaires, including the field edit and recontact of households, verification and validation procedures were instituted. Verification was a simple field and mail check to insure that the correct household was contacted and that the head of the household was interviewed. Validation included the verification procedure and reinterviews on selected questions. The numbers of questionnaires verified and validated are summarized in Tables 2.2 and 2.3.

Data tabulation revealed some differences between responses to questionnaires and those of the validation forms. This was noticeable particularly with regard to household income and acknowledged participation in welfare programs. Variations also were noted, though in fewer cases, in answers regarding employment of family members other than the household head, the family structure, and years of residence in home county.

Differences were expected in responses concerning income. However, some variations were significant enough to suggest question-

TABLE 2.2

Number of Completed Interviews and Number
and Percentage Verified, Field Contact and
Mail, 1974[a]

County	Completed Interviews	Field Verifications[b]		Mail Verifications[b]		Total Verifications	
		Number	Percent	Number	Percent	Number	Percent
Dodge	894	138	15.7	276	36.5	414	46.3
Natchitoches	851	99	11.6	224	30.1	323	38.0
Sunflower	851	162	19.0	259	37.6	421	49.5
Starr	826	88	10.7	214	29.4	302	36.6
Total	3422	487	14.2	973	33.2	1460	42.7

[a]The numbers of completed interviews reported differ from the final totals because of additional completions obtained during the cleanup and editorial processes and exclusions of certain questionnaires on the basis of data inconsistencies.

[b]Approximately 10 percent of the sample were verified by interview. In addition, a return postcard verification form was sent to all households interviewed.

TABLE 2.3

Number of Completed Interviews and Number
and Percentage Validated, 1974*

County	Completed Interviews	Number Validated	Percentage
Dodge	894	109	12.2
Natchitoches	844	51	6.0
Sunflower	851	47	5.5
Starr	826	45	5.4
Total	3415	252	7.4

*The numbers of completed interviews reported differ from the final total by virtue of additional completions obtained during the cleanup and editorial processes and the exclusion of certain questionnaires because of data inconsistencies.

able interviewing techniques. In some cases, errors were found and corrected. In others, the respondents simply refused to give the information. No error pattern was established for any interviewer, supporting the conclusion that interviewing techniques were acceptable.

On the basis of the verification procedures (involving 42.7 percent of all respondents) and the validation surveys (involving 7.4 percent of all respondents), it may be concluded that the surveys were conducted in accordance with specifications.

BIAS AND NONRESPONSE

The nonresponse rate for this study averaged 34.2 percent for the four counties, resulting primarily from refusals to participate and from failure to contact heads of households. Although this is a fairly high level of nonresponse in absolute terms, it is no more than has been commonly observed in other household surveys conducted during the 1970s. For example, a 1974 report of a conference on population surveys reports average response rates between 60 and 65 percent.[1]

The refusal rate in this survey is lower than expected when compared with the pretest. As expected, the refusing households were essentially middle- to upper-income households.* Except for this possible bias, it appears that those refusing did not differ significantly from those who responded.

REPRESENTATIVENESS OF THE SAMPLE

Although procedures used in this work have sought a minimum bias, it is impossible to state categorically that the sample is totally representative. A partial evaluation may be obtained by comparing summaries of demographic information for the four sample counties for 1970 with the household sample based on interviews conducted in 1974 (see Table 2.4).

It is immediately apparent that the components of the sample data (1974) generally parallel those for 1970 for the four counties. For example, it may be seen that the proportions of the total populations in the civilian labor force are about the same. The proportions

---

*Further contacts with the head of each refusing household were attempted in all cases; few additional interviews were obtained. A short form, based on interviewer observations, was completed for each household for use in comparing nonrespondents with participants.

TABLE 2.4

Distribution of Population, Labor Force, Employment
and Unemployment, Sex and Race, Four Sample
Counties, 1970, and the Survey Sample, 1974

	Total	Male	Female	Chicano	Black
Four counties					
Total population (16 years and over)	100.0	100.0	100.0	100.0	100.0
Labor force (as percent population)	49.6	57.3	35.6	40.3	42.0
Civilian labor force (as percent population)	43.0	53.6	35.5	40.2	41.9
Employed (as percent civilian labor force)	93.1	93.4	92.6	93.8	88.0
Private wage and salary	59.5	61.2	56.9	59.7	64.2
Government	24.0	19.4	30.7	25.7	20.0
Self-employed	9.1	12.4	4.2	8.2	3.6
Unpaid family workers	0.5	0.4	0.7	0.2	0.1
Unemployed	6.9	6.6	7.4	6.2	12.0
Not in labor force (as percent population)	50.2	39.0	60.3	59.7	58.0
Institutional inmates	2.6	4.7	0.8	0.0	4.2
Sample					
Total population (16 years and over)	100.0	100.0	100.0	100.0	100.0
Labor force (as percent population)	42.3	59.5	28.1	39.7	38.4
Civilian labor force (as percent population)	42.3	59.5	28.1	39.7	38.4
Employed (as percent civilian labor force)	94.9	94.1	96.4	95.2	88.9
Private wage and salary	*	*	*	*	*
Government	*	*	*	*	*
Self-employed	*	*	*	*	*
Unpaid family workers	*	*	*	*	*
Unemployed	5.1	5.9	3.5	4.8	11.1
Not in labor force (as percent population)	57.7	40.5	71.9	60.3	61.6
Institutional inmates	*	*	*	*	*

*Not available.

Source: U.S. Department of Commerce, Bureau of the Census, United States Census of Population: 1970, Characteristics of the Population, Pt. 20, Louisiana, Tables 121/126, pp. 20-328, 20-358; Pt. 45, Texas, Table 121, p. 45-968; Pt. 26, Mississippi, Tables 121/126, pp. 26-288, 26-323.

of the civilian labor force employed and unemployed are similar, although those for the sample are smaller than those for the counties in total. The proportion not in the labor force is larger for the sample than for the four counties, probably because of the over-representation of the older and minority populations in the incorporated areas, providing easier availability for interview during the day.

There are some differences in the relative sizes of subcomponents within the totals, such as the higher proportion of men and lower proportion of women in the sample labor force as compared with the same items for the four counties. Similarly, the proportion of women out of the labor force in the sample was higher than that for the similar group for the four counties. This difference probably results from lower proportions of the sample population in the prime labor force ages than those reported for the four counties, while the older-age categories (45 and older) were larger for the sample than for the four counties (see Table 2.5). This, too, resulted from this group's relative availability for interviewing, since the oldest category was mostly outside the labor force and therefore most likely to be at home during the day. The data also suggest that, except in the case of Chicanos, families with young children are slightly underrepresented in the sample population.

Education levels also differ. The education levels of blacks and Chicanos in the sample are below the average levels reported for the four counties and the total sample (see Table 2.5).

In general, the sample is representative of the four counties with the exceptions described above. Recognizing the time span between the compared reports, with consequent differences in the levels of economic activity, the variations are understandable.

COUNTY BUSINESS AND INSTITUTIONS SURVEY

Information from employers and government officials was obtained from an unstructured questionnaire administered in all four counties. The nature of some of the data made them difficult to quantify and evaluate. Much of the material can be described as impressionistic, and to a large extent it is used anecdotally.

Employers were categorized by numbers of employees and samples of each employer group selected for interview. The criteria used to select employers included: (1) all employers of 100 or more, (2) all employers of 35 or more who had entered the county since 1970, and (3) two employers for each major industrial group combinations of Standard Industrial Classification (SIC) major categories

TABLE 2.5

Total Population, by Age and Education Level, Four Sample Counties, 1970, and the Sample, 1974

(percent)

	Total Population		Black Population		Chicano Population[a]	
	Four Counties	Sample	Four Counties	Sample	Four Counties	Sample
Age						
0–14	36.9	33.0	37.6	29.4[b]	39.2[b]	39.2[b]
15–24	20.5	18.0	17.7	25.9[c]	16.7[c]	16.7[c]
25–44	23.9	18.4	20.6	17.2	19.0	19.0
45–64	10.5	18.5	15.2	14.8	15.8	15.8
65 and over	8.5	11.9	8.9	13.6	9.4	9.4
Education Level[d]						
Less than 8 years	44.3	35.2	65.2	44.3	63.0	48.4
8–11 years	26.7	31.5	20.6	34.1	15.2	24.2
12–15 years	21.7	27.8	10.1	18.5	15.9	22.6
16 or more years	7.3	5.5	4.1	3.2	5.9	3.8

[a]The four county totals for Chicanos are the same as for Starr County.
[b]Ages 0–15.
[c]Ages 16–24.
[d]Education is calculated differently for the four counties and the sample. For the four counties in 1970, only those persons who are 25 years of age or more are included, whereas in the sample persons 16 years of age or older are included.

Source: U.S. Department of Commerce, Bureau of the Census, United States Census of the Population: 1970, Characteristics of the Population, Pt. 20, Louisiana, Tables 121/126, pp. 20-328, 20-358; Pt. 45, Texas, Table 121, p. 45-968; Pt. 26, Mississippi, Tables 121/126, pp. 26-288, 26-323.

employing eight or more, including all employers drawn in items 1 and 2 above.*

In appraising county development patterns and related data, a number of public, quasi-public, and social institutional groups also were selected for interview, including officials in city and county government, chamber of commerce officials, area economic-development-authority officials, ministers, leaders of social clubs, and officials of community action agencies.

The major financial institutions in each county also were interviewed because of their direct relationship to the economic-development process. These interviews dealt with the development potential of the county, including financial and other services available to support development.

Also interviewed were welfare and employment security agencies; they provided data on training programs, job placement, conditions of employment, types of job information available, aids available to assist the unemployed in securing employment, and numbers receiving assistance. Considerable difficulty was encountered in obtaining information on program evaluation and program performance due to refusals of some state, local, and regional officials to cooperate.

No attempts were made to check the accuracy of sample data with the results of other studies, as no reasonably comparable data base could be found. Where appropriate, other study findings were utilized for purposes of comparison.

Considerable use was made of secondary data from the Census of Population, Census of Agriculture, the Census of Business, and the Census of Housing, as well as the statistics published by various other federal agencies. These data were utilized both as rough checks on primary survey results and for comparative purposes. Published and unpublished data were also obtained from various departments of state and county governments.

COMPARABILITY OF THE HOUSEHOLD SAMPLE WITH THE RURAL SOUTH

By the nature and purpose of the selection criteria, the population of the four counties is not representative of the rural South in

---

*A list of the combinations of major SIC groups used in compiling this sample is as follows: agriculture, forestry, and fishing; mining, contract, and other construction; manufacturing; transportation and public utilities; wholesale and retail trade; finance, insurance, and real estate; service, excluding government; and government. The number of interviews varied from county to county, ranging from 20 to 50, depending on the number eligible for inclusion.

TABLE 2.6

Total and Rural Population, Selected Characteristics,
South and Rural South, 1970, and the Sample, 1974
(number and percent)

Categories	1970 South	1970 Rural	1974, Sample
Total population	62,795,367	22,255,406	11,685
Male	30,587,841	11,044,454	5,485
Female	32,207,526	11,210,952	6,200
Total labor force	24,711,178	7,963,652	3,164[a]
Male	15,483,150	5,218,306	2,010
Female	9,228,028	2,745,346	1,154
Civilian labor force	23,728,727	7,852,709	3,164[a]
As percent of population	37.8	35.3	27.1
Male	14,524,446	5,109,774	2,010
As percent of population	23.1	23.0	17.2
As percent of labor force	58.8	64.2	63.5
As percent of male labor force	93.8	97.9	100.0
Female	9,204,281	2,742,935	1,154
As percent of population	14.7	12.3	9.9
As percent of labor force	37.2	34.4	36.5
As percent of female labor force	99.7	99.9	100.0
Employment	22,797.477	7,521,871	3,003
As percent of civilian labor force	96.1	95.8	94.9
Male	14,051,822	4,932,258	1,890
As percent of civilian labor force	59.2	62.8	59.7
As percent of male civilian labor force	96.7	96.5	94.0
Female	8,745,655	2,589,613	1,113
As percent of civilian labor force	36.9	33.0	35.2
As percent of female civilian labor force	95.0	94.4	96.4
Unemployment	931,250	330,838	161
As percent of civilian labor force	3.9	4.2	5.1
Male	472,624	177,516	120
As percent of civilian labor force	2.0	2.3	3.8
As percent of male civilian labor force	3.3	3.5	6.0
Female	458,626	153,322	41
As percent of civilian labor force	1.9	2.0	1.3
As percent of female civilian labor force	5.0	5.6	3.6
Age (as percent of total)			
0-14	28.9	30.1	36.1[b]
15-24	18.1	16.7	15.2[c]
25-44	23.5	22.8	18.4
45-64	19.9	20.3	18.4
65 and over	9.6	10.1	11.9

[a]Assumed to be the same.
[b]0-15.
[c]16-24.

Source: U.S. Department of Commerce, Bureau of the Census, United States Census of Population: 1970, Characteristics of the Population Pt. 1, United States Summary, sect. 1, Tables 57, 132, 137, pp. 1-286, 288, 453, 463.

the same manner as would be true for a random sample drawn from the entire rural Southern population. The greatest disparities are found in the racial composition and the proportion of the county population below the poverty level. In addition, labor force participation was approximately ten percentage points lower than for the entire rural South. However, with respect to many important economic characteristics, such as labor-force composition, industrial structure, and wage levels, the four counties together resemble the rural South as a whole. In other respects, the four counties individually are representative of broad areas of the rural South. Despite the racial diversity, most characteristics of the population, the operation of local institutions, and the attitudes of community leaders toward economic development and social change in all of the counties are surprisingly similar. Differences are generally in degree rather than in substance. As a result, the findings of the study should provide valuable insight into the economic and social conditions that exist in the rural South. Further, the study findings should serve as indicators of the nature and extent of problems faced by many Southern rural economies and by many of the people in the rural South, as well as the difficulties in finding solutions. (Table 2.6 contains selected population and labor force data for the South and rural South for 1970 and for the sample.)

NOTE

1. American Statistical Association, "Report on the ASA Conference on Surveys of Human Populations," *American Statistician* 28 (February 1974): 30-34.

CHAPTER

3

DEMAND IN RURAL SOUTHERN LABOR MARKETS

Rural labor markets in the South remain significantly influenced by the changes brought about by agricultural mechanization since the end of World War II. It is not possible to understand fully the contemporary problems of rural labor markets stemming from the demand side of the employment equation without having some understanding of the rapid changes that have occurred in the entire industrial structure of the rural South. Although individual areas have been affected in differing degrees, there is hardly a rural county in the South that has not felt the impact of the adaptation of machinery to agriculture and the resulting rapid decline in employment opportunities in the agricultural sector.

Technological change and labor displacement has had a tremendous impact on all four counties included in this study (see Table 3.1). Because agriculture-related skills are not easily transferable to nonagricultural jobs, there is a serious labor-market adjustment dilemma, complicated by the large reduction in employment opportunities that has taken place in the past 20 years. It is apparent that the nonagricultural sector has not been able to provide employment for many displaced workers. The result has been a high rate of outmigration from the rural South and some degree of withdrawal from the labor market by some who have remained behind.

EMPLOYMENT TRENDS AND INDUSTRIAL STRUCTURE

Data in Table 3.2 support a number of observations that are indicative of trends in the counties under study and in other areas of the rural South. Rural employment as a percentage of total employ-

TABLE 3.1

County Employment Data, Total and Four Counties, 1950 and 1970

County	1950		1970		Percentage Change, 1950-70	
	Total Civilian Labor Force	Number Employed	Total Civilian Labor Force	Number Employed	Total Civilian Labor Force	Number Employed
Dodge	6,373	6,234	5,890	5,637	-7.6	-9.7
Natchitoches	10,371	10,022	10,915	10,081	5.2	0.6
Starr	3,693	3,130	4,280	4,016	15.9	28.3
Sunflower	17,089	16,637	10,695	9,851	-37.4	-40.8
Total	37,526	36,023	31,780	29,585	-15.3	-17.9

Source: U.S. Department of Commerce, Bureau of the Census, United States Census of Population: 1950, General Social and Economic Characteristics, Final Report PC(1)-C11 Georgia, PC(1)-C18 Louisiana, PC(1)-C43 Texas, PC(1)-C24 Mississippi; United States Census of Population: 1970, General Social and Economic Characteristics, Final Report PC(1)-C12 Georgia, PC(1)-C20 Louisiana, PC(1)-C45 Texas, and PC(1)-C26 Mississippi.

TABLE 3.2

Selected Rural Employment Data, 1950 and 1970

County	Rural Employment as Percent of Total		Rural Employment Percentage Change, 1950-70	Rural Farm Employment Percentage Change, 1950-70	Rural Nonfarm Employment Percentage Change, 1950-70	Rural Nonagricultural Employment as Percent of Rural Employment, 1970
	1950	1970				
Dodge	63.3	60.4	-13.9	-75.2	120.0	84.1
Natchitoches	58.9	48.4	-17.3	-80.1	88.5	86.5
Starr	63.5	62.6	26.6	-26.0	58.4	66.7
Sunflower	89.5	59.5	-60.6	-85.7	8.3	69.3
United States	31.7	24.4	4.7	-51.8	50.5	89.4
South	50.7	33.0	-9.6	-65.4	44.7	89.2

Source: U.S. Department of Commerce, Bureau of the Census, United States Census of Population: 1950, General Social and Economic Characteristics, Final Report PC(1)-C11 Georgia, PC(1)-C18 Louisiana, PC(1)-C43 Texas, PC(1)-C24 Mississippi; United States Census of Population: 1970, General Social and Economic Characteristics, Final Report PC(1)-C12 Georgia, PC(1)-C20 Louisiana, PC(1)-C4 Texas, PC(1)-C26 Mississippi.

ment declined from 1950 to 1970 for all four survey counties, for the South, and for the entire United States. In terms of the percentage change for the 20-year period, three counties experienced a decline in rural employment as did the South. Only Starr County experienced a growth in rural employment, which was the trend for the United States as a whole. The growth in Starr County was due to its location on the United States-Mexico border, and the population migration increase has been occurring all along the border region since the end of World War II. In both cases the growth resulted from a large increase in rural nonfarm employment and a relatively small decline in rural farm employment. The last two columns of Table 3.2 illustrate the large nonfarm employment gains of 58.4 percent and 50.5 percent for Starr County and the United States, respectively.

All counties showed a decline in rural farm employment and increases in rural nonfarm employment. The magnitude of the changes, however, differed from county to county.

Employment by Industry

Review of the data in Table 3.3 reveals that, in spite of the dramatic decline in agricultural jobs, agriculture remains an important source of employment in the rural South and is a major source of employment in all but one of the study counties (that is, Natchitoches County). Agriculture exerts a major influence in other ways besides providing employment. The agricultural sector generates a disproportionate amount to total yearly income in the counties and therefore has a strong influence on job opportunities in the retail and service sectors.

As anticipated, manufacturing employment is of less significance in the rural counties than it is in the entire South or in the United States. Only in Dodge County is manufacturing employment comparable to that of the South as a whole. However, both Census data and the primary sample revealed that a substantial portion of the county labor force commutes to surrounding counties to work primarily in manufacturing employment. Thus, in actuality, Dodge is not significantly different from the other rural counties studied in terms of the characteristics of employment opportunities in manufacturing within the county.

The financial, real estate, and insurance sector is a small source of employment in rural areas. Furthermore, it is low in all four counties relative to the South and the United States, a reflection of the low income levels in the rural South.

TABLE 3.3

Industry of People Employed: 1970 Percentage Distribution of Total Employed, Selected Areas

Category	Dodge	Natchi-toches	Starr	Sunflower	Four Total Counties	South	United States
Agriculture, fishing, and forestry	11.2	7.7	24.6	20.7	15.0	4.5	3.5
Mining and construction	6.4	9.8	10.0	4.5	7.5	8.8	6.3
Manufacturing	27.5	7.5	3.2	15.1	13.2	23.2	24.4
Transportation, communications, and public utilities	3.7	6.2	4.1	3.3	4.5	6.8	6.3
Wholesale	2.5	2.8	2.7	4.5	3.3	19.9	18.9
Retail	14.2	17.2	15.3	15.5	15.8		
Financial, real estate, and insurance	2.2	1.8	1.5	1.8	1.8	4.4	4.7
Services	8.0	12.6	6.1	11.1	10.3	9.6	8.0
Health	4.7	3.8	1.6	4.5	3.9	12.8	16.5
Education	5.0	20.5	19.8	12.4	14.8		
Public services	14.5	9.9	11.1	6.6	9.8	10.1	5.2
Total	100.0	100.0	100.0	100.0	100.0	100.0	100.0

Source: U.S. Department of Commerce, Bureau of the Census, Census of Population: 1970, General Social and Economic Characteristics, Final Report PC(1)-C12 Georgia, PC(1)-C20 Louisiana, PC(1)-C45 Texas, PC(1)-C26 Mississippi.

LABOR DEMAND

Employment in health and education for the four counties combined is higher in percentage terms than that of the United States and the South. Employment in education and health is higher in Natchitoches than in the other three counties as a result of location of a four-year university in the parish. It is also relatively high in Starr County (more than 21 percent of total employment in 1970) because of the lack of alternative sources of nonagricultural private-sector employment.

Government employment is high in all four counties relative to both the South and the United States. However, the high proportion of employment is not reflective of an unusually large number of employees in the public sector, given the population size; in fact, the opposite is true. In part, it reflects stability in governmental employment in spite of the general decline in employment opportunities in the counties. It also reflects the small number of jobs available in other sectors and the low labor-force participation rates.

Potential for Increases in Labor Demand

Insight into the sectors of the Southern rural economy that have the greatest potential for increased employment opportunities may be gained by examining those sectors that have grown during the past 20 years. Table 3.4 contains data that relate to the growth in employment by sector for selected areas from 1950 to 1970.

As expected, agriculture experienced a large decline in employment in all four counties. This decline was larger than that experienced by the South and the United States. Starr County felt the least impact from the displacement of agricultural workers.

Manufacturing has been an important sector in providing new jobs in most of the counties in the past 20 years. The four-county total experienced significantly greater growth than did the South or the United States. Natchitoches Parish was the exception, experiencing a small decline; Sunflower County had the largest percentage growth, having started from a very small base in the 1950s.

Surprisingly, growth in services for the four counties combined was greater than that for the South or for the United States. However, Dodge and Sunflower experienced a decline in this sector between 1950 and 1970. Part of this decline may be due to black out-migration in both counties. Black females provided a large source of available labor for personal services. The decline is also a result of reduced general demand as a result of substantial population decline.

Other areas of significant growth were health, education, and public services. Growth in the health sector is apparently greater than that for the South and the United States; education grew at lower

TABLE 3.4

Industry of People Employed: Percentage Change of Total Employed, 1950–70, Selected Areas

Category	Dodge	Natchi-toches	Starr	Sunflower	Four Total Counties	South	United States
Agriculture, fishing, and forestry	-79.3	-81.1	-21.8	-82.4	-78.0	-69.3	-61.5
Mining and construction	46.6	71.4	-18.9	12.8	28.6	25.9	10.4
Manufacturing	88.6	-11.4	64.6	575.9	98.8	74.0	29.5
Transportation, communications, and public utilities	6.1	1.1	85.4	27.2	24.8	35.1	12.3
Wholesale	93.2	85.2	296.3	90.5	100.6	56.9	38.5
Retail	41.1	58.7	53.6	9.0	35.1		
Financial, real estate, and insurance	115.5	77.0	136.0	51.3	79.5	141.8	90.6
Services	-22.4	36.5	50.3	-13.5	41.2	21.0	12.5
Health	315.6	363.4	170.8	387.9	342.5	135.2	173.4
Education	44.8	145.7	374.4	172.8	164.4		
Public services	255.7	190.6	168.0	52.2	149.2	188.2	63.0
Total	-9.7	0.6	28.3	-40.8	-17.9	38.2	37.5

Source: U.S. Department of Commerce, Bureau of the Census, United States Census of Population: 1950, General Social and Economic Characteristics, Final Report PC(1)–C11 Georgia, PC(1)–C18 Louisiana, PC(1)–C43 Texas, PC(1)–C24 Mississippi; United States Census of Population: 1970, General Social and Economic Characteristics, Final Report PC(1)–C12 Georgia, PC(1)–C20 Louisiana, PC(1)–C45 Texas, PC(1)–C26 Mississippi.

rates. Public-service employment increased significantly more rapidly for the four counties combined than for the United States, but the rate of increase was less than that for the South. Growth in this sector was especially low in Sunflower County; the rate for Dodge County was relatively and absolutely high.

Despite the various patterns of growth in the four counties (primarily in manufacturing, health, and education), total employment declined. It is significant that the decline in agricultural employment was so great that it offset completely the employment growth in other sectors in the combined four counties.

OCCUPATIONAL LABOR DEMAND

Additional insight into the nature of the labor demand in rural areas can be obtained from an analysis of occupational profiles. The data in Table 3.5 show that occupational profiles of study counties differ significantly from those of the South and the United States.

As expected, the percentage of sales workers employed in the counties was low relative to the South and the United States. This reflects limited wholesale and retail markets in rural areas as well as relatively lower purchasing power of rural households. Clerical occupations were also relatively low and, similar to sales, indicate a lack of large business interests and thriving large industrial and commercial sectors.

Craftsmen were a relatively lower percentage in all counties except for Dodge County. The existence of a large number of operatives in this county is due to the presence of a considerable number of apparel and related industries. In general, the lack of skilled craftsmen and operatives is typical of rural areas.

Most of the occupations in which the four counties in 1970 had larger relative percentages than the South and the United States were those reflecting agricultural interests or those requiring unskilled labor. These occupations include general laborers, farm laborers and unpaid workers, farmers and farm managers, and private household workers. Despite tremendous declines in the number of persons employed in these occupations, a quarter of the total employment for all counties in 1970 was in these occupations. By counties these percentages were as follows: Dodge, 20.1 percent; Natchitoches, 18.3 percent; Starr, 30.3 percent; and Sunflower, 29.9 percent. These percentages perhaps indicate that Starr and Sunflower counties are both the most rural and the most agriculturally dependent of the four counties.

Percentage changes in occupational employment from 1950 to 1970 are divided into three categories: those occupations showing a

TABLE 3.5

Total Employment, by Major Occupational Groups, Selected Areas, 1970
(percent)

Category	Dodge	Natchi-toches	Starr	Sunflower	Total	South	United States
Professional and technical	9.5	16.2	14.1	12.0	13.2	13.6	14.8
Managers and administrators	6.1	8.5	8.5	7.1	7.5	8.4	8.3
Sales workers	4.9	5.2	6.0	5.0	5.2	6.9	7.1
Clerical	12.1	14.9	12.6	10.7	12.6	16.4	18.0
Craftsmen and such	14.0	11.6	8.3	9.4	10.9	14.2	13.9
Operatives	26.1	12.6	10.7	15.3	15.8	18.3	17.6
Laborers, except farm	6.7	5.8	5.6	4.1	5.4	5.1	4.5
Farmers and farm managers	4.6	2.2	3.0	5.2	3.8	1.9	1.9
Farm laborers and unpaid workers	4.6	3.8	20.8	13.6	9.4	1.8	1.2
Service workers	7.3	12.8	9.4	10.6	10.6	10.6	11.3
Private households	4.2	6.5	0.9	7.0	5.6	2.5	1.5
Total employment	100.0	100.0	100.0	100.0	100.0	100.0	100.0

Source: U.S. Department of Commerce, Bureau of the Census, Census of Population: 1970, General Social and Economic Characteristics, Final Report PC(1)-C12 Georgia, PC(1)-C20 Louisiana, PC(1)-C45 Texas, PC(1)-C26 Mississippi.

decline, a small gain, or a large gain. As expected, farmers and farm managers (that is, most tenant farmers) declined greatly in all four counties at rates similar to those of the South and the United States (see Table 3.6). The same is true of farm laborers and unpaid workers, with the exception of Starr, although Sunflower had a smaller decline than did Dodge County or Natchitoches Parish. General laborers showed small increases in two counties and declined in the other two. The national pattern for laborers was down, but the South showed a slight increase for the period. Private household workers in the four counties combined increased in employment, contrary to regional and national trends. In total, the number of workers employed in agriculture and related unskilled activities in these rural counties declined and is consistent with regional and national trends (see Table 3.4). Nevertheless, the existence of a relatively large percentage of the population that is still dependent on agriculture for a livelihood (see Table 3.3) in the four counties is still an important factor in the determination of the occupational distribution and trends.

Small gains were experienced in the operatives, craftsmen, sales, and managerial and administrative classifications. Gains in sales and in manager and administrators were low relative to the South and the United States; at the extremes, Starr had considerable gains, and Sunflower had net losses in both categories. Again, Starr County increases are attributed to health and educational programs in the county; the reductions in Sunflower County are related to the decline in importance of agriculture and related activities.

Large gains occurred in services, clerical, and professional and technical classifications. Increases in the professional and technical category occurred in all counties; however, with the exception of Starr County, the increases were lower than those for the South and the United States. Nevertheless, as a percentage of total employment, clerical occupations were low in the three counties and parish relative to the South and the United States. Service-worker increases were comparable to increases in the region and at the national level.

NATURE AND ASPECTS OF CURRENT LABOR DEMAND

A number of factors determine what will be the present or future demand for labor in a particular county. Among these are market demand for the final product, the number and size of firms, technology, production methods, and the level of wage rates or change in the level of wages.[1]

TABLE 3.6

Total Employment, by Major Occupational Groups, Selected Areas—
Percentage Change, 1950-70

Category	Dodge	Natchi-toches	Starr	Sunflower	Total	South	United States
Professional and technical	84.1	109.6	192.3	90.6	108.0	151.7	131.1
Managers and administrators	1.5	30.8	45.3	-3.7	15.1	44.2	27.0
Sales workers	2.6	19.4	112.4	-5.6	14.2	50.3	38.6
Clerical	212.9	247.6	275.6	125.3	198.9	136.0	99.3
Craftsmen and such	93.1	60.7	23.2	45.6	57.4	65.6	36.3
Operatives	99.4	31.6	16.5	47.1	51.1	41.6	20.8
Laborers, except farm	-41.2	-29.9	0.1	23.1	-20.9	1.8	-10.0
Farmers and farm managers	-85.2	-91.6	-71.3	-93.8	-72.0	-78.5	-66.9
Farm laborers and unpaid workers	-73.2	-71.0	-10.8	-50.1	-96.0	-64.7	-60.3
Service workers	93.9	139.9	170.7	93.1	118.5	112.1	101.2
Private households	-20.2	64.2	-5.3	3.6	15.7	-13.7	-18.2
Total employment	-9.7	0.6	28.3	-40.8	17.9	38.2	36.1

Source: U.S. Department of Commerce, Bureau of the Census, United States Census of Population: 1950, General Social and Economic Characteristics, Final Report PC(1)-C11 Georgia, PC(1)-C18 Louisiana, PC(1)-C43 Texas, PC(1)-C24 Mississippi; United States Census of Population: 1970, General Social and Economic Characteristics, Final Report PC(1)-C12 Georgia, PC(1)-C20 Louisiana, PC(1)-C45 Texas, PC(1)-C26 Mississippi.

LABOR DEMAND

Market demand for the final product is the most important factor affecting the demand for labor. The demand for most products produced by firms in the four counties studied is dependent primarily upon national business conditions and to some extent upon regional and foreign conditions, as few products are consumed in the counties. Therefore, conditions that affect the demand for the final product (and therefore the derived demand for labor) are exogenously determined. Knowledge of current nationwide business conditions is important in ascertaining demand and may also provide some insight into future demand levels.

At the time that the household survey for this study was undertaken (spring of 1974) the national unemployment rate was high, but unemployment rates were much lower in the four rural counties. Most of the industries in the four counties are either agricultural or agriculture-related. Although a few durable-goods industries do exist in the four counties, most are nondurable-goods industries, which tend to be the least affected by business recessions, as the goods produced are the least postponable. Sectors in the counties that tend to be affected more by the business slump are manufacturing, sales, and clerical. Relatively immune from economic fluctuations are the governmental and service sectors.

More internal to the counties and more likely to affect the short-run demand for workers is the number and size of firms. Table 3.7 shows this information for the survey counties. Of all firms in the four counties combined, 91.2 percent employed fewer than 20 workers. Combined figures for the counties reveal that 74 percent of the establishments employed seven or fewer. Only 18 firms employed 100 or more employees.

The number of firms in the counties is small when expressed in terms of how many are available to "serve" the respective populations. In Georgia, the ratio of population to establishments was reported as 3.19, but in Dodge County one establishment serves 57.6 persons. Similar figures are 4.08 for Louisiana and 68.5 for Natchitoches Parish; 3.35 for Texas and 98.9 for Starr County; and 4.30 for Mississippi and 97.5 for Sunflower County. Small firms, and not many of them, clearly limit the employment possibilities in the four counties.

The type of labor that is demanded is largely dependent upon the technology utilized in the productive process. Although agriculture has been mechanized and manufacturing has grown substantially, the labor demand in the study counties is predominantly for unskilled or semiskilled workers. Many of the industries located in the study counties were attracted to the area by the abundance of unskilled labor that could be purchased at low prices—for in spite of the greater use of capital in agriculture, wages for agricultural labor remain low.

TABLE 3.7

Number of Firms, by County and by Employment Size, 1973

	Total Reporting Units	Number of Employees						
		1-3	4-7	8-19	20-49	50-99	100-249	250-499	500 and over
Dodge	272	137	64	43	15	6	4	3	0
Natchitoches	514	243	123	100	38	8	2	0	0
Starr	179	98	47	23	7	3	1	0	0
Sunflower	382	209	72	69	21	3	3	4	1
Total	1347	687	306	235	81	20	10	7	1

Source: U.S. Department of Commerce, Social and Economic Statistics Administration, County Business Patterns, 1973, CBP-73-12 Georgia, CBP-73-20 Louisiana, CBP-73-45 Texas, CBP-72-26 Mississippi.

TABLE 3.8

Industrial Indexes for Rural Study Counties

County	1970 Census Data	1973 County Business Patterns	1974 Primary Household Data
Dodge	0.94	1.01	0.97
Natchitoches	0.94	1.07	0.92
Starr	0.87	0.95	0.87
Sunflower	0.87	1.01	0.87

Source: U.S. Department of Commerce, Bureau of the Census, *Census of Population: 1970, General Social and Economic Characteristics*, Final Report PC(1)-C12 Georgia, PC(1)-C20 Louisiana, PC(1)-C45 Texas, PC(1)-C26 Mississippi; U.S. Department of Commerce, Social and Economic Statistics Administration, *County Business Patterns, 1973*, CBP-73-12 Georgia, CBP-73-20 Louisiana, CBP-73-45 Texas, CBP-72-26 Mississippi.

In order to obtain a more accurate or relative picture of the industrial structure and wage structure in the four counties, an industrial index was constructed. The industrial index measures variations in the structure of industries among counties. Three sources of data were used in constructing three indexes for each county (see Table 3.8). Depending upon the base year used (that is, the source of the data), annual average hourly earnings were used in constructing the index.[2]

Data contained in County Business Patterns, due to the lack of agricultural workers covered in its annual survey, overstate relatively the indexes for all four counties. Nevertheless, a pattern emerges from the industrial indexes. Starr and Sunflower are low-wage counties—no doubt because of the relative importance of agriculture in the two counties—relative to the two other rural counties in the study and to the United States as a whole. Dodge and Natchitoches have a relatively more diversified industrial base than do the other two counties and therefore have higher indexes. However, indexes for these two counties also indicate that relative to the United States they are low-wage counties. The employer survey conducted in the counties found wages to be low in Sunflower; wages were also low in Natchitoches and Dodge, but they were higher in those counties than in Sunflower.*

---

*Due to the small number of private establishments in Starr County, wage data collected in the employer survey were inadequate for that county.

By occupation, the lowest paid were laborers, ranging from a minimum of $1.60 per hour in Dodge and Sunflower and $2.00 in Natchitoches to $2.40 in Sunflower, $3.40 in Dodge, and $3.75 in Natchitoches. Service-worker ranges were surprisingly low: $1.25 to $4.00 in Dodge and $1.06 to $2.50 in Natchitoches. Operator and craftsmen ranges started low (slightly above the minimum wage) but also ranged up to the highest of any occupation (approximately $4.00). The exceptions to this were Sunflower, which was low on the upper range, and Natchitoches, which, by and large, had both higher low and upper ranges. Most workers in these two occupational categories, however, tended to be grouped towards the lower range.

Farm wage data were sparse, but in Natchitoches wages started at the federal minimum ($1.30 for covered agricultural workers at the time of the survey in early 1974) and peaked early at $2.35 per hour. Sales workers also started low in all counties (close to the federal minimum wage of $1.60 at the time of the survey) but ranked with operatives and craftsmen at the upper end. Clerical workers started out in all counties with jobs above the minimum wage and peaked just below operatives and craftsmen. Reported wage ranges are misleading in that many of the manufacturing companies listed the upper ranges based on piece rate systems, which many workers have difficulty in achieving.

Employers also were queried about the bonus or pay incentives they provided their employees. Of the 22 replying, approximately half offered little more than small Christmas bonuses. Two businesses offered profit-sharing plans, but they were small companies in terms of number of employees.

Fringe benefits offered by employers in the rural counties were limited. Most consisted of life insurance and medical insurance. Life-insurance benefits were small, but the premiums were often paid by employers. Medical insurance was usually cost shared for the worker only (there were family options to be paid entirely by the worker). Another common benefit was paid vacations, which usually averaged one to two weeks, depending upon length of service. Paid holidays averaged five to six days per week. A few firms offered discounts to employees on the products they produced. Some furnished transportation in the line of duty that also was used personally. One agricultural concern provided free housing, water, telephones, and livestock feed for its employees. An even smaller number of firms provided disability or accident insurance for their workers. Twenty employers had some sort of retirement program, the quality of which, however, was not assessed in this survey. The paucity of such programs in manufacturing is quite noticeable. The lack of fringe benefits is due no doubt to the almost total absence of unionism in these counties.

Thus, not only are most firms low-wage, but when the overall wage package is considered, they are even lower relative to national averages. The type of labor that such firms expect to hire is obvious: not highly educated or highly trained.

Recruitment and Selection Procedures in Rural Labor Markets

As might be expected, recruitment techniques utilized by employers are basically compatible with those utilized by employees in finding jobs. Employer interviews indicate that this results because of little actual recruitment effort by employers. In essence, employers allow potential employees to determine recruitment patterns. Table 3.9 contains employers' indications of the methods they utilized in finding employees. No distinction was requested with respect to white-collar or blue-collar. In addition, multiple responses were tabulated.

It is obvious that the most important channels of job acquisition or search in rural areas are the informal ones. Utilization of either walk-ins and referrals by relatives or friends accounted for over 53 percent of the employer responses (see Table 3.9). Detailed discussion with employers revealed that relative or friend referrals were usually a result of a plant official's informing current workers that there was a need for additional employees. Uses of state employment services and newspaper advertisements were far behind but close to each other, with each accounting for approximately 13 percent of the responses.

Employers also were asked to indicate which of the methods used had been the most effective in acquiring the best workers. Of the small number who replied, the overwhelming majority was most satisfied with the informal methods. Walk-ins and referrals accounted for over 83 percent of employer responses.

Some employers were exceptionally critical of state employment services and suggested that many of those referred were not qualified. Employers often claimed that many of the referrals appeared to be going through the formality of job interview as a prelude to drawing unemployment compensation. Only two of the study counties had permanently located public employment-service offices within their boundaries.

A significant number indicated that they utilize the state employment service for testing and screening of workers. Others professed to have at one time used tests and formal selection procedures that had come under severe criticism from various government agencies for the way in which they had been administered. Consequently,

TABLE 3.9

Employee-Recruitment Methods Used by Employers

Method Used	Dodge		Natchitoches		Starr		Sunflower		Totals	
	Number	Percent	Number	Percent	Number	Percent	Number	Percent	Number	Percent
At gate	26	47.3	10	26.3	4	44.4	13	22.8	53	33.3
Referred by relatives and friends	11	20.0	9	23.7	4	44.4	8	14.0	32	20.1
Ads	9	16.4	4	10.5	—	—	9	15.8	22	13.8
Private employment agencies	1	1.8	3	7.9	—	—	8	14.0	12	7.5
Hiring halls	—	—	2	5.3	—	—	—	—	2	1.3
State employment agencies	6	10.9	4	10.5	1	11.1	10	17.5	21	13.2
Other governmental agencies	1	1.8	—	—	—	—	—	—	1	0.6
Letters of application	—	—	2	5.3	—	—	—	—	2	1.3
Other	1	1.8	4	10.5	—	—	9	15.8	14	8.8
Total	55	100.0	38	100.0	9	100.0	57	100.0	159	100.0

most employers had substituted informal qualitative selection procedures that were difficult to quantify or evaluate for this work. Many smaller employers had personal knowledge of most prospective employees or of their families. Some employers primarily hired persons known by present employees.

Sources of Skill Training

To identify further the type of employee sought, employers were asked where they believed most of their employees obtained the skills necessary for performance of their present jobs. More than one response was possible from each employer (see Table 3.10), but the general conclusion was that on-the-job training (OJT) was the source of most skills obtained by the present employees. Not surprisingly, just over 50 percent of the employees believed it was their OJT programs that had provided the training. The importance of formal training was downgraded by many employers. Employers cited the limited application of general training received through formal channels and generally preferred specific OJT to be part of a training program. Employers preferring such an arrangement were most often in manufacturing. These same employers were often critical of overmotivated employees (often the younger ones) who expected "too much too soon." Employers indicated a high propensity for this behavior on the part of employees who had participated in formal training programs.

Specific employer training methods are shown in Table 3.11. Again, OJT dominates; only 15 employers mentioned formal training methods. Small-scale work-experience programs existed in only Dodge and Sunflower counties. Probing of employers also indicated that most of what they referred to as apprenticeship programs tended to be informal and, in fact, often constituted nothing more than a trial period for new employees.

Seasonal Labor Demand

Employers estimated that the combined labor force in the four counties expands 7 to 10 percent during the summer months. Most of this expansion is in agriculture and manufacturing. Manufacturing employment increases occur especially in textiles and apparel due to seasonal demand fluctuations. Dodge, Natchitoches, and Sunflower especially experience increased demand for agricultural workers in the summer and spring. Starr County is unique in that it experiences a sharp increase in demand for agricultural workers (for harvesting

TABLE 3.10

Sources of Employee Training, as Cited by Employers

Method Used	Dodge		Natchitoches		Starr		Sunflower		Totals	
	Number	Percent	Number	Percent	Number	Percent	Number	Percent	Number	Percent
OJT (present job)	21	50.0	9	52.9	5	83.3	11	52.4	46	53.5
OJT (elsewhere)	11	26.2	4	23.5	–	–	4	19.0	19	22.1
At a school	5	11.9	1	5.9	–	–	1	4.8	7	8.1
Government sponsored program	3	7.1	1	5.9	–	–	–	–	4	4.6
Formal apprenticeship	–	–	2	11.8	1	16.7	1	4.8	4	4.6
Other	2	4.8	–	–	–	–	4	19.0	6	7.0
Total	42	100.0	17	100.0	6	100.0	21	100.0	86	100.0

TABLE 3.11

Specific Training Methods Cited by Employers

Methods Used	Dodge		Natchitoches		Starr		Sunflower		Totals	
	Number	Percent	Number	Percent	Number	Percent	Number	Percent	Number	Percent
Work-experience program	3	16.7	–	–	–	–	4	25.0	7	13.5
OJT	13	72.2	9	64.3	3	75.0	11	68.8	36	69.2
Apprenticeship training	2	11.1	4	28.6	1	25.0	1	6.2	8	15.4
Other	–	–	1	7.1	–	–	–	–	1	1.9
Total	18	100.0	14	100.0	4	100.0	16	100.0	52	100.0

and shipping) that lasts only two weeks. It is often able to tap labor supply sources from Mexico to meet this need.

Absenteeism and Turnover

Often mentioned by employers were problems of absenteeism and labor turnover. Almost 31 percent of the employers complained about excessive absences by employees. No patterns were evident in the data with respect to sex, race, or age of those employees claimed to be involved. Of the 18 firms experiencing such problems, 13 were in manufacturing.

A 1973 study conducted by Prentice-Hall in cooperation with the American Society for Personnel Administration found that manufacturing firms had the highest rate of absenteeism.[3] Reasons for absenteeism were similar to those found in the four rural counties (illness and personal problems), with alcoholism and drug abuse being minor factors.

Turnover rates cited by employers in the rural counties ranged from a low of 25 percent of the annual labor force to as high as 300 percent. However, the most often quoted turnover rates were 40 to 50 percent of the employer's annual labor force. A number of employers stated that these rates were quite conservative estimates.

Absenteeism and turnover are problems that are no doubt related. Some employers showed unusual insight into understanding or explaining the basis for the problems. As these problems primarily were reported by manufacturing industries, additional probing by the interviewers revealed that some problems were due to the high expectations of workers on the one hand and low motivation on the other. Although seemingly a contradiction, it should be noted that nonsatisfaction of goals or expectations often turns into poor motivation.

Four manufacturing employers cited the inability of rural workers to become acclimated to an industrial society as the basis for their turnover problem. These employers claimed that workers, in a throwback to agricultural traditions, often did not show up when it was raining. Furthermore, if something occurred on the job that dissatisfied the worker, instead of complaining, his reaction was to quit on the spot or simply not to return the next day. In sum, many of the unskilled workers (according to employers) view a somewhat more structured labor market (with rules and regulations) as an unstructured labor market (such as agriculture) with which they are familiar. In essence, many employers attributed high absenteeism and high turnover rates to the type of labor they hired and rarely to the fact that wages paid might be low. However, none of those interviewed revealed any indication to a change in hiring standards, nor did any show significant concern for the problem. The comment by employers that workers were relatively easily replaced was common.

CONCLUDING OBSERVATIONS

Based on the data obtained from employers in this work and the analysis in this chapter, some general observations concerning the demand for labor in the rural South can be made.

The demand side of the labor market in the rural South is dominated by low-wage firms in manufacturing, services, and agriculture. The outlook for short-term expansion of total labor demand is concentrated in sectors with such low wages that immediate improvement in the quality of jobs available (in terms of compensation) is unlikely. Any substantial increase in employee compensation will have to originate from external pressure.

In spite of large-scale out-migration, the demand for labor is still vastly exceeded by the available and potential supply of labor. Employer attitudes with respect to turnover, absenteeisms, and training reflect this situation. Job training is deficient in rural jobs, due primarily to the nature of the work. As a result, reduction of the human capital deficiency is not likely to come from skills learned on the job.

Demand for highly trained labor in public employment is likely to expand little in the short run. Even if upgrading of the labor force is possible, this sector will not be able to account for any significant employment increase.

NOTES

1. Richard A. Lester, "Shortcomings of Marginal Analysis for Wage-Employment Problems," <u>American Economic Review</u> 36 (March 1946): 63-82.

2. This index is an adaptation of one used by Lester Thurow in <u>Poverty and Discrimination</u> (Washington, D.C.: The Brookings Institution, 1969), p. 32. The index used was:

$$I_j = Y_{ij} \frac{X_i}{\bar{X}}$$

where:

I_j = industrial index for county j
Y_{ij} = percent of employment in industry i in county j

LABOR DEMAND

X_i = average hourly earnings in industry i for the United States for a given year (year depends on data used)

$\bar{X}$ = average hourly earnings in the United States for a given year (year depends on data used).

3. Jack Brannan, "Job Absenteeism Rated 9 Days," Commercial Appeal, February 3, 1974.

CHAPTER 4

LABOR SUPPLY: CHARACTERISTICS AND DETERMINANTS

Many factors have been influential in shaping the characteristics of both the potential and the actual labor force. The nature of the population in terms of labor market skills, as well as its behavior regarding labor market activities, affects not only the present situation in the rural South but in large measure determines the needs of the future.

Table 4.1 contains the distribution of several characteristics of the potential and actual labor force in the survey counties. All have important implications for the study of the operation of rural labor markets.

The male-female characteristics of both the potential and actual labor force are similar to those of the South as a whole, which has an over-16 population that is 47.7 percent male and a labor force that is 62 percent male. The sex distribution is reflective of the continued lower percentage of the labor force made up of women, not only in the rural South but in the entire United States labor force (38 percent). Although not reflected in data in Table 4.1, the sex distribution of the labor force is substantially the same for the Anglo, black, and Chicano segments of the 16-and-over population.

Figures in Table 4.2 show the proportions of blacks and Chicanos of labor force age in the rural survey counties to be significantly greater than the proportion for the South as a whole, which are 16.9 percent and 3.9 percent, respectively. These differences are reflected in the racial composition of the labor force. Racial composition is particularly important when the education and age characteristics of the 16-and-over age group in the sample population are discussed.

The age distribution of the sample population reflects the decades of out-migration from the rural South and illustrates the human-resource problem that has resulted. The age of the rural labor force

TABLE 4.1

Characteristics of the Potential Labor-Force-Age
Population and the Actual Labor Force in the
Four Counties
(percent)

Characteristic	Persons 16 Years of Age and Over	Persons in Labor Force
Sex		
Male	45.1	63.6
Female	54.9	36.4
Race		
Anglo	43.0	47.0
Black	30.2	29.0
Chicano	26.8	24.0
Education		
Less than 8 years	35.2	24.8
8-11	31.5	28.9
12-15	27.8	37.3
16 or more	5.5	9.0
Age		
16-24	23.9	19.6
25-34	15.1	22.8
35-44	13.6	20.1
45-54	14.5	19.6
55-64	14.3	14.3
65 and over	18.5	3.6
Total (number)	7,480	3,164

population contains a disproportionately large number of persons under 25 years and over 54 years of age. The disproportionately high number of blacks and Chicanos is particularly important as an explanation for the differing racial composition of younger persons (16 to 24 years) in the rural sample counties relative to the entire rural South. The overrepresentation, however, highlights the problem that black and Chicano youth pose for the rural South. The significantly greater percentage of the population that is found in the older-age categories—particularly in the 65-and-over group—is consistent across racial classifications.

TABLE 4.2

Characteristics of the Population of Labor Force
Age, by Race, for Survey Counties
(percent)

Characteristic	Anglo	Black	Chicano
Sex			
Male	46.3	42.9	45.7
Female	53.7	57.1	54.3
Education			
Less than 8 years	20.6	44.3	48.4
8-11	33.7	34.1	24.2
12-15	37.5	18.5	22.6
16 or more	8.2	3.2	3.8
Age			
16-24	18.1	28.9	27.4
25-34	15.1	14.9	15.5
35-44	13.5	11.8	15.7
45-54	16.3	11.8	14.7
55-64	17.1	13.3	11.2
65 and over	19.9	19.3	15.5

HUMAN CAPITAL ENDOWMENT

The amount of human capital possessed by the average worker not only affects the earning capacity of the labor force but significantly influences the types of industries and occupations that will develop in a region. Accordingly, it sets the pace for economic growth in the area. It is difficult to measure the actual amount of human capital embodied in the labor force of a given area. Nevertheless, there are measures that can give a general indication. Educational attainment is one measure; participation in formal skill-training programs is another. Both are useful in discussing the present earnings potential of the labor force and in assessing the potential for economic development.

The figures in Table 4.2 indicate that the human capital embodied in this rural sample is extremely low. They are indicative of the severe restrictions placed on the economic activities of the rural South by the relatively poor quality of the labor force. Over half (53.7 percent) of the labor force had less than a high school education. In fact, a quarter had fewer than eight years of formal education.

The average educational attainment was only ten years. These difficulties are compounded by the fact that the educational attainment of those in the active labor force is significantly superior to that of the total sample labor force age population. Thus, the reserve from which potential labor force members could be drawn is inferior to an already educationally deficient labor force. These figures are somewhat biased by the low educational attainment of the older population segments, who are not prime candidates for labor force activity. Over 65 percent of the 65-and-over age group and almost 60 percent of the 55-to-64 age group have fewer than eight years of educational attainment.

The paucity of human capital endowment is demonstrated further by the fact that less than 10 percent of the 16-and-over population had ever participated in a formal training program. The two largest single sources of training were the military and vocational schools. Unfortunately, it is difficult to translate military training programs into civilian skills; the nature and transferability of these military program skills cannot be accurately assessed. The skills obtained through vocational education are more easily classified. The majority of these were either automotive or small engine repair or clerical in nature.

Less than 1 percent of the potential labor force had ever participated in a formal apprenticeship or OJT program. Similarly, less than 1 percent had been involved in a government manpower training program. The problem is even more serious than these distressing figures reveal, because many (60 percent) of the small number who had participated in a training program had a high school education or better. Nevertheless, the majority of the potential labor force have neither education nor training. Survey results show that job-related skills gained through formal education or training are not prevalent among people in the labor force of the rural South.

Human capital also can be obtained through job experience without formal training programs. One indication of the extent of human capital gained from this source in the rural labor force can be found by examining the length of time an individual has been engaged in the same type of occupational activity. Although an imperfect measure of occupational tenure, the fact that 27 percent of all those in the labor force have been in their current job for less than one year and 57 percent have tenure of less than five years is a strong indication that significant human capital development through specific job experience has not occurred. Farming, professional, and administrative occupational classifications exhibited the greatest job-occupational stability for employees. Occupations such as manufacturing and construction (where blue-collar skills are most likely to be found) exhibit both relatively small percentages of long tenure and high percentages of persons with less than one year on the job.

48   INCOME AND WELFARE IN THE RURAL SOUTH

In general, the data lead to the conclusion that job experience has not offset the skill deficiencies resulting from low levels of education and training. In fact, on a relative basis, the nature of job experience has probably added to the overall low quality of the labor force. The most striking factor concerning human capital in the rural South is not its source or its nature, but its absence.

LABOR FORCE PARTICIPATION IN RURAL LABOR MARKETS

One important area of labor market behavior that is affected by the nature and characteristics of the labor force age population is the decision to participate in the labor force. Previous research has found that certain population characteristics—such as age distribution, educational distribution, and marital status—are associated with variations in labor force participation.[1]

Based on previous research, it could be anticipated that the labor force participation rates will be lower for the rural sample population than for the entire United States. An age distribution concentrated at the upper and lower ends and a low educational level both lead to this expectation. In addition, over a quarter of the population over 16 years of age reported health problems of a sufficient magnitude to prevent activity in the labor force. Over 50 percent of those with a health problem were under 65 years of age. The fact that labor force participation rates found in this study were relatively low was, therefore, not surprising (see Table 4.3). What was unexpected was the magnitude of the difference between the rates found in this study and the rates for the entire South.

Table 4.4 contains labor force participation rates for several subgroups in the study population. Not only is the overall rate (42.3 percent) for the rural study area extremely low (see Table 3.15), but it is significantly lower than that which the 1970 Census reflects for the South (57 percent). The various rates recorded in Table 3.16 in general represent the anticipated intergroup relationships and are similar in this respect to the 1970 Census results. However, rates found for all the rural study groups are extremely low relative to the entire South.

The labor force participation rates (LFPRs) for household heads across both sex and racial lines are lower in the rural areas than for the national population (see Table 4.4). Several possible reasons for this discrepancy merit consideration. On the demand side, rural workers typically face a smaller quantity and diversity of jobs; therefore, it is easier to become discouraged or disenchanted with the possibility of getting a job—especially an enjoyable one. As a result,

TABLE 4.3

Labor Force Participation Rates of Survey Respondents 16 Years of Age and Older, by Race

Characteristic	Total	Anglo	Black	Chicano
Sex				
Male	59.5	63.2	54.7	58.9
Female	28.0	32.3	28.5	21.0
Education				
Less than 8 years	29.9	28.9	30.5	30.0
8-11 years	28.8	41.3	40.0	31.4
12-15 years	56.6	57.7	54.0	56.3
16 or more	69.6	63.3	76.3	84.2
Age				
16-24	34.6	39.5	30.7	34.4
25-34	63.6	67.8	65.2	55.3
35-44	62.5	68.8	61.7	54.3
45-54	57.2	63.5	58.6	44.7
55-64	42.1	44.6	40.1	38.8
65 and over	8.4	9.8	8.3	5.8
Total	42.3	46.6	39.7	38.4

more potential workers drop out of the labor force in rural areas. From a supply standpoint there are several mitigating factors against favorable LFPRs in rural areas. Two are relatively of greatest importance. The rural sample has an age distribution skewed much more toward the upper age brackets than is the case in the national population. For example, the mean age of household heads in rural areas is 52 years. The well-documented out-migration of younger people from rural areas has left a sizable block of individuals near retirement age and the time in life when health problems cause labor force withdrawals. The latter characteristic was an important deterrent to labor-force participation in the rural sample. Of the household heads interviewed, 32 percent indicated they had some sort of health problem. Of those who were classified as "out of the labor force," 62 percent had health problems.

The greatest differences between rural and national LFPRs occurs for Chicanos (see Table 4.4). This is true for both men and women and no doubt can be traced to the significant incidence of migrant workers among the Chicano labor force in our sample.

TABLE 4.4

Labor Force Status and Labor Force Participation Rates, by Race and Sex, Rural versus National Population, 1973

	Labor Force Status			Labor Force Participation Rate
	Employed	Unemployed	Out of Labor Force	
Men				
Anglos				
Rural	67.8	1.3	30.8	69.2
National[a]	78.7	2.9	18.4	81.6
Blacks				
Rural	64.0	2.7	33.3	66.7
National[b]	72.3	5.9	21.8	78.2
Chicanos				
Rural	62.7	7.4	29.9	70.1
National[b]	80.6	5.3	14.1	85.9
Women				
Anglos				
Rural	31.2	1.4	67.4	32.6
National[b]	39.2	4.3	56.5	43.5
Blacks				
Rural	32.3	6.2	61.5	38.5
National	43.1	8.5	48.4	51.6
Chicanos				
Rural	17.2	5.0	77.8	22.2
National[b]	33.9	7.2	58.9	41.1

[a]Rates shown for rural are for household heads only. National population rates are for women and men 20 years of age and older. Primary data generated by study.

[b]U.S. Department of Labor, <u>Manpower Report of the President</u>, April 1975, Table A-7, p. 214.

While the absolute and relative magnitudes of the LFPRs differ between the two sex groups, the relative rankings across racial lines remain the same for the rural and national data. For women, blacks have the highest LFPR, Anglos second, and Chicanos third in both populations. Among men, Chicanos have the largest LFPRs, followed by Anglos and then blacks.

Finally, though LFPRs are lower within the rural sample, rural unemployment rates are superior to those of the national population, with the single exception of Chicano men. It is possible that those who decide to participate in the labor force in rural areas either find it easier to secure a job or become discouraged more quickly in their job search and drop out of the labor force faster than is the case for the general population. It is also possible that the knowledge of job opportunities is good among potential rural workers, in part because of the limited number of available job slots. Note, too, the significant difference in unemployment rates across racial lines in the rural counties. For the most part these patterns are the same as those existing for the general population.

THE LABOR FORCE STATUS MODEL

In the past decade there has been considerable investigation by economists of the factors that determine whether a person will participate in the labor force.* Most of these inquiries have used as the dependent variable in the models the LFPR of some subgroup within the population.[2] The nature of the data was such that these investigations sought to explain either variations in LFPRs across standard metropolitan statistical areas (in the cross-section studies) or variations in LFPRs of the national population over time.

A smaller number of models were based on data involving observations across individuals, with the objective of isolating those factors determining the labor force status (LFS) of the group involved. That is, the dependent variable in these studies was dichotomous, taking on a value of 1 if the person was in the labor force and a 0 otherwise.[3]

A common characteristic of all these studies is their concentration on either urban populations or the population in general (which is 60 to 70 percent urban, depending on one's definition of "rural").[4] None deals specifically with the participation decision of rural residents. In an attempt to isolate those factors that determine whether a rural resident participates in the labor force, the following regression model is given:

$$LFS = a_0 + a_1 EWAGE + a_2 WED + a_3 HEALTH + a_4 OINCOME + u \quad (4.1)$$

---

*This section draws heavily on: Loren C. Scott, Lewis H. Smith, and Brian Rungeling, "Labor Force Participation in Southern Rural Labor Markets," in <u>Amer. J. Agr. Econ.</u> 59 (May 1977): 266-74. Reprint permission is granted and copyrighted © by the American Agricultural Economics Association.

LFS is a dichotomous dependent variable taking on a value of 1 if the individual is participating in the labor force and 0 otherwise.[5]

EWAGE in Equation 4.1 is the expected wage of the individual if working. One would think that the greater the EWAGE, the greater the individual's inducement to enter the labor force. Measurement is a practical problem. The approach that was chosen uses an expected wage across all individuals in the sample.[6] The following model was derived in order to determine a person's EWAGE:

$$EWAGE = b_0 + b_1 SEX + b_2 ANGLO + b_3 BLACK + b_4 AGE + b_5 AGESQ + b_6 ED + b_7 TRAIN + b_8 DODGE + b_9 SUN + b_{10} NATCH + u \quad (4.2)$$

A person's expected wage is dependent on several factors in the labor market. Marginal productivity theory suggests that those persons with more education, training, and work experience would be expected to earn higher wage rates. Hence, ED is entered as a continuous variable measuring years of formal education attained; TRAIN is a dummy variable taking on a value of 1 if the person participated in a government-sponsored training program, and a 0 otherwise; and serving as proxies for amount of work experience are AGE and AGESQ, which are the individual's age (in continuous form) and age squared. (AGE and AGESQ are employed in Equation 4.2 since most empirical studies of the relationship between age and earnings find it to be nonlinear.)

Several variables are included in Equation 4.2 to account for possible discriminatory behavior on the part of employers (SEX, ANGLO, BLACK) and for differences in economic conditions in the counties (DODGE, SUN, NATCH). SEX is a dichotomous variable assuming a value of 1 for men and 0 for women. Possible racial discrimination is measured by using ANGLO (1 = Anglo; 0 = non-Anglo) and BLACK (1 = black; 0 = nonblack). The omitted racial category is Chicano; hence the coefficients on ANGLO and BLACK will measure Anglo and black wage rates relative to those of Chicanos. As proxies for differences in economic health and industrial mix between the counties, DODGE (1 = resides in Dodge County; 0 = otherwise), SUN (1 = resides in Sunflower County; 0 = otherwise), and NATCH (1 = resides in Natchitoches Parish; 0 = otherwise) were inserted into Equation 4.2. The omitted county is Starr. Thus, the coefficients on each of the county variables will measure how wage rates in that county compare to those of Starr.

Equation 4.2 was estimated using as observations the rural residents who were employed. Once estimated, both employed and nonemployed persons' characteristics were inserted into Equation 4.2, and the value of EWAGE was then established for use in the LFS equation.

Returning now to Equation 4.2, it is asserted that those persons who are married have greater financial and family responsibilities than do those who are single; thus, the former are more likely to be in the labor force. WED (1 = married; 0 = otherwise) is included in the LFS equation to capture this phenomenon. Problems with health should be negatively associated with labor force participation; hence HEALTH (1 = indicated a health problem; 0 = otherwise) is inserted in Equation 4.1.

The extent to which a person has sources of income other than earnings on his job (that is, earnings of other family members, transfer payments, and so forth) should act as a pure income effect, causing him to choose more leisure time and less participation in the labor force. To control for differences in other income between household heads, OINCOME, the amount of income from sources other than earnings on the job, was used. For married women and teenagers the other income measure is HINCOME: household head's income from all sources.

Two variables are employed in the LFS equation for married women and teenage women. Since women traditionally have assumed responsibility for the care of children in the home, the presence of children should have a negative influence on the woman's decision to enter the labor force. The presence of children in the home, in effect, raises the woman's "at home wage" and induces her to remain out of the labor force. Hence, the variable CHILD (1 = has responsibility for children at home; 0 = otherwise) is added to the LFS equations involving women. The presence or absence of child-care facilities nearby may reduce some of the costs of child care and induce some women to enter the labor force at the margin. Thus, CARE (1 = child-care facilities available nearby; 0 = otherwise) is also added to these equations.

Finally, an obvious and important alternative to work for teenagers is school attendance. SCHOOL (1 = presently attends school; 0 = otherwise) is used in the teenager equations to capture this effect.

In Table 4.5 the results of estimating the EWAGE equation are presented. All of the signs of the coefficients are in the direction suggested by a priori reasoning. The indications are that men tend to earn more per hour than women, things being equal, and that Anglos earn more per hour than blacks and Chicanos (note that the difference between black and Chicano wages is insignificantly different from zero). Labor force experience and educational attainment improved the EWAGE of a rural resident. However, once racial, sex, and human capital differences have been controlled for, variations in economic activity and industrial mix between counties had no significant influence on the EWAGE.

TABLE 4.5

Regression Coefficients for the EWAGE Equation
(t-values in parentheses)

Independent Variable	Regression Coefficient (t-value)
Constant	−3.05
SEX	1.17
	(11.16)[a]
ANGLO	0.57
	(2.33)[b]
BLACK	−0.28
	(1.10)
AGE	0.13
	(7.66)[a]
AGESQ	−0.001
	(6.93)[a]
ED	0.19
	(19.70)[a]
TRAIN	0.11
	(1.08)
DODGE	0.20
	(0.82)
SUN	0.04
	(0.16)
NATCH	0.19
	(0.48)
R^2	.37
F	95.65[a]
Sample size	1656

[a] Significant at the 0.01 level.
[b] Significant at the 0.05 level.

The ultimate objective of this section is to discover those factors that determine whether a rural resident will participate in the labor force. In Table 4.6 statistical results are presented not only for household heads but also for five other subgroups within the rural population: prime-age men; older men; married women; teenage men (who are not household heads); and teenage women. (These five subgroups were chosen because their LFPRs have experienced the most unusual behavior at the national level since the turn of the

TABLE 4.6

Regression Results: Labor Force Status Equations
(t-values in parentheses)

Independent Variables	Sample Subgroups					
	Household Heads	Men, 25-54	Men, 65+	Married Women	Teenage Men, 16-19	Teenage Women 16-19
Constant Term	0.52	0.97	0.13	0.12	0.52	0.23
EWAGE	0.03	-0.003	0.04	0.14	0.02	0.03
	(4.75)a	(0.04)	(2.50)b	(13.53)a	(0.59)	(1.19)
WED	0.27	0.03	0.04	—c	0.41	0.11
	(16.72)a	(1.03)	(1.08)		(5.21)a	(2.46)b
HEALTH	-0.51	-0.44	-0.12	-0.20	-0.24	-0.02
	(33.33)a	(24.49)a	(6.37)a	(8.71)a	(3.40)a	(0.30)
OINCOME	-0.02	-0.01	-0.01	—	—	—
	(0.69)	(2.88)a	(2.69)a			
SCHOOL	—	—	—	—	-0.50	-0.24
					(16.19)a	(7.83)a
HINCOME	—	—	—	-0.005	-0.002	-0.001
				(3.08)a	(1.01)	(0.52)
CHILD	—	—	—	-0.08	—	-0.27
				(3.98)a		(4.46)a
CARE	—	—	—	0.08	—	0.12
				(2.86)a		(1.71)
R^2	0.36	0.34	0.10	0.14	0.43	0.19
F-statistic	460.27a	153.91a	14.92a	71.47a	70.61a	15.27a
Sample size	3158	1190	560	2186	480	471

aSignificant at the 0.01 level.
bSignificant at the 0.05 level.
cDashes indicate variable not included in this equation.

century.) Perhaps the most consistent phenomenon in Table 3.18 is the importance of health in the participation decision of the rural population. The only equation in which health is shown to have no significant effect on the desire to work is for teenage women. HEALTH not only is highly significant in all the adult equations, but its coefficient is also noticeably larger than the coefficients on the other independent variables in this equation. (In addition the beta coefficient on Health was much larger than those on the other independent variables in all the adult equations. The beta coefficient permits a comparison of the relative strengths of the independent variables in explaining variations in the dependent variable.) This discovery confirms the findings in other investigations of the LFS decision based on urban and nation samples and suggests that expanded health services in rural areas could significantly improve labor force participation there.[7]

EWAGE has the expected positive influence on the LFS decision, though its coefficient is statistically significant for only three of the subgroups: household heads in total, older men, and married women. The influence of EWAGE tends to be the greatest in the married-women equation; this is not an altogether surprising discovery, since this subgroup typically has the greatest freedom in choosing between participation and nonparticipation in the labor force. Given their presumed responsibility for child care and housework, married women are more likely to be drawn into the labor market by higher wages. (Though it is not shown here, EWAGE is also highly significant in the LFS equation for the 848 female household heads in the sample.) Prime-age men, on the other hand, whose chief responsibility is that of breadwinner, have less freedom of choice in the LFS decision and are more prone to work no matter what the expected wage.

Because racial, sex, and human capital factors were found to be significantly related to EWAGE, these factors influence the participation decision of household heads, older men, and married women indirectly via their influence on EWAGE. In Table 4.5 Anglos were found to earn higher wage rates than blacks and Chicanos. To the extent that this was due to discrimination on the part of employers, such behavior has a negative influence on the LFS decision of blacks and Chicanos in the three subgroups involved. To get some notion of the order of magnitude of the effect of racial discrimination on the LFS decision, consider three men, one Anglo, one black, and one Chicano, each of whom is a 35-year-old household head, a high school graduate with no participation in governmental training programs, a resident of Dodge County, single, with no health problems or other sources of income. The probability that each would participate in the labor force would be 0.74, 0.67, and 0.69 for the Anglo, black, and Chicano, respectively.

LABOR SUPPLY

The possibility exists that sex discrimination also might play a role in the participation decision of household heads. Men were shown to earn higher wages than women in the EWAGE equation, and EWAGE exerts a positive influence on participation for this group. For example, if the probability of participating in the work force were estimated for three female household heads with the same characteristics as the men mentioned earlier, the results would be 0.64, 0.56, and 0.59 for the Anglo, black, and Chicano, respectively. These numbers are from 10 to 11 points lower than for men of comparable characteristics. There is the problem, however, of determining whether the lower wages earned by women are the result of employer discrimination or of occupational preferences of women. There is evidence from another study using a national sample that shows that national male-female wage differentials are more a function of female occupational preferences than of sex discrimination.[8] The reasoning used is that because women have responsibility for housework and child care, in addition to possible market-work responsibilities, they choose those types of jobs that involve low pay but which have work schedules that allow them to perform their housework. Data from this study do not permit a direct resolution of this issue.

The same reasoning used above indicates that additions to one's human capital, either through formal schooling (ED) or through more work experience (AGE), increase the probability of participating in the labor force for household heads, older men, and married women.

The pressure of family responsibilities has the expected positive influences on participation among all groups except for prime age and older men. (WED obviously could not be used in the married-women equation.) Being married had a particularly strong impact on the LPS decision of both teenage groups, being surpassed in its influence only by the school-attendance variable.

Responsibility for children in the home had a detrimental effect on the participation decision of married women and teenage women (66 of the female teenagers were married and thus were also included in the married women regression equations). However, the results show that if child-care facilities are made available, they tend to have a positive influence on a married woman's desire to work. Such cannot be surmised for the female teenagers, though, since CARE is not significantly related to their LFS variable. Income from sources other than the job (INCOME and HINCOME) has the expected negative influence on the desire to work for all adult groups. However, the size of the coefficients on the other income variables suggests that its influence is quite marginal. Surprisingly, the household head's size of income was not shown to affect the LFS of the teenagers.

DEMOGRAPHIC CHARACTERISTICS OF JOB SEEKERS IN RURAL LABOR MARKETS

The limited job opportunities in rural labor markets and the large potential labor force make job search an unusually important aspect of labor market behavior.* In addition, the job-search behavior of rural workers may help explain the low labor force participation rates found in this work.

Job-search behavior usually will vary according to the characteristics of the job seeker. A brief profile of job seekers interviewed for this work is therefore appropriate. The decision was made to conduct an analysis not only on total job seekers but on the subgroup household heads. The differences in job-search methods that could arise from the pressures that unemployment places on a household head were the bases for this decision.

In Table 4.7 are data that break down the job seekers (total and household heads) by sex and county. Men represented over 75 percent of all job seekers who were household heads, but were only 53 percent of the total job seekers. Difference arises, as should be expected, from the ratio of men to women household heads in the sample. Sex distributions, however, do differ among counties. The distribution in Dodge and Natchitoches counties is similar to the total distribution for the sample. Job seekers in Sunflower County were disproportionately female household heads (52 percent); Starr County's household head job seekers were disproportionately male (93 percent).

Table 4.8 contains information pertaining to the racial breakdown of the job seekers across counties. One obvious peculiarity is that almost 43 percent of the job seekers are Chicanos, whereas this group comprises only 24 percent of the total sample interviewed (see Table 4.1). One possible explanation for this phenomenon is the migrant character of a substantial portion of the Starr County work force. It is reasonable to assume that migrant workers engage in job search more often than the less mobile labor force of the other counties.

Within the counties, the racial composition of job seekers reflects the general character of the population. Only Sunflower County (with

---

*The following discussion on job search in rural areas draws largely from: Brian Rungeling, Lewis H. Smith, and Loren C. Scott, "Job Search in Rural Labor Markets," presented at the 28th Annual Meeting of the IRRA in New York, December 1975. Reprinted by permission from Proceedings of the 28th Annual Winter Meeting, © 1976 by the Industrial Relations Research Association, Madison, Wisconsin.

LABOR SUPPLY

TABLE 4.7

Sex of Job Seekers
(percent)

Sex	Total	Dodge	Natchitoches	Sunflower	Starr
Heads of households					
Male	75.5	67.9	69.7	48.1	92.9
Female	24.5	32.1	30.3	51.9	7.1
Total number	367	60	94	53	160
All over age 16					
Male	53.1	59.7	55.2	35.4	71.8
Female	46.9	40.3	44.8	64.9	28.2
Total number	957	169	213	166	409

TABLE 4.8

Race of Job Seekers
(percent)

Race	Total	Dodge	Natchitoches	Sunflower	Starr
Heads of households					
White	28.6	71.7	50.0	22.6	1.9
Chicano	42.8	–	–	–	98.1
Black	28.6	28.7	50.0	77.5	–
Total number	367	60	94	53	160
All over age 16					
White	27.8	69.2	46.0	25.3	2.2
Chicano	42.3	–	2.3	–	97.8
Black	29.9	30.8	51.6	74.7	–
Total number	957	169	213	166	409

77.4 percent black job seekers) appears to have a racial composition of job seekers that is out of line with the racial population mix as a whole.

When distributed by age, household heads tend to be in the older age brackets, as would be expected in a rural area (see Table 4.9). Almost 58 percent of all job seeking household heads were over 34 years of age. One deviation from the typical was Dodge County,

TABLE 4.9

Age Distribution of Job Seekers
(percent)

Age	Total	Dodge	Natchitoches	Sunflower	Starr
Heads of households					
16-19	2.5	1.7	4.3	3.8	1.3
20-24	13.6	8.3	18.1	24.5	9.4
25-34	26.2	40.0	28.7	28.3	18.8
35-44	21.3	13.3	21.3	13.2	26.9
45-64	30.5	31.7	21.3	22.6	38.1
65-99	6.0	5.0	6.4	7.5	5.6
Total number	367	60	94	53	160
All over age 16					
16-19	25.3	31.4	22.1	27.5	23.5
20-24	21.5	18.9	26.8	25.1	18.3
25-34	19.8	21.9	20.2	21.6	18.1
35-44	14.5	12.4	15.0	10.2	16.9
45-64	16.4	13.6	12.7	12.6	21.0
65-99	2.5	1.8	3.3	3.0	2.2
Total number	958	169	213	167	409

where 50 percent of the job seekers were under 35 years of age. Still, there were few job seekers in the lower age brackets in that county. In Starr County, most job seekers were older, in the age bracket 45 to 64 years, with a few in the younger age brackets. Natchitoches and Sunflower had distributions similar to the total distribution.

Of job-seeking household heads, 71 percent were not high school graduates. The relatively limited job opportunities for persons with low education, together with normally high turnover rates for uneducated and unskilled workers, explains the high percentage.

In an effort to ascertain skills of job seekers, household heads were asked what their industry of employment was during 1973, or the industry in which they were employed when they had jobs. Over 30 percent of all workers indicated agricultural activities as their primary employment. Agriculture was followed by government, services, and manufacturing (see Table 4.10).

Table 4.11 portrays the occupational preference of heads of households who were job seekers. Most job seekers (29.8 percent) listed an agricultural activity as their preferred vocation; the second-most mentioned occupation was construction (14.7 percent). For the most part, the occupational differentials mentioned between the counties reflect the contrasting industrial mixes of the areas. The primary industry in Sunflower and Starr counties is agriculture; hence, it is not surprising to find that most of the job seekers in these two counties list farming activities as their primary occupation. Among the four counties, Dodge is the most industrially oriented; thus construction ranks highest among the preferred occupations of its job seekers.

Seventy percent of the household heads who engaged in job search activity had earnings of less than $4000 annually; less than 5 percent earned over $10,000 per year. By county, Dodge, with its more industrial economic base, had the most favorable income distribution; the agriculturally-oriented Starr and Sunflower counties had the poorest distributions.

Additional family income (that is, income in addition to that of the household head) is extremely important to low-wage household heads particularly during periods of unemployment. Income from other family members helped families in all four counties break through the $4000 income barrier (see Table 3.26). However, in Sunflower County this additional income moved about 6 percent of

TABLE 4.10

Industry of Head-of-Household Job Seekers
(percent)

Industry	Total	Dodge	Natchi-toches	Sun-flower	Starr
Agriculture, forestry, and fishing	30.4	1.9	15.2	32.6	47.4
Mining	1.5	1.9	2.5	0	1.3
Construction	12.6	13.5	13.9	4.7	13.8
Manufacturing	13.2	25.0	16.5	25.6	3.9
Wholesale trade	2.5	3.8	1.3	0	3.3
Retail trade	8.0	7.7	10.1	7.0	7.2
Finance, insurance, and real estate	1.2	3.8	2.5	0	0
Services	14.1	19.2	27.8	16.3	4.6
Government	14.4	17.3	10.1	11.6	16.4
Transportation, communications, and utilities	2.1	5.8	0	2.3	2.9
Total number	326	52	79	43	152

TABLE 4.11

Occupational Preference of Head-of-Household Job Seekers
(percent)

Occupation	Total	Dodge	Natchi-toches	Sun-flower	Starr
Professional	4.9	5.8	8.9	4.5	2.6
Administrative and managerial	2.1	3.8	3.8	2.3	0.7
Clerical	3.7	1.9	5.1	6.8	2.6
Sales	4.9	5.8	7.6	4.5	3.3
Domestic services	4.6	11.5	6.3	6.8	0.7
Food-beverage preparation	3.7	5.8	2.5	6.8	2.6
Service workers	6.1	5.8	8.9	6.8	4.6
Plant farming	21.2	1.9	3.8	25.0	36.4
Animal farming	2.5	–	2.5	–	4.0
Miscellaneous agricultural, forestry and fishing	6.1	–	6.3	4.5	7.9
Manufacturing—raw	4.6	5.8	7.6	6.8	2.0
Manufacturing—durables	3.7	3.8	8.9	4.5	0.7
Manufacturing—assembly	5.2	11.5	3.8	6.8	3.3
Construction	14.7	25.0	10.1	4.5	16.6
Transportation	6.7	7.7	10.1	–	6.6
Packaging	4.0	3.8	–	9.1	4.6
Mining, logging, and extraction	1.2	–	3.8	–	0.7
Total number	326	52	79	44	151

the families over this rough poverty line. In other counties the percentage improvement was at least 11 percent or higher. The majority of job seekers are still in low income households after total income sources are considered.

JOB-SEARCH METHODS

It is helpful to classify research efforts in the area of job search into two categories: (1) the predominantly theoretical efforts designed to bring marginal analysis to bear on job-search behavior, with emphasis on models of the relationship between aspiration wages and the duration of unemployment, and (2) the more voluminous empirical efforts that have concentrated on determining the methods of job search used by various subgroups of the population and explaining any existing differences among groups and differentials in the effectiveness of various methods.[9] The analysis of job search in rural labor markets falls into the latter classification.

In Table 4.12 data are presented on the percent of job seekers using various methods of search not only in the rural study but in two general population studies and an urban investigation as well.

Several interesting points are evident from a perusal of the table. First, no matter which population sample is considered, direct application to employer (DE) is the source most used. Second, with the exception of the Bradshaw study, friends and relatives (F-R) is the second source most mentioned. The state employment service (ES) is definitely third in the rural study, but this may not be the case in the other three. The manner in which the data were presented in these latter investigations prevents a calculation of the percentage using the "other" category of search methods. This is unfortunate,

TABLE 4.12

Comparison of Job-Search Methods Used by Job Seekers
(percent)

	Rural Study		Bradshaw Unemployed Workers (1971)	Rosenfeld Nationwide Sample (1973)	Hilaski Urban Poor (1968-69)
	Household Heads	All Over Age 16			
ES	30.8	26.5	30.8	33.5	46.9
DE	76.0	75.5	71.6	66.0	75.9
F-R	54.8	44.1	15.2	50.8	64.4
Other	21.5	20.7	*	*	*
Sample size	367	958	4117	10,437,000	142,500

*Cannot be directly calculated.

Note: Percentages do not add to 100 because some job seekers used more than one method.

Sources: Thomas F. Bradshaw, "Job Seeking Methods Used by Unemployed Workers," Monthly Labor Review 96 (February 1973): 36; Carl Rosenfeld, "Job Seeking Methods Used by American Workers," Monthly Labor Review 98 (August 1975): 40; Harvey J. Hilaski, "How Poverty Area Residents Look for Work," Monthly Labor Review 94 (March 1971): 43.

since later in this study evidence will be presented suggesting that the "other" category would probably be mentioned more often than the ES in these nonrural studies, because the "other" category includes such methods as newspaper ads, union hiring halls, and private employment agencies. Rural areas use these methods less because most newspapers are not geographically specific to the rural area, and unions and private employment agencies are not as prevalent in rural areas as in urban areas.

It is not surprising to find the ES well down the list among search methods mentioned in rural areas. Only two of the counties in this study, Natchitoches Parish and Sunflower County, have a full-time ES office.

Note that in the one study that is strictly urban-specific (Hilaski's) the population mentions use of the ES office significantly more than do the populations of the other studies. No doubt, accessibility is an explanation for the greatest part of this difference. The data in Table 4.13 lend further credence. In the two counties without an ES office, the percentage using that method is low relative to the other two counties. On the other hand, the two containing ES offices have a "percentage-using method" for ES which is comparable to that found in Hilaski's urban study.

Search Method Most Used

In addition to information on the number of methods used, the rural residents were asked which method they used the most (see Tables 4.14 and 4.15). Given the earlier results illustrated in Table 4.13 it is not surprising that DE was the most often used method, followed by F-R, the state ES, and "other." Differences are minor in search method most used between household heads and all over age 16. Differences do exist, however, between the sexes.

TABLE 4.13

Search Methods Used by Household Heads
(percent)

Method	Dodge	Natchi-toches	Sun-flower	Starr
ES	13.3	41.5	50.9	23.7
DE	81.6	78.7	67.9	71.2
F-R	45.0	67.0	47.2	49.4
Other	28.3	25.5	11.3	15.0
Total number	60	94	53	160

LABOR SUPPLY

TABLE 4.14

Search Methods Most Used
(percent)

Method	Heads of Households	All Over Age 16
ES	11.7	11.4
DE	54.2	58.8
F-R	25.3	21.2
Other	8.8	8.6
Total number	367	958

TABLE 4.15

Search Methods Most Used, by Race and Sex
(percent)

Search Method	Anglo	Chicano	Black	Anglo	Chicano	Black
Head of Household						
ES	4.9	0	26.4	8.0	10.9	11.5
DE	58.8	80.0	45.3	58.0	48.9	59.6
F-R	17.6	15.0	18.9	25.0	30.7	25.0
Other	17.7	5.0	9.5	9.1	9.5	3.9
Total number	17	20	53	88	137	52
All over age 16						
ES	5.2	5.8	27.0	7.3	8.1	14.6
DE	65.2	69.6	49.7	60.9	53.0	59.3
F-R	17.4	15.8	14.1	24.5	31.2	19.5
Other	12.2	8.8	9.1	7.3	7.7	6.5
Total number	115	171	163	151	234	123

Women tend to rely more on the ES and "other" and less on F-R than do men. Unfortunately, a direct comparison of these findings with other studies is not possible since other investigations did not tabulate their findings according to most-used techniques. With one exception, however, the results from other inquiries blend well with the rural findings. The exception is that other studies have found that men use the ES more than do women.[10]

The racial distinction between search methods most used resulted in no surprises (see Table 4.15). As in other studies, blacks are found to use the ES more than Anglos. A possible explanation has been posited by Lurie and Rayack:

> The public employment service is legally committed to
> equal opportunity and the Negro feels he is more likely
> to get equal treatment there. However, he suspects
> that the private employment service, the newspaper ads
> and the union are less likely to place him in "good" em-
> ployment and furthermore, that any attempt by him to use
> these sources may result in embarrassment to him.[11]

Anglos, on the other hand, tend to use the "other" category—private employment agencies, newspaper ads, union hiring halls—relatively more than do blacks.

A straightforward comparison of Chicano search intensity with the other two racial categories is not possible, since virtually all Chicanos reside in Starr County, which has no ES office. One noteworthy observation is the rather large proportion of Chicano women, in both the household-heads and the all-over-age-16 categories, who applied directly to the employer in their job search. A possible explanation for this is the presence of one large corporate farm in Starr County that during the harvest season each year hires a large number of wives and teenagers. In all probability a significant number of the female job seekers in Starr County were ones who were household heads who exhibited search intensity measures quite similar to those of Anglo male household heads.

Search Method by Which Job Obtained

The rural-study columns in both Tables 4.12 and 4.16 show that DE was the search method mentioned the most often in this survey. Table 4.16 indicates that the largest percentage of job seekers found a job using that method; F-R remained second in both tables.

The ES and "other" are closely ranked in both tables. However, their positions are reversed: ES is ranked third among methods mentioned most often but is fourth in terms of method by which job was obtained. The implication is that the "other" methods are somewhat more efficient in obtaining jobs than is the ES.

Additional data are supplied in Table 4.16 for making comparisons of the results from the rural study with those from four urban inquiries and an investigation by Rosenfeld of the general population. Several interesting points are evident from an examination of this table. First, it is apparent that the "other" category is a significantly more important job-search method in urban areas than it is in rural areas. It bears repeating that this is because the "other" category includes newspaper ads, union hiring halls, private employment agencies, and community action agencies. Newspapers in rural areas

TABLE 4.16

Comparisons of Methods of Search by Which Job Was Found: Percent of Sample Using Each Method

Method of Search	Rural Study (1973)		Urban Males (1965)[a]	Urban Males (1968)[b]	Urban Males (1965)[c]	Urban Males (1964)[d]	U.S. Job Seekers (1973)[e]
	Household Heads	All over Age 16					
ES	6.3	4.7	7.1	11.2	7.0	6.0	5.1
DE	59.0	63.5	33.4	12.1	15.0	50.0	34.9
F-R	26.3	24.0	23.7	33.5	35.0	33.6	26.2
Other	8.3	7.8	35.8	43.2	43.0	10.4	33.8
Sample size	315	761	1106	349	60	250	10,437,000

[a]David W. Stevens, "Racial Differences in Migration and Job Search: A Case Study—Comment," Southern Economic Journal 33 (April 1967): 574–76.

[b]Edward C. Koziara, Karen S. Koziara, and Andrew G. Verzilli, "Racial Differences in Migration and Job Search: A Case Study," Southern Economic Journal 37 (July 1970): 97–99.

[c]Joseph R. Rocha, Jr., "The Differential Impact of an Urban Labor Market upon the Mobility of White and Negro Potentially Skilled Workers," Ph.D. dissertation, MIT, August 1967.

[d]Melvin Lurie and Elton Rayack, "Racial Differences in Migration and Job Search: A Case Study," Southern Economic Journal 23 (July 1966): 81–95.

[e]Carl Rosenfeld, "Job Seeking Methods Used by American Workers," Monthly Labor Review 98 (August 1975): 39–42.

are typically delivered from urban publishing sites, concentrate their coverage on the urban center, and more often their want ads are not geographically specific to the rural areas. Further, rural areas simply do not have the other three institutions in the quantity (or quality) that exists in urban areas.

Accessibility is a second major factor evident in Table 4.16. The ES does not rank as favorably in rural areas as in the urban areas. Of all job seekers in rural areas, only 4.7 percent obtained their job via ES. Comparable figures for urban areas range from 6 percent to 11.2 percent. That this variance is due to inaccessibility to ES offices is further supported by the data in Table 4.17, where county results are shown. Note that in Sunflower and Natchitoches counties, where ES offices are located, the percentage finding jobs via ES (9.3 percent and 8.2 percent for household heads) is comparable to the percentages reported for the urban areas in Table 4.16. It is the minimal performance of the employment service in Starr and Dodge counties, where no local offices exist, that lowers the overall ES record in the rural study.

Finally, the data in Table 4.16 indicate that in rural areas direct application to employers is more important and asking friends and relatives is less important in obtaining jobs, as compared to urban areas. One possible explanation for this is that the greater population density of the urban areas increases the number of daily contacts with "friends or relatives" and makes this network more widely used than in rural areas.

TABLE 4.17

Search Method by Which Job Was Obtained, by County
(percent)

Method	Dodge	Natchitoches	Sunflower	Starr
Household head				
ES	0	8.2	9.3	6.7
DE	76.0	46.6	62.8	58.4
F-R	14.0	32.9	27.9	26.8
Other	10.0	12.3	0	8.1
Total number	50	73	43	149
All over age 16				
ES	0.7	5.4	10.6	4.2
DE	79.1	48.0	64.6	63.4
F-R	11.5	35.1	23.0	24.7
Other	8.7	11.5	1.8	7.8
Total number	139	148	113	361

TABLE 4.18

Search Method by Which Job Was Obtained,
by Sex
(percent)

	Total	Male	Female
Heads of households			
ES	6.3	6.3	6.6
DE	59.0	58.7	60.7
F-R	26.3	28.0	19.7
Other	8.3	7.1	13.1
Total number	315	254	61
All over age 16			
ES	4.7	5.1	4.2
DE	63.5	60.7	67.4
F-R	24.0	27.5	19.2
Other	7.8	6.7	9.3
Total number	761	448	313

Table 4.18 illustrates, according to sex, the search method by which employees obtained their jobs. Table 4.15 shows both sexes using direct application to employers the most. Table 4.16 indicates that this method was also ranked first by both sexes in terms of obtaining a job. Asking friends and relatives ranks second for both men and women. It is interesting to note, however, that although women tended to use ES more than men, the success rate for women with ES is virtually the same as that for men. It would appear from this evidence that ES is less efficient in finding jobs for women than for men.

Racial differences in the methods by which jobs were obtained are given in Table 4.19. Given the earlier analysis of methods most used by race, it is not surprising that among household heads a larger percentage of blacks found jobs through ES than did Anglos (8.9 percent for blacks versus only 3.3 percent for Anglos). All three races had the greatest success with DE; F-R ranked a distant second. On the whole, the variations in job-search success across racial lines are rather slight.

JOB-SEARCH EFFECTIVENESS

Earlier, allusion was made to the "effectiveness" or "efficiency" of various job-search methods. In the job-search literature these words often are used interchangeably. This is unfortunate, as the

TABLE 4.19

Search Method by Which Job Was Obtained, by Race
(percent)

	Anglo	Black	Chicano
Heads of households			
ES	3.3	8.9	6.8
DE	58.9	60.8	58.2
F-R	28.9	22.8	26.7
Other	8.9	7.5	8.3
Total number	90	79	146
All over age 16			
ES	4.1	7.0	3.9
DE	64.5	61.8	63.7
F-R	25.0	22.0	24.5
Other	6.3	9.2	7.9
Total number	220	186	355

only measures derived so far have been effectiveness measures. From an economic standpoint, no one has yet measured the comparative efficiency of different search methods. This would require data on the amount of time spent using each method, the total cost (both money and psychic) of using each method, the payoffs for each method in terms of starting wages, and reductions of duration of unemployment. The standard approach has been to calculate some sort of effectiveness measure as a means of establishing the relative worth of the various search techniques.

Two Measures of Effectiveness

Previous investigations have employed two different effectiveness measures; these are referred to in this work as Method I and Method II. Method I, which was employed by Rosenfeld, uses the following formula:

$$\text{Effectiveness Method I} = \frac{\text{number obtaining job by method}}{\text{number who reported using the method}}$$

In Table 4.20, the effectiveness rates for household heads and all over age 16 in the rural study are calculated using Method I. The rates are quite comparable across both groups. DE clearly ranks above the other three search methods, with F-R and "other" ranking second and third, respectively. Of interest is the poor score of ES. Even though ES ranked third in terms of users, it ranks a distant fourth by this measure of effectiveness. It is also instructive to note that the effectiveness figures for ES in this rural study—17.7 percent and 14.2 percent for heads of households and all over 16, respectively—are comparable to the figure for ES in Rosenfeld's study (13.7 percent). It would appear that the ineffectiveness of ES is not just a rural phenomenon.

Effectiveness Method II is the one employed by Hilaski. He uses the following formula:

$$\text{Effectiveness Method II} = \frac{\text{number who obtained job using method}}{\text{number who used method the most}}$$

Table 4.21 illustrates the results of applying this formula to the rural data. There is more noticeable clustering of the rates for DE, F-R, and "other" using Method II, particularly for household heads. However, ES remains a very distant fourth again, even though it ranked third among the most used sources. Once again, the effectiveness rates for ES in Table 4.21 (46.5 and 33 percent) are similar to that of the Hilaski study of the urban poor, in which ES received a score of 51 percent. This is further evidence implying effectiveness difficulties for ES that extend beyond rural areas.

A New Measure of Effectiveness

One glaring shortcoming of the aforementioned measures of effectiveness is their failure to consider ceteris paribus factors. That is, the ES office may have had a poorer record than the other search methods because its clientele possessed smaller embodiments of human capital than did the clients of the other methods. Or perhaps the people who used ES were ones who were more susceptible to adverse discriminatory behavior in the labor market than were users of other methods. A more scientific test of effectiveness would be to select individuals with comparable socioeconomic characteristics, have them try the various search methods, and then compare results. Controlling for differences in socioeconomic characteristics of the users may be critical in making effectiveness comparison among methods. Regression analysis has been employed to obtain this isolation.

Two measures of search success of effectiveness were used: (1) whether or not the job seeker found a job (JOB) and (2) the duration

TABLE 4.20

Effectiveness of Job-Search Methods: Method I

Method	Number Using Methods		Methods Used in Obtaining Job		Effectiveness Rate, Method I, Household Head	Effectiveness Rate, Method II, All over Age 16
	Household Head	All over Age 16	Household Head	All over Age 16		
State employment service	113	254	20	36	17.7	14.2
Direct application to employer	279	723	186	483	66.6	66.8
Friends or relatives	201	422	83	183	41.3	43.4
Other	79	198	26	59	32.9	29.8
Total number	672	1597	315	761	—	—

TABLE 4.21

Effectiveness of Job-Search Methods: Method II

Method	Number Using Methods		Methods Used in Obtaining Job		Effectiveness Rate, Method I, Household Head	Effectiveness Rate, Method II, All over Age 16
	Household Head	All over Age 16	Household Head	All over Age 16		
State employment service	43	109	20	36	46.5	33.0
Direct application to employer	199	563	186	483	93.5	85.8
Friends or relatives	93	203	83	183	89.2	90.1
Other	32	83	26	59	81.3	71.1
Total number	367	958	315	761	—	—

of unemployment of those who found a job (DURA).* The following regression equations were estimated:

$$JOB = b_0 + b_1 DE + b_2 F\text{-}R + b_3 OTHER + b_4 SEX + b_5 WHITE + b_6 BLACK + b_7 ED + b_8 AGE + b_9 TRAIN + b_{10} HEALTH + u \quad (4.3)$$

$$DURA = c_0 + c_1 DE + c_2 F\text{-}2 + c_3 OTHER + c_4 SEX + c_5 WHITE + c_6 BLACK + c_7 ED + c_8 AGE + c_9 TRAIN + c_{10} HEALTH + c_{11} OTHERY + c_{12} WEALTH + u \quad (4.4)$$

where:

- JOB = 1 if the job seeker obtained a job; 0 otherwise†
- DURA = duration of unemployment in weeks
- DE = in Equation 4.3 a 1 is inserted if the job seeker applied directly to employer the most among the search methods; a 0 is used otherwise. In Equation 4.4, a 1 is inserted if "applied directly to employer" was the method that got the job; a 0 was used otherwise.
- F-R = a dummy variable in Equation 4.3 with a 1 if "asked friend or relatives" was most used technique and 0 otherwise. Similarly, in Equation 4.4, F-R equaled 1 if this technique was the one by which job obtained; 0 otherwise.
- OTHER = a dummy variable with a value of 1 in Equation 4.3 if the "other" category was the most used search technique; 0 otherwise. In Equation 4.4, c had a value of 1 if it was the search method by which job obtained; 0 otherwise.

---

*A third measure of search success was to be used: the starting wage on the job obtained. Unfortunately, data on the initial wage were not collected from the sample. Regression equations using the present wage rate as a proxy for the initial wage yielded unsatisfactory results in terms of significance of independent variables and overall explanatory power of the equation.

†A similar problem with respect to a dichotomous dependent variable exists as it did in the labor force status model (see p. 51).

Since the search category ES is being omitted from both equations, an attempt is made to determine—via b_1, b_2, b_3, c_1, c_2, and c_3—whether the three included job seeking methods have a significantly different impact on the success measures relative to the state employment service.

Three independent variables are included in each equation to control for discrimination in the labor market. SEX equals 1 if the job seeker is a male; 0 otherwise. ANGLO equals 1 if the individual is Anglo, 0 otherwise; and BLACK equals 1 if the person is black, and 0 otherwise. Among the racial-discrimination variables, Chicano is the omitted category, so the coefficients on ANGLO and BLACK are measuring the success differentials for Anglos relative to Chicanos and blacks relative to Chicanos.

Several variables are included to control for differences in human-capital embodiment among the job seekers. ED is a continuous variable measuring the total years of formal schooling obtained. AGE is the age of the individual in continuous form and serves as a proxy for amount of labor market experience. TRAIN is a dummy variable having a value of 1 if the person participated in a government sponsored training program, and 0 otherwise. HEALTH is also a dummy variable with a value of 1 if the individual indicated that he had a health problem, and 0 otherwise.

Finally, two additional variables were added to the duration of unemployment equations. Both measure items that should enable a job seeker to endure longer periods of unemployment while seeking the most preferred job. OTHERY is a dummy variable having a value of 1 if the household head had income coming in other than his own earnings (that is, earnings of other family members or rent on a house). If there was no other income, this variable was 0. WEALTH similarly had a value of 1 if the respondent indicated that he had some stock of wealth, for example, a savings account, bonds, a credit union membership, or life insurance policies; WEALTH had a value of 0 if none of these was mentioned.

The results of estimating Equations 4.3 and 4.4 are shown in Table 4.22. Since the primary reason for estimating these equations was to determine whether there are significant differences in payoffs for using alternative search techniques, the most interesting coefficients are those associated with search-method variables. Since ES is the omitted category, DE, F-R, and "other" are being examined to see how well they perform relative to the employment service, other things being held constant. In the JOB equation DE, F-R, and OTHER all have positive values, indicating that the probability of finding a job through these methods exceeds that of the "other" technique. However, only the coefficient for DE is significantly different from zero, and it is not large. In the DURA equation none of the

TABLE 4.22

Job-Search-Effectiveness Equations
(t-values in parentheses)

Independent Variable	Found–Did Not Find Job (JOB) N = 369	Duration of Unemployment (DURA) N = 312
Constant	0.81	33.92
DE	0.12	-3.04
	(2.69)a	(1.30)
F-R	0.10	-1.09
	(1.90)	(0.41)
OTHER	0.11	-3.62
	(0.73)	(0.46)
SEX	0.19	-11.84
	(4.14)a	(5.14)a
WHITE	-0.07	-7.15
	(1.46)	(3.00)a
BLACK	-0.12	-1.49
	(2.53)a	(0.66)
ED	-0.001	-0.21
	(0.21)	(0.81)
AGE	-0.002	0.06
	(1.54)	(0.80)
TRAIN	-0.07	-0.51
	(1.50)	(0.20)
HEALTH	-0.15	7.82
	(3.42)a	(3.48)a
OTHERY	—	0.57
		(0.32)
WEALTH	—	-3.97
		(2.10)b
R^2	0.16	0.24
F	6.99a	7.93a

aSignificant at the 0.01 level.
bSignificant at the 0.05 level.
cDashes indicate variables not included in this equation.

coefficients on the search method variables is significantly different from zero. Compare these results to the prior effectiveness measures illustrated in Tables 4.20 through 4.22. There it appeared that the state employment service was a significantly inferior search approach relative to the other three methods. However, the data in Table 3.38 suggest that that conclusion overstates the case considerably. Apparently, the reason the ES has such a poor effectiveness record is because its clientele are less job ready by virtue of education or training or are more likely to be discriminated against than are the users of the other search methods. That is, it is simply more difficult to find jobs for those who use the ES. This may be in part a result of the Talmadge Amendment, since employers in this study expressed a reluctance to hire persons on welfare.

OCCUPATIONAL STRUCTURE AND STATUS

Whether making an initial career decision or contemplating a midcareer shift, occupational decisions, by nature, are long-run decisions. Obviously, if occupational movement were costless, wage differentials would be the sole criteria for occupational change. Such is not the case, however, because most occupational decisions involve some type of cost—for example, lost wages, training costs, or moving expenses.

Analysis of initial occupational choices is made difficult by the fact that such decisions are made by most workers at a relatively early age, with limited knowledge, and are usually only made between broad occupational categories. Additional difficulties arise because there are many factors that limit occupational access, such as lack of knowledge of opportunities, educational or training requirements, and discrimination of various kinds. Given the nature of the data generated by this work, it would be impractical to attempt to analyze the process of occupational choice. It is, however, both possible and useful to analyze the occupational choice among various population subgroups, as well as to attempt to perceive possible barriers to occupational movement. It can be argued that limitations on information about entry channels and various restrictions to occupational entry, whether justified by the nature of the occupation or artificial, are the most important factors shaping the occupational decision.[12]

Occupational Variation by Worker Characteristics

Tables 4.23 and 4.24 show the current occupational structure of household heads by race and by sex. Obviously, both Anglos and

TABLE 4.23

Occupational Distribution of Employed
Household Heads, by Race, 1974
(percent)

Occupation	Anglo	Black	Chicano	Total
Professional	10.5	4.7	9.3	8.8
Administrative and managerial	15.2	2.7	11.1	10.9
Clerical	7.8	1.9	3.5	5.2
Sales	7.0	1.2	4.0	4.8
Domestic service	0.7	9.9	0.5	3.1
Food-beverage preparation	1.0	4.9	2.8	2.5
Service workers	5.3	9.3	6.8	6.7
Plant farming	3.2	16.9	10.3	8.5
Animal farming	2.2	1.0	7.1	2.9
Miscellaneous agricultural, forestry, and fishing	8.1	6.4	8.1	7.8
Manufacturing—raw	2.9	4.9	2.5	3.4
Manufacturing—durables	9.5	6.4	3.8	7.4
Manufacturing—assembly	9.3	5.6	3.8	7.0
Construction	8.2	9.5	13.9	9.8
Transportation	6.6	8.8	7.6	7.4
Packaging	1.2	4.5	2.5	2.4
Mining, logging, and extraction	1.3	1.4	2.5	1.7
Total number	903	486	397	1786

Chicanos have disproportionately large percentages employed in the professional and administrative categories relative to blacks. In fact, blacks are underrepresented on a relative basis in all "white-collar" occupations and are substantially overrepresented in agricultural and service categories. It is apparent from the data that considerable occupational segregation exists between blacks and Anglos. The difference between the occupational structure of Anglos and blacks suggests that the relative low average education of blacks hinders their occupational entry. It also is likely, given the social history of the rural South, that racial discrimination continues to be a formidable barrier to entry in some occupations.

The occupational structure of the Chicano household heads appears to be "intermediate" between Anglo and black structure. In fact, it probably reflects the industrial structure of Starr County more than does any other single factor.

TABLE 4.24

Occupational Distribution of Employed
Household Heads, by Sex and Race, 1974
(percent)

Occupation	Female			Male		
	Black	Anglo	Total	Black	Anglo	Total
Professional	7.8	27.0	18.1	3.8	8.4	7.2
Administrative and managerial	3.5	11.7	7.1	2.4	15.7	11.5
Clerical	1.7	13.5	8.3	1.9	6.9	4.7
Sales	0.9	9.0	5.1	1.3	6.7	4.7
Domestic service	37.4	3.6	19.3	1.3	0.3	0.5
Food-beverage preparation	18.3	3.6	13.0	0.8	0.6	0.7
Service workers	16.5	11.7	13.4	7.0	4.4	5.6
Plant farming	0	1.8	1.2	22.1	3.4	9.7
Animal farming	0	1.8	0.8	1.1	2.3	3.3
Miscellaneous agricultural, forestry, and fishing	0.9	0.9	0.8	8.1	9.1	8.7
Manufacturing—raw	1.7	1.8	2.0	5.9	3.0	3.6
Manufacturing—durables	0.0	3.6	1.6	8.4	10.3	8.3
Manufacturing—assembly	7.2	7.2	6.7	4.9	9.6	7.1
Construction	0.9	0.0	0.4	12.1	9.3	11.3
Transportation	1.7	1.8	1.6	11.1	7.3	8.4
Packaging	0.9	0.9	0.8	5.7	1.3	2.7
Mining, logging, and extraction	0	0	0	2.2	1.5	1.7
Total number	115	111	254	371	795	1535

Occupational segregation on the basis of sex is even more apparent than for race (see Table 4.24). Women are heavily concentrated in professional and service occupations—one normally considered a "good" category, the other a less preferred one. The professional category reflects the relatively large number of women in the teaching and health care professions. The heavy concentration in the service occupations reflects the disproportionately large number of black female household heads.

Table 4.25 contains data distributing current occupation by age of household head. The results are generally as anticipated. They are indicative of the reluctance of younger workers to go into such occupations as farming, domestic service, and food services. The data also reflect the difficulties that older workers have in changing occupations, evidenced by the high percentage of older workers in farming and the relatively small percentage in manufacturing. In general, however, when the structure of occupations is compared among age categories, differences are surprisingly small.

As would be expected, the distribution of occupations by education revealed that those in white-collar occupations had the highest level of educational attainment. Farming, service occupations, and construction give evidence of requiring the least.

The occupational structure found in the sample is very similar to that found in another study of rural workers.[13] The structure reflects the type of limited industrialization that has occurred in the rural South. The occupational distribution by race conforms to a racially segregated structure that is nationwide, although more pronounced in the rural South.[14]

TABLE 4.25

Occupational Distribution of Employed
Household Heads, by Age, 1974
(percent)

Occupation	16-24	25-34	35-44	45-54	55-64	64+
Professional	6.7	11.4	9.0	7.7	8.7	4.9
Administrative and managerial	6.7	9.1	11.0	12.5	12.2	11.8
Clerical	6.7	5.3	7.0	3.9	3.2	7.8
Sales	3.7	5.6	5.0	4.1	4.4	5.9
Domestic service	2.2	1.5	1.0	5.1	4.1	7.8
Food-beverage preparation	0.7	2.0	2.3	4.3	1.2	3.9
Service workers	3.7	5.6	6.5	8.7	7.0	6.9
Plant farming	9.0	9.1	8.3	7.5	9.3	7.8
Animal farming	1.5	1.3	2.5	1.9	4.7	10.8
Miscellaneous atricultural, forestry, and fishing	4.5	7.1	4.8	8.7	9.9	12.7
Manufacturing—raw	4.5	4.5	3.8	2.4	2.9	1.0
Manufacturing—durables	12.7	7.1	7.0	8.2	6.1	3.9
Manufacturing—assembly	10.4	7.8	7.3	7.2	5.2	3.9
Construction	7.5	9.8	12.5	6.7	12.5	4.9
Transportation	10.4	7.8	7.5	8.2	5.8	3.9
Packaging	5.2	3.0	2.3	1.9	1.7	1.0
Mining, logging, and extraction	3.7	2.0	2.3	1.0	0.9	1.0
Total number	134	396	399	415	343	102

Occupational Movements

The prevailing occupational structure is in large part a reflection of the industrial structure of the study area and should change as the industrial mix shifts. In fact, this is the case with a substantial increase in white-collar and manufacturing employment and a decrease in agricultural employment, as reflected in the differences between the data in Table 4.23 and the first occupation of the sample household heads (see Table 4.26). From a theoretical standpoint, it should be expected that change in occupational structure would be distributed proportionately among racial groups. It is obvious, however, that such is not the case, especially for blacks. For persons remaining in the same county, movement out of agriculture has been proportionately greater for Anglos than for blacks or Chicanos, as has movement into manufacturing. The most notable difference, however, is the lack of movement by blacks into the white-collar occupations. In fact, the percentage of employed blacks in the professional category actually declined.

The present occupational structure, as well as the occupational movement of household heads, suggests that blacks particularly have not shared equally, in terms of occupational upgrading, in the movement of the study area from one totally dependent on agriculture toward a more balanced economy. That is, blacks remain concentrated in the lower "status" occupations and are excluded from those of higher "status."

Occupational Status

The esteem with which the community in general holds members of a given occupation is one of the important factors that influence occupational decisions. In general, higher-status occupations are preferred and are therefore more difficult to enter. These occupations may also be of "high" status because of educational or other requirements that significantly limit the ability of most workers to enter them. Analysis of occupations by status helps to delineate barriers that may exclude individuals or groups and yields additional insight into the nature and degree of occupational segregation.

Although a wide variety of factors at a given time may influence occupational status, there are two that are generally believed to be the most important: educational requirements and average earnings.[15] Based on this assumption, a simple index was constructed by adding a standardized value for average educational level and average yearly earnings of sample members in each of the 17 occupational categories used in this work. After construction of the index, the categories

TABLE 4.26

Occupational Distribution of Employed
Household Heads for First Job Held,
by Race, as Reported in 1974
(percent)

Occupation	Anglo	Black	Chicano	Total
Professional	9.1	5.2	6.7	7.3
Administrative and managerial	4.7	1.1	1.6	3.0
Clerical	8.6	1.5	4.3	5.5
Sales	7.3	1.7	4.0	5.1
Domestic service	0.5	6.5	0.5	2.3
Food-beverage preparation	2.1	3.5	2.1	2.3
Service workers	4.7	5.2	4.0	4.6
Plant farming	4.8	34.4	29.2	19.4
Animal farming	0.8	0.0	5.9	1.7
Miscellaneous agricultural, forestry, and fishing	20.0	21.6	16.1	19.2
Manufacturing—raw	3.0	2.6	2.1	2.6
Manufacturing—durables	8.0	3.3	2.4	5.6
Manufacturing—assembly	6.6	2.8	2.7	4.6
Construction	6.7	2.4	6.2	5.4
Transportation	6.8	3.7	8.3	6.2
Packaging	4.4	3.3	1.9	3.5
Mining, logging, and extraction	1.8	1.1	1.9	1.5
Total number	903	486	397	1786

were reduced to seven broader classes. Several of the categories were so close that attempts to differentiate would have been meaningless, making some combination necessary. In addition, a few categories contained a small absolute number of observations. The combinations were as follows:

Class 1 = professional and administrative-managerial
Class 2 = clerical-technical and sales
Class 3 = all manufacturing and construction
Class 4 = service workers, packaging, and transportation
Class 5 = mining-extractive and miscellaneous agriculture, forestry, and fishing
Class 6 = animal and plant farming
Class 7 = food and beverage and domestic services.

TABLE 4.27

Current Occupational Status of Employed
Household Heads, by Race
(percent)

Occupational Status	Anglo	Black	Chicano
Class 1	26.1	7.5	20.6
Class 2	14.8	3.1	7.6
Class 3	30.1	26.5	23.9
Class 4	13.2	22.9	17.1
Class 5	9.4	7.9	10.7
Class 6	5.1	17.7	17.1
Class 7	1.5	14.4	3.0
Number	899	480	393

Both education and income were important factors in differentiating Classes 1 and 2 as well as Classes 6 and 7 from the remaining classes and from each other. However, in Classes 3, 4, and 5 the educational pattern was such that income became the important differentiating factor.

Data in Table 4.27 shows the distribution of employed household heads by occupational status and by race. Clearly, Anglos have a disproportionate share of the highest-status occupations, and blacks and Chicanos are overrepresented in the lowest. Classes 3 and 4 contain the largest percentage of employed household heads regardless of race. These two classes also contain individuals who have an average 10 to 12 years of education and whose income, while above the poverty level, is not really "middle" income by national standards.

The distribution by sex reveals that women are disproportionately represented at both ends of the status scale (see Table 4.28). The relatively large number of women in the highest status group reflects the fact that most elementary and secondary school teachers in the sample are females; the high percentage in the lowest status category reflects the employment of women exclusively in domestic service. Both figures also are influenced by the small absolute number of females employed.

Equally important as current occupational status is the worker's ability to move to a higher-ranked occupation during his or her lifetime. Table 4.29 contains data by race on the percentage of workers who moved into their present occupational class from a lower class. It is apparent that there has been considerable occupational movement among all workers. However, blacks appear to have a relatively

LABOR SUPPLY 83

small probability of moving into the highest occupational category. The considerable movement into the middle occupational groups shown by blacks and Chicanos would indicate a lesser ability to obtain such jobs initially. In addition, changing attitudes have opened these occupations to minority groups on a greater scale than existed prior to the 1960s.

TABLE 4.28

Current Occupational Status of Employed Household Heads, by Sex
(percent)

Occupational Status	Men	Women
Class 1	18.9	25.9
Class 2	9.4	13.8
Class 3	30.4	10.9
Class 4	16.7	15.8
Class 5	10.7	0.4
Class 6	12.6	2.0
Class 7	1.2	31.1
Number	1525	247

TABLE 4.29

Upward Occupational Movement of Employed Household Heads as Percentage of Total in Occupation, by Race

Occupational Status	Anglo		Black		Chicano	
	Moved from Lower Class	Number in Class	Moved from Lower Class	Number in Class	Moved from Lower Class	Number in Class
Class 1	59.7	211	33.3	33	60.8	74
Class 2	54.0	68	53.8	13	71.4	28
Class 3	46.9	121	65.9	123	67.4	89
Class 4	33.6	38	53.8	104	50.8	65
Class 5	44.3	35	15.8	38	32.5	40
Class 6	0.0	46	2.4	83	0.0	64
Class 7	0.0	14	0.0	65	0.0	13

The majority of the occupational movement was from a given class to the class immediately above; a much smaller percentage of household heads moved up two classes. Upgrading by more than two classes was negligible, indicating that initial access to a given occupation is very important. In fact, race and initial occupation appear to be the two most important factors in determining current occupational status.

In an effort to isolate the individual effect of factors such as race and first occupation on current occupational status, the status index was used as the dependent variable in a regression equation. Independent variables included in the analysis were: race, sex, age, training-program participation, county, and occupational status of first job. (For a description of the form taken by these variables, see the labor force participation discussion in this chapter. The occupational status variable is that discussed earlier in this section.)

Table 4.30 contains the results of the regression analysis. In light of the previous discussion the results are as anticipated. The possible exception is the finding that, other things constant, age does not exert any influence on occupational status. The regression results attest to the importance of access to a relatively high-status occupation initially. The results definitely support the conclusion that occupational segregation based on race and sex exists in the rural areas studied. Unfortunately, it is impossible to separate the effects of discrimination as a barrier to occupational entry from other factors, such as education, that are related to race.

GEOGRAPHIC MOBILITY

The out-migration of population from the South and particularly from the rural South for the past several decades is well documented. It has had a heavy impact on the population composition of the rural South. Because this book is based on a cross-section of the population currently residing in the rural South, primary data are not available on out-migrants. Nevertheless, the current economic and labor market status of the sample can be correctly understood only in light of past migration patterns.

Estimates based on Census data reveal that net out-migration of over 15 percent occurred between 1960 and 1970 for the area covered in this work. Both Anglos and blacks experienced net out-migration. However, the rate was substantially less for Anglos (approximately 7 percent) than for blacks (approximately 32 percent). More significantly, net out-migration rates for both blacks and Anglos were extremely high in the 20-to-34 age category, ranging between 30 and 85 percent depending on the age breakdown and county

TABLE 4.30

Regression Results: Occupational Status of Household Heads

Independent Variables	Regression Coefficient	t-values
Male	0.3402	2.06[a]
Anglo	0.3489	7.62[b]
Chicano	0.3862	2.76[b]
Training	0.0947	2.08[a]
Age	-0.0002	0.12
Status of first occupation	0.4668	22.95[b]
Dodge	0.1095	0.80
Natchitoches	0.1143	0.83
Sunflower	0.0905	0.67
Constant	0.7898	—

[a]Significant at the 0.05 level.
[b]Significant at the 0.01 level.

being considered. The higher-than-average net out-migration of this age group is not unexpected, but it perpetuates the problem of a population of labor force age with disproportionate representation at the upper and lower age brackets. It also removes from the rural labor force some of its potentially most productive members.

The nature of the problem this continued net out-migration produces is perhaps better understood when it is realized that the result does not come from a very active in- and out-migration stream but from a high out-migration rate and a very low rate of in-migration. It is paradoxical that one of the major problems of the rural South, which gave birth to one of the great human migratory movements in the nation's history, resulted in immobility of the population that remains.

Over 85 percent of the persons 16 years of age and over in the sample lived in the same county five years prior to the time of interview, and almost 75 percent were born in that county, an indication of substantial immobility. A more direct measure of immobility is reflected in the figures contained in Table 4.31. Household heads in the survey were asked whether they could conceive of circumstances that would make them move from their present county of residence. Over 85 percent said "no." Moreover, as the data indicate, the negative response of all groups, except for those from 16 to 24 years of age, was 75 percent or more.

TABLE 4.31

Willingness to Move of Household Heads in
Rural Survey, by Race, Sex, and Age
(percent)

Characteristic	Willing to Move	
	Yes	No
Race		
Anglo	13.8	86.2
Black	11.2	88.8
Chicano	19.9	80.1
Sex		
Male	16.4	83.6
Female	9.3	90.7
Age		
16-24	35.3	64.7
25-34	25.0	75.0
35-44	22.9	77.1
45-54	14.5	85.5
55-64	10.2	89.8
65 and over	2.9	97.1

Not surprisingly, the most often cited reason (41 percent) for this answer was, "this is my home." An unexpected finding was that this answer was as prevalent among household heads from 15 to 34 years old as it was among those 55 years of age and older. A relatively small percentage (8.5) indicated that job attachment was an influence in their answer. Less than 1 percent stated that preference for living in a rural area was a factor. From the earlier description of the present population of labor force age in the rural South and the results discussed immediately above, it is apparent that out-migration is probably not a viable alternative for a significant portion of the population.

The present population has engaged in a significant type of residential mobility. Over 62 percent of the population was born on a farm in the county. By 1973 over half had moved to a nonfarm residence. A substantial amount of this movement took place in the past ten years.

Estimates of migration rates for the latter part of the 1960s and the first years of the 1970s show a reversal of the South-to-North migration patterns. There is considerable discussion of possible

LABOR SUPPLY 87

return migration as a major factor in the future population growth of the South. No evidence of such a trend was found for the rural Southern counties included in this work.

Less than 5 percent of the households, containing a similar population percentage, moved more than 50 miles in the past five years. Moreover, only 35 percent of this group moved from another state. Most moves involved a change in the county of residence but not the state and were almost exclusively an Anglo (82.8 percent) phenomenon. In addition, over 50 percent of the household heads involved were over 35 years of age.

Return migration may indeed be a factor for the South as a whole in the future, but it does not appear to be important for Southern rural areas. Even with the small number involved in this study, only 28 percent of those who had moved more than 50 miles gave returning home as the reason. If return migration does occur in an amount that is significant, it is likely to be to the urban South. Such a trend could further complicate the problems of the rural areas by restricting the opportunities for rural-to-urban migration within the South.

CONCLUDING OBSERVATIONS

It is possible to make several general observations from the preceding analysis relating to the supply of labor in rural Southern labor markets.

In many ways, the rural Southern labor market bears a resemblance to the dual labor market found in urban centers. Most of the characteristics of secondary labor markets can be observed for a substantial proportion of employment opportunities when viewed from the demand side and from employer attitudes. There is considerable difficulty, however, in identifying the relevant primary labor market, making the dual labor market concept itself hard to apply to rural areas.

The need for alternative employment opportunities seems obvious, and with the reduction of opportunities through migration, development of the rural South must be the answer. Clearly, however, developmental efforts will be handicapped by deficiencies in the quality of the indigenous labor supply.

Several observations relating to the labor force participation analysis are significant.

1. Labor force participation rates in the rural South tend to be significantly lower than those for the nation as a whole. This is attributable in part to lower educational attainment, greater incidence

of health problems, and an age distribution skewed toward the upper age levels in rural labor markets. It also is indicative of the limited number of job opportunities available in rural areas and signals the probable existence of a substantial discouraged-worker problem.

2. Health plays a prominent role in the participation decision of all groups considered, except for teenage women. For adults, the existence of health problems is by far the major determinant of labor force participation.

3. The existence of child-care responsibilities has a strong negative influence on the desire to work of married women and of teenage women. However, the evidence shows that the provision of nearby day-care facilities can work to encourage participation among married women.

4. The presence of family responsibilities—being married—is a very important factor in the labor force participation decision of teenagers. Marital status also influences the participation decision of household heads as a group.

5. Because of their influence on the expected wage, investments in human capital through formal education and work experience increase the probability of labor force participation for all adult groups except for prime-age males.

Rural labor markets appear to operate relatively well in the dissemination of employment information. There is evidence that rural workers possess quite accurate knowledge of the type of jobs and the wages available. This also may be true for potential labor force participants. In fact, evidence suggests that to be effective in rural areas, the employment service must concentrate more on expanding the type and variety of placements it can make and the type of clientele it services.

The out-migration from the rural South to metropolitan areas is well documented. In large part this movement resulted from the pull of available jobs and the hope for better earnings and a high living standard. The metropolitan areas offered opportunities in the form of primary labor market jobs. In effect, migration formed a bridge between regional labor markets and an avenue for jobs of poor to better quality. Although the possibility of geographic movement remains, the prospects for achievement of significant economic improvement has greatly diminished. As a result, the rural South has become, in effect, a secondary labor market characterized by low labor force participation, high labor turnover, and a poorly educated and poorly trained labor force with low earnings capacity, required to work in dead-end jobs.

The analysis of rural labor market behavior reveals indirect evidence of racial and sex discrimination. There is evidence that racial and possibly sex discrimination indirectly affect (via the expected wage) the labor force decision of black men, female household heads, and married women. Additionally, the finding of occupational segregation by both sex and race suggests an additional effect of discrimination on the labor force decisions of the same groups. Both factors help explain lower earnings and income of black families and of households with female heads. Such results also indicate that antidiscrimination efforts in rural areas need to be upgraded, and that if they are, alterations in labor market behavior of affected groups can be expected.

Cursory analysis of the existing industrial structure, which is supported by an examination of employers' attitudes, indicates that private employer training is not likely to occur. Yet lack of training, even for the limited variety of jobs available, is evident among the rural labor force. The earning capacity of many rural workers is thereby severely restricted. In addition, limited job opportunities reinforce, as well as contribute directly to, the low levels of labor force participation.

The lack of sufficient available jobs, the low quality of existing jobs, the human-capital deficiencies in much of the population of labor force age, as well as the numerous institutional restrictions, help explain the nature and operation of rural Southern labor markets. The same factors also clearly indicate that the private sector is limited in its ability to provide for the population.

NOTES

1. A complete discussion of the findings of previous research regarding the impact of various population characteristics of labor force participation can be found in Herber S. Parnes, "Labor Force and Labor Market," in A Review of Industrial Relations Research, vol. 1, Woodrow L. Ginsburg et al. (Industrial Relations Research Association, 1970): 1-78.

2. This, for example is the approach used in the classic study by W. G. Bowen and T. A. Finegan, The Economics of Labor Force Participation (Princeton, N.J.: Princeton University Press, 1969), and in Glen G. Cain, Married Women in the Labor Force (Chicago: The University of Chicago Press, 1966).

3. See, for example, Byron G. Spencer, "Determinants of the Labor Force Participation of Married Women: A Micro-Study of Toronto Households," Canadian Journal of Economics 6 (May 1973): 222-38. Wendy L. Gramm employed discriminant analysis on data of this type in "The Labor Force Decision of Married Female Teachers: A Discriminant Analysis Approach," Review of Economics and Statistics 55 (August 1973): 341-48.

4. Ray Marshall, Rural Workers in Rural Labor Markets (Salt Lake City, Utah: Olympus, 1974), p. 14.

5. The use of a dichotomous dependent variable introduces heteroskedasticity into the equation with the result that variances of the coefficients are biased in a direction that may lead to rejection of some coefficients that may in fact be statistically significant. Also, the resulting estimate of the conditional probability of participation is not constrained to fall within the 0 to 1 range. Several methods of data transformation are available for correcting this problem. Gunderson, however, has shown that the differences in results from use of ordinary least squares are trivial. See Morley Gunderson, "Statistical Models for Dichotomous Dependent Variables," mimeographed (Toronto: Center for Industrial Relations, University of Toronto, 1972. Thus, the analysis given here proceeds with the ordinary least squares techniques.

6. This methodological approach was followed in several of the studies contained in Glen Cain and Harold Watts, eds. Income Maintenance and Labor Supply (Chicago: Rand-McNally, 1973).

7. See, for example, Harold S. Luft, "The Impact of Poor Health on Earnings," Review of Economics and Statistics 57 (February 1975): 43-57; James W. Morgan et al., Income and Welfare in the United States (New York: McGraw-Hill, 1962); Joseph M. Davis, "Impact of Health on Earnings and Labor Market Activity," Monthly Labor Review 95 (October 1972): 46-49.

8. James Gwartney and Richard Stroup, "Measurement of Employment Discrimination According to Sex," Southern Economic Journal 39 (April 1973): 575-87.

9. Indicative of the theoretical works are George Stigler, "Information in the Labor Market," Journal of Political Economy (Supplement) 70 (October 1962): 95-105; Armen A. Alchain, "Information Costs, Pricing and Resource Unemployment," in Microeconomic Foundations of Employment and Inflation Theory, ed. Edward Phelps et al. (New York: Norton, 1970), pp. 29-52. Examples of the empirical efforts are seen in H. L. Sheppard and A. H. Belitsky, The Job Hunt (Baltimore: The Johns Hopkins University Press, 1966); Edward C. Koziara, Karen S. Koziara, and Andrew G. Verzilli, "Racial Differences in Migration and Job Search: A Case Study," Southern Economic Journal 37 (July 1970): 97-99; Harvey J. Hilaski, "How Poverty Area Residents Look for Work," Monthly Labor Review 94 (March 1971): 41-45; Thomas F. Bradshaw, "Job Seeking Methods Used by Unemployed Workers," Monthly Labor Review 96 (February 1973): 35-40; Carl Rosenfeld, "Job Seeking Methods Used by American Workers," Monthly Labor Review 98 (August 1975): 39-42; Albert Rees, "Information Networks in Labor Markets," American Economic Review 56 (May 1966): 559-66.

10. These are the results reported in Rosenfeld, "Job Seeking Methods Used by American Workers," and Bradshaw, "Job Seeking Methods Used by Unemployed Workers," which are studies dealing with the general population. Hilaski, "How Poverty Area Residents Look for Work," a study of the urban poor, found no significant difference in search and behavior along sex lines.

11. Melvin Lurie and Elton Rayack, "Racial Differences in Migration and Job Search: A Case Study," Southern Economic Journal 23 (July 1966): 81-95.

12. For an informative analysis of the process of occupational choice, see Donald R. Kaldor and Donald G. Zytowski, "A Maximizing Model of Occupational Decision-Making," Personnel Guidance Journal 47 (April 1969): 781-88.

13. Marshall, Rural Workers in Rural Labor Markets.

14. See, for example, Robert Houser and David Featherman, "White-Non White Differentials in Occupational Mobility among Men in the United States, 1962-1972," Demography 11 (May 1974): 274-66. Richard B. Freeman, "Changes in the Labor Market for Black Americans 1948-72," Brookings Papers on Economic Activity 1973, no. 1, A. K. Okun and George Z. Perry, eds. (Washington, D.C.: Brookings Institution, 1973), pp. 67-120.

15. For a discussion of occupational indexes and an example of a generally accepted index, see Otis Dudly Duncan, "A Socioeconomic Index for all Occupations," in Occupations and Social Status, ed. Albert J. Reiss et al. (New York: Free Press, 1961), pp. 109-38.

CHAPTER

5

INCOME
AND
EARNINGS

Income is the most common measure of the well-being of an individual or family. Although other factors (such as wealth) may actually be involved, the command over goods and services and the ability to choose among various options of life is limited by the level of current income for most families. In the rural South few families have command over more than one economic resource, the human resource, measured in terms of their own physical and mental capacities. As a result, the capacity to earn and the level of current earnings should be the focal point of any analysis of household income in the rural South.

In addition, the level and distribution of personal income and per capita income may serve as a measure of the economic well-being of a region and its inhabitants. Analysis of the sources of individual incomes, as well as the absolute levels, may also be utilized to investigate the potential for internally financed regional economic growth. Further, comparison of income sources and levels among population subgroups (such as age, race, and education) yields insight into the causative factors of unequal income distribution. Such a comparison also indicates the extent to which human-capital endowment and labor market discrimination influence the current level and distribution of income.

DISTRIBUTION OF CURRENT INCOME

The average household income for the rural sample was $6,353 in 1973. This is substantially below the mean income for the South and for the United States, even in 1969.[1] The mean income for the sample, although indicative of the overall low income levels, fails to show many important factors influencing level and distribution.

TABLE 5.1

Mean Incomes of Households, by Race, Sex,
Age, and County, 1973
(dollars)

Category	Mean Income
County of residence	
Dodge	7772
Natchitoches	6167
Sunflower	6023
Starr	5409
Race of head	
Anglo	8490
Black	4037
Chicano	5197
Sex of head	
Male	7479
Female	3286
Age of head	
16-24	5452
25-34	7907
35-44	8619
45-54	9225
55-64	6137
65 and over	3553

Substantial variation in mean income by race, sex, and age is obvious (see Table 5.1). Thus, if average income is used as a basis for decision, Dodge County would be preferable as a place of residence to any of the other three. Starr would be the least preferable. Although the mean-income figures reveal important information about the relative income of population subgroups, they cannot answer two important questions: What is the distribution of personal income, and what is the extent of variation among subgroups?

Although not shown by mean figures, almost 70 percent of the sample households had a total income below the 1973 mean income of $6353. In part, the result reflects variations between racial subgroups; the within-group variation was less extreme (see Table 5.2). It appears that not only are Anglos absolutely better off than Chicanos or blacks in terms of income, but for Anglos the distribution of personal income is less skewed toward the lower levels.

There is considerable variation in the income of black households between counties in percentage terms. However, blacks are not substantially better off in absolute terms in any one county, as indicated by the low county means for blacks: Dodge, $4746; Natchitoches, $4097; and Sunflower, $3745. Differences in mean income across counties are more pronounced for Anglos (Dodge, $8571; Natchitoches, $7558; Sunflower, $9593; and Starr, $11,053). When mean income figures are compared directly between Anglos and non-Anglos, it appears that Anglos are in the most favorable income positions in counties where they constitute a relatively small proportion of the population.

Clearly, female-headed households are in an adverse position with respect to income (see Table 5.2). Not only is their mean income absolutely low ($3,286), but over 65 percent of female-headed households had an income in 1973 below the mean. The distribution of income for male-headed households is also skewed toward the lower-income categories, but the higher mean around which the distribution is centered is significant in terms of relative well being.

As anticipated, younger and older households have relatively low income levels. Those in the prime earnings years (25 to 54)

TABLE 5.2

Total Income of Sample Households, by Race and Sex, 1973
(percent)

Income Category (dollars)	Anglo	Chicano	Black	Male	Female	Total
0-999	1.7	5.2	7.7	2.3	10.0	4.3
1000-1999	11.8	17.7	25.3	10.6	35.4	17.3
2000-2999	12.0	17.1	19.9	14.3	19.2	15.6
3000-3999	8.0	14.8	12.9	11.5	9.9	11.1
4000-4999	6.1	8.2	7.1	7.5	5.3	6.9
5000-5999	6.4	7.8	7.1	7.4	5.8	6.9
6000-6999	6.5	6.1	4.8	6.7	3.7	5.9
7000-7999	5.5	3.4	3.7	5.3	2.1	4.5
8000-8999	5.0	4.5	2.8	4.8	2.5	4.2
9000-9999	5.0	3.6	1.7	4.2	2.0	3.6
10,000-14,999	18.7	7.0	5.3	15.0	3.2	11.8
15,000-24,999	10.2	3.7	1.6	7.9	0.8	6.0
25,000 and over	3.3	0.8	0.2	2.4	0.1	1.8
Total number	1445	755	957	2310	848	3158

TABLE 5.3

Total Household Income, by Age, 1973
(percent)

Income Category (dollars)	Age Category					
	18-24	25-34	35-44	45-54	55-64	65 and over
0-999	4.5	1.3	3.3	3.6	6.5	5.5
1000-1999	12.3	9.7	7.9	9.1	18.4	31.3
2000-2999	12.8	8.4	8.9	9.8	12.8	28.6
3000-3999	12.3	10.6	7.5	11.5	11.4	12.6
4000-4999	8.9	7.1	6.2	8.2	6.8	6.0
5000-5999	9.5	7.8	7.9	9.1	7.4	3.9
6000-6999	10.6	7.6	7.5	6.2	5.8	3.2
7000-7999	7.3	5.4	5.0	6.6	4.6	1.9
8000-8999	4.5	6.7	5.0	5.5	4.6	1.4
9000-9999	4.5	5.2	5.2	3.8	4.2	1.4
10,000-14,999	10.6	20.3	21.1	14.0	11.0	2.1
15,000-24,999	2.2	7.6	12.4	9.8	4.4	1.3
25,000 and over	0.0	2.2	2.3	2.7	2.3	0.8
Total number	179	462	483	549	571	913

have the highest levels (see Table 5.3). The relatively poor position of the 65-years-and-over group is related to family size and limited access to earned income.

SOURCES OF INCOME

The current level of income is determined largely by the sources of household income or, as is the case of many households, the sources to which it is restricted. In general, household income is generated by two sources: earnings and transfers. A more useful delineation, however, is provided by dividing these two major categories into several subgroups. Therefore, in this work, earned income is divided into wages and salaries and business income (that is, proprietor's earnings). Other income is classified as government transfers or other private sources. Because of the importance of Social Security in the rural South, Old Age Survivors Disability and Health Insurance (OASDHI) is shown as a separate category.

County Distributions of Sources

Table 5.4 contains the distribution of the sources of income by county. Obviously, earned income in the form of wages and salaries is by far the most significant, but as a percent of the total income it is somewhat low when compared with findings of national studies.[2] The percentage of the households in the sample receiving business income is also lower than the national figure. Only Starr County displayed a percentage of households with wage and salary incomes that were sufficiently different from the total to merit comment. In all probability the higher proportion of income accounted for by wages and salaries in Starr County reflects the relatively smaller percentage of older households in the county as well as the higher labor force participation for Chicano men. In general, however, the variation in percentage of households with earned income is not great across counties.

Although a lack of significant differences was characteristic of earned income, the opposite is true for other sources of income. Both "other-private" and government transfers vary among the counties by substantial amounts. Variations in private sources probably reflect the industrial structure of the counties as well as the relative wealth. The differences in percentage of households receiving Social Security are a function of age distribution of the population and of industrial structure (that is, covered employment). Accordingly,

TABLE 5.4

Source of Income of Households
Receiving, by County, 1973
(percent)

Source	Total	Dodge	Natchitoches	Sunflower	Starr
Wages and salaries	63.0	62.7	57.4	62.6	69.7
Business income[a]	11.7	15.4	10.0	9.8	11.6
Other-private[b]	11.1	16.4	12.2	6.8	9.0
Transfers-government[c]	27.9	27.1	36.3	23.2	24.0
Social Security	28.3	31.9	31.2	28.2	21.6

[a]Includes farm income for those who own and operate a farm.
[b]Includes interest and dividend payments, rental income, private pensions, private donations.
[c]Includes Veterans Benefits, OAA, AFDC, Workman's Compensation, ABD, and Unemployment Insurance.

INCOME AND EARNINGS

TABLE 5.5

Source of Household Income, by Race, 1973
(percent)

Source	Anglo	Chicano	Black
Wages and salaries	61.7	67.1	61.3
Business income	16.3	11.6	4.7
Other—private[a]	17.0	8.9	4.1
Transfers—government[b]	20.7	25.0	40.9
Social Security	30.7	20.8	29.4

[a]Includes interest and dividend payments, rental income, private pensions, private donations.
[b]Includes Veterans Benefits, OAA, AFDC, Workman's Compensation, ABD, and Unemployment Insurance.

the variations are as expected. It is more difficult to explain differences among the counties in government transfers. Racial distribution within the counties may be a factor.

In order to gauge the effect of race and county variations, income source was distributed by race of household (see Table 5.5). Several important observations may be made by comparing data in Table 5.4 with those in Table 5.5. First, race alone does not explain inter-county variations in government transfers. If this were the case, Sunflower County should have contained the largest percentage of households with this income source; in fact, however, it contained the smallest. Second, the variations across counties in "other-private" sources probably are a function of race. It is obvious that private income sources apply to relatively few blacks; that is the case also for business income. In terms of number of recipients, government transfers are more significant as an income source for blacks than for Anglos or Chicanos, but they are an important source for all groups.

The relative impact of access to various sources of income is illustrated by comparing the means of income received by various sources. The mean wages for the sample was $6411 (1973); the mean of business income was $7732. These are more than twice the mean figures for any other source.

The mean private transfer income for the sample in 1973 was $2521, compared with $1135 for government transfers and $1844 for Social Security. The importance of these figures is accentuated by the fact that private transfers usually represent a supplement to earned income, but government transfers and Social Security are more likely to be the major source of household income.

Government transfers, Social Security, and, to a lesser extent, private transfers are distributed on the basis of factors over which the individual or household exercises little control. Even the fact of receipt or nonreceipt may be outside the individual's ability to influence, as it is determined by a political process in which the recipient seldom is an effective part.

In contrast, the level of earned income is influenced by direct actions of the individual or household. Additionally, individual characteristics such as sex, education, and training may be important determinants of the level of earnings.

Sources of Earned Income

Almost 70 percent of the households in the sample had some earned income in 1973, in the form either of wages and salaries or of proprietor's income. This is low compared with national figures. However, in light of an age distribution that has a disproportionately small number in working-age categories and a labor force participation rate of 42.3 percent for the over-16 population (57 percent for household heads), it is surprising that there were not even fewer households with earned income.

The mean value of earned income for the 3158 households reporting some income earned was $6618 ($6411 for wages and salaries and $7732 for proprietor's income). These figures, relative to total income distribution, lead to the hypothesis that for the majority of those with earned income, this source should account for a significant percentage of total income. For the majority (71 percent) of the sample households with earned income, it is the major determinant of their current income level. This was true for all four counties (Dodge, 64.5 percent; Natchitoches, 68.6 percent; Sunflower, 75 percent; and Starr, 75.6 percent.

Findings regarding income sources and the mean income levels by source in the sample counties allow several inferences about the role of earnings in total income. First, there appears to be relatively little current income generated by accumulated wealth. Second, the restrictions placed on earned income associated with many government transfers make it unlikely that earnings are a major income source for families with government transfer income.* These factors coupled with low means of government transfer income and private

---

*OASDHI, Aid to Families with Dependent Children (AFDC), and, at the time of this study, Old Age Assistance (OAA) were major government programs having earnings restrictions.

INCOME AND EARNINGS 99

transfers suggest that the greater the percentage of income accounted for by earnings, the higher is the total current income. Table 5.6 contains data on the percent of current income derived from earnings, by current income categories. The hypothesis tendered appears true.

As the level of income rises, in general the percentage of income earned rises. The major exceptions are the highest and lowest income categories. The relative decline in percentage of total income earned by households with current income in excess of $25,000 probably reflects the relationship between high current earnings and wealth. Nevertheless, 72 percent of the households in this category received between 90 and 100 percent of their income from earnings.

It is difficult to explain why earnings accounted for 90 to 100 percent of the total income for 80 percent of households with less than $1000 current income. Most of these households may not be eligible for any of the federally financed welfare programs.* Although the absolute number of households involved is small, the extremely low income level indicates a serious unresolved problem.

The importance of earned income to a majority of households in the sample is obvious. It is also apparent that the level of earnings is subject to considerable variation among households. Earned income of a given household can be separated into two components: earnings of the household head and earnings of other household members. Most households with more than one wage earner are husband-wife households. In the rural sample over 85 percent of the secondary family workers were wives. Analysis of earned income of household members other than the head will, therefore, be confined to working wives.

Earnings of Household Head

For most households the income of the household head is a major portion of the total family income. Since earnings are the major income source for a majority of families, it follows that the earnings of the head will be a major determinant of total family income. Sixty-three percent of the household heads in the rural sample had some earnings during 1973. For those 1995 households, the earnings of the head were a relatively large component of total income, as the data in Table 5.7 indicate. Although less than half the total households derived all of their income from the head's earn-

---

*A number appeared to be eligible but were not receiving any type of support. The programs referred to are OAA, AFDC, Aid to the Blind, and Aid to the Permanently and Totally Disabled (or ABD, referring to the last two programs combined).

TABLE 5.6

Earned Income as a Percentage of Total Income,
by Income Category, 1973

Income Category ($)	Percent Earned										Total Number
	0–10	11–20	21–30	31–40	41–50	51–60	61–70	71–80	81–90	91–100	
0–999	0.0	3.6	1.8	5.4	1.8	3.6	0.0	1.8	1.8	80.4	56
1000–1999	5.5	6.6	7.7	6.1	3.3	6.6	1.1	3.3	3.3	56.4	181
2000–2999	4.9	5.8	5.3	5.3	4.4	6.8	7.3	4.4	2.9	52.9	206
3000–3999	2.8	3.3	1.2	4.5	3.7	8.1	6.5	4.9	4.5	60.6	246
4000–4999	2.3	2.8	1.1	4.0	4.5	6.2	3.4	4.5	6.2	65.0	177
5000–5999	0.0	1.6	2.7	3.8	3.8	2.2	5.9	8.6	4.9	66.5	185
6000–6999	0.6	2.3	1.2	0.6	5.8	4.0	4.0	8.7	5.8	67.1	173
7000–7999	1.5	0.0	0.8	3.8	2.3	0.8	2.3	1.5	6.8	80.5	133
8000–8999	1.7	0.0	1.7	2.5	1.7	5.0	0.0	4.1	5.0	78.5	121
9000–9999	0.0	0.9	4.5	0.9	3.6	0.9	2.7	2.7	1.8	81.8	110
10,000–14,999	1.1	0.0	0.6	0.6	1.1	1.7	1.4	2.5	4.5	86.5	356
15,000–24,999	0.5	1.1	1.1	1.1	1.1	1.6	2.0	4.3	5.9	81.3	187
25,000 and over	1.9	7.4	0.0	1.9	5.6	0.0	2.7	3.7	3.7	72.2	54

TABLE 5.7

Earnings of Household Head as a Percentage
of Total Household Income, 1973

Percent of Income	Total	Dodge	Natchitoches	Sunflower	Starr
1-10	2.0	2.6	2.3	1.8	1.3
11-20	2.4	2.0	4.0	0.8	2.9
21-30	3.7	4.0	4.4	3.9	2.5
31-40	5.1	4.2	5.3	6.1	4.8
41-50	7.9	7.2	8.4	7.5	8.4
51-60	9.9	10.4	9.7	10.2	9.3
61-70	9.1	11.4	8.4	8.9	7.6
71-80	9.2	9.8	8.4	8.3	10.1
81-90	7.8	8.8	9.0	6.5	7.0
91-100	43.1	39.7	40.1	45.9	46.2
Total number	1995	501	476	492	526

ings, 80 percent obtained the majority of 1973 income from this source. These figures varied only slightly across counties.

The level of earnings varies substantially with the specific characteristics of an individual household head. For example, the mean earnings figure was $6002 for all household heads, but female heads of household earned half that figure ($3049). Similar variation in mean earnings is found among racial groups, as the data in Table 5.8 indicate. Anglo mean earnings were substantially above those of Chicanos and blacks. Variations by age appear to conform to the normal pattern associated with low earnings for young workers, rising earnings into the prime labor-age categories, and a decline in later years.

Analysis of variations in earned income by race and sex of the household head revealed that the two most important factors are the relatively small percentage of blacks and Chicanos with earnings above $10,000 (2.4 percent and 7.5 percent, respectively) and the large percentage of female heads with under $3000 income (62.8 percent). The most important factor, however, is the overall low earnings distribution that is accentuated for black, Chicano, and all female household heads.

The percentage of total income not accounted for by earnings of household heads must come from one of three sources: transfer payments to the head, earnings of other family members, or transfer payments to other family members. Most household heads (83 percent) who had earnings derived 90 to 100 percent of their total income

TABLE 5.8

Mean Earnings of Household Heads, by
Selected Characteristics, 1973

Characteristic	Mean Earnings (dollars)	Sample Size (number)
Sex		
Male	6569	1677
Female	3049	322
Race		
Anglo	8244	938
Black	3403	551
Chicano	4587	520
Age		
16-24	4149	166
25-34	6685	421
35-44	7048	427
45-54	6558	461
55-64	4995	371
65 and over	3983	153

from this source. Transfer payments were a relatively small part of the household head's income. Therefore, income generated by other family members is the most important factor accounting for differences between the total income and the earnings of the household head.

Earnings of Working Wives

The earnings of a wife can be extremely important to the economic well-being of a family.[3] The hypothesis has also been asserted that earnings of wives have a "favorable" effect on the overall distribution of family income.[4] With increased labor force participation of women generally, and married women particularly, earnings of the wife are becoming an extremely important income source for many families.

Just under a quarter (24.2 percent) of all married women in the sample had some earned income in 1973. This is 30 percent of all the married women under 65 years of age. Although the wife's earnings are important to most families, they take on added significance if the wife is the only wage earner in the household. Twenty-nine percent of the working wives were the sole source of household earnings. However, in less than 1 percent of the cases did the wife's earnings represent the only income source. Table 5.9 shows the distribution of the earnings of wives as a percentage of total family income. Clearly, for most households in which the wife is employed, her earnings are a secondary, supplemental income source. In 75 percent of these households the wives' earnings accounted for less than one-half of the total family income.

There is a high probability that a household with two wage earners will be in one of the three upper-income categories, as indicated by the fact that 43.9 percent of the families in the $10,000 to $14,999 bracket had two wage earners, as did over 50 percent of those in the $15,000-and-higher category. There is, however, a significant percentage of households in the lower categories that have two wage earners. In the rural South, multiple wage earners in one household do not assure a relatively high income.

Several other important observations may be made concerning earnings of wives. The mean earnings ($4226) do not display the wide variation by race found in the mean earnings of household heads, although Anglo wives have substantially higher earnings ($4565) than do black ($3707) or Chicano ($3839) wives. However, for all races the mean earnings of wives exceeds the mean for female household heads ($3049).

In general, it can be stated that households with two wage earners were better off in terms of total income than were households with

TABLE 5.9

Wives' Earnings as a Percentage of Total Household Income, by County, 1973
(percent)

Percent of Income	Total	Dodge	Natchitoches	Sunflower	Starr
1-10	5.7	4.2	7.4	6.7	4.1
11-20	10.3	15.0	10.1	7.4	7.1
21-30	17.7	14.4	14.2	15.4	20.4
31-40	20.8	24.0	22.3	21.5	12.2
41-50	22.2	21.6	18.9	22.1	28.6
51-60	13.0	7.8	14.2	14.1	18.4
61-70	6.4	6.0	5.4	9.4	4.1
71-80	3.4	4.8	3.4	2.7	2.0
81-90	2.0	1.2	3.1	0.7	3.1
91-100	0.5	1.2	0.7	0	0
Total number	562	167	148	149	98

only one. The wide variation in earned income among households implies that factors such as race, sex, and age have a significant impact on the earnings level.

DETERMINANTS OF EARNINGS

Research into factors influencing earnings and, therefore, income has been extensive. Numerous studies have investigated the impact on income of productivity-related factors, such as formal education, apprenticeship programs, and vocational training. Others have concentrated on personal characteristics, such as race, sex, age, and health.[5] Analysis of the tremendous volume of research leads to the conclusion that there are three determinants of earnings: labor force participation, wage rates, and time engaged in work activities. The effect of such factors as race, sex, education, and age on earnings results from their influence on one, two, or all three of these determinants.

The influence of labor force participation is self-evident. Earnings come only from employment and, by definition, labor force participation is a precondition for employment. Factors that influence the labor force status of household heads as well as of all household members of working age affect the total household earnings. The discussion of determinants of labor force participation in Chapter 4 and the subsequent findings help explain differentials in earned income among households.

The variations in labor force participation by age and sex are particularly important in explaining the low income levels of elderly households and female-headed households. A similar conclusion seems warranted with respect to the effect that age and sex differences have on the distribution of income among racial groups, although the relatively low labor force participation for blacks by no means can account for the total variations in income. This is particularly true in light of the wide variations in earnings. It is necessary to analyze both the determinants of wage rates and the determinants of hours worked in order to construct an accurate picture of the impact which earnings have on income.

Wages in the Rural South

The standard method of determining the effect of variables on wage rates begins with classification of the variables into three broad groups: individual variables, labor market variables, and national variables.[6] In practice the three sets of factors are likely to be highly intercorrelated.

INCOME AND EARNINGS

The estimating equations developed to determine the wage effect of individual factors have usually explained no more than 30 to 40 percent of the variation about the mean of the analyzed wage rates.[7] The variables used to capture the individual effects are generally of the following type: years in present job, race, age, sex, years of education, manpower-development training, and marital status. Individual variables stress the importance of the human-capital accumulation of the individual. To some extent this approach reflects supply elements of wage determination. However, it is inadequate to assume that individual characteristics represent inherent productivity. These variables may also reflect institutional characteristics, which may in turn reflect elements of discrimination and payments above minimum levels required to keep resources in their present uses, more than mere productivity of human capital.

The supply explanation of the functioning of labor markets assumes a homogeneous labor force in which institutional realities of discrimination are ignored. The human-capital approach introduces the individual characteristics of the labor force into the problem.

The labor market factors usually refer to differences in industrial mix among labor markets. This approach reflects demand elements of the wage-determination model. Factors that typically have an impact on wage structure are occupation and industry, size of labor market, geographic region of employment, and extent of union membership in the labor market area.

The traditional demand function ignores the effect of labor market variables on the formation of individual wage rates. However, any model of wage-rate determination should take these factors into account.

Finally, national factors also have an impact on the individual wage rate. This can be represented in many ways, but one of the more obvious is the coincident movement of employment and unemployment in labor market areas across the United States. During a business expansion, there tends to be a high positive correlation among labor market areas for changes in both employment and unemployment, a tendency that suggests that underlying national forces have an impact on individual wage rates.[8] However, the cross-sectional nature of the data dictates that no attempt be made to catch the impact of national and/or regional factors on local wage rates.

In general, mean wage rates for heads of households in the rural county study are considerably higher than for all employed individuals 16 years and older (see Table 5.10). However, there are four exceptions: black women in the Dodge, Natchitoches, and Sunflower labor market areas and Chicano women in the Starr labor market area. In contrast, Anglo female heads of households make higher average wages than employed Anglo women age 16 and over in the Dodge,

TABLE 5.10

Mean Wage Rate, by County, Race, and Sex

	Employed Heads of Household		Employed, 16 Years and Over	
	Wage Rate (dollars)	Sample Size (number)	Wage Rate (dollars)	Sample Size (number)
Dodge	3.460	437	2.951	746
Anglo	3.760	351	3.154	237
Female	2.449	47	2,331	237
Male	3.963	304	3.699	358
Black	2.234	86	2.151	151
Female	1.565	19	1.935	68
Male	2.424	67	2.328	83
Natchitoches	3.339	376	2.961	616
Anglo	3.833	240	3.377	379
Female	2.820	30	2.687	138
Male	3.978	210	3.772	341
Black	2.364	134	2.219	234
Female	1.517	35	1.832	111
Male	2.664	99	2.569	123
Sunflower	2.663	454	2.486	720
Anglo	3.621	183	3.102	317
Female	2.701	22	2.512	127
Male	3.476	161	3.497	190
Black	2.016	271	2.001	403
Female	1.813	60	1.957	151
Male	2.074	211	2.027	252
Starr	2.660	394	2.358	683
Chicano	2.660	394	2.358	683
Female	1.953	31	1.989	230
Male	2.720	363	2.546	453
Total	3.025	1661	2.686	2765

Natchitoches, and Sunflower labor market areas. It should be noted that the sample of the Starr labor market area included all of the Spanish-surname household heads and individuals.

Based on the preceding sections, it can be argued that minority women who are heads of households have been forced to cut short their education and take lower-paying jobs in order to support their families. The more stable family status of Anglo women probably results in fewer Anglo women who are household heads at an early age. When Anglo women do enter the labor force, their educational background is superior to that of black female heads of households.

In all cases, as shown in Table 5.10, Anglo mean wages exceed mean wages for blacks. Also, the dispersion of wage rates for Anglos is much greater than that for blacks. This indicates that blacks' wages tend to be concentrated at the lower wage levels.

Fairly large wage-rate differences also exist between men and women of the same race or cultural background, with the exception of blacks in Sunflower County. It also should be noted that in the predominantly black Sunflower labor area and in the largely Chicano Starr labor market area, the mean wages are less than those in the predominantly Anglo labor market areas.

It is apparent from Table 5.11 that the average mean wage is directly related to years of education. In each of the four labor market areas the differentials in wage rates associated with educational attainment are significantly large. In all four labor market

TABLE 5.11

Mean Hourly Wage Rate, by Years of Education, by County

Years of Education	Heads of Households		Age 16 Years and Over	
	Wages (dollars)	Number	Wages (dollars)	Number
Dodge	3.460	437	2.951	746
1-7	2.591	105	2.371	128
8-12	3.585	277	2.894	515
13-26	4.488	55	3.903	103
Natchitoches	3.339	376	2.961	616
1-7	2.439	93	2.256	109
8-12	3.151	184	2.691	334
13-26	4.533	99	3.928	173
Sunflower	2.663	454	2.486	720
1-7	1.863	159	1.827	196
8-12	2.821	239	2.520	412
13-26	4.259	56	3.511	112
Starr	2.660	394	2.358	683
1-7	1.811	179	1.748	246
8-12	2.873	153	2.343	304
13-26	4.584	62	3.523	133
Total	3.025	1551	2.686	2765

areas, wage rates are significantly higher for heads of households than for other individuals at a given level of attained education. This probably reflects the fact that household heads having the same educational level as do other individuals generally would have been employed longer in their present jobs. For household heads it appears that wage differences are minor across labor market areas.

More specifically, heads of households in the largely Anglo Dodge labor market area with one to seven years of education receive an average $2.59 per hour. In the Sunflower labor market area, which is largely black, the corresponding wage rate is $1.86. For persons having some college training, the average wage rate in the Dodge labor market area is $4.49, as opposed to $4.26 in the Sunflower labor market area.

This closing of the wage gap between Anglos and minorities, resulting from education, occurs only in the case of heads of households. Mean wage rates of employed persons 16 years and older show differentials at all educational levels.

The Wage-Determination Model

The model to be investigated is of the following form:

$$W = f(\underline{C}, \underline{L}) \tag{5.1}$$

where W is the individual wage rate, $\underline{C}$ is a matrix of individual characteristics variables, and $\underline{L}$ is a matrix of local labor market variables. The variables in $\underline{C}$ consist of continuous variables representing age, years in present job, and years of education, as well as qualitative (dummy) variables representing race, marital status, job training status, job status, receipt of payments in kind, number of jobs held, health status, and receipt of cash for farm work. The variables in $\underline{L}$ consist of dummy variables representing local labor market conditions and industrial structure.

The method employed to estimate Equation 5.1 is that of ordinary least squares for multiple linear regression. The specific variables utilized are:

W	= Wage rate
AGE	= Age
ED	= Years of Education
UPJ	= Years in present job
DODGE	= Dummy variable for Dodge County labor market; DODGE = 1 if Dodge County, 0 otherwise
NATCH	= Dummy variable for Natchitoches Parish labor market; NATCH = 1 if Natchitoches Parish, 0 otherwise
SUN	= Dummy variable for Sunflower County labor market; SUN = 1 if Sunflower County, 0 otherwise

INCOME AND EARNINGS 109

	$DODGE = NATCH = SUN = 0$ if Starr County labor market
SEX	= Dummy variable for male, SEX = 1 if male, 0 otherwise
ANGLO	= Dummy variable for Anglo, ANGLO = 1 if White, 0 otherwise
BLACK	= Dummy variable for black, BLACK = 1 if black, 0 otherwise
	$ANGLO = BLACK = 0$ if Chicano
WED	= Dummy variable for marital status; WED = 1 if married, 0 otherwise
TRAIN	= Dummy variable for job-training status, TRAIN = 1 if training completed, 0 otherwise
FTD	= Dummy variable for job status; FTD = 1 if employed full time (over 35 hours per week), 0 otherwise
PDK	= Dummy variable for payments in kind; PKD = 1 if received payments in kind, 0 otherwise
SJD	= Dummy variable for second job; SJD = 1 if held second job, 0 otherwise
HEALTH	= Dummy variable for health problem HEALTH = 1 if experiencing health problems, 0 otherwise
FWPD	= Dummy variable for farm work for pay; FWPD = 1 if receiving farm work pay, 0 otherwise
IAD	= Dummy variable for agricultural industry; IAD = 1 if employed in agriculture, 0 otherwise
IED	= Dummy variable for mining industry; IED = 1 if employed in mining, 0 otherwise
ICD	= Dummy variable for construction industry; ICD = 1 if employed in construction, 0 otherwise
IMD	= Dummy variable for manufacturing industry; IMD = 1 if employed in manufacturing, 0 otherwise
ITD	= Dummy variable for transportation industry; ITD = 1 if employed in transportation, 0 otherwise
IWD	= Dummy variable for wholesale trade industry; IWD = 1 if employed in wholesale trade, 0 otherwise
IRD	= Dummy variable for retail trade industry; IRD = 1 if employed in retail trade, 0 otherwise
IFD	= Dummy variable for finance industry; IFD = 1 if employed in finance, 0 otherwise
ISD	= Dummy variable for service industry; ISD = 1 if employed in service, 0 otherwise

The linear stochastic form of Equation 5.1 is:

$$W_i = B_0 + B_1 AGE_i + B_2 ED_i + B_3 YPJ_i + B_4 DODGE_i +$$
$$B_5 NATCH_i + B_6 SUN_i + B_7 SEX_i + B_8 ANGLO_i +$$
$$B_9 BLACK_i + B_{10} WED_i + B_{11} TRAIN_i =$$
$$B_{12} FTD_i + B_{13} PDK_i + B_{14} SJD_i + B_{15} HEALTH_i +$$
$$B_{16} FWPD_i + B_{17} IAD_i + B_{18} IED_i + B_{19} ICD_i +$$
$$B_{20} IMD_i + B_{21} ITD_i + B_{22} IWD_i + B_{23} IRD_i +$$
$$B_{24} IFD_i + B_{25} ISD_i + u_i \qquad (5.2)$$

where u_i is a stochastic error term. An equation of the form 5.2 is estimated for employed heads of household and for employed individuals (16 years and older). In addition, Equation 5.2 is computed for the individual counties utilizing each of the two sets of data.

Wage Rates for Employed Heads of Households

Table 5.12 presents the results of the wage equation for employed heads of households for the combined labor market areas. The equation explains about 42 percent of the variation in individual wage rates. The overall F-ratio is significant at the 1-percent level, and the standard error of the estimate is $1.41. The average wage rate for all four labor market areas is $3.03. The present study uses three continuous independent variables, two of which proved to be significant, and 22 dummy variables. Eleven of the dummy variables are significant at either the 5- or 1-percent levels. Of the 25 independent variables used in this analysis, the coefficients of the two variables FTD and FWPD carry a sign that requires further explanation. All of the other independent variables have the expected sign.

In the case of FTD, the regression coefficient of -0.00480 indicates that household heads reporting full-time employment received $0.0048 less per hour than individuals reporting part-time employment; this appears to be inconsistent. However, the small t-value recorded for this coefficient indicates that little meaning can be attached to this perverse sign. The FWPD coefficient of -0.28879 indicates that, all other things being equal, an individual receiving cash payments for farm work made $0.28879 per hour less than a person who did not do any farm work for cash wages. In this case, the coefficient is highly significant. The probable explanation is that individuals employed at lower wage rates are more likely to seek outside employment or second jobs. Individuals in rural areas who engage in seasonal agricultural work receive low wages and are likely to supplement their regular income through off-season nonagricultural employment.

TABLE 5.12

Regression Results: Relation between the Wage Rate of Employed Heads of Households in Rural Areas to Selected Individual Characteristics

Variable	Regression Coefficient	t-Value
Constant	0.25505	—
AGE	0.00260	0.76470
ED	0.16364	15.93379[a]
YPJ	0.06792	7.80690[a]
DODGE	0.25012	1.00952
NATCH	0.29392	1.18421
SUN	0.21965	0.88348
SEX	0.64455	3.57111[a]
ANGLO	0.44452	1.83785
BLACK	-0.32873	-1.29488
WED	0.40039	2.47506[b]
TRAIN	0.16125	1.54810
FTD	-0.00480	-0.03976
PKD	-0.31298	-2.6585[a]
SJD	-0.07466	-0.48605
HEALTH	-0.23786	-1.99196[b]
FWPD	-0.28879	-2.06323[b]
IAD	-0.66035	-4.24799[a]
IED	-0.12937	-0.50654
ICD	0.12666	0.78827
IMD	-0.64572	-4.92728[a]
ITD	-0.33607	-1.58554
IWD	-1.01443	-4.77784[a]
IRD	-1.03428	-7.75671[a]
IFD	0.68953	2.47827[b]
ISD	-0.59209	-4.68945[a]

Note: $R^2 = 0.42289$; $S_e = 1.4138$; F-Ratio = 45.575.[a]
[a]Significant at the 0.01 level.
[b]Significant at the 0.05 level.

The three continuous variables used in this analysis, AGE, ED, and YPJ, are typically viewed as important explanatory variables in explaining the variation in individual wage rates. However, in the presence of all independent variables, the age of the head of household proves not to be a significant variable.

On the other hand, the human capital variables, years of education and years in present job, are highly significant. Each year of education adds $0.16364 to the hourly wage scale of employed workers, and the longevity of the worker in his present job accounts for $0.06792 per hour for each year of seniority.

The 22 dummy variables represent two distinct forces at work in determining the individual wage rates in the four labor market areas. The following dummy variables reflect individual influences on the wage rates of heads of households: SEX, ANGLO, BLACK, WED, TRAIN, FTD, PKD, SJK, HEALTH, and FWPD. Five of these dummy variables proved to be significant at the 5- and 1-percent levels: WED, SEX, PKD, HEALTH and FWPD.

The married head of household makes 40 cents an hour more than the unmarried household head, and the male household head averages 64 cents per hour more than a female head of household, after the other independent variables have been taken into account. Household heads receiving payments in kind earn an average of 31 cents an hour less than persons who work only for cash payments. Household heads experiencing health problems typically make about 24 cents an hour less than persons without health problems. Heads of households receiving pay for farm work make 29 cents an hour less than other workers.

Here again, the importance of the human-capital variables is evident in the form of the reduced average wages of workers with health problems. However, the most important dummy variables in this analysis reflect institutional factors rather than human capital. Clearly, sex and marital status have a major impact on the wage rates of heads of households.

Twelve dummy variables show the effect of the local labor market and the industrial structure on the wage rate of head of households. None of the specific labor market dummies proved to be significant, but of the industrial structure variables, IAD, IMD, IWD, IRD, IFD, and ISD were significant at the 5- or 1-percent levels. The contribution of the nine industrial dummy variables is calculated using the government sector as the base. A regression coefficient of -0.66035 means that an agricultural worker, on average, makes about 66 cents per hour less than an individual working in government. On the other hand, a household head employed in the finance sector makes about 69 cents an hour more than a person employed in the government sector.

Despite the fact that the four rural labor market areas were drawn from very diverse geographic surroundings, the labor market did not exert a significant impact on head-of-household wage rates. One might have expected that Starr County with its heavy concentration of Chicanos and Sunflower County with its large black population would have had labor market characteristics different from the predominantly Anglo Dodge County and Natchitoches Parish. However, from this analysis there is every indication that low-income rural counties in the Southwest and Southeast are homogeneous with regard to the workings of the labor market. This was confirmed by the labor market wage equations estimated for the individual labor market areas.[9]

Two differences between the county equations and the total equations merit brief comment. One of the salient differences between the individual labor market equations and the composite estimating equations is the significance of the race variable. Where wage rates for heads of households are lowest, a significant difference in wages exists between Anglos and blacks in Sunflower and between Anglos and Chicanos in Starr labor market areas. A similar wage difference, also statistically significant, exists between Anglos and blacks in the Dodge labor market areas.

The variable for job-training status shows interesting differences among the four labor market areas. The regression coefficient is highly significant for the Dodge labor market area but is not significant in the other three. Apparently either there are higher-quality labor inputs to training programs in the Dodge labor market area relative to the other three areas or management in the Dodge area has a greater appreciation of worker training programs. Specifically, training in the Dodge labor market area was worth, on average, a pay differential of 54 cents per hour.

Wage Rates for Employed Individuals (16 and Older)

The composite estimating equation for employed individuals presented in Table 5.13 explains about 41 percent of the variation in wage rates. In general, the regression coefficients are similar in size and sign to those for employed heads of households. However, there are several exceptions that require explanation.

The age variable is significant in explaining wage rates for employed individuals, but the regression coefficient is quite small in this case, adding only $0.006 to wage rates for each year of age. This variable is not significant for heads of households.

The coefficient of the sex variable is significant for both employed individuals and household heads. However, the wage differential is much larger in the case of employed individuals. Employed male workers made about 89 cents more than their female counterparts; in the case of employed heads of households, men make approximately 64 cents more than women. This difference is due in part to the fact that employed women are likely to be secondary wage earners with less attachment to the labor force and receiving lower wages.

TABLE 5.13

Regression Results: Relation between the Wage Rate of Employed Individuals (16 Years and Over) in Rural Areas and Selected Individual Characteristics

Variable	Regression Coefficient	t-value
Constant	−0.16128	—
AGE	0.00690	2.92373[a]
ED	0.15670	20.35065[a]
YPJ	0.06611	10.13957[a]
DODGE	0.26164	1.43901
NATCH	0.31975	1.76921
SUN	0.20600	1.14597
SEX	0.88973	14.50729[a]
ANGLO	0.26838	1.52212
BLACK	0.26746	−1.46121
WED	0.32553	5.19601
TRAIN	0.22135	2.80048[a]
FTD	−0.01790	−0.21211
PKD	−0.22500	−2.46412
SJD	0.03256	0.24590
HEALTH	−0.22978	−2.46043[b]
IAD	−0.75379	−7.72168[a]
IED	0.02437	0.10919
ICD	0.19044	1.48746
IMB	−0.49616	−5.36215[b]
ITD	−0.21056	−1.29225
IWD	−0.77897	−4.61366[b]
IRD	−0.87962	−9.55797[b]
IFD	0.17725	0.99926
ISD	−0.45017	−5.32809[b]

Note: R^2 = .48045; S_e = 1.2677; F-Ratio = 71.504[a]; n = 2510
[a]Significant at the .01 level.
[b]Significant at the .05 level.

Training programs do not significantly increase the earnings of employed heads of households. However, employed individuals significantly benefit from such programs.

There appears to be one significant difference among the industrial dummy variables. The finance sector dummy variable does not possess a significant coefficient for employed individuals. This reflects the fact that individuals are employed in the lower-paying jobs in the finance sector, even though the finance sector in rural areas is characterized as a high-wage industry.

It should be noted that the variable "farm work for pay" was not included in the analysis of employed individuals. This variable did appear in the wage regression for employed heads of households and was statistically significant.

Regression analysis was conducted on each of the four county labor market areas. Generally, these individual wage equations are in line with composite findings.[10]

The results strongly support a hypothesis already formulated in Chapter 4 that substantial racial and sex discrimination exists in rural Southern labor markets. Such a finding leads to the conclusion that much of the income differences, particularly between Anglos and blacks, is not based on productivity differences. The surprising lack of significance attached to the training variable as a factor in explaining the wage rate of household heads holds an important implication for manpower policy.

Time Worked in Rural Labor Markets

One important aspect of labor market experience involves the amount of work time an individual participant may choose within a given time frame. Traditional economic theory views this aspect of labor market behavior as a voluntary worker choice between income and leisure. It is obviously important to investigate the nature of the process by which the work-leisure decision is made. However, it is perhaps of more value to try to identify those factors that limit or restrict a worker in this decision and to estimate the nature and degree of their impact on actual work time.

In this study the analysis of work time was divided into two parts: hours worked per week and weeks worked per year. This decision was dictated partially by the nature of the data and partially by the belief that factors affecting the number of hours worked per week, such as child-care responsibilities, availability of overtime, and certain types of health restrictions, probably were different from the factors which determined the number of weeks worked in a year, particularly in a rural area.

Hours of Work

Hours-of-work preference of rural residents has not been specifically examined; however, there are two urban studies on this topic.[11] These have concentrated on explaining the variation in working hours of the general population, although some of the earlier inquiries were undertaken to discover whether the supply curve for labor is backward bending. Generally, their findings supported this notion.[12] Others have estimated the hours of work function in an effort to isolate a dynamic component in the discouraged worker effect.[13]

More recently, the determinants of hours of work have come under more intensive investigation as policy makers have sought to discover the effect on work effort of a guaranteed annual income scheme like the negative income tax. For the most part, these investigations used micro data from the <u>1967 Survey of Economic Opportunity</u>. The consensus of findings supports the economist's presumption that positive income transfers will increase a person's consumption of leisure (or cause him to work less).[14] However, there is considerable disagreement over the magnitude of this income effect.

The studies mentioned above do have one methodological advantage over this one. The hours-of-work variable was collected in continuous form. However, in many of those studies hours worked were estimated rather than secured directly from the interviewee. The data in the rural sample, on the other hand, were collected on a <u>categorical</u> basis. The three categories are: (1) 1-34 hours, (2) 35 to 48 hours, and (3) 49+ hours.

Such a data configuration suggests basically two approaches to analyzing rural hours of work preferences. One can use a cross-tabular presentation. Although useful, this approach makes it difficult to hold constant all the important factors influencing hours of work so that the influence of any one variable might be determined. Nonetheless, the cross-tabular approach is used for descriptive purposes. A greater reliance will be placed on regression analysis, as this method makes a more rigorous allowance for ceteris paribus factors.

<u>Individual Variations in Hours Worked</u>. Approximately 55 percent (1864) of the household heads interviewed during this study reported that they were employed. These individuals were asked how many hours they worked at all jobs in the week prior to the interview. The responses were tabulated in the categories mentioned above. Useful replies were secured from 1760 household heads (1516 men and 244 women).

The breakdown of weekly hours worked by sex is shown in Table 5.14. Not surprisingly, the data indicate that men tend to work longer hours than women. Although the percentage working in the standard work-week range (35 to 48 hours) is quite close, a signifi-

TABLE 5.14

Distribution of Hours Worked, by Sex and Race,
Rural Household Heads, 1973
(percent)

Hours Worked	Male	Female	Anglo	Chicano	Black
1-34	13.9	31.2	8.8	16.1	29.4
35-48	62.1	58.6	60.0	65.8	61.0
49+	24.3	10.2	31.2	18.1	9.6
Total number	1516	244	886	392	479

cantly smaller percentage of men work short hours (13.6 percent versus 31.2 percent for women), and a larger percentage work long hours (24.3 percent versus 10.2 percent for women). No doubt, part of this variance in working hours can be attributed to the additional nonmarket house-care responsibilities of the women. However, all female household heads in this sample, by definition, are unmarried,* so the variance in work behavior across sexes cannot be attributed wholly to differences in family responsibilities. It may be due to sex discrimination, differentials in health problems, education, training, and/or age.

Table 5.14 shows that Anglos tend to work longer hours than Chicanos, and Chicanos work longer hours than blacks. The distributions by race are basically the same between races. It is at the extreme ends that the differences occur. Anglos tend to have a much higher percentage working "overtime" hours (31.2 percent, as compared with 18.1 percent and 9.6 percent for Chicanos and blacks, respectively). Once again, it is not possible to tell via cross-tabular analysis whether these differences are due to racial discrimination, to variances in human-capital embodiments, and/or to diverse preferences for leisure.

It is conventionally assumed that younger and older workers have a greater preference for leisure time than do prime-age workers and that, as a result, younger and older workers tend to work fewer hours per week. To a small extent the rural data reveal such a phenomenon. There are few young (16 to 24-year-old) household heads in the sample. With the exception of the eight teenage men,

---

*In accordance with the U.S. Census definition, married women are not considered household heads except under certain selective circumstances (for example, if the husband is overseas, in the military).

the younger household heads do tend to work fewer hours per week than do those in the middle-age range. The differences, however, are slight. The variances for older workers on the other hand—particularly those 65 years of age and older—are more pronounced. Some 31 percent of elderly men and 65 percent of elderly women work 1 to 34 hours per week. Those persons of both sexes aged 55 to 64 also tend to work significantly fewer hours per week than the prime-age workers.

One way in which workers can satisfy their performances for hours of work is through occupational and industrial mobility. It is apparent from the figures in Table 5.15 that when one looks across occupations in these four rural counties, considerable dispersion exists in the typical work hours. Short work weeks (fewer than 35 hours) appear to be common in plant farming, food and beverage preparation, mining-logging-extraction, and construction trades.

TABLE 5.15

Hours Worked by Household Heads, by Occupation, 1973
(percent)

Occupation	Hours Worked		
	1–34	35–48	49+
Professional	4.6	70.4	25.0
Administration and managerial	5.7	59.3	35.1
Clerical and technical	9.7	77.4	12.9
Sales	9.9	54.3	35.8
Domestic service	67.3	26.5	6.1
Food and beverage preparation	31.0	54.8	14.3
Service workers	19.0	61.2	19.8
Plant farming	35.5	44.7	19.7
Animal farming	15.6	51.1	33.3
Miscellaneous agriculture, forestry, and fishing	17.0	45.2	37.8
Manufacturing—new materials processing	10.0	73.3	16.7
Manufacturing—durables	11.5	71.0	17.6
Manufacturing—assembly production	5.6	79.4	15.1
Construction trades	20.7	68.4	10.9
Transportation	15.0	59.4	25.6
Packaging	4.7	81.4	14.0
Mining, logging, extraction	26.7	46.7	26.7

TABLE 5.16

Hours Worked by Household Heads, by Industry, 1973
(percent)

Industry	Hours Worked			Sample Size
	1–34	35–48	49+	
Mining	5.6	61.1	33.3	36
Construction	27.3	58.6	14.1	128
Manufacturing	15.5	59.8	24.7	219
Transportation, communication, and public utilities	0.0	85.7	14.3	56
Wholesale trade	8.1	54.8	37.1	62
Retail trade	6.4	56.8	36.8	185
Finance, insurance, and real estate	12.4	68.8	18.8	32
Service	13.3	67.0	19.7	188
Government	6.6	78.7	14.7	273
Other	16.7	66.6	16.7	6

The domestic-service occupation is almost totally a short work-week field and, no doubt, is comprised mainly of females.

Several occupations also exist in which overtime hours can be worked, including miscellaneous agricultural pursuits, animal farming, sales, and the administrative-managerial fields. An overtime wage premium is not always paid, however. Less than 10 percent of the household heads reported receiving a premium wage for overtime work. It should be noted that agricultural workers are still not covered by the overtime provision of the Fair Labor Standards Act. Most occupations had the largest percentage of their members working in the standard work-week range. Only four occupations—domestic services, mining-logging-extraction, miscellaneous agriculture, and plant farming—had less than 50 percent of their members within the standard work-week range.

In Table 5.16 the distribution of hours worked within broad industrial classifications is shown: The table yields several interesting findings. First, the government and transportation-communication-public-utilities fields are almost totally standard work-week industries. Apparently, the institutional character of these industries allows little in the way of overtime or short-time work. Second, overtime work seems common in both wholesale and retail trade and in the mining industries. It is not unusual to find work in the mining sector—particularly petroleum extraction—to be seven-day-a-week shift work.

Finally, short work weeks are most common in construction, manufacturing, services, and finance-insurance-real estate.

Causes of Variation in Hours Worked. An important weakness of cross-tabular analysis is that in analyzing the influence on hours worked of any one factor (such as race), it is difficult to hold constant other influences without the tool becoming cumbersome and unwieldly. Because of data-tabulation problems, it was necessary to assign some value to the dependent variable for each category. The following values were chosen:

Category (hours)	Assigned Value
1 to 34	30
35 to 48	41
49+	52

The regression model designed to isolate the determinants of hours of work in rural labor markets is of the following form:

$$\text{HOURS} = a_0 + a_1 W + a_2 OY + a_3 SEX + a_4 ANGLO + a_5 BLACK + a_6 ED + a_7 WED + a_8 HEALTH + a_9 YOUNG + a_{10} OLD + a_{11} OTIME + a_{12} SJD + a_{13} DODGE + a_{14} SUN + a_{15} NATCH + u \quad (5.3)$$

Traditional work-leisure analysis suggests that the number of hours people work is dependent on the wage (WAGE) they receive. The direction of causation, however, is ambiguous. An increase in the wage rate increases the price of leisure time and thereby induces the individual to work more. This is called the substitution effect. On the other hand, a wage increase raises real income and, since leisure is a normal good, the person is induced to purchase more of it (that is, he works less). This is the income effect of a wage change. Thus, the effect of a wage change on hours worked depends on the relative strengths of the income and substitution effects. OY (1 if the person has income from sources other than his job; 0 otherwise) should be negatively related to hours worked, since "other income" has a pure income effect on work effort.

Sex and racial discrimination in the marketplace may also influence hours worked. Women and racial minorities are more likely to find employment in the more menial, dirty, and/or unrewarding jobs. Consequently, their preferences for working longer hours could be diminished by this factor. Also, to the extent that blacks and Chicanos are discriminated against in how they spend their money, through restrictions on hotels, restaurants, and entertainment activities they can comfortably attend, the payoff to work effort is reduced, and they are induced to work fewer hours. To capture the effects of sex discrimination, SEX (1 = male; 0 = female) is included in the regression equation. Two racial variables are included to isolate the effects of racial discrimination: ANGLO (1 = Anglo; 0 = non-Anglo) and BLACK (1 = black; 0 = nonblack). Since Chicanos is the omitted racial category, the analysis measures via the coefficients on ANGLO and BLACK how the work hours behavior of these two groups compares with that of Chicanos.

Finegan has suggested that the more educated the person, the more pleasant and rewarding the job for which he is eligible, and hence the longer the hours he would be willing to work.[15] ED, the number of years of formal education attained, is used to control for this effect. Married household heads (WED = 1 if married; 0 otherwise), because of their greater financial responsibilities, would be expected to desire more hours of work per week than would unmarried household heads. Poor health should have a detrimental effect on work effort. To account for this variable, HEALTH (1 = had a health problem; 0 otherwise) was created. It was argued earlier that younger and older persons have a greater preference for leisure time than do prime-age individuals. YOUNG (1 if age 16 to 24; 0 otherwise) and OLD (1 if age 54+; 0 otherwise) are dummy variables designed to test this hypothesis.

Generally speaking, it would be expected that if a person is paid a premium wage for overtime hours, the person will work more.[16] OTIME (1 = premium paid for overtime work; 0 otherwise) is a premium-wage variable. Based on evidence from a study of the general population,[17] longer work hours are also presumed to be positively associated with moonlighting (SJD = 1 if had a second job; 0 otherwise).

Finally, it might be argued that differences in economic conditions in the four counties at the time of the survey may have some marginal influence on hours worked. County-location dummy variables (DODGE, SUN, and NATCH) were inserted in the regression equation for all but Starr County. Thus the coefficients on the county dummies are comparing each county's effect on hours worked vis-à-vis Starr County.

It might be argued that occupational and industrial dummy variables should be included in the regression model. Such variables have been omitted because shifts between occupations and industries are the primary vehicles workers use to satisfy their hours preferences. What this suggests is that workers, in general, are able to find jobs consistent with their hours preferences and that differences in demand have no systematic influence on their hours choice.[18]

TABLE 5.17

Regression Coefficients for Hours-Worked Equation

Independent Variable	Coefficient	t-Value
Constant	37.33	
W	-0.18	1.69
OY	0.004	0.75
SEX	2.31	3.01[a]
WHITE	2.23	2.14[b]
BLACK	-1.20	1.09
ED	0.23	5.40[a]
HEALTH	-1.61	3.18[a]
WED	0.77	1.11
YOUNG	-1.25	2.13[b]
OLD	-0.99	2.48[b]
OTIME	1.05	1.81
SJD	2.73	4.20[a]
DODGE	-0.61	0.57
SUN	-0.26	0.25
NATCH	-2.17	2.05[b]

Note: $R^2 = 0.16$; F-Ratio = 19.58[a]; Sample size = 1604.
[a] Significant at the 0.01 level.
[b] Significant at the 0.05 level.

The empirical estimates of the coefficients in Equation 5.3 are shown in Table 5.17. All of the variables that are significantly related to hours have the expected signs. It is disappointing to find that neither WAGE nor OY is related to hours at acceptable confidence levels. It would have been useful to observe how rural workers might respond to income transfers, as compared with the response of urban residents. The insignificance of OY suggests that such transfers would have no effect on rural work efforts. Two factors make us hesitant in concurring with that conclusion; both deal with the way OY is specified in Equation 5.3. First, OY is in dummy-variable rather than continuous form. Inserting the absolute value of OY might impart significance to its coefficient. Second, OY does not include <u>all</u> the other income received by the family; it includes earnings and transfer payments received by other members of the family.

INCOME AND EARNINGS 123

More satisfactory results were achieved with the other independent variables. Regression estimates indicate that men work significantly more hours per week than women. It is not possible to determine from the data whether this difference is a result of sex discrimination on the part of employers or a greater female preference for fewer hours. The latter is quite possible in the rural sample, since all female household heads were unmarried and thus would have responsibility for house care in addition to market work. Because of additional nonmarket responsibility, a woman may desire a short-hours job.[19]

Differentials in hours worked also exist across racial lines after controlling for other socioeconomic factors. Data in Table 5.14 show Anglos working longer hours than blacks or Chicanos. Once again, it is not possible to determine directly whether this is due to the effects of racial discrimination or to a greater preference for leisure on the part of the minority groups. The case is somewhat stronger for racial discrimination, since no scientific evidence of basic racial differences in tastes for leisure time exist.

Poor health conditions turn out to have a significant negative influence on hours worked. In Chapter 4 it was shown that health also is a critical factor in the labor force participation decision. It is important to note that this factor remains important even after age is held constant across interviewees. That is, the significance of the health variable cannot be attributed to a sample heavily weighted with older people who are prone toward health problems.

Once other factors are held constant, younger and older members of the rural workforce tend to work fewer hours per week than do their prime-age counterparts. Also, rural moonlighters tend to work more hours per week than do those who hold only one job. Both results are in keeping with conclusions from other studies.[20] In addition, increases in educational attainment have a slight positive effect on hours worked.

Finally, once other relevant worker characteristics are held constant, residents of Natchitoches tend to work fewer hours per week than do residents of the other three counties. There are no glaring differences across counties in the occupational distribution of the rural workers, so it can be presumed that the lower hours of activity in Natchitoches is due primarily to slightly poorer general economic conditions at the time of the interview.

Weeks Worked

Most previous analyses dealing with time worked during a full year have converted weeks per year into hours per year for purposes of analysis. This adjustment has caused reservations concerning the results in other studies. In the four-county sample the nature of the data is such that the assumptions that would be required to transform weeks worked per year into hours per year are unwarranted. The following section, therefore, analyzes the weeks worked by those in the household survey for the primary purpose of identifying factors that cause differences in weeks worked for subgroups of the sample.

Data on weeks worked for the nonrural South, for the South as a whole, or for the United States covering the year 1973 are not currently available. Consequently, it is not possible to make direct comparisons between such data and the results of the household survey. Census data for the United States for 1969 do reveal that during that year over 58 percent of those 16 years of age and over worked 50 weeks or more; 18 percent worked fewer than 26 weeks. Similar figures for the household sample are 41.9 percent and 43.9 percent, respectively. It is important, therefore, to discuss why workers in the rural South work substantially less in a year than does the country as a whole.

During 1973 the average number of weeks worked by members of the household survey who worked at all was 43.8 weeks. This average hides a substantial variation by county, as follows: Dodge, 47.5 weeks; Natchitoches, 44.9 weeks; Sunflower, 42.4 weeks; and Starr, 40.4 weeks. Much of the variation between counties is due to the greater dependence in two of the counties on agriculture as a major employer. Both Starr and Sunflower counties have relatively high percentages of their labor force employed in agriculture and, as should be expected, the percentage of agricultural workers who worked fewer than 48 weeks was greater than for any other occupational category (see Table 5.18). Further, Dodge, which had the highest average weeks worked also was the most "industrialized" of the survey counties. In fact, analysis of Table 4.25 reveals an expected pattern of weeks worked by occupation. Agriculture and construction showed the largest number, with fewer than 25 weeks worked and with 25 to 44 weeks worked, with most white-collar, manufacturing, and extractive occupations having the highest percentage working more than 48 weeks per year.

Factors other than occupational distribution—for example, race and sex—are important in determining weeks worked. The finding that stands out most in this work is the relatively large percentage of Anglos, both men and women, who worked 49 to 52 weeks. In the case of men, this reflects occupational differences between Anglos and non-Anglos and may also reflect preferential work treatment. Chicano women had the lowest percentage working 49 to 52 weeks, as well as the highest percentage working zero weeks. This probably reflects the employment opportunities available to women in Starr County, but it may also be indicative of cultural pressure against women working in the Chicano community.

TABLE 5.18

Distribution of Weeks Worked within
Occupations, Household Heads
(percent)

Occupation	Weeks Worked					
	1-12	13-24	25-34	35-44	45-48	49-52
Professional	0	1.3	8.3	8.3	2.5	79.0
Administration and managerial	1.5	1.5	3.6	2.6	2.1	88.7
Clerical and technical	0	1.1	1.1	5.4	4.3	87.1
Sales	0	2.4	3.6	3.6	3.6	86.9
Domestic service	8.9	10.7	5.4	3.6	5.4	60.7
Food and beverage preparation	9.1	6.8	18.2	9.1	2.3	50.0
Service workers	0.8	2.5	7.5	8.3	5.0	74.2
Plant farming	1.3	13.8	23.7	9.9	9.2	41.4
Animal farming	7.7	1.9	3.8	3.8	1.9	75.0
Miscellaneous agriculture, forestry, and fishing	1.5	2.9	8.1	4.4	4.4	77.9
Manufacturing—new materials processing	1.7	3.3	1.7	3.3	6.7	83.3
Manufacturing—durables	0.8	2.3	4.5	8.3	3.0	81.1
Manufacturing—assembly production	0.8	0.8	5.6	2.4	3.2	87.2
Construction trades	3.4	4.6	13.1	9.1	7.4	62.3
Transportation	0	1.5	8.3	7.5	3.8	78.9
Packaging	2.3	7.0	2.3	4.7	4.7	76.7
Mining, logging, extraction	0	6.7	10.0	0	0	83.3

Note: Those who worked zero weeks are excluded, therefore columns may not total 100 percent in all occupations.

It also is relevant that a slightly higher percentage of Anglo than black women worked 49 to 52 weeks, even though a significantly greater percentage of black women worked at some time during 1973. It is obvious that in the rural South, minority household heads have substantially greater difficulty obtaining year-round employment than do their Anglo counterparts.

The high percentage of household heads who did not work at all during 1973 (36.2 percent) is somewhat misleading inasmuch as age as an influencing factor is not considered. The importance of age is shown by the following information: in 1973, 83.9 percent of the household heads over 65 did not work at all, and only 9.2 percent worked 42 weeks or more. As anticipated, of those who worked 42 weeks or more, the greatest percentage fell in the 25-to-54 age category.

Although it would appear that one could conclude that race, age, sex, and occupation were the major factors causing differences in weeks worked, such an inference is not valid based on cross-tabular analysis alone. In order to separate the impact of various factors on weeks worked in 1973, the following regression model was formulated:

$$\text{WEEKS} = b_0 + b_1 \text{WED} + b_2 \text{AGE} + b_3 \text{BLACK} + b_4 \text{ANGLO} + b_5 \text{MALE} + b_6 \text{ED} + b_7 \text{TRAIN} + b_8 \text{HEALTH} + b_9 \text{FTIME} + u \qquad (5.4)$$

The importance of the variables AGE, BLACK, ANGLO, and MALE has previously been discussed (they assume the same form as they did in Equation 5.3). WED, which takes the value of 1 if the household head is married and zero otherwise, was included because the pressure of family responsibilities should decrease the probability of fewer than maximum available weeks worked voluntary. HEALTH (1 if head has a health problem; 0 otherwise) was included because health problems that cause entire weeks of no work may be different from those causing reduced hours per week. Thus, the results of the hours equation do not assume a similar finding with respect to weeks worked.

The remaining three variables were included instead of occupational variables. ED (years of education in continuous form) and TRAIN (1 if head had skill training; 0 otherwise) along with race and sex are significant factors in determining occupational status. It was decided to measure these directly and, thereby, draw inferences as to occupational effects.

Table 5.19 contains the results of regression analysis on household heads with the same hours worked. All signs are as expected, and the results in general support the inferences drawn from the cross-tabular analysis. The lack of significance of the variable MALE, although unexpected, is probably an indication that occupational differences between men and women may be more significant than sex as a determinant of weeks worked.

In general, the results of the preceding analysis are similar to those found in other studies that have not concentrated on rural areas. It can be concluded that poor health is probably the most significant

TABLE 5.19

Regression Coefficients for Weeks-Worked Equation

Independent Variable	Coefficient	t-Value
Constant	19.79	
WED	2.27	-2.07[a]
AGE	0.03	1.26
BLACK	1.86	2.53[a]
ANGLO	5.15	7.41[b]
MALE	2.24	1.86
ED	0.36	5.11[b]
TRAIN	1.63	2.10[a]
HEALTH	-7.53	9.99[b]

Note: $R^2 = 0.49$; F-Ratio = 52.46; Sample size = 2129.
[a]Significant at the 0.05 level.
[b]Significant at the 0.01 level.

single factor causing less than full-time employment in terms of hours worked per week as well as weeks worked per year. This further highlights the difficulties that health problems present for rural Southern families.

In terms of race and sex, minorities work less in hours and weeks. Although in the case of women there is reason to believe that some of the differential may be voluntary, there is strong support that discrimination plays an important role.

The form of discrimination is important, for it is unlikely that the differentials in hours and weeks worked result to any large degree from overt discrimination. Rather, the results suggest that the important factor is the occupational structure of black, Chicano, Anglo, and female workers, which itself may be a function of past as well as present discrimination.

INCOME FROM OTHER THAN CURRENT EARNINGS

Although earnings represented the major income source for the majority of sample households, over half the households received some income from another source. Moreover, for 30 percent of the sample households, transfer income represented their entire 1973 income.

Private Sources

Of the households in the rural sample, only 12 percent received income via private transfer payments. More importantly, for no households did interest, rent, or private transfers represent the sole income source. Table 5.20 shows the percentage of households receiving other private income by source. Several important facts can be inferred from the data.

Obviously, private transfers are associated primarily with the Anglo segment of the population, as are the other two private sources. Seventy-six percent of all private transfer payments went to Anglos in 1973, and almost three-quarters of all income associated with wealth (interest and rent) went to Anglos. What accumulated wealth does exist in the rural sample is concentrated in a few Anglo households.

Mean income from all sources of private transfers was $2,621. The mean for private pensions was $3,184. This figure assumes importance because, unlike earned income, it does not reduce Social Security payments. Most households receiving a private pension also received Social Security income. Like the other private transfers, pensions were predominantly an Anglo phenomenon.

Government Transfers

Government transfers are important in the rural South not only because they are received by such a large percentage of the population, but also because they are the sole income source for a significant number of households. Table 5.21 contains a breakdown of government transfer programs and the percentage of total households receiving each. Social Security is the most important government transfer, with OAA second, a result not unexpected in light of the

TABLE 5.20

Households Receiving Private Income, by Race, 1973
(percent)

Source	Total	Anglo	Black	Chicano
Interest payments	2.6	4.4	0.2	1.9
Rental income	2.8	4.2	1.3	1.8
Pensions	4.5	7.3	1.8	2.6
Gifts	2.1	2.5	0.9	0.5

TABLE 5.21

Households Receiving Government-Transfers
Income, by Race, 1973
(percent)

Source	Total	Anglo	Black	Chicano
Social Security	28.3	30.7	29.4	20.8
OAA	12.6	10.0	17.6	13.8
AFDC	6.9	2.0	15.9	4.9
Veterans benefits	5.2	7.7	3.9	1.9
ABD*	3.8	2.8	5.4	3.5
Unemployment Insurance	0.9	1.0	1.3	0.9
Worker's Compensation	1.1	0.9	0.6	1.0

*Aid to the Blind or Disabled (ABD) refers to the combined category of Aid to the Blind and Aid to the Permanently and Totally Disabled.

age distribution of the sample. In addition, Social Security and OAA do not have a significant racial bias in terms of percentage of each racial group receiving income from these two sources. Chicanos are less likely to be receiving Social Security than are Anglos or blacks, a fact accounted for by a slightly "younger" age distribution and the concentration of Chicanos in agriculture. Mean incomes from Social Security and OAA are $1,844 and $1,124, respectively. In spite of these low mean incomes, only 20 percent of the Social Security households were able to supplement their income through earnings. Even for those households with earnings, incomes were not increased substantially. In over 65 percent of the households, earnings were less than $2000, which is below the point at which earnings are penalized.

Unlike OAA and Social Security, AFDC, the third largest government transfer program, consists mainly of black recipient households (70 percent). The mean AFDC income ($1143) was extremely low in light of the fact that the program is designed exclusively for families with children under 18 years of age. Slightly over half the AFDC households were able to supplement their income through earnings; but of these households, 82 percent earned less than $2000 in 1973. Perhaps the most significant factor relating to AFDC as an income source is that only 6.9 percent of the households were receiving income from this source in a sample population with over a quarter of the households headed by a woman.

The remaining sources of government transfer require little explanation or evaluation, with the possible exception of unemployment insurance and worker's compensation. These are most notable by their absence. The lack of these programs in the sample is attributable to the industrial structure of the study areas—that is, the small amount of employment covered under these programs relative to the nation as a whole.

An attempt to evaluate transfer income in a manner similar to earned income is difficult, if not impossible. Private transfers are largely a function of accumulated wealth or, in the case of pensions, past employment. Not only is it difficult to conceive of a manner in which this income source could be utilized to improve the general income position of the total population, but the absolute size of these income sources renders them relatively unimportant.

A similar statement is not true with respect to government transfers. They are a major income factor in the rural South, as reflected by the sample. However, the factors that determine the level of government transfers are generally unaffected by the actions of individual households, are a function of decisions made outside the rural South, and are highly political in nature. A significant portion of the households find that their annual income, in whole or in part, is beyond a person's ability to affect. Yet decisions made concerning various government transfer programs have a substantial impact on the rural South. Further, because of the numbers involved, the labor market effects of government transfer programs in rural areas should receive considerable attention in decisions concerning changes in the benefit level or coverage of such programs. In particular, given the extremely low benefit levels coupled with the low household income levels, the existing restrictions on earned income need to be reevaluated.

DISCRIMINATION IN SOUTHERN RURAL LABOR MARKETS

The income comparisons made in the first section of this chapter make it clear that significant differences exist between the incomes of Anglo and non-Anglo households, as well as between male-headed and female-headed households. Subsequent analysis revealed that much of this differential was the result of wage-rate differentials that could not be explained by productivity differences. One possible and plausible explanation could be discrimination with respect to race and sex. The considerable amount of literature that has developed since the early 1960s leaves little doubt that labor market discrimination on the basis of race or sex or both exists in many if not most segments of the U.S. economy.21 The exact nature and the extent of such discrimination remains an area for which information is deficient. If any meaningful policy relating to labor market operations or economic welfare in the rural South is to be formulated, the effect of discrimination on earnings and employment must be considered.

Wage Discrimination: Race*

It is difficult, if not impossible, to isolate the effect of racial discrimination on the economy of the rural South or on individual members of minority groups who reside in the South. In the area of current labor market activity, past discrimination may be as important a factor as discrimination that is currently being practiced. However, the nature and extent of past discrimination is difficult to measure. Further, it can be argued that elimination of continued discriminatory practices is of greater immediate importance in terms of short-run improvements in economic welfare.

One possible measure of discrimination is the ratio of wages of blacks to wages of Anglos. Calculation of such a simple ratio for the sample reveals that average wages for black men are only 60 percent of the average for Anglo men; the ratio of black women to Anglo women is 78 percent. However, the purpose of measuring wage discrimination is to isolate the differential that is solely the result of race. Therefore, differentials that result from differences in productivity factors not directly related to discrimination must be identified and removed from the unadjusted difference.

The method utilized here to hold constant productivity differences is ordinary least squares regression. By estimating the parameters of a wage equation, the influence of productivity differences can be removed and an adjusted and meaningful wage ratio computed.

The adjusted ratio becomes the ratio of the sum of the coefficients of the black-wage equation applied to mean values of the variables for Anglos and a similar computation involving the Anglo equation. If no discrimination is present, the adjusted ratio would equal 1. Deviations of the ratio from unity can be interpreted as a relative measure of discrimination in wage rates.22 The form of the adjusted ratio is as follows:

---

*This section involves analysis of Anglo-black differences only. The concentration of Chicanos in a single county makes Anglo-Chicano or Chicano-black comparisons relatively meaningless.

$$\text{Adjusted Wage Ratio} = \frac{\Sigma R_{bi} M_{Ai}}{\Sigma R_{Ai} M_{Ai}} \tag{5.5}$$

where:

R_i = ith coefficient from the regression equation
M_i = mean value of ith independent variable
b is a subscript denoting black
A is a subscript denoting Anglo

The following independent variables were entered into the wage equations:

AGE = actual age
ED = years of formal education
YPJ = years employed in present job
HEALTH = 1 if individual has a health problem; 0 otherwise
TRAIN = 1 if individual has participated in a formal training program; 0 otherwise
FARM = 1 if individual is employed in agriculture; 0 otherwise
FTD = 1 if individual is a full-time employee

The variables included in the equation were chosen not only because they are generally accepted as influencing wages, principally through productivity effects, but also because they are relatively free from the direct effects of labor market discrimination. A variable important in wage determination—occupational status—was not included in the equation; the exclusion was necessary because of the strong possibility that occupational status was directly affected by racial discrimination in the labor market.

Four equations were used to estimate coefficient values: one for Anglo men; one for black men; one for Anglo women, and one for black women. The results of estimating the adjusted wage ratios are as follows:

$$\text{Male Adjusted Ratio} = \frac{2.784}{3.677} = 0.757$$

$$\text{Female Adjusted Ratio} = \frac{2.26}{2.47} = 0.915$$

In comparing the simple wage ratios with the adjusted ratios (0.60 versus 0.76 for men and 0.78 versus 0.92 for women), it is clear that the simple ratios overstate the extent of wage discrimination. Even after adjustment, however, there is significant wage discrimination between Anglo and black men.

Occupational Discrimination

Overt discrimination in wage rates may not be the only source of Anglo-black wage differentials that result from current labor market discrimination. Substantial discrimination that limits the occupational choice of blacks could account for part of the observed unadjusted wage differential. To test the extent of occupational segregation between blacks and Anglos in the rural South, a linear probability approach using regression analysis was chosen. Utilizing a dichotomous dependent variable (1 if in a given occupation; 0 otherwise), regressions were computed for 13 occupational classes for each of the race-sex groups. In addition to a variable measuring racial probabilities (1 if black; 0 if Anglo), independent variables measuring the effect on occupational status of age, education, and training were included in the equation. The sign of the race coefficient will indicate the direction of segregation if the coefficient is statistically significant.

The hypothesis that significant occupational segregation for both men and women exists based on race is borne out by the results shown in Table 5.22. In general, black men have a high probability of being in a relatively low-wage occupation. The probability of black employment is lower in such occupations as clerical, sales, and administrative and higher in farm, services, and packaging.

For women, nine occupational categories were found to be affected by racial discrimination. In general, black women had a greater probability of being in those occupations that are traditionally lower-paying with more restricted advancement opportunities. The glaring exception was the category "professional." Black women had a significantly greater probability than Anglos of being in this category. This result may reflect the large number of elementary and secondary school teachers and licensed practical nurses in the category, as well as the small absolute number of "professional" in the rural South.

Wage Discrimination: Sex

As significant as racial discrimination may be with respect to wages, there appears to be substantial support for the position that the effect of sex discrimination is greater.[23] One study places the estimated differential (adjusted for productivity differences) at 0.55.[24]

The unadjusted male-female ratios for Anglos and blacks, respectively, are 0.67 and 0.86. This reflects less wage discrimination than was found between racial groups. However, when productivity adjustments are made in a manner similar to that utilized to investigate racial wage differences, the resulting ratios are lower,

TABLE 5.22

Anglo-Black Estimates of Employment Probabilities
(t-values in parentheses)

Occupation	Male Regressions	Female Regressions
Professional	0.0355 (2.469)[b]	0.11324 (4.59)[a]
Administrative	-.0623 (-3.45)[a]	-0.02077 (1.41)
Services	0.0419 (3.19)[a]	0.06306 (2.81)[a]
New materials manufacturing	0.0266 (2.06)[b]	-[c]
Clerical	-0.0400 (-2.78)[a]	-0.25050 (-9.63)[a]
Durables manufacturing	-0.0369 (-2.01)[b]	-0.03231 (-2.55)[b]
Assembly line workers	-0.0450 (-2.634)[a]	-0.06342 (-3.08)[a]
Construction	-0.0256 (-1.31)	0.00720 (1.70)
Transportation	0.0130 (0.75)	0.00692 (0.88)
Package	0.0341 (3.02)[a]	-0.02409 (-2.75)[a]
Food and beverage	-.0039 (-0.71)	0.07698 (4.13)
Farm	0.1012 (4.15)[a]	-0.01206 (-1.57)
Sales	-0.046 (-3.245)[a]	-0.06650 (-3.77)[a]
Domestic service	-[c]	0.06300 (2.81)[a]

[a]Significant at the 0.01 level.
[b]Significant at the 0.05 level.
[c]Dashes indicate no regression run on this occupational category.

INCOME AND EARNINGS 135

not higher as would normally be expected. The adjusted ratio for Anglos is 0.65 and for blacks 0.70. The unadjusted ratios actually mask a superiority in productivity-related factors on average among both Anglo and black women.

Observations on Discrimination

Analysis of wage discrimination in the rural sample supports the hypothesis that elimination of wage discrimination in the rural South should lead to substantial earnings improvements for black men and for women regardless of race. The results of this analysis clearly indicate that substantial efforts to find and remedy overt wage discrimination between black and Anglo women in the rural South will do little to improve the earning capacity of black women.

In terms of wage discrimination, the greatest problem for black women in the rural South is the same as that for Anglo women: discrimination on the basis of sex. It is the elimination of this form of labor market discrimination that will be most beneficial to black and Anglo women alike.

Elimination of occupational discrimination could lead to substantial improvements in the earnings of black men. The same is not true for black women. Although evidence of occupational segregation was found and should be remedied, it is unlikely that this would help substantially. The conclusion is based on the limited numbers of females, black or Anglo, in higher-paying occupations and a concentration of black women in the lowest-paying occupations. The latter factor will probably not change even if occupational segregation is attacked because of the first factor.

HEALTH PROBLEMS AND INCOME

Throughout the analysis of labor market behavior, income, and earnings, health constantly appears as an important variable, particularly with regard to such matters as labor force participation, wages, and work time. Although the effect of poor health on labor force status has been discussed in Chapter 4, the effect of health on other aspects of labor market behavior deserves additional investigation. In general, the benefits to be derived from improving the health of a workforce (or workforce-age population) center around productivity. A healthy worker is expected to be more productive, and better overall health improves the average probability that a worker can perform productive work at all.

The manner in which health affects productivity has received increasing attention in the past decade. Recent studies have adopted the human-capital approach; that is, they have made health a part of the total stock of human capital. In a pioneering article, Mushkin attempted to estimate the returns to better health care by estimating the number of additional workers that may be attributed to an increasing life expectancy as it rises over a period of years.[25] More recent studies have emphasized actual productivity differences between persons with and without health problems.[26]

The essence of health in a human-capital context is contained in the following statement: ". . . [A] person's stock of knowledge affects his market and non-market productivity while his stock of health determines the total amount of time he can spend producing more in earnings and commodities."[27] Thus, the major effect of health problems on a labor force is to shorten the available time for productive activity. However, previous analysis of wage rates indicates that health may also affect earnings. Both possibilities must be explored if the total effect of health problems is to be discovered.

Analysis is restricted to household heads under age 65. Although there is a high incidence of health problems in those over 65 years of age, the effect on labor force activity is minimal. Table 4.31 shows the incidence of health problems in the under 65 population. The most notable fact shown by Table 5.23 is the higher incidence of health problems among females, regardless of race. This is particularly important in that it further compounds the labor market and earnings problems of the female head of household by adding the problem of bad health to the already existing burden of sex discrimination in job opportunities and pay. As would be expected, those with health problems are concentrated in the 45-to-64 age bracket. Age was found to be especially significant in the case of women.

Generally, the health problems faced by the persons in the rural survey are long term in nature. In all groups, at least half or more of the individuals have had the particular problem over five years. For example, 56.6 percent of all Anglo men have had problems for over five years. For black men the percentage rises to 57.4 percent. Part of the reason for this is certainly the nature of the ailments. The most prevalent problems in all race-sex groups were cardiovascular and renal ailments, especially among respondent black women, of whom 49.6 percent were affected. Other ailments prevalent in all race-sex groups were arthritis, rheumatism, and intestinal disorders. These problems tend to linger over a period of years.

The major effect of health problems on labor market behavior should be reflected in time worked. Table 5.24 compares those with health problems and those without in terms of no work in 1973 and

TABLE 5.23

Household Heads under Age 65 with Health Problems, by Race and Sex, 1973

	With Health Problems		Without Health Problems	
	Number	Percent	Number	Percent
Anglo	223	20.1	888	79.9
Male	172	18.6	752	81.4
Female	51	27.3	136	72.7
Black	168	24.0	532	76.0
Male	80	17.9	366	82.1
Female	88	34.6	166	65.4
Chicano	161	27.5	424	72.5
Male	123	25.5	359	74.4
Female	38	36.9	65	63.1
Total	552	23.0	1884	77.0
Male	375	20.2	1477	79.8
Female	177	32.5	367	67.5

work of less than 26 weeks during the same time period. The differences in work activity between those with and those without health problems can be clearly seen. However, accurate assessment of the impact of health on work activity can be made only if other influencing factors are removed. The most useful technique for this purpose is regression analysis, which allows the productive loss associated with health problems to be estimated for the average person.[28]

The technique utilized involves estimating separate regression equations for the portion of the sample with health problems and for the portion without. The independent variables selected for inclusion represent factors, primarily productivity-associated, that are expected to influence the two dependent variables: wage rates and weeks worked in 1973. Independent variables included were sex, race, age, education, training, and occupation.

Regression coefficients from the equations of those with health problems were applied to the mean values of each independent variable for those persons without health problems. A ratio was constructed that compared the adjusted mean with the actual mean of the group without health problems for both wage rates and weeks worked as follows:

$$\text{Adjusted Wage Ratio} = \frac{\Sigma (URC_i \times HM_i)}{HMR} \qquad (5.5)$$

$$\text{Adjusted Work Ratio} = \frac{\Sigma(URC_j \times HM_j)}{HMT} \tag{5.6}$$

where:

URC_i = the regression coefficient of the ith independent variable from the wage equation for those with health problems

HM_i = the mean value of the ith independent variable (wage analysis) for those without health problems

HMR = the mean value of the hourly rate of pay for those without health problems

URC_j = the regression coefficient of the ith independent variable from the weeks equation for those with health problems

HM_j = the mean value of the ith independent variable (weeks analysis) without health problems

HMT = the mean time (weeks) worked for the sample without health problems.

Substituting into the equation produced the following results:

$$\text{Hourly Rate of Pay} = \frac{2.7946}{3.1378} = 0.8906$$

$$\text{Weeks Worked Per Year} = \frac{26.4443}{42.2200} = 0.6263.$$

TABLE 5.24

Work Activity by Household Heads, by Health Status, Race, and Sex, 1973

	Worked Less than 26 Weeks		Worked Zero Weeks	
	Health Problem	No Health Problem	Health Problem	No Health Problem
Anglo	61.7	9.3	53.6	6.1
Male	57.3	4.9	47.9	2.5
Female	76.5	33.5	72.5	25.5
Black	68.4	22.5	52.9	9.9
Male	57.4	11.8	42.5	1.1
Female	78.4	46.4	62.5	27.7
Chicano	61.4	20.3	37.8	9.2
Male	52.7	11.1	28.4	1.1
Female	89.3	70.7	68.4	53.8

INCOME AND EARNINGS

The ratio for hourly rate of pay indicates than an individual with health problems but with other characteristics identical to those of a healthy person can be expected to earn 89 cents for every dollar that a healthy person would make. Similarly, a person with health problems with the other identical characteristics of a healthy person will be expected to work only 62 percent of the time a healthy individual works. To see the combined effect of the differences in hourly rate of pay and weeks worked per year on the annual earnings of unhealthy workers, yearly average income figures need to be calculated. In this calculation, an assumption must be made concerning the hours per week. Data limitations do not permit a regression to be run on hours per week similar to those for the other two variables. Thus, it is necessary to assume that the average work week is 40 hours. Given this assumption, the yearly income figures are computed as follows:

	No Health Problem	Health Problem
Hourly wage X	$ 3.14	$ 2.79
Hours per week (assumed)	40	40
Gross pay per week X	$125.60	$111.60
Weeks per year	42.22	26.44
Annual earnings	$5302.83	$2950.70
Difference: $5302.83 − $2950.70 =	$2352.13	

A cursory analysis of this difference indicates that the amount of time worked is the factor that most affects the earnings of the individual with health problems in contrast to that for the healthy person. The wage rate and time effects can be broken down into more precise terms.

If it is assumed that an unhealthy individual works the same amount of time as a healthy person, the health effect on wage will be given by the following equation:

$$HPW[HMT (HMR - UAR)] = \text{wage component} \quad (5.7)$$

where:

HPW = hours per week (assumed)
UAR = unhealthy adjusted hourly rate

Substituting the appropriate values into the equation produces:

$$40[42.22 (3.14 - 2.79)] = \$591.08.$$

Thus, even if an individual with health problems were to work the same number of hours as a healthy person, there still will be a difference of almost $600 in earnings. This differential in wage rates may be caused by the fact that the individual with health problems does not have the range of opportunities available to him that would pay a higher wage or the fact that employers are reluctant to place workers with disabilities at certain types of jobs.

The wage component explains about a quarter of the differential in earnings. Given that the worker is paid less per hour, there is an additional component of the difference in earnings that can be explained by the amount of time worked, using the following formula:

$$HPW[UAR (HMT - UAT)] = \text{time component} \qquad (5.8)$$

where:

HPW, UAR, and HMT are defined as above and UAT = adjusted weeks worked.

Substituting the appropriate values into the equation yields:

$$40[2.79 (4.22 - 26.44)] = \$1761.05.$$

This final formula is important in that it shows the strong effect of the time component in the differential earnings of the two groups. The total differential of $2352.13 is made up of a time component of $1761.05, or roughly 75 percent of the total difference, and a wage component of $591.08, which accounts for the remaining 25 percent.

The results obtained thus far can be roughly compared with those obtained in similar studies of the economic costs of poor health. In a study conducted by Joseph Davis, a sample of 1,583 Anglo respondents was drawn from the civilian, noninstitutional population of men between the ages of 45 and 54.[29] A much more elaborate study was carried out by Harold S. Luft, using a large sample drawn from the Current Population survey.[30] Holding constant all factors that may have a consequent effect on earnings, Luft obtained an estimate of the differential in earnings caused by health. The comparative results for these three studies in terms of wage income and weeks worked differentials between healthy and unhealthy workers follows:

	Weeks Worked	Hourly Wage	Annual Earnings
Rural Study	15.78	0.35	$2352
Luft	6.45	0.23	$1068
Davis	3.65	0.32	$1379

INCOME AND EARNINGS 141

Results of interstudy comparisons reveal that workers in the rural South who have health problems are penalized almost twice as much as is the case on a national level. Further, this difference is explained primarily in terms of work weeks lost due to poor health.

The preceding analysis reveals the magnitude of the health problem in rural areas in terms of labor market activity. Not only do health problems result in lower productivity because of an increased probability of nonwork time, but wage rates on average are lower for workers with health problems. Both factors have an effect on the potential income of households in which the head is in poor health.

The results support the existence of a need for improved health care in rural areas of the South. Better health care for rural areas should increase the chances that certain individuals will be able to participate in the labor force at all, and for others may enhance their productivity on the job.

SUBEMPLOYMENT IN RURAL AREAS

The analysis pertaining to earnings, particularly that relating to time worked, makes it clear that unemployment and part-time employment constitute significant problems in rural areas. In addition, the number of persons of labor force age outside the labor force is indicative of an underemployment problem. Present unemployment-rate computations are poorly suited to measure this problem. Further, the low earnings levels found for many sample households give evidence that employment and economic well-being are not synonymous. The magnitude of the entire problem is difficult to ascertain with economic measures currently in general use. However, one measure which has been suggested is the "subemployment index" (SI).

Beginning in the late 1960s, concern was expressed over the adequacy of the unemployment rate as a "social indicator." While acknowledging that it was certainly useful as an "economic indicator," critics questioned the use of the unemployment rate because it takes no account of the income adequacy of employment. That is, in addition to unemployment figures, it is necessary to know how many people are employed in jobs that do not permit their families to live at minimum levels of decency for this society.[31]

To fill this statistical void, Secretary of Labor Willard Wirtz was directed by President Johnson to provide some measure of the severity of employment problems in urban slums. Since an appropriate measure was not available, Wirtz directed his staff to develop a "subemployment index" which would take into account not only those who have difficulty finding employment, but also those who are employed but at inadequate wage rates. The reason for this marriage of earnings and employment data into a single index was the view that workers with low earnings may have problems of as much concern from the viewpoint of manpower policy as those of many workers with substantial unemployment.[32]

Unfortunately, there is no general agreement on the precise components of an SI. "Inadequate income" is a quite normative phrase, and disagreement over its precise definition has led to different definitions of the SI. Differences of opinion also have arisen over whether the SI should cover all persons 16 years of age and older, or family heads only.[33]

The SI constructed for the rural sample will correspond to that developed by Levitan and Taggart.[34] This index is oriented toward the problem of family poverty and is based on the total earned income contributed by the family head. The precise definition of the index is:

$$SI = \frac{U + DW + PT + Y}{E + U + DW} \qquad (5.9)$$

where:

- U = number of officially unemployed family heads
- DW = number of family heads that are discouraged workers (that is, not in the labor force but desire to work)
- PT = family head employed part-time involuntarily
- Y = family head (not included in U, DW, or PT) whose annual income, adjusted for family size, falls below the official poverty line
- E = total employed family heads.

Excluded from E, U, DW, PT, and Y are family heads over 65 and older and family heads 16 to 21 years of age who are students. Older persons and students are excluded because most persons in these groups have less attachment to the labor force since their income needs are normally provided by other sources. These exclusions are subject to question, but Levitan and Taggart feel the index will be less biased with their exclusion than by including them.[35]

The purpose of this index is to focus on the number of jobs needed to upgrade the social status of entire families. There appears to be a strong case for also including secondary workers along with family heads in the index, since many families headed by a low-wage earner have enough other wage earners in the family to pull the group out of poverty. However, Vietorisz, Mier, and Giblin argue:

> . . . focusing the definition on family income from multiple sources breaks the direct connection between

the index and the labor market and therefore deprives the index of relevance for the unavailability of jobs and for crucial dimensions of available jobs: the full time aspect, pay, career aspects, and productivity. Such a definition would confuse remedial policy choices because it obscures the cause of family income shortfall. We believe, therefore, that a properly defined inadequacy index must consider as potentially subemployed only one person per family.[36]

The SI does not address the question of underemployment. There is no comparison of the skill-achievement level of the worker with the skill level required for his job. A person with a Ph.D. in physics may be earning $7500 a year as a truck driver, but because he is employed at a wage above the official poverty level he would not be included in the numerator of the SI.

For the 1973 sample of rural household heads the following values existed for the variables in Equation 5.9: $U = 48$; $DW = 166$; $PT = 134$; $Y = 462$; $E = 1748$. Plugging these values into Equation 5.9 results in an SI of 41.3 percent for the rural sample. This compares to an unemployment rate of only 2.7 percent for this subgroup of household heads. Clearly, the unemployment rate serves as a very poor indication of the employment problems of rural household heads.

It would be instructive to compare the SI results for the rural sample with those for the United States as a whole. Levitan and Taggart computed an SI for the U.S. population using data from the Current Population Survey for March 1972.[37] Because their data were collected a year earlier than data in this study, the results are not directly comparable. Comparative figures are shown in Table 5.25. There are two glaring differences in the results across the two samples.

First, the SI is much larger—almost four times greater—in the rural areas than for the U.S. sample. What makes this difference even more startling is that general economic conditions were more favorable the year of the rural survey (for example, the average U.S. unemployment rate was 5.6 percent in 1972 and 4.9 percent in 1973).

A second obvious difference between the two groups is the reversed importance of the unemployed vis-à-vis the discouraged workers in the subemployment numbers. Discouraged workers constitute a significantly greater part of the subemployed in rural areas than in the United States as a whole; the reverse is the case for the unemployed. Apparently, discouragement over the prospects of finding a job is much more pervasive in rural areas—perhaps because the number of employment opportunities is considerably more restricted. If this sample is indicative of the magnitude of the

TABLE 5.25

A Comparison of SI Components for the
United States and the Rural Sample

Component	U.S. Sample (1972)		Rural Sample (1973)	
	Number	Percent	Number	Percent[a]
Adjusted labor force[b]	86,122,000	–	1,962	–
Total number unemployed or with inadequate income	9,942,000	100.0	810	100.0
Unemployed	2,731,000	27.5	48	5.9
Discouraged workers	542,000	5.5	166	20.5
Employed part-time involuntarily	1,113,000	11.2	134	16.5
Employed full-time at inadequate earnings level	5,656,000	55.8	462	57.1
Subemployment index		11.5		41.0

[a] Percentage of those employed or with inadequate income.
[b] "Adjusted labor force" is the sum of those employed, those actively seeking work, and the discouraged workers. The adjusted labor force is the denominator of the SI.

Source: U.S. Sample from Sar A. Levitan and Robert Taggart, "Employment and Earnings Inadequacy: A Measure of Worker Welfare," Monthly Labor Review 96 (October 1973): 23.

discouraged-worker effect in rural areas as a whole, the "hidden unemployment" is a much more serious problem in rural than in nonrural areas of the country. This, in turn, means that the unemployment rate is a particularly poor measure of manpower underutilization in rural areas.[38]

CONCLUDING OBSERVATIONS

Although the mean income of the rural sample is low relative to the entire South or the United States, substantial variation exists, with the result that female-headed households, elderly households, and non-Anglo households are on average substantially below the average in terms of annual income.

INCOME AND EARNINGS

Some, although by no means all, of the problems of female-headed households and black households are associated with wage discrimination. As none of the states in the South has a state antidiscrimination law with any form of associated enforcement agency, responsibility for achievement of a climate of equal opportunity depends entirely upon the actions of the U.S. Equal Employment Opportunity Commission (EEOC). To date, this agency has shown little interest in discrimination in rural areas. The findings of the present work indicate that EEOC must become active in the rural South if the pervasive racial and sex discrimination is to be eliminated.

One possible way in which income of rural households may be increased in the short run is through the employment of more secondary workers, primarily wives. Households in which both husband and wife are working are, on average, in a superior income position. Programs, such as child care, that make it easier for the wife to be in the labor market could be beneficial. Certainly, manpower-training programs should not ignore the benefits, in terms of increased family income, that could result from increasing the productivity of wives through training. Such a policy will be limited of course by availability of employment opportunities. In fact, the SI indicates that a substantial number of households are in an adverse income position in spite of the full-time employment of the household head.

One aspect of the income-limiting problem that can be attacked in the short run is poor health. Based on the findings of this study, a call for increased health-related expenditures in the rural South is warranted in terms of the potential effect on the labor market activity of a significant percentage of the rural population of labor force age. Efforts to expand employment opportunities also may be helpful in this regard by increasing the number of employment opportunities that are not physically arduous. This could expand the work life of many people in the rural South.

Although much of the analysis in this chapter has been directed toward earnings-related problems, the importance of transfer payments, particularly government transfers, should not be relegated to a secondary position. The percentage of households dependent on welfare payments is sufficiently large for there to be a need for a careful analysis of the role of this income source in all its aspects in the rural South.

One finding of this work relates to the level of payments. For almost all government transfer programs the average annual payment levels are so low that the earnings restrictions associated with the programs appear ludicrous. Regardless of the original intent of a specific program, it is difficult to understand why any aid program should be designed so as to assure that the recipients remain below a level of income that denotes poverty. Yet the restrictions on earnings associated with AFDC and Social Security yield precisely this result for many households in the rural South. A reevaluation of the earnings restrictions is definitely in order.

There are many specific routes that could be taken to improve the income position of rural households in the South, in addition to the few mentioned above. For example, the wage analysis indicates that improvement in the quantity, and probably the quality, of education should have a positive effect on earnings. Such a policy also would improve the relative position of individuals who migrate from the rural South to metropolitan areas.

What is true in the long run assumes even greater significance in the short run. Because of the nature of the industrial structure, the political structure, and the distribution of wealth in the rural South, it is unlikely that improvements in the income position of households in the lower half of the distribution can come from earned income unless a major effort is made in the area of public employment. Given the large number of low-income household heads who are either unemployed, out of the labor force, or employed with earnings below the poverty level, public employment opportunities should be open to all who are in the above-designated groups.

If it is assumed that funds from the federal level are to be utilized, the measures by which the distribution of federal programs is determined assume major significance. Currently utilized measures of need, particularly the unemployment rate, shortchange the rural South. Not only do such measures fail to reflect accurately the extent of economic difficulties for rural areas, they actually mask the nature as well as the magnitude of the problem.

NOTES

1. Census figures show that the mean family income for the United States in 1969 was $9,590, and for the South it was $9,486. The mean for all families and unrelated individuals in the South was $7,933. Census data also show that mean family income for rural nonfarm and rural farm was $7,800 and $7,388, respectively, in 1969. In four years, average income in the rural sample counties had failed to reach the 1970 Census levels. U.S. Department of Commerce, Bureau of the Census, United States Census of Population: 1970, General Social and Economic Characteristics (Washington, D.C.: U.S. Government Printing Office, 1972).

2. For example, a 1962 study of a national sample found that 78 percent of all households had some wage and salary income. Dorothy S. Projector, G. S. Weis, and E. T. Thoresen, "Composition of Income as Shown by the Survey of Financial Characteristics

of Consumers," in Papers on the Size Distribution of Wealth and Income, ed. Lee Scanlon (New York: National Bureau of Economic Research, 1969), pp. 107-56.

3. See for example, Elizabeth Waldmen and Robert Whitemore, "Children of Working Mothers, March 1973," Special Labor Force Report 165 (Washington, D.C.: U.S. Department of Labor, 1974).

4. For a discussion of the validity of this point, see Herman Miller Income Distribution in the United States (Washington, D.C.: U.S. Government Printing Office, 1966); James A. Sweet, The Employment of Wives and the Inequality of Family Income, Discussion Paper (Madison, Wisconsin: Institute for Research on Poverty, 1971).

5. Jacob Mincer, "The Distribution of Labor Incomes: A Survey with Special References to Human Capital Approach," Journal of Economic Literature 8 (March 1970): 1-26; this article illustrates some of the productivity factors and contains an excellent bibliography. See also James W. Morgan et al., Income and Welfare in the United States (New York: McGraw-Hill, 1962); James Gwartney, "Discrimination and Income Differentials," American Economic Review 63 (June 1973): 396-408; Malcolm S. Cohen "Sex Differences in Compensation," Journal of Human Resources 6 (1971): 434-47; Cynthia Lloyd, ed., Sex, Discrimination and the Division of Labor (New York: Columbia University Press, 1975); Stanley Masters, "The Effect of Educational Differences and Labor Market Discrimination on the Relative Earnings of Black Males," Journal of Human Resources 9 (Summer 1974): 342-60.

6. Albert Rees and George D. Shultz, Workers and Wages in an Urban Labor Market (Chicago: The University of Chicago Press, 1970); Howard M. Wachtel and Charles Betsey, "Employment at Low Wages," Review of Economics and Statistics 54 (May 1972): 121-29; Paul M. Ryscavage, "Measuring Union-Nonunion Earnings Differences," Monthly Labor Review 97 (December 1974): 3-9.

7. Ibid.

8. Jeffrey, E. Casetti, and L. King, "Economic Fluctuations in a Multi-regional Setting: A Bi-factor Analytic Approach," Journal of Regional Science 9 (December 1969): 397-404.

9. Labor market wage equations for the individual labor market areas are contained in the original study, Adarns et al. "Labor Markets in the Rural South," prepared for U.S. Department of Labor, Employment and Training Administration March 31, 1977, under R & D Grant no. 51-13-72-10.

10. Ibid.

11. Raymond J. Struyke, "Explaining Variations in Hourly Wage Rates of Urban Minority Group Females," Journal of Human Resources 8 (Summer 1973): 349-64; C. Russell Hill, "The Determinants of Labor Supply for the Urban Working Poor," in Income Maintenance

and Labor Supply, ed. Glen Cain and Harold Watts (Chicago: Rand McNally, 1973), pp. 182-204.

12. However, alternative evidence has been found; in addition, the econometric techniques used by some authors have come under attack. Note, for example, Martin S. Feldstein, "Estimating the Supply Curve of Working Hours," Oxford Economic Paper 20 (March 1968): 74-80; A. C. Rayner, "On the Identification of the Supply Curve of Working Hours," Oxford Economic Papers 21 (July 1969): 293-98.

13. Stuart O. Schweitzer and Ralph E. Smith, "The Persistence of the Discouraged Worker Effect," Industrial and Labor Relation Review 27 (January 1974): 249-60.

14. Glen Cain and Harold Watts, eds. Income Maintenance and Labor Supply (Chicago: Rand-McNally, 1973), pp. 328-67.

15. T. A. Finegan, "Hours of Work in the U.S.: A Cross Sectional Analysis," Journal of Political Economy 70 (October 1962): 452-70.

16. This is not necessarily the case, however. If a worker is a "leisure-preferer," he may not respond to this inducement. For a theoretical treatment of this case see Leon Moses, "Income, Leisure, and Wage Pressure," Economic Journal 72 (June 1962): 320-34; Richard Perlman, "Observations on Overtime and Moonlighting," Southern Economic Journal 33 (October 1966): 237-44.

17. Vera C. Perrella, "Moonlighters: Their Motivations and Characteristics," Monthly Labor Review 93 (August 1970): 62.

18. This approach is consistent with the methodology followed in Cain and Watts, Income Maintenance and Labor Supply.

19. Gwartney and Stroup have found evidence on wage differentials across sexes that can be attributed to female occupational preferences rather than to sex discrimination. James Gwartney and Richard Stroup, "Measurement of Employment Discrimination According to Sex," Southern Economic Journal 39 (April 1973): 575-87.

20. See Perrella, "Moonlighters: Their Motivations and Characteristics"; Schweitzer and Smith, "The Persistence of the Discouraged Worker Effect."

21. See, for example, Ray Marshall, "The Economics of Racial Discrimination: A Survey," Journal of Economic Literature 12 (September 1974): 849-72.

22. For application of similar methodology to the problem of public sector discrimination, see James E. Long, "Public-Private Sector Differences in Employment Discrimination," Southern Economic Journal 42 (October 1975): 89-96.

23. See, for example, Isabel V. Sawhill, "The Economics of Discrimination against Women: Some New Evidence," Journal of Human Resources 8 (Summer 1973): 383-95; Gwartney and Stroup, "Measurement of Employment Discrimination According to Sex."

24. Sawhill, "The Economics of Discrimination Against Women."

25. Selma J. Mushkin, "Health as an Investment," Journal of Political Economy (Supplement) 70 (October 1962): 129-57.

26. R. E. Baldwin and Burton Weisbrod, "Disease and Labor Productivity," Economic Development and Cultural Change 22 (April 1974): 414-35. See also E. M. Popkin, "Economic Benefits from the Elimination of Hunger in America," Public Policy 20 (Winter 1972): 133-53.

27. Michael Grossman, "On the Concept of Health Capital and Demand for Health," Journal of Political Economy 80 (March-April 1972): 224.

28. The method employed here draws heavily on that utilized by Luft in Harold Luft, "The Impact of Poor Health on Earnings," Review of Economics and Statistics 57 (February 1975): 43-57.

29. Joseph M. Davis, "Impact of Health on Earnings and Labor Market Activity," Monthly Labor Review 95 (October 1972): 46-49.

30. Luft, "Impact of Poor Health."

31. The concept of subemployment first appeared in the United States Department of Labor, Manpower Report of the President, 1968 (Washington, D.C.: U.S. Government Printing Office, 1968).

32. Herman P. Miller, "Measuring Subemployment in Poverty Areas of Large U.S. Cities," Monthly Labor Review 96 (October 1973): 11.

33. This controversy is summarized in T. Vietorisz, R. Mier, and J. Giblin, "Subemployment: Exclusion and Inadequacy Indexes," Monthly Labor Review 96 (May 1973): 3-12.

34. Sar A. Levitan and Robert Taggart, "Employment and Earnings Inadequacy: A Measure of Worker Welfare," Monthly Labor Review 96 (October 1973): 19-27.

35. Ibid., pp. 24-25.

36. Vietorisz, Mier, and Giblin, "Subemployment: Exclusion and Inadequacy Indexes," p. 6. These authors agree with Levitan and Taggart that only family heads should be included in this particular index, but they disagree with the exclusion of the aged and the student family heads.

37. Levitan and Taggart, "Employment and Earnings Inadequacy."

38. Bowen and Finegan estimated the number of "hidden unemployed" in urban areas of the United States in 1962 at 718,000. The unemployment rate that year was 5.2 percent. See W. B. Bowen and T. A. Finegan, "Labor Force Participation and Unemployment," Employment Policies in the Labor Market, ed. Arthur M. Ross (Berkeley: University of California Press, 1965), p. 155. The data on the relative magnitude of the discouraged worker effect in rural areas shown in Table 5.25 suggests that Bowen and Finegan's estimate would have to be revised upward very significantly if the rural sector were added to their tabulations.

CHAPTER

6

POVERTY

In 1967 the President's National Advisory Commission on Rural Poverty concluded a comprehensive study with the finding that "rural poverty is so widespread and so acute, as to be a national disgrace."[1] The report also stated that "most of the rural South is one vast poverty area."[2] The South remains the most impoverished region in the United States, with 16.2 percent of all families in poverty.[3] This rate was more than twice that for the nation in 1970.

Through analysis of absolute levels of income and distributions of personal and per capita income, this chapter provides a description of the magnitude and character of Southern rural poverty.

DEFINITION OF POVERTY

Debate over the conceptual and specific definitions of poverty has existed since the "Poor Laws" of the late 1700s in Great Britain. This work has adopted the definition of poverty utilized by most federal agencies as modified further by the Bureau of Census.[4] The use of this particular poverty definition has the advantage of making the results of this work comparable with those of other research.

The Census definition measures poverty in terms of the ability of a family to purchase some quantity of items (a minimum market basket) with current family income.[5] Poverty levels are determined by calculating the amount of income a family needs to provide itself with a diet judged to be minimally adequate in a nutritional sense. Estimates of the costs per person of such a diet are furnished annually by the U.S. Department of Agriculture. In addition to food expenditures, nonfood expenditures are included as a multiple of food expenditures. Nonfood expenditures, on the basis of survey data, are

POVERTY

estimated to be twice those of food expenditures. These guidelines are revised annually to incorporate cost-of-living changes.

INCIDENCE OF POVERTY

The federal poverty guidelines in existence in 1973 (see Table 6.1) were applied to the total households in the rural survey. Using these guidelines, 1,306 (43.1 percent) of the survey households were found to be living below the poverty level in 1973.

Among the survey counties there was considerable variation in the incidence of poverty. Almost 18 percent of the total poverty households resided in Dodge County, and 24.5 percent resided in Natchitoches Parish. Most of the poverty households were found in Starr and Sunflower counties, which accounted for 32 percent and 25.5 percent, respectively, of the poverty households in the study.[6] The number of households in poverty as a percent of all households in each county were: Dodge, 29.2 percent; Natchitoches, 39.0 percent; Starr, 54.4 percent; and Sunflower, 43.4 percent.

Regardless of how these statistics are viewed, it is obvious that Starr and Sunflower counties have the highest incidence of poverty. This high incidence is partially explained by the relatively high proportion of minorities in the counties' population. The probability of a black or Chicano household living in poverty is almost 2.5 times that of an Anglo family. In fact, 58.5 percent of all black households in the survey and 55.4 percent of the Chicano households were in poverty. The county patterns reflect the fact that a high incidence of minority population was one of the county-selection criteria. Although Southern rural poverty in these counties seems to be pri-

TABLE 6.1

Federal Poverty Income Guidelines, 1973
(dollars)

Family Size	Nonfarm	Farm
1	2100	1800
2	2725	2325
3	3450	2950
4	4200	3575
5	4925	4200
6	5550	4725
7 or more	6200	5275

Source: Monthly Labor Review 96:3 (March 1973): 60.

marily a problem of minorities, it should be noted that the 1970 Census revealed that in absolute terms most of the Southern rural poor (approximately two-thirds) were Anglo.

CHARACTERISTICS OF POVERTY

Almost 61 percent of all poverty households in the survey were headed by men (see Table 6.2). The distribution varied significantly by county, from 44.6 percent for Dodge County to 73.6 percent for Starr County. Most of the differences, however are accounted for by race, in that 55 percent of Anglo and black poverty households were headed by a man, compared with 73.7 percent for Chicano households (see Table 6.3).

Though smaller in number, poverty households headed by women appear to be relatively worse off than those headed by men. In this study, 60.6 percent of all households headed by women are poor, compared with 34.2 percent for men. Furthermore, compared with

TABLE 6.2

Personal Characteristics of Poverty Household Heads in the Survey Counties, 1974

Characteristic	Percent
Sex	
Male	60.6
Female	39.4
Race	
Anglo	25.1
Black	42.9
Chicano	32.0
Years of Education	
Less than 8	68.3
8-11	24.1
12-15	7.0
16 or more	0.6
Age	
16-24	4.5
25-34	11.2
35-44	13.1
45-54	14.7
55-64	16.9
65 and over	39.6

TABLE 6.3

Selected Characteristics of Poverty Household Heads in the Survey Counties, 1974
(percent)

Characteristic	Anglo	Black	Chicano
Sex			
Male	54.1	54.6	73.7
Female	45.9	45.4	26.3
Education			
Less than 8 years	55.1	67.6	79.3
8–11	31.7	26.6	14.9
12–15	12.0	5.6	5.0
16 or more	1.2	0.2	0.7
Age			
16–24	4.6	4.8	4.1
25–34	4.5	13.6	13.2
35–44	5.5	14.1	17.7
45–54	11.0	14.3	18.2
55–64	19.0	16.8	15.3
Over 65	55.4	36.4	31.6

37.7 percent for male heads of households, approximately 75 percent of female heads of households had less than $2000 income. Mean household income for poverty female heads was $1696, or 67 percent of that for men. It is obvious that the availability of improved earnings through better-paying jobs (and access to higher-paying occupations) is much more limited for female heads of households. As amplified in Chapter 3, women, regardless of income, tend to be adversely affected by occupational segregation and discrimination.

Examination of other characteristics of poverty households reveals that in addition to the large percentage of household heads 65 years of age and older (18.5 percent), 17 percent were between 55 and 64 years of age. Therefore, the existence of a relatively large number of elderly heads of poor households was expected (see Table 6.2). The fact that 39.6 percent of poverty household heads are 65 years of age and over in rural areas indicates a critical social problem.

The existence of a potentially more productive group of heads of household in poverty is an equally important policy problem. Specifically, 39 percent of all heads of poor household heads are in the category of prime labor force age (25 to 54 years of age).

Race is another characteristic of poverty households that provides insight into the nature and incidence of poverty (see Table 6.3). Approximately 43 percent of the poor households were headed by blacks. As expected, almost all of the poor in Starr County were Chicano (98.3 percent); most of the poor in Sunflower and Natchitoches counties were black: 86.8 and 56.4 percent, respectively. Although Anglo poverty accounted for only one-quarter of all poverty in the survey, it is a significant problem in those counties with smaller numbers of minorities. Almost 62 percent of the poor in Dodge County and 42 percent of the poor in Natchitoches Parish were Anglos.

Educational attainment is another personal characteristic of poverty households that was found to be very low in the four rural counties. Almost 70 percent of the poverty household heads have eight years or fewer formal education. Relative to men, women tended to achieve higher educational levels, with 26.1 percent (19.9 percent for men) reporting nine years of education or more.

Although educational attainment of the poor was low in all counties, two counties, Starr and Sunflower, had extremely low levels of educational attainment, with 85.8 percent and 77 percent, respectively, of the poor in those counties having completed only the eighth grade or lower. In Starr County, the dominance of agricultural employment, the large numbers of migrant farm workers, and the infusion of legal and illegal immigrants from Mexico are possible explanatory factors for the inordinately low educational levels. In Sunflower County, past racial discrimination in education is a partial explanation of low educational attainment by the poor.

Economic Characteristics of the Poor

The severity of poverty in the rural study area is clearly shown by analysis of personal income of poor households (see Table 6.4). These data reveal that over 90 percent of the poor households received less than $4000 income in 1973.

There was substantial variation in income among poverty households by sex of the household head regardless of race (for males means were $2497 for Anglos, $2412 for blacks, and $2726 for Chicanos; for females the means were $1581 for Anglos, $1741 for blacks, and $1748 for Chicanos). The poverty households in Starr County tended to have slightly higher incomes, with the mean total incomes for Chicano households (Starr County) for both male and female heads of households slightly greater than for similar groups in the other three counties. Such a finding is associated with larger family sizes in Starr County and therefore greater potential for income generated by household members other than the head. In

TABLE 6.4

Distribution of Poverty Households by Income,
by County, 1973
(percent)

Income Bracket (dollars)	Dodge	Natchi-toches	Starr	Sun-flower	Total
0-999	7.7	9.3	9.4	15.0	10.5
1000-1999	48.5	48.0	31.9	43.7	41.8
2000-2999	30.0	30.5	26.1	23.7	27.3
3000-3999	6.4	5.3	17.5	9.6	10.5
4000-4999	6.0	4.0	7.7	4.2	5.6
5000-5999	0.9	2.8	6.5	3.3	3.8
6000-6999	0.4	0	1.0	0.6	0.5
Total	100.0	100.0	100.0	100.0	100.0

fact, a slightly higher percentage of the Chicano households (compared to Anglo and black households) had more than one income recipient.

The sources of household income shown in Table 6.5 indicate that government transfer payments are the most often mentioned source of income to the poor; wages and salaries are second. In those counties with the greatest dependency on agriculture (Starr and Sunflower), wages and salaries are the most important source, with government transfer payments second. Third in importance in all counties are Social Security benefits. The data in Table 6.6 reveal that wages and salaries are the most mentioned income sources for the Chicano poor; government transfer payments ranked first for the black poor; and Social Security is the major income source for the Anglo poor.

Government transfer payments (including Social Security) are definitely more important to the poor than to the nonpoor, primarily a reflection of the overrepresentation of the aged in poverty. The importance of specific government transfer payments varies among racial groups. Social Security and OAA are especially important to Anglos; government transfer payments, in general, are relatively less important to the Chicano poor (they are less important to all Chicano families). As sources of income, the former adult welfare programs and AFDC are generally of equal importance in all counties. The major exception is Sunflower County, which had 37 percent of all AFDC participants.

Income from business and private transfers was received by fewer poor families than by nonpoor. These income sources are especially infrequent for blacks, regardless of income.

TABLE 6.5

Distribution of Households by Sources of Income,
by County, 1973
(percent)

Source	Total		Dodge		Natchitoches		Starr		Sunflower	
	Poor	Nonpoor	Poor	Nonpoor	Poor	Nonpoor	Poor	Nonpoor	Poor	Nonpoor
Wages and salaries	44.9	75.7	32.6	75.1	31.2	74.2	58.3	83.3	50.0	72.3
Business income	5.6	16.0	6.0	19.3	5.3	13.0	7.0	17.0	3.9	14.3
Transfers–private	6.4	15.8	11.6	20.3	6.8	16.8	6.2	13.3	2.4	11.3
Transfers–government	47.0	18.9	56.2	19.3	61.4	26.5	39.5	15.3	42.2	12.5
Social Security	35.1	23.5	49.4	24.9	41.4	24.6	24.5	18.1	32.3	24.9

TABLE 6.6

Sources of Income of the Poor and Nonpoor
Households, by Race, 1973
(percent)

Source	Anglo		Chicano		Black	
	Poor	Nonpoor	Poor	Nonpoor	Poor	Nonpoor
Wages and salaries	23.2	71.7	57.4	84.0	48.2	80.0
Business income	6.4	18.9	7.2	18.2	3.9	6.0
Transfers— private	12.2	19.9	7.0	10.4	2.8	6.0
Transfers— government	48.0	17.2	35.2	17.2	55.2	30.0
Social Security	52.9	23.8	24.6	17.0	32.5	24.9

Wages and salaries are significantly less important as a source of income for poor families than for the nonpoor. Nevertheless, wages and salaries are mentioned as income sources more than twice as many times by the black and Chicano poor than by the Anglo poor, an indication that labor market activities are more important to minority group households as a source of income.

Most of the wages and salaries earned by poverty households are generated by the household head. Therefore, the number of weeks worked by the head greatly affects the amount of income generated by wages and salaries. Almost 38 percent of the poverty heads of households who had worked in 1973 indicated they worked 26 weeks or less; only 37 percent had full-time employment. Chicano heads of households worked the least number of weeks (44 percent worked 26 weeks or less) and also had the least full-time employment (33.2 percent). Blacks faired only slightly better than Chicanos (36.4 percent worked 26 weeks or less, and 40 percent worked full-time). Surprisingly, only 14 percent of poverty heads of households working 26 weeks or less cited health as a problem.

These findings indicate that there are a number of factors, including health, seasonal jobs, low-wage-paying industries, and the general lack of jobs in rural areas, that result in wages and salaries being a less important source of income to the poor than to the non-poor. In spite of these factors that contribute to low labor force participation of the poor, 34 percent of the heads of households in poverty were employed in 1974, and 5.1 percent were unemployed. Almost 71 percent of those who were employed were in Starr and Sunflower counties.

Household Size of the Poor

A number of insights into poverty are gained by examining the number of persons in poverty households. Over 51 percent of the poverty households contained two or fewer persons (27.4 percent contained only one person). The percentage of one- and two-person households in poverty by counties is as follows: Dodge, 25.8 percent; Natchitoches, 23 percent; Sunflower, 16.2 percent; and Starr, 12 percent. Many of these households have heads over the age of 65. However, there are a number of one- and two-person households with heads under the age of 65 existing in a state of poverty. Over 18 percent of the poor are made up of one- and two-person households that are not eligible for Supplemental Security Income (SSI) and some of whom are probably not eligible for AFDC.

Mean household income for the poor (shown in Table 6.7) reveals, as expected, that as family size increases, family income also increases. Data in Table 6.8 show that 29 percent of the poor households contained five or more family members. Most of these households were in Starr and Sunflower counties, which had the largest poverty households.

RELATED DIMENSIONS OF POVERTY

It is a logical expectation that some important dimensions of poverty are not economic but are strongly related to labor force

TABLE 6.7

Mean Household Income for the Poor, by Household Size, 1973
(dollars)

Number in Family	Mean Household Income
1	1365
2	1887
3	2102
4	2460
5	2697
6	3106
7	3381
8	3280
9	3526
10 or more	3525

TABLE 6.8

Total Income of the Poor, by Household Size, 1973
(percent)

Income Category (dollars)	Household Size									
	1	2	3	4	5	6	7	8	9	10 or more
0–999	22.1	6.1	7.7	8.7	6.2	1.0	2.7	15.4	6.1	2.6
1000–1999	71.2	44.2	36.1	26.0	25.8	15.6	20.3	12.8	18.2	13.2
2000–2999	6.7	49.7	39.4	29.8	22.7	30.2	20.3	17.9	18.2	18.4
3000–3999	0	0	16.8	26.9	24.7	27.1	16.2	15.4	15.2	26.3
4000–4999	0	0	0	8.7	20.6	13.5	18.9	12.8	9.1	23.7
5000–5999	0	0	0	0	0	12.5	17.6	20.5	30.3	15.8
6000–6999	0	0	0	0	0	0	4.1	5.1	3.0	0
Total number	358	310	155	104	97	96	74	39	33	39

behavior. Among the most notable are those relating to health, housing conditions, and place of residence. Health problems, in general, appear to be an important reason for nonparticipation in the labor force by the poor. Almost 50 percent of the poor heads of households indicated health problems. Health problems were cited by almost 57 percent of the Anglo poor (41.4 percent for Chicanos and 47.5 percent for blacks), which largely reflects the disproportionate number of elderly Anglo poor. In fact, over 52 percent of all those with health problems were 65 years of age and over, although one-quarter of the poor with health problems were in the prime working-age categories.

Another fact reflecting poverty is the quality of housing and the quality of those services usually associated with housing. Data from the Census of Housing indicate for all survey counties that the quantity of available housing has increased and housing conditions in general have improved since 1950.[7] Nevertheless, these same data reveal that rural areas, relative to other areas of the country, have serious problems in terms of the quality of housing and sanitation. This study of rural areas found that almost 40 percent of the poverty households do not have hot and cold running water.

In addition, the poor also have more sanitation problems associated with their housing. It is highly probable that these conditions are related to the health problems discussed earlier. Lack of public sewers or septic tanks is indicated by a significant percentage of poor households. Over 28 percent of the households had neither public sewers nor septic tanks. Starr and Sunflower counties had the fewest facilities.

Data for both the poor and nonpoor in the survey counties are consistent with Census of Housing data, which reflect the existence of poor-quality housing and associated services in rural areas. This study specifically indicates, however, that the poor live in the worst housing in those counties where the general level of housing is poor anyway.

Most poverty households in all four counties had electricity (98.6 percent). Telephone services, however, appear to be much more restricted in rural areas. Only 46.8 percent of the poor households had telephones. The installation of communications systems in rural areas has not benefited from a federal program similar to the Rural Electrification program.

One of the most interesting findings of this study is the discovery that rural poverty and farm poverty are not synonymous. In fact, only 73 of the poverty households (5.6 percent) in the rural areas in this study are located on farms. Most of these rural poor farm households are headed by men (78.1 percent), and most are elderly. In fact, 60.3 percent of these household heads are 65 years of age

POVERTY   161

or older, and 16.1 percent are between 55 and 64 years of age. Almost
58 percent of the rural farm poor are Anglos; one-quarter of the households are headed by blacks; the remainder are Chicanos.

THE WORKING POOR

One concept usually agreed upon by that portion of humanity called
"Western Civilization" is that to be employed is a good thing. This
rationale evolves from the "Protestant Ethic," which holds that work
is good and that idleness is evil. Consequently, most Americans—
including most of the poor—see work not only as a means of providing
income but also as a way of contributing to self-respect and status
in society and adding meaning to life.[8]

Just over 34 percent (448) of the poverty household heads were
employed at the time of the survey. Selected characteristics of these
working poor-household heads are compared with the nonworking poor
in Table 6.9. The figures indicate that working poor household heads,
when compared with those not working, are more likely to be male,
black, and younger than 65. As expected, most of the nonworking
poor are 65 years of age and over. However, physical disability and
other health problems and forced early retirement are reflected in
the relatively large number (17 percent) of nonworking heads of households in age brackets of 55 to 64 years.

Training for the working poor is practically nonexistent. Only
44 of the rural, working poor-household heads (9.8 percent) had ever
participated in any type of training program, and only 35 of these
completed the program. Unfortunately, many of the jobs available
to the working poor are for either low-skilled or semiskilled and are
found in agriculture and certain types of manufacturing. Many of
these jobs are low-wage, low-skilled, dead-end jobs that contribute
to poverty. Further, many of these jobs hold out a false hope for
overcoming poverty.[9]

The largest group of the employed poverty household heads work
in agricultural jobs (35.6 percent). Only two other occupations employ
more than 10 percent of the poor: construction (10.6 percent) and
domestics (10.6 percent). The majority of all agricultural jobs (80
percent) are in Starr and Sunflower counties. Otherwise, occupational
distribution is similar across counties.

As discussed earlier, wages and salaries are an important source
of income to the poor. Still, it comes as a surprise to learn that a
considerable number of the working poor earn less than the agricultural or the nonagricultural federal minimum wage. At least 36 percent of the working poor received wages that were equal or close to
the $1.60 per hour federal minimum wage for nonagricultural workers

TABLE 6.9

Characteristics of Working and Nonworking
Poor, 1974
(percent)

Characteristic	Working	Nonworking
Sex		
Male	77.5	51.8
Female	22.5	48.2
Race		
Anglo	13.2	31.3
Chicano	37.3	29.3
Black	49.5	39.4
Age		
16-24 years	8.5	2.5
25-34 years	20.8	6.2
35-44 years	23.9	7.5
45-54 years	24.8	9.5
55-64 years	16.7	16.9
65 and over	5.3	57.5

in effect at the time of the survey. Approximately 22 percent of the poor received earnings averaging less than the prevailing agricultural minimum wage of $1.30 per hour. Even when business income is added to earnings produced by wages and salaries, 55 percent of the working poor still had an annual income of less than $3000 during 1973.

Unfortunately, if a head of household works 40 hours every week for 50 weeks at the federal minimum wage, it is probable that this household (assuming no other income) would be classified as poor. For example, any nonfarm household with more than two members under similar circumstances would be a poverty family (more than three members for farm households in 1973). As the Manpower Report of the President, 1972 succinctly pointed out: "Included among the poor is a significant proportion of families whose heads work full time throughout the year but who still do not earn enough to lift themselves and their dependents above the poverty level."[10] Clearly, the federal minimum wage (agricultural and nonagricultural) as an antipoverty device has been a failure.

THE NEAR POOR

Studies that have examined poverty families over time show that although the percentage of the poverty population of a given area may remain constant over a considerable period of time, there may be significant changes in specific families.[11] Families often move in and out of poverty at various stages of the family life cycle, with the probability of poverty varying considerably from stage to stage. The greater the number of people close to the poverty line in a given area, the greater the probability that a particular area's poverty population will change over time. Although any family can fall into poverty under adverse personal circumstances, the probability of such occurrence to those families near the poverty level is much greater. Not only does it take a smaller financial "push" to send these families into poverty, but they are less likely to possess those factors, such as education, training, or personal savings, that might keep them above the poverty level in time of personal crisis. Of the households included in this study, over 50 percent were found to have incomes less than 125 percent of the poverty level. Similar data from the 1970 Census were 12.5 percent for the nation and 17 percent for the South. It is in this respect that the potential poverty problem of the South is the greatest.

The application of the 125-percent poverty index to the total survey sample increased the number of poor households by 301 (23 percent). Application of the index by sex gave an increase in the number of female and of male heads of households: 15.9 and 27.7 percent, respectively. Most of the increase by race was Anglo, with this particular group of poverty households increasing by 38.2 percent. Although the number of heads of households over age 65, regardless of race, increased by 24 percent, equal or larger percentage increases were recorded for age brackets 16-to-24, and 25-to-34 and 55-to-64.

Important in determining the number of families close to or in poverty is the definition or guideline that establishes the existence of poverty. As discussed earlier, the various definitions or guidelines tend to be controversial, with some considered conservative and some others liberal in ascertaining the incidence of poverty. Arbitrariness also enters into the establishment of guidelines. For example, a (nonfarm) family of four earning a few hundred dollars more than $4200 in 1973 can hardly be considered to be out of poverty (see Table 5.1).

All of this indicates that a considerable number of families are very close to living in poverty, with entrance and exit depending upon a variety of factors. Significantly, some of the demographic characteristics of those close to poverty may differ from those presently in poverty. That is, many of those close to being in poverty are elderly and are Anglo.

SPECIAL CASE OF THE ELDERLY

The high incidence of poverty among those over 65 years of age makes poverty of the aged a special problem in rural areas. As mentioned previously, 40 percent of the poor in the survey are 65 years of age and over. The next largest grouping of the poor is found in the age bracket 55-to-64 (17 percent). Social Security and SSI payments keep a large number of aged households barely above the poverty threshold. Furthermore, George Thomas, in a study published in 1973 based on the 1967 Survey of Economic Opportunity, claims that the population over 65 years of age in the South has increased 14 percent in the eight-year period 1959-67, with Anglos registering the largest gain.[12]

Old-age and retirement for most individuals means a serious reduction in income. Those individuals who were below the poverty line before retirement are forced down even further by retirement. Those over 65 years of age in rural areas usually have less access to both earned and unearned income (low Social Security and OAA payments). Other studies indicate that access to earnings by the elderly in the South is lower than in other areas of the country.[13] This phenomenon, in part, is a result of the high percentage of the aged who formerly received their income from agricultural sources. It also results from the general poverty of the area that, in turn, has resulted in inadequate government services, including low public assistance benefits and relatively low participation rates in the food-stamp program (to be discussed in Chapter 7).

Incomes of elderly persons are usually substantially below those of younger persons and are generally derived from transfer payments. Low incomes are, in part, due to low rates of labor force participation. Factors such as "forced retirement, age discrimination in the labor market, and high illness rates have combined to remove 72 percent of the men and 90 percent of the women over 65 from the active labor force."[14] Furthermore, the existence of large numbers of "discouraged workers" in the rural South probably reduces the access that those over 65 years of age have to supplemental earned income. Obviously, additional retirement or improved government benefits and supplements will be necessary to prevent a large segment of the elderly population from spending the remaining years of life in poverty.[15]

CORRELATES OF POVERTY

Poor productivity (low marginal productivity) and lack of investment in human capital provide a common structure for models that attempt to explain the correlates of poverty.[16] One model, utilizing Census data for states, found that poverty in the United States is directly affected by the number of families living on farms, the number of families headed by blacks, low labor force participation rates, low educational attainment, the amount of full-time employment, and the prevailing industrial structure.[17] A number of similar correlates of poverty in the rural South have also been identified in the primary data of this work.

Any analysis of poverty in the rural South must take into account the release of thousands of workers from agricultural employment through mechanization. Neither out-migration nor increase of nonagricultural jobs has kept pace with the growth in population. Thus the supply of unskilled labor has grown in spite of the thousands of persons leaving the South. Also, a lack of nonagricultural employment has resulted in low wages, low salaries, and a large surplus of low-skilled labor. The existence of a significant number of "discouraged workers" in rural areas attests to this fact, and this large group outside of the labor force is not reflected in the relatively low unemployment rates of rural areas.

Obviously, poverty in rural areas does not affect all groups equally. In general, the poorest households are headed by females or by the aged and racially by blacks or Chicanos. Consequently, as expected, those households with double handicaps—for example, black females—have a high incidence of poverty.

Households headed by blacks and Chicanos were found to have higher rates of poverty than those headed by Anglos. Years of discrimination, social deprivation, and inferior separate schools have contributed to the poor educational attainment of blacks and Chicanos in most parts of the United States.[18] These correlates of poverty assume even greater importance in rural areas of the South where the problems have been more severe. For example, blacks not only receive lower earnings, but occupationally they are segregated into those jobs that are lower-paying and require the fewest skills.

Low levels of completion and inferior quality of instruction are common characteristics of the educational experiences of poverty populations.[19] For not only do education and training enhance income through higher productivity, but persons with higher educational attainment are, in general, better able to find and to hold jobs.[20] It is therefore expected that the relationship between the level of education and the incidence of poverty in the rural South is negative.[21]

This study reveals that in addition to low educational attainment, there has been little occupational training for members of poor rural families. This is due to the lack of available programs and/or lack of information about the few programs that do exist in rural areas and not to the lack of ability of initiative of individuals.

The social and family structure of households also may affect levels of poverty. At present, too little is known about the structure and importance of female-headed poverty households. Such households are expected to compete for earnings on an equal basis with male-headed households in the labor market. This study does indicate that, in general, such households are disadvantaged in attempting to maintain an income above the poverty level, in spite of greater access to AFDC benefits.

Health and housing facilities available to rural workers also are important aspects of poverty. Both health and housing facilities of the poor are significantly inferior to those of the nonpoor. This finding is crucial, considering that such facilities in rural areas are, to begin with, relatively inferior.

It should be noted that almost 50 percent of the poor heads of households in the survey area had health problems. Even though lack of full-time jobs is probably the most important factor contributing to low earnings and income, disability and health problems also have affected the low level of employment and, in turn, the income of the household. Health and poverty interact. Poor health may lead to poverty (cannot work); poverty leads to poor health (no medical care). The primary survey results have indicated that health and physical disability problems are important factors in keeping poor people in rural areas out of productive activities altogether, or in affecting the number of weeks worked. This study and another study, by the Institute for Research on Poverty at the University of Wisconsin, found that persons with one or more chronic health conditions are more likely to report low family incomes than are those without these conditions.[22] The extent to which access to proper medical care could alleviate this situation may be an important factor in the reduction of rural poverty. Nevertheless, as was true for the elderly, the types of jobs that many of the disabled could fill are lacking in rural areas.

Rural workers, in general, appear to have low annual earnings, due in part to less than full-time employment during the year. This is especially true for rural poor workers, for whom seasonal factors contribute to irregularity of work and earnings during the year. Furthermore, many of the poor heads of households are paid salaries in conformity with either the agricultural or the nonagricultural federal minimum wage.

In order to have earnings, even low earnings, one must have had some sort of job during the previous year (1973) to report this source of income. This study found, however, that despite low unemployment rates, a large surplus of labor exists in the rural South. Although "discouraged workers" have been discussed and analyzed by many writers from a case-study point of view, a considerable number

POVERTY 167

of these have been empirically isolated by this study. Allowing for
the aged, the sick, and disabled, it would appear that some of the
"discouraged" poor would be able to work if jobs were available in
rural areas. However, such jobs would have to pay higher than the
present various federal minimum wages if they were to keep the poor
out of poverty.

The nature of poverty and many of the characteristics of the poor
in the study area affect and are affected by the area's industrial structure,
which has been discussed in detail in Chapter 3. Employment
in rural areas is dominated by traditionally low-paying, labor-intensive
manufacturing industries and by agriculture. Not only is
such an industrial base associated with low pay, it contains a disproportionately
large number of jobs subject to seasonal and/or casual
employment and higher general unemployment. Such jobs have not
prevented the existence of poverty in rural areas. Nevertheless,
due to the inadequacy of government transfer payments, the amount
of income received by the poor from low-wage-paying industries is
important to their survival. In sum, wages and salaries from low-wage
industries and government transfer payments have not eliminated
poverty in rural areas of the South.*

The relationships between the factors discussed above and the
high rate of poverty in the rural South are strongly indicated by this
study. It therefore is perhaps unnecessary to stress that a significant
portion of our nation's current rural poverty and welfare problems
is found in the rural South and should be dealt with there.[23]

The incidence of poverty in the rural South is high, for certain
groups extremely high. Those groups with a high incidence of poverty
are blacks, Chicanos, female heads of households, and the aged in
general. This study also strongly supports the findings of others
that indicate that much of rural poverty is associated with poor health,
inadequate schooling, limited human-resource programs, and limited
economic development relative to the rest of the nation.[24] In spite
of the governmental policies that have existed since the 1930s (mostly
in the area of agriculture) and some improvement in relative incomes,
Michael Harrington's labeling of rural poverty as the "harshest and
most bitter poverty" in existence is still true today.[25]

It should be obvious that no one policy will solve the multifaceted
problems associated with poverty. Furthermore, a case can be made

---

*Application of the poverty guidelines to the total income of the
rural households in the study less income generated by AFDC, OAA,
and ABD resulted in the addition of only 100 households to the poverty
group. This indicates that the importance of these types of government
transfers in keeping persons out of poverty is exaggerated.

that the rural sector should be viewed as an interdependent, though somewhat different, part of the total economy and social order. Perspectives on income distribution, the organization of the economic system, social stratification, and welfare should be interrelated to allow a viable policy to emerge.[26]

NOTES

1. President's National Advisory Commission on Rural Poverty, The People Left Behind (Washington, D.C.: U.S. Government Printing Office, 1967), p. ix.

2. Ibid., p. x.

3. Derived from data contained in the U.S. Department of Commerce, Bureau of Census, United States Census of Population; 1970, General Social and Economic Characteristics (Washington, D.C.: U.S. Government Printing Office, 1972).

4. Absolute definitions of poverty on which the federal guidelines are based, although official and widely used, involve substantial value judgments about what constitutes an adequate level of income. Consequently, there are those who feel that the guidelines set the poverty level of income too low, and those who think it is too high. For further critical discussion of this poverty index and other definitions, see Mollie Orshansky, "Counting the Poor: Another Look at the Poverty Profile," Social Security Bulletin 28 (January 1965); Mollie Orshansky, "Who's Who among the Poor: A Demographic View of Poverty," Social Security Bulletin 28 (July 1965); Lowell E. Galloway, Poverty in America (Columbus, Ohio: Grid, Inc., 1973), pp. 1-14; Rose Friedman, Poverty: Definition and Perspective (Washington, D.C.: American Enterprise Institute for Public Policy Research, 1965), pp. 2-42.

5. A complete discussion of the version used by the Bureau of Census can be found in the U.S. Department of Commerce, Bureau of the Census, "Revision in Poverty Statistics," Current Population Reports, series P-23, no. 28 (Washington, D.C.: U.S. Government Printing Office).

6. These poverty rates by county are significant higher than those for the South and the United States, where the poverty rates in percent were 16.2 and 10.7, respectively, in 1970. Bureau of the Census, Census of Population: 1970.

7. Adams et al., Labor Markets in the Rural South, U.S. Department of Labor, Employment and Training Administration (Washington, D.C.: U.S. Government Printing Office, 1977).

8. Leonard Goodwin, Do the Poor Want to Work? (Washington, D.C.: The Brookings Institution, 1972), p. 1.

9. Dennis P. Sobin, The Working Poor (Port Washington, N.Y.: Kennikat Press, 1973), p. 5.

10. U.S. Department of Labor, Manpower Report of the President, 1972 (Washington, D.C.: U.S. Government Printing Office, April 1972), p. 22.

11. For a discussion of movement in and out of poverty and differential rates of movement associated with different family characteristics, see Terence F. Kelly, "Factors Affecting Poverty: A Gross Flow Analysis," in The President's Commission on Income Maintenance Programs—Technical Studies (Washington, D.C.: U.S. Government Printing Office, 1970), pp. 1-81.

12. George Thomas, "Regional Migration Patterns and Poverty among the Aged in the South," Journal of Human Resources 8 (Winter 1973): 78-79.

13. Joseph W. McGuire and Joseph A. Pichler, Inequality: The Poor and Rich in America (Belmont, Calif.: Wadsworth, 1969), p. 76.

14. Ibid.

15. Juanita M. Kreps, ed., Employment, Income and Retirement Problems of the Aged (Durham, N.C.: Duke University Press, 1963), p. 126.

16. David M. Gordon, Theories of Poverty and Underemployment (New York: Heath, 1972), pp. 28-29; Edward P. Denison, The Source of Economic Growth in the United States and the Alternative before Us, Supplementary Paper no. 13 (New York: Committee for Economic Development, 1962).

17. Lester C. Thurow, Poverty and Discrimination (Washington, D.C.: The Brookings Institution, 1969).

18. Bradley R. Schiller, The Economics of Poverty and Discrimination (Englewood Cliffs, N.J.: Prentice-Hall, 1973), p. 121.

19. Kelly, "Factors Affecting Poverty," pp. 88-89; Alan B. Batchelder, The Economics of Poverty (New York: Wiley, 1973), pp. 88-94.

20. President's Commission, The People Left Behind, p. 41.

21. Thomas I. Ribich, Education and Poverty (Washington, D.C.: The Brookings Institution, 1968), pp. 1-16.

22. Myron J. Lefcowitz, Poverty and Health (Madison, Wisc.: Institute for Research on Poverty, The University of Wisconsin, 1970), pp. 1-3.

23. Brian Rungeling and Lewis H. Smith, Rural White Poverty in the Mid-South (Report to OEO, December, 1973), pp. 119-29.

24. Oscar Ornati, Poverty amid Affluence (New York: The Twentieth Century Fund, 1966), p. 56.

25. Michael Harrington, The Other America: Poverty in the U.S. (New York: Macmillan, 1962), pp. 39-48.

26. James H. Copp, "Poverty and Social Order: Implications and Reservations," *American Journal of Agricultural Economics* 52 (December 1973): 743.

CHAPTER

7

**THE WELFARE
SYSTEM
IN THE
RURAL SOUTH**

During the 1960s the welfare system of the United States emerged as a controversial public issue. A system conceived in the 1930s as a humane program had become the object of criticism and scorn by recipients, taxpayers, and program administrators.[1] The pervasive discontent of these groups differed in specific cause but, in general, they related to such issues as costs, coverage, equity, benefit levels, and administrative arbitrariness.

For purpose of clarity, the "welfare system" as defined in this study includes the four categorical welfare programs that existed in 1973—Aid for the Blind (AB), Aid to the Permanently and Totally Disabled (APTD), the Old Age Assistance Program (OAA), and Aid to Families with Dependent Children (AFDC)—as well as the food-stamp program and the general assistance programs that directly transfer cash or add to spendable income. There are other programs—most notably, medicaid—that operate in these counties, but it is difficult to measure the impact on individual families, since these programs represent entitlements and not a direct addition to family incomes.

Of the categorical programs, three are referred to as the "adult" programs (AB, APTD, and OAA); the other is known as the "family" program (AFDC). Until January 1, 1974, all four of these programs were administered by the separate states and trust territories of the nation on a federal-state matching of funds basis. As a result, there were 54 different programs with varying benefits levels, coverage, and eligibility standards. These programs were subject only to minimum federal criteria.

Moreover, these programs were financed by separate formulas for each program, with funds matched by the federal government. Within each state, individual counties actually administered the programs. Obviously, this type system invites inequities, injustices, and abuses. The South had no monopoly on such problems, but it did have its share.

In the 1970s an effort was made to eliminate the problems created by such an amorphous system by turning the categorical programs over to the federal government.[2] Eventually, the political debate over the proposal centered primarily over the family program. When the dust had cleared, the federalization of the family program had been deleted, and responsibility for the three adult programs was assumed by the federal government. As of January 1, 1974, the elderly, the blind, and the disabled (who collectively numbered over 6 million) became eligible for SSI benefits as administered by the Social Security Administration. The minimum income benefits are set by a uniform scale that applies across the nation and are provided without regard to whether the recipient ever contributed to the Social Security system. The principle of a federal income guarantee was established.

The present chapter reviews the findings of the surveys of households and community officials and leaders concerning the operation of the welfare system in the rural South. Most discussion of categorical programs will be devoted to the AFDC, as this is the only one that retains the same structure it had at the time of the interviews in early 1974. The data on the federalized adult programs are included also, because they indicate social need. Little attention is given to general assistance in the following analysis because this program has almost no impact in the survey counties.

In addition to the categorical aid programs, the food-stamp program has become an integral part of the nation's assistance effort to low-income families. Although the history of food stamps dates back to the 1930s, it was not until enactment of the Food Stamp Act of 1964 that the program became permanent. Implementation under that act, however, depended upon the willingness of the counties to participate, and many Southern rural counties did not exercise this option. In 1973 the federal government passed legislation that required all counties to participate in the food-stamp program by July 1, 1974.

THE CATEGORICAL PROGRAMS

Table 7.1 presents a distribution of the number of recipients in the four counties for each of the old categorical programs for 1973 or 1974 (see note for Table 7.1). Of special significance is the high number of individuals who were receiving OAA. The figures would suggest that since 1974 SSI benefits have become an important source of income to the Southern rural economy. The analysis that follows

TABLE 7.1

Participation in Categorical Welfare Programs in the Four Counties, 1973 and 1974

	AFDC		OAA Recipients	ATPD Recipients	AB Recipients	General Assistance Recipients
	Families	Recipients Children				
Dodge	483	1550 1166	738	276	30	No program
Natchitoches	743	2757 2097	2248	398	36	121
Starr	390	1491 1063	1030	124	26	No program
Sunflower	1563	5754 4545	1781	536	56	17

Note: The data on AFDC and General Assistance are as of February 1974. OAA, ATPD, and AB were federalized as of January 1, 1974; hence the data for these programs are for February 1973.

Source: U.S. Department of Health, Education, and Welfare, Recipients of Public Assistance Money Payments by Program, State, and County, reports for 1973 and 1974 (Washington, D.C.: Government Printing Office, 1973, 1974).

focuses on the AFDC program more than the others because, as previously stated, it is the only program remaining under the local control and influence.

It is probably not the case that most of the abuses and inadequacies of AFDC have been substantially reduced since the welfare debates of the 1960s. The lack of a uniform minimum income floor still leads to wide variations in average benefits from state to state. In the South, local administration invites arbitrariness in determining eligibility in a region where overt racial discrimination is less than a generation in the past. The exclusion from AFDC of families of the working poor and of families in which the male household head is present remains the general pattern in the South. As a result, if viewed as an antipoverty device, the AFDC program is a failure. The words of Daniel P. Moynihan's description are as adequate today as they were almost a decade ago:

> <u>The true issue about welfare is not what it costs the taxpayers, but what it costs the recipients</u>. Evidence— as usual—is practically nonexistent, but the probability is strong that the present welfare system is serving to maintain the poorest groups in society in a position of impotent fury. Impotent because the system destroys the potential of individuals and families to improve themselves. Fury because it claims to do otherwise.[3]

Hopefully, the following analysis provides some of the needed "evidence" referred to by Moynihan concerning this deepening crisis.

PERSONAL CHARACTERISTICS OF RECIPIENTS

Table 7.2 shows the racial distributions of AFDC recipients in the four counties. The high percentage of racial minorities is partly reflective of their higher incidence of poverty, but also of the fact that the sample counties were chosen because of their racial concentrations.

Nonetheless, in each county the percentage of black and Chicano recipients is higher than their percentage of the total population in their respective counties.

The racial distributions for OAA are contained in Table 7.3. The numbers of participants in OAA are more nearly equal across racial categories than was the case for AFDC. Due to the long domination of agriculture (which for many years did not provide Social Security coverage for its workers), OAA became an income-

TABLE 7.2

Recipients of AFDC, by Race, by County
and Total, 1973
(percent)

	Anglo	Black	Chicano	Total
Dodge	32.4	67.6	0	100.0
Natchitoches	8.1	91.9	0	100.0
Starr	0	0	100.0	100.0
Sunflower	2.0	98.0	0	100.0
Total sample	10.4	69.5	20.0	100.0
Sample size (number)	16	107	31	154

maintenance program in the rural South. The high incidence of OAA recipients in the South (for example, one-third of the aged population of Louisiana were OAA recipients in February 1973—a percentage exceeded only in Mississippi) and the high Anglo participation rate in OAA were two factors that no doubt explained the ease by which OAA was federalized in 1973.[4]

Because of the low numbers involved, the figures for participation in the AB and the APTD are combined in the tabulation of the survey data throughout this chapter. Accordingly, the racial characteristics of AB and APTD are contained in Table 7.4. As in the case of OAA, the participation rate of Anglose in these two programs is significantly higher than their rate for AFDC; the proportion for blacks is considerably lower; and Chicanos, slightly higher.

TABLE 7.3

Recipients of OAA, by Race, by County
and Total, 1973
(percent)

	Anglo	Black	Chicano	Total
Dodge	61.8	38.2	0	100.0
Natchitoches	45.7	54.3	0	100.0
Starr	2.1	0	97.9	100.0
Sunflower	17.4	82.6	0	100.0
Percent of total sample	31.0	41.7	27.3	100.0

TABLE 7.4

Recipients of AB and APTD, by Race,
by County and Total, 1973
(percent)

	Anglo	Black	Chicano	Total
Dodge	65.2	34.8	0	100.0
Natchitoches	42.9	57.1	0	100.0
Starr	0	0	100.0	100.0
Sunflower	5.9	94.1	0	100.0
Total sample	30.0	43.4	26.5	100.0
Sample size (number)	25	36	22	83

The sex distribution of recipients of categorical welfare is contained in Table 7.5. In general, the survey data for these rural counties is consistent with the expected profile. That is to say, AFDC recipients were overwhelmingly female-headed households, whereas the other adult programs were generally male-headed households.

The age distribution of the recipients of each program is contained in Table 7.6. The figures for OAA show a mean of 73.8 years of age. With the mean age being well above the normal age for labor

TABLE 7.5

Recipients of Categorical Welfare Assistance,
by Sex and County, 1973
(percent)

	AFDC	OAA	ABD
Dodge			
Female	73.0	60.3	43.5
Male	27.0	39.7	56.5
Natchitoches			
Female	83.8	42.5	28.6
Male	16.2	57.5	71.4
Starr			
Female	87.1	38.3	45.5
Male	12.9	61.7	54.5
Sunflower			
Female	87.1	44.1	58.8
Male	12.9	55.9	41.2

TABLE 7.6

Average Age of Recipient Household Head of
Categorical Welfare Assistance, by County, 1973
(years)

	AFDC	OAA	ABD
Dodge	43.7	72.8	59.8
Natchitoches	40.4	74.4	57.4
Starr	39.0	72.8	55.6
Sunflower	39.4	75.5	55.6
Mean value for all counties	40.6	73.8	57.2

force participation, it is apparent that this group generally cannot be expected to work. The mean age of the household heads with dependent children of 40.6 years seems higher than one would expect. These means, however, are consistent in all four counties, with Dodge County recipients somewhat older than the others.

Any evaluation of the adequacy of welfare assistance must consider the size of the recipient's family. Table 7.7 gives the mean sizes of recipient family size for each of the categorical programs. Of special note is the mean for AFDC recipients, which was 4.8 persons per family (with Sunflower county families being considerably higher). These figures will become more significant in subsequent discussions of benefit levels.

Mean levels of educational attainment for recipient household heads of various categorical welfare programs are shown in Table 7.8. These means are considerably below the already low educational

TABLE 7.7

Mean Family Size of Recipients of Categorical
Welfare Assistance, by County, 1973
(number of persons)

	AFDC	OAA	ABD
Dodge	4.3	1.6	2.6
Natchitoches	4.2	1.6	1.7
Starr	4.4	1.9	2.8
Sunflower	5.8	1.6	2.7
Mean value for all counties	4.8	1.7	2.4

TABLE 7.8

Mean Values of Educational Attainment for
Household-Head Recipients of Categorical
Welfare Assistance, by Program and
by County, 1973
(years)

	AFDC	OAA	ABD
Dodge	7.6	7.2	4.8
Natchitoches	8.1	5.4	4.4
Starr	5.6	3.0	2.5
Sunflower	6.8	5.1	4.3
Mean value for all counties	7.1	5.2	4.0

means for the population as a whole. Program recipients in Starr County, Texas, have the lowest education mean for each categorical program. In all but one program (AFDC in Natchitoches), the means are considerably below the eighth-grade minimum that is required for participation in most manpower programs.

Thus, the profile of personal characteristics is complete. In these rural Southern counties, the AFDC recipients are overwhelmingly middle-aged, are from racial minorities, have relatively large numbers of dependent children, and have very low levels of educational attainment. The most significant finding of this portrait is the magnitude of each of the characteristics rather than the characteristics themselves. For the adult programs relative to AFDC, the recipients are more likely to be older men; there is a relatively higher incidence of Anglos; the family size is considerably smaller. It is only with respect to educational attainment that the adult program recipients are consistently more disadvantaged than the AFDC recipients.

ECONOMIC CHARACTERISTICS OF RECIPIENTS

Significant labor market participation characteristics for the recipients of the various categorical welfare programs are presented in Table 7.9. The adult programs show what could be expected: virtually no labor force participation. The data for AFDC recipients also show a very high percentage (60.2 percent) of the recipients not in the labor force. On the other hand, 40 percent of the AFDC recipients did report themselves to be either employed (28 percent)

THE WELFARE SYSTEM

or unemployed (12 percent). Although there are no available national data with which to compare these figures, the labor force participation rate of AFDC recipients in these counties is higher than had been expected. If this is actually the case, it is most probably so because the level of benefit payments to AFDC recipients in Southern rural counties is notoriously low. Some AFDC recipients have no choice but to supplement their AFDC benefits through work if they are to survive.

A rough measure of the work history of those household heads who were AFDC recipients, constructed from responses to three questions (which are categorized), is presented in Table 7.10. The

TABLE 7.9

Labor Force Status of Recipients of Categorical Welfare Assistance, by County, 1973
(percent)

	AFDC	OAA	ABD
Dodge			
Employed	29.7	0	0
Unemployed	10.8	0	13.0
Not in the labor force	59.5	100.0	87.0
Natchitoches			
Employed	29.7	0.8	0
Unemployed	5.4	0.8	4.8
Not in the labor force	64.9	98.4	95.2
Starr			
Employed	19.4	2.1	0
Unemployed	19.4	0	4.5
Not in the labor force	61.2	97.9	95.5
Sunflower			
Employed	30.6	1.7	0
Unemployed	10.2	0	0
Not in the labor force	59.2	98.3	100.0
Total, all counties			
Employed	27.9	1.1	0
Unemployed	11.9	0.3	6.0
Not in the labor force	60.2	98.6	94.0

TABLE 7.10

Occupational Employment History of Household
Heads Who are Recipients of AFDC Payments,
All Counties Combined, 1973
(percent)

Occupational Category	First Occupation after Leaving School	Longest-Held Occupation since Leaving School	Current Occupation
Professional	0.7	0.7	0
Managerial	0	0.7	0.7
Clerical	1.3	0.7	0.7
Sales	1.3	0.7	0
Domestic service	21.2	21.7	8.6
Food and beverages	4.6	5.9	4.6
Service workers	1.3	3.9	2.0
Plant farming	26.5	19.7	0.7
Animal farming	0	0	0
Miscellaneous agriculture	11.9	12.9	0.7
Manufacturing—new materials	0.7	0.7	0.7
Manufacturing—durables	1.3	2.0	0.7
Manufacturing—assembly line	3.3	3.9	3.3
Construction	2.0	1.3	1.3
Transportation	0	2.0	1.3
Mining, logging, and extracting	1.3	0	0.7
Recreation	0.7	0	0.7
Never worked	21.9	21.9	21.9
Not presently working	–	–	51.8
Total	100.0	100.0	100.0

questions sought information on (1) the occupation of the head of the household for the first job after leaving school, (2) the occupation held for the longest time since the recipient left school, and (3) the current occupation, if any, of the recipient. First, the data show that 21.9 percent of the AFDC recipients have never worked and therefore have no work experience. A very high percentage (73.7

THE WELFARE SYSTEM   181

percent) of all AFDC recipients were not working at the time of the
survey. This means that AFDC benefits are the primary source of
income for most of these households. The data in Table 7.10 show
that over half of all employed AFDC recipients were in the unskilled
occupations (domestic service or agricultural occupations), both when
they first left school and as their longest occupation since leaving
school. One-third of all AFDC recipients reported agricultural jobs
as their longest-held occupations since they left school. Thus, there
is one clear difference between rural and urban AFDC recipients:
The former have a work history of employment in agriculture. Of
those AFDC recipients who also are currently employed, however,
one-third hold jobs in domestic service and very few (about 5 percent)
hold jobs in agriculture.

ASSESSMENT OF THE EXISTING CATEGORICAL WELFARE

As shown in the preceding section, the recipients of the various
forms of categorical welfare have very low levels of labor force
participation. This means, of course, that the welfare benefits could
be expected to account for a significant portion of the total income of
families. Table 7.11 presents the mean dollar value of the annual
benefits received from each program in each county. When it is
recalled that the AFDC recipients had much larger family sizes, it
is obvious that they are worst-off on a per capita basis and that these
benefits are grossly deficient. In fact, the average annual per capita
figure for AFDC recipients ($250) is less than that for OAA ($549) or
ABD ($563).

The gross inadequacy of the benefits from AFDC is most vividly
seen from an examination of the total family income levels for the

TABLE 7.11

Mean Dollar Value of Annual Benefits
Received from Categorical Welfare
Assistance Programs, by County, 1973
(dollars)

	AFDC	OAA	ABD
Dodge	1193.92	794.87	1904.74
Natchitoches	1431.14	985.24	1088.91
Starr	1265.13	970.45	1269.64
Sunflower	1001.00	920.64	1028.12
Total	1203.86	933.13	1350.43

TABLE 7.12

Mean Value of Total Income of All Families That
Were Recipients of Welfare Assistance, by
Category of Assistance, by County, 1973
(dollars)

	AFDC	OAA	ABD
Dodge	3140.73	2224.34	4284.52
Natchitoches	2691.92	2195.78	3043.62
Starr	2424.35	2353.63	1894.18
Sunflower	2149.71	2297.19	2299.71
Total	2573.37	2261.09	2930.46

recipients of the categorical welfare programs. Table 7.12 contains the findings from the survey. These figures combined the welfare benefits with all other income earned by everyone in the households. Again, when reference is made to family size (review Table 7.7), the income levels are so low as to make questionable the possibility of survival. Clearly, the level at which recipients or their family members are able to supplement their benefits still leaves them with insufficient income. The inability may be due to lack of job opportunities, lack of work experience, low levels of human-capital endowment, program regulations that discourage seeking work, or some combination of all four factors. Regardless of the explanation, however, results show extremely low levels of family income for all welfare recipients, but especially so for those families receiving AFDC.

A more vivid picture of the inadequacy of AFDC and OAA payments in the rural South is highlighted by the data presented in Table 7.13. No payment to an AFDC family is sufficient to maintain that family above the federally stipulated poverty level. In fact, most AFDC payments leave the recipient substantially below the poverty threshold. In total, almost 75 percent of the families receiving AFDC would be $2500 or more below the poverty level if that were the only source of income. The severity of this low payment level is further emphasized by the figures in Tables 7.11 and 7.12. Payments under the AFDC program represent, on average, 46.8 percent of the total income of recipient families. It is obvious that even where there is another income source involved, AFDC payments generally will not be sufficient to lift the family above the poverty level.

Analysis of those receiving OAA payments leads to the conclusion that a problem also exists regarding adequacy of benefits, but

THE WELFARE SYSTEM 183

it is much less severe than was the case for AFDC recipients. As Table 7.13 reveals, payments were such that OAA benefits left all families below the poverty level. In the case of OAA recipients, 75 percent were within $2000 of the poverty level. This result differs from that found for AFDC recipients primarily because of differences in family size—as would be expected by the nature of the two programs. In terms of total income, OAA payments constituted only 41.3 percent of all income for the average recipient family. Thus, even though it took less total income for the average OAA recipient's family to be above the poverty level than it took for the average AFDC family to be so, the OAA recipient had to secure a larger percentage from some source other than the welfare program.

The figures cited above leave little doubt as to the inadequate level of welfare payments in the rural Southern counties in this sample, whether viewed absolutely or relative to other areas.[5] In general, the payment structure is typical of the entire rural South. If the welfare programs discussed above are evaluated as an anti-poverty effort, it is clear they constitute a dismal failure in the rural South.

TABLE 7.13

Difference between Welfare Payments and Poverty Level for AFDC and OAA Recipients, Distribution by County, 1973
(percent)

Amount below Poverty Level (dollars)	Dodge	Natchi-toches	Sun-flower	Starr	Total
AFDC					
0-500	0	8.1	0	3.2	2.6
501-1000	8.1	0	2.0	3.2	3.3
1001-1500	18.9	16.2	4.0	12.9	12.3
1501-2000	13.5	16.2	6.0	19.4	12.9
2001-2500	8.1	8.1	2.0	12.9	7.2
2501-3000	51.4	51.4	86.0	48.2	61.7
OAA					
0-500	2.9	8.1	10.9	4.6	6.6
501-1000	17.4	17.8	7.3	5.8	12.8
1001-1500	21.7	23.4	38.2	37.9	29.3
1501-2000	26.1	26.6	27.3	26.4	26.6
2001-2500	15.9	18.6	9.1	13.8	15.2
2501-3000	15.9	5.7	7.3	11.5	9.6

Another aspect of evaluating the adequacy of welfare programs concerns overage. In general, programs such as AB, APTD, and even OAA to some extent, do not suffer from problems of coverage. Those who are eligible are usually encouraged to enroll by persons in a community and by social workers and program administrators. In most areas the attitude toward AFDC is much more restrictive. In addition, eligibility criteria are such that local case workers have considerable latitude in the eligibility decision.

By nature and intent, AFDC is a restricted program. Only 15.9 percent of all female household heads in the sample were receiving AFDC payments (an additional 7.8 percent of the female household heads were eligible but were not receiving AFDC). Such figures make it appear that coverage is not a problem. But when one looks at coverage in terms of eligible households only, the results are somewhat different. Of the total eligible (229), 32.7 percent were not receiving AFDC benefits at the time of the survey. By county, the percentage eligible but not receiving benefits was as follows: Dodge, 22.9; Natchitoches, 33.9; Starr, 39.2; and Sunflower, 33.3. Despite the restrictive nature of AFDC eligibility requirements limiting the number who could participate, a substantial portion of those eligible was not covered. More importantly, a majority of female household heads were not eligible even though the average income levels of all groups, including those employed, was very low.

Most welfare recipients were able to supplement their real income to some extent through the purchase of food stamps during the time of the survey. All the counties had established food-stamp programs (although one had done so only within the preceding few months). Table 7.14 shows that in each county categorical welfare recipients had a high participation rate in the food-stamp program. The lower participation rate by OAA recipients is most likely due to disqualification because of asset holdings accumulated over their lifetimes.

FOOD-STAMP PROGRAM IN THE RURAL SOUTH*

The food-stamp program has become the most important federal aid program in the United States in terms of persons covered and dollar amounts involved. The food stamp program represents an

---

*Supplemental data utilized in this section were collected with the aid of a grant from the Income Security Policy/Analysis Branch, U.S. Department of Health, Education, and Welfare.

TABLE 7.14

Receipt of Food Stamps by Recipients of
Categorical Welfare Assistance,
by County, 1973
(percent)

	AFDC		OAA		ABD	
	Yes	No	Yes	No	Yes	No
Dodge	86.5	13.5	72.7	27.3	90.7	9.1
Natchitoches	84.2	15.8	52.6	47.4	88.9	11.1
Starr	83.9	16.1	68.1	31.9	86.4	13.6
Sunflower	87.8	12.2	61.0	39.0	58.8	41.2

income supplement available to low-income families, making it a major antipoverty effort.[6] Because of the high number of low-income families in the South, both absolutely and relative to other regions of the United States, the food-stamp program is particularly important in this region. In 1972, with 11.6 percent of the total population, the Southeast contained 17.2 percent of the food-stamp recipients in the United States and received 20.6 percent of the total dollar subsidy (Bonus Food Coupons).[7] Given the relative position of the rural South to the total South, the potential importance of the food-stamp program in the rural South is self-evident.

There is one specific aspect of the food-stamp program that substantially increases its importance as an aid program: It is the only program that provides an income supplement to low-income families regardless of the sex or employment status of the household head. In fact, it is the only aid program that does not have some specific qualifier other than income.

The amount of subsidy a household receives under the program varies with the income level and size of the household involved. For example, in the spring of 1973 a one-person household with no income could receive $42 in food stamps free per month, and a household of 20 persons with zero income could receive $482 in stamps. On the other hand, if the single person had an income of between $100 and $110 and the 20-person household had an income of $250 to $270, each household unit would be eligible for the same dollar value of food stamps as previously but would have to pay $18 and $75, respectively, to receive the coupons. Table 7.15 shows the variation in purchase cost of food stamps as income changes for a family of four.

The food-stamp program was fully operational in all four sample counties at the time of this survey. Reports from food-stamp officials in the four counties indicated that as of March 1974 participation in

TABLE 7.15

Food-Stamp Purchase Schedule for
Four-Person Household, February 1, 1974
(dollars)

Monthly Net Income	Purchase Price
0 to 19.99	0.00
20 to 29.99	0.00
30 to 39.99	4.00
40 to 49.99	7.00
50 to 59.99	10.00
60 to 69.99	13.00
70 to 79.99	16.00
80 to 89.99	19.00
90 to 99.99	22.00
100 to 109.99	25.00
110 to 119.99	28.00
120 to 129.99	31.00
130 to 139.99	34.00
140 to 149.99	37.00
150 to 169.99	41.00
170 to 189.99	47.00
190 to 209.99	53.00
210 to 229.99	59.00
230 to 249.99	65.00
250 to 269.99	71.00
270 to 289.99	77.00
290 to 309.99	83.00
310 to 329.99	89.00
330 to 359.99	95.00
360 to 389.99	104.00
390 to 419.99	113.00
420 to 474	118.00

Note: Coupon allotment, with nonassistance maximum monthly income of $473 is $142.

Source: Food Assistance Manual, Food Stamp Section, Food Stamp Program Revisions for Volume 12, Department of Public Welfare, State of Mississippi, Division of Food Assistance, Jackson, Miss., as revised February 1, 1974.

THE WELFARE SYSTEM

each county was as follows: Dodge County, 1022 households and 3283 persons; Natchitoches Parish, 2215 households and 7318 persons; Sunflower County, 1831 households and 9733 persons; and Starr County, 2190 households and 8500 persons. In terms of persons served, the food-stamp program is by far the largest aid program in any of the four counties.

Characteristics of Food-Stamp Participants

By the nature of the program, food-stamp recipients fall into what is normally called the low-income population. This means that such households as those headed by an elderly person, by a female, or by a welfare recipient would probably be overrepresented in the food-stamp program relative to their respective population proportion. Table 7.16 contains selected data on households in the study sample who were receiving food stamps. The distributions of the various characteristics reflect the overrepresentation of particular subgroups,

TABLE 7.16

Current Food-Stamp Recipients in Sample,
Selected Characteristics, by County,
Spring 1974
(percent)

Characteristic of Household Head	Dodge	Natchi- toches	Sun- flower	Starr	Total
Sex					
Male	48.6	57.6	51.3	73.6	61.5
Female	51.4	42.4	48.7	26.4	38.5
Race					
Anglo	59.0	37.0	7.8	1.4	19.7
Black	41.0	63.0	92.2	0.0	37.9
Chicano	0.0	0.0	0.0	98.6	42.4
Age					
16-24	1.7	3.0	4.7	4.4	3.8
25-44	19.7	28.5	53.2	33.4	30.5
45-64	32.9	30.3	31.6	36.9	33.9
65-99	45.7	38.2	28.5	25.2	31.8
Married	45.9	49.4	49.7	70.3	57.7
Total number of households	173	165	193	401	932

as anticipated. For example, although female-headed households constitute only 27.3 percent of the total sample, they account for 38.5 percent of the households receiving food stamps. Similarly, black families comprise 29.9 percent of the sample and 37.9 percent of the food-stamp recipients. The obviously inferior income position of these groups is reflected in the above figures.

One explanation for the inordinately high participation rate in Starr County is the high incidence of migrant workers. The migrant workers receive information on various programs and possibly receive program-registration assistance both while in Starr County and while "on the road." Information concerning food stamps is included in the services provided. While in Starr County during the "off season," many of the migrants are qualified by food-stamp administrators as "zero-income persons." Technically, officials are supposed to prorate the annual income over the year to determine eligibility amount. In practice, however, the officials say this is impossible to do since many migrants have no income for the months they spend in the county. Hence, say the officials, it is impossible to deny these people assistance. Their income, therefore, is often considered "zero," which means they pay nothing for the stamps they receive. Moreover, officials state it is very difficult to verify the annual income of many Starr County recipients (both migrants and nonmigrants), since income levels of many families are so low that they do not pay any income taxes. The officials are of the impression that a number of people are receiving more food stamps than they should, but they claim it is almost impossible to rectify.

Another plausible explanation for the higher incidence of food-stamp recipients in Starr County relative to the other counties in the survey is the fact that the program administrators are Chicano serving Chicano recipients. In the other counties the program is often administered by Anglos to predominantly black recipients. As a result, in Starr County it is unlikely that there is racial stigma associated with the food-stamp program, nor is it likely that there is racial discrimination associated with the administration of the program. These factors are likely to be present to some degree in the other three counties.

Household size and income are important factors in determining eligibility as well as coupon bonus in the food-stamp program. Table 7.17 contains this information for the sample as well as data on employment for heads of families receiving food stamps. As the data reveal, household size is larger on average in Sunflower and Starr than in the other two counties. This reflects, in part, the relatively larger percentages of households with the head over 65 years of age in Dodge County and Natchitoches Parish (see Table 7.16).

TABLE 7.17

Household Size, Income, and Employment of
Head for Food-Stamp Households in Sample,
by County, Spring 1974
(percent)

Characteristic of Household	Dodge	Natchitoches	Starr	Sunflower	Total
Persons in household					
1	26.6	23.0	10.2	12.4	16.0
2	26.6	26.1	16.7	17.6	20.4
3	13.3	12.7	13.5	8.3	12.2
4	8.1	7.3	12.0	10.9	10.2
5	5.2	9.7	13.5	9.3	10.4
6	8.1	6.7	12.2	5.7	9.1
7	3.5	4.8	7.5	11.9	7.2
8	2.9	3.6	5.2	6.2	4.7
9	2.1	2.4	3.2	6.7	3.6
10 or more	3.5	3.6	6.0	10.9	6.1
Mean household size	2.9	3.2	4.3	4.6	3.8
Mean household income, 1973 (dollars)	2836	2691	3251	2283	2876
Household head employed	19.7	19.4	36.2	38.3	30.5
Sample size (number)	173	165	401	193	932

The larger average household size as well as the large number of participants found in Starr County help explain why the average income of recipients is highest in the county where the average income of the total sample was the lowest. This logic, however, should lead to the expectation of a relatively high average income for recipients in Sunflower County—a result not supported by the data. The fact that almost 99 percent of the food-stamp recipients in Sunflower County were black is the most likely explanation for the low average income of recipients in this county—low even in relation to that of recipients in the other counties.

It is interesting to note that employment of the household head is highest in the two counties that have the lowest and the highest mean income of recipients. This helps explain the high average in Starr County but is contradictory with respect to Sunflower County. The overall percentage of household heads employed across counties (30.5) is sufficiently high to support the contention that food stamps represent an income supplement to a significant number of working poor households.

As shown in Table 7.14, food stamps represented an important income supplement for households receiving cash payments under other aid programs. The most surprising finding is that all households with AFDC and OAA payments were not receiving food stamps, since the probability of eligibility is extremely high. Although elderly households may be more reluctant than younger households to participate in any aid program, this obviously is not a factor where a household is already receiving OAA. Some possible explanations will be offered in a later section of this chapter.

Changes in Food-Stamp Participation

Because eligibility for participation in the food-stamp program is based on monthly income and recertification of eligibility is required quarterly, it is reasonable to expect that in rural areas with high seasonal employment there would be substantial movement in and out of the program during a given year. In fact, participation was surprisingly stable. Table 7.18 shows data pertaining to the total number of households receiving food stamps during 1973 and the number of months they received them.

Inclusion of Starr County makes the total figures misleading because the food-stamp program was not operating in Starr County until the fall of 1973. This helps explain why more households (401) were receiving stamps in Starr County at the time of the survey than had done so at any time during 1973.

When Starr County is removed from the analysis, the remaining counties show corresponding traits. In all these counties the number who received food stamps at some time during 1973 exceeds the number receiving stamps at the time of the survey (see Table 7.15). In all counties, over three-quarters of those who participated in the program during 1973 received stamps in all 12 months of that year, and all in this group were still receiving stamps at the time of this survey. This indicates that participation in the food-stamp program tends to be quite stable and of relatively long duration for the majority of households—not a totally unexpected result when the characteristics of recipients are considered.

TABLE 7.18

Number of Months Food Stamps Purchased
During 1973, by County
(percent)

Months	Dodge	Natchi-toches	Sun-flower	Starr	Total
1	1.6	5.0	1.5	13.2	6.8
2	2.7	2.8	2.2	27.7	12.6
3	2.2	3.3	3.4	39.8	17.7
4	2.2	1.7	1.5	10.3	5.1
5	1.1	2.8	1.9	6.3	3.7
6	2.7	4.4	1.9	1.6	2.4
7	0.5	0.6	3.4	0	1.1
8	1.1	1.7	0.1	0	0.7
9	2.7	0.6	1.5	0	0.9
10	1.6	1.7	0.0	0	0.6
11	1.6	0.6	1.5	0	0.7
12	80.0	75.1	79.6	0	47.1
Total households purchasing food stamps, 1973	185	181	205	376	947

Eligible Nonparticipants

The preceding analysis clearly indicates the importance of the food-stamp program to the sample population, with 28 percent of the total households participating in the spring of 1974. The potential importance is even greater. An additional 853 sample households were estimated to be eligible for food stamps but not participating in the program, making 53 percent of the total households in the sample eligible for food stamps.*

---

*The total number of households estimated to be eligible to receive food stamps was 1,787. Those eligible but not participating were estimated by adjusting reported income by deductible expenditures (rent, utilities, medical expenses, and education expenses) and excluding those with certain types of assets. Data limitations required some arbitrary decisions that probably resulted in conservative estimates.

TABLE 7.19

Households Eligible for and Percent Receiving
Food Stamps, by County and by Race

	Number Eligible	Percent Receiving
County		
Dodge County	346	50.0
Natchitoches Parish	433	38.1
Sunflower County	432	44.7
Starr County	574	69.9
Race		
Anglo	488	37.7
Black	700	50.4
Chicano	574	69.9

Table 7.19 shows participation rates by county and by race. The wide variety in participation rates is surprising. There would seem little doubt that some of the variations must stem from differing efforts by local program officials to contact and enroll those eligible in the counties. It also is possible that those eligible but not participating have higher incomes than participants. This would mean, on average, smaller absolute benefits from participation. However, the average income of $2943 in 1973 for eligible nonparticipants is not sufficiently greater than the $2876 average for participants to make this a viable explanation. Only in Sunflower County is the difference large enough to support such logic: $3869 for nonparticipants versus $2283 for participants. However, the $2869 is still lower than the average for participants in Starr County (see Table 7.17).

The two counties in which populations contained a relatively high percentage of blacks displayed the lowest participation rates—a fact that is unlikely to be coincidental. In both Natchitoches Parish and Sunflower County the participation rates for Anglos were very low: 25.4 percent and 19.5 percent, respectively. This supports the impression that interviewers received that the programs were considered "black" programs by most Anglos.

Discussions with welfare officials in Natchitoches Parish and Sunflower County and subsequent interviews with eligible nonparticipants led to the conclusion that participation in the food-stamp program was not encouraged. No provision for program outreach existed in either county.

THE WELFARE SYSTEM 193

While it is apparent that the food-stamp program is of considerable importance to low-income households in the rural South, it is equally apparent that numerous eligible households are not benefiting from the program. Because the reason for nonparticipation can be as important as the fact of nonparticipation itself, the following section contains an analysis of factors influencing the decision not to participate.

Causes of Nonparticipation[8]

Participation in the food-stamp program was so low in three of the survey counties that investigation of factors contributing to nonparticipation was imperative. This required a supplemental interview of a sample of eligible nonparticipants in Dodge County, Natchitoches Parish, and Sunflower County. A total of 206 households were involved in the subsample: 48 in Dodge County, 80 in Natchitoches Parish, and 78 in Sunflower County. Table 7.20 contains selected data on the subsample. In general, reasons given for nonparticipation were found to vary little by individual household characteristics, with the exception of elderly households.

Table 7.21 contains the distribution of primary responses for nonparticipation during the survey period. Inability to meet the costs of food stamps was cited most often as the reason why respondents had not applied during the study period. Over a quarter of those who answered indicated that costs prohibited them from participating. Almost half of the respondents in this group had actually participated in the program. The higher the household income, the less benefit a household will receive from participating because of the cost of stamps. Therefore, it is at first surprising that almost 65 percent of those who cited "cost too much" as a reason for nonparticipation had a monthly income of between $100 and $300. However, almost 90 percent of this income group were households in which the heads were over 65 years of age, and households that had only one or two persons.

The category "cost too much" can be separated into two unique responses. Of those who cited cost as a factor in nonparticipation, 21.3 percent indicated that they could not or would not put the necessary amount of money into the purchase of food stamps. The remaining respondents stated that the differential between the dollar value and the purchase price (bonus) was not sufficient to induce them to participate.

Several of those in the first group stated that they could not afford food stamps and claimed to have difficulty in meeting the

TABLE 7.20

Eligible Nonparticipants Subsample,
Selected Characteristics of
Household Heads

Characteristic	Percent
Race	
Black	65.0
Anglo	35.0
Sex	
Male	68.0
Female	32.0
Married	63.6
Household size	
1	22.3
2	31.1
3	11.2
4	8.3
5	6.8
6	7.3
7	4.4
8	2.4
9	1.0
10 or more	5.4
Age	
16-24	2.9
25-34	6.8
35-54	23.3
55-64	15.5
65 and over	51.5
Monthly income of household (dollars)	
1-50	1.5
51-100	4.9
101-200	40.3
201-300	21.4
301-400	16.5
401-500	7.3
500 and over	8.3

Source: Center for Manpower Studies, Factors Affecting Food Stamp Nonparticipation in the Rural South, A Report to the Income Security Policy/Analysis Branch, Department of Health, Education and Welfare (University of Mississippi, 1975).

TABLE 7.21

Primary Reasons for Not Applying for
Food Stamps, Spring 1974

Reason	Percent
Did not think they needed them	9.9
Does not want to accept welfare	2.2
Cost too much	26.0
Did not think they were eligible	18.2
Lack of transportation	6.6
Too much trouble, red tape, not worth the effort	6.1
Been turned down before	16.0
Other	15.0

Source: Brian Rungeling and Lewis H. Smith, Center for Manpower Studies, Factors Affecting Food Stamp Nonparticipation in the Rural South, A Report to the Income Security Policy/Analysis Branch, Department of Health, Education and Welfare (University of Mississippi, 1975).

cash-purchase requirements. The answers given by those respondents indicated that they simply did not have $30 or $40 in cash on hand at any one time to purchase stamps. Some were not aware that a partial purchase could be made. Others were aware of this alternative but still stated that they never had the necessary cash at one time.

The respondents who stated that the bonus was too small may be making a rational decision if the monthly cost of purchasing food stamps exceeds the normal monthly family food expenditures. A significant number of those responding indicated this to be true and, for some, calculations of the bonus they would have received tended to support this. However, for the majority of those respondents, calculations of potential bonuses indicated that the bonus was substantial, in some cases several times the purchase price. These families must either be basing their decision not to participate on erroneous information or making it in an irrational manner from an economic viewpoint.

Problems of poor information are not restricted to cost data. The responses indicate other informational problems. A total lack of information, however, was not a major problem, as only one respondent professed to be completely unaware of the program.

Belief that the household was not eligible to participate was the primary response of 18.2 percent of those interviewed. This response was prevalent among those with monthly incomes exceeding $300 and among those households in which someone was employed and earning an hourly wage rate exceeding the federal minimum wage (at the time of the interviews the minimum wage was $1.60 per hour). This is one indication that detailed eligibility requirements are not generally known to the public. Many feel that the program applies only to those on welfare or to those who are not employed.

There were several reasons given that were a reflection of the attitudes of the respondents both toward the program and toward themselves. Ten percent of those who had not applied for stamps stated that they did not need them in spite of the fact that their financial situation made them eligible. Several indicated that they would apply when they felt that stamps were needed. All of those who stated that they did not need stamps were over 35 years of age, perhaps indicating that older people have a different attitude toward food stamps and welfare in general than do younger people. Surprisingly, there was no discernible relationship between the level of income and the response "didn't think they needed them."

In addition to those in the above response category, four persons stated that they had not applied because they did not want to accept welfare. This response is probably closely related in meaning to the response discussed above. Not only had most of the respondents in these two groups not applied during the study period, but they had in fact never applied for food stamps.

"Too much trouble or red tape" is a reason given for nonparticipation that relates both to attitudes and to administrative problems. Of the 6 percent of the sample who gave this response half had never applied for stamps, and half had applied at sometime in the past. For those who had never applied, this response is an indication of a negative attitude toward program administrators that is probably based on information obtained from friends and neighbors. For those who had previously applied, this attitude was based on more concrete information. Several interviewees told of waiting all day in a food-stamp office to file application, only to be told to return the next day. One respondent related that this happened three days in a row, after which he simply gave up. Several interviewees mentioned the rudeness of administrative personnel as a secondary reason for not applying, and a few simply stated that the information requested was "nobody's business."

One major category of response that may affect the attitudes of potential participants is "been turned down before." Sixteen percent of those responding gave this as their primary reason for not applying. As might be expected, this response was cited most often by those

TABLE 7.22

Secondary Reasons for Nonparticipation
in Food-Stamp Program

Reasons	Number of Responses	Percent of Total Responses
Didn't think they needed them	34	13.7
Doesn't want to accept welfare	6	2.4
Cost too much	51	20.6
Didn't think eligible	36	14.5
Lack of transportation	20	8.1
Too much red tape	27	10.9
Been turned down before	30	12.1
Other	44	17.7

Source: Brian Rungeling and Lewis H. Smith, Center for Manpower Studies, Factors Affecting Food Stamp Nonparticipation in the Rural South, A Report to the Income Security Policy/Analysis Branch, Department of Health, Education and Welfare (University of Mississippi, 1975).

with a relatively high monthly income. During the interviews it became apparent that many believed that once turned down, reapplication was not possible. Thus, although those who received stamps were well aware of recertification, information concerning reapplication apparently is not explained at all or is explained inadequately to those who are initially ineligible.

A significant number of respondents gave secondary reasons for not applying for stamps during the study period. Table 7.22 shows the distribution of reasons by the total number of times they were mentioned. Transportation difficulties, excessive red tape, and attitudes toward the need for food stamps were cited more often as secondary consideration than as primary one.

Food Stamps and the Elderly

Throughout the study, special problems of the elderly in relation to food-stamp participation became increasingly apparent. Half of the nonparticipants over 65 years of age had never applied for food stamps. By contrast, in no other age group did those who had never applied exceed a third of those in the group. This was true despite the fact that almost 60 percent of the elderly households had a monthly income of less than $200. Therefore, the reasons for nonparticipation among the elderly are based on less first-hand knowledge of the program than are those for other age groups.

One response that was significant only among the elderly was "lack of transportation." Seventy-five percent of the respondents who gave this reason for not applying during the study period were over 65. Most of the respondents exhibited some knowledge of the program by indicating that the prohibiting factor was not the problem of securing transportation in order to apply, but the lack of transportation on a regular basis to pick up the monthly stamp allotment. Most indicated that securing transportation would require payment, thus adding to the true cost of participating in the food-stamp program. Furthermore, several households indicated that the local office would not allow someone else to secure the stamps for them (if true, this is contrary to regulations).

As the previous analysis might lead one to believe, "cost too much" was the single response cited most often by the elderly for nonparticipation, as it was for all respondents. However, for the elderly the process by which this conclusion was reached may be somewhat different. Although most elderly households fell in the income category between $100 and $300 per month, most also contained one or two persons.* Consequently, although incomes were low, the food-stamp bonus was not significant in the majority of cases. For example, a single person with $150 a month income would receive a bonus of only $11; a household of two with a $210 income would receive a bonus of only $22.† Thus, although qualifying for food stamps, elderly individuals and couples on Social Security or OAA would normally receive only a small bonus, or, as several elderly individuals stated, "the extra just isn't worth it."

The normal food consumption of an elderly person is also likely to be less, for many reasons, than that of younger individuals, yet age is not a consideration in the food-stamp allotment formula. Additionally, other expenses, particularly medical expenses, tend to increase with age, thus reducing the portion of a fixed income that is available to be spent on food. This latter logic is more closely related to the reason why older age groups gave "cost too much" as a response.

The elderly also cited other reasons common to all age groups. However, it should be apparent that there are some unique difficulties

---

*This statement holds for both gross income and net income calculated for eligibility purposes.

†Scale as of January 1, 1974.

with the program insofar as the elderly are concerned. In fact, the program as currently constituted seems poorly equipped to aid the elderly poor.

Generally, in spite of the great impact the food stamp program is having on the low-income population in the rural South, nearly half of those eligible are not being served. In part, this results from misinformation or lack of information and from individual attitudes. However, evidence is sufficiently strong to support the belief that in parts of the rural South there is little sympathy on the part of program administrators for outreach, and in some cases there is suspicion of overt efforts to discourage enrollment.

There is also support for the belief that administrative rules and the structure of the program discourage many eligible households from participation. The fact that normal household expenditures on food, as well as the cash flow of the household, are not considered in the program design appears to be a problem for many households, particularly among the elderly.

Such problems would be difficult to overcome in any practical manner, given the nature and structure of the food-stamp program. The most logical alternative would be to replace the current system with a direct cash disbursement instead of food coupons.

PERCEPTIONS OF THE WELFARE SYSTEM IN THE RURAL SOUTH

Inadequate benefit levels and incomplete coverage are in part the result of attitudes by government officials and the general public toward welfare programs. Additional problems arise due to the nature of program administrative practices and the attitudes held by program administrators.

The programs most affected by adverse attitude on the part of the public are AFDC and food stamps. These two programs do not fit into the traditional view—need created through no fault of the recipients—as do programs relating to age or disability. AFDC particularly suffers from this problem. The public more and more has come to view the AFDC recipient as being part of a socially undesirable group. Illegitimacy, divorce, and desertion are viewed as personal inadequacies, allowing the problem to be dismissed from public responsibility.[9] There is also a widespread belief that "welfare cheating" exists on the part of recipients of AFDC and, more recently, food stamps. This feeling reflects in part the eligibility of those not traditionally believed to be "needy."

Such attitudes on the part of the general public may influence program administrators, adding to the problems inherent in the administrative structure of many welfare programs.[10] The requirement of a needs test is humiliating to recipients. The nature of the AFDC and food-stamp programs fosters an adversary relationship between those who administer the programs and the individual recipients. As one author put it:

> The relations of those who give assistance and those who receive it are strained. The caseworker is likely to distrust the recipient of aid, to view his dependency with disdain. As an adviser, he may be condescending. As an investigator he becomes an enemy. The recipient is likely to regard the caseworker with scorn, as one whose function is to maintain docility among the poor. When request for supplementary grants are denied, when he is disqualified and aid cut off, his scorn turns into hatred. Between the caseworker, and the recipient of aid there is a perpetual state of war.[11]

Given the latitude a caseworker has in determining both eligibility and benefit levels, the structure described above is indeed a problem.

The disproportionate number of minority poor has made welfare a racial issue, particularly in the case of AFDC.[12] Problems associated with this issue will be as great in the rural South as anywhere in the United States. In Natchitoches, Dodge, and Sunflower the incidence of participation in the AFDC and the food-stamp programs was considerably higher by blacks than was their proportion of the population. The same was true for Chicanos in Starr County. In each county the participation rates were consistent with the higher poverty rates for minority groups. Nonetheless, the high participation rates by these minority groups have given the program the stigma of being conceived primarily for these groups. The issue is less significant in Starr County, probably because the county's population is almost entirely Chicano. In the other three Southern counties, there was a widespread attitude that equates AFDC and food-stamp programs as "black programs."

In all of the counties there was a widely held view that there are people who genuinely need both family assistance and food stamps. But there also is a strong belief that the ranks of the recipients are swollen beyond the actual number of needy people. This feeling was especially widespread with respect to food stamps. As one food-stamp administrator observed, the "statistical number of people in poverty in this county greatly exceeds the actual number of poor people." With respect to AFDC, there were allegations that its rolls also contained some household heads who really could and should work.

THE WELFARE SYSTEM

There were no feelings that there might be eligible people not being served. There was no interest manifested in trying to bolster outreach efforts to assure participation of all who were eligible. Administrative loyalties clearly favored the interests of taxpayers to reduce total costs rather than the interests of the potential clientele. In fact, many practices deterred wide participation. For example, in most instances there was only one office for the food-stamp and AFDC programs. In some instances, the office hours were irregular. In all cases, the hours were limited to the normal business day. With respect to food stamps, the fact that stamps could be purchased only during business hours of weekdays led a number of employers to complain of high absenteeism on the days that food stamps could be purchased. For many rural residents the distance to food-stamp offices was considerable. In at least one instance there was only one official to administer the program, and she was often absent. Hence, a long trip to that office might be futile for any would-be purchaser. It would be necessary to come another day and risk a repeat of the same experience. In most cases, waiting lines were common at food-stamp offices because of shortages of clerks and lengthy red-tape requirements. One may conclude fairly that the effectiveness of the food-stamp and AFDC programs suffers from the negative attitudes of local program administrators. Administrative concern tends to be more with program operations than with the needs of the recipients. In fact, the officials do not mention the inadequacies of benefits. Rather, they tend to imply the opposite—that they feel benefits are ample relative to the low income levels of the rest of the local population and in some instances are excessive and eligibility requirements are too liberal. In no case did program administrators feel that informational or administrative barriers existed that might preclude wider participation.

There was universal support for the idea that job training should be available to AFDC household heads, although the concept had more abstract support than specific statements as to the types of training and where such trainees would ultimately be employed. There were no special training programs for AFDC household heads (that is, Work Incentive, or WIN, Program) in two of the counties. WIN programs did operate in Dodge and Sunflower. In Dodge, 120 participants were enrolled in 1973; slightly over 60 percent received training under WIN. About a third were found unsuitable for training, and 7 percent were placed in jobs without training. In Sunflower County the ES appraised 160 WIN referrals (from the welfare office). Of this number, 54 were placed directly in unsubsidized employment, 15 got on-the-job contract training (one-half wages subsidized), and 4 entered public-service employment (all wages subsidized). The remainder were determined to be suited neither for placement nor for training.

Unfortunately, no follow-up evaluation is available for either of the counties. Information concerning occupations and wage rates for those placed in jobs was not available. Further, there is no way to determine how long those placed remained employed or whether they returned to the AFDC roles. The importance of this type of data collection and analysis was not recognized by the rural program officials. Nevertheless, it is unlikely that WIN could have a major impact in rural areas, given the lack of employment opportunities that exists.

There was no suggestion made by any of the private employers that they would provide jobs for any AFDC-recipient household heads. It was assumed either that other employers would be willing to hire these people or that it was the responsibility of the public sector to do it. Local government officials, however, showed little inclination to accept responsibility for absorbing the employment problems of household heads who were receiving AFDC assistance. Obviously, if any serious effort is to be made to provide employment opportunities for any significant number of AFDC household heads, a program of job creation that is federally financed and administered will be required. Presently, at the local level there is mostly lip-service given to the importance of the idea of employment of welfare heads of households.

In all but Starr County, the administrators were usually Anglos and most of the recipients were blacks. These officials were of the general impression that Anglos more often sought welfare services (for example, information, family planning, health services) than did blacks, who were more likely to seek cash assistance. In all four of the counties a paternalistic attitude permeated the AFDC administrative practices. In one instance, an official referred to AFDC as being exclusively "a mama's program." There was a general attitude throughout that the recipients should be grateful for what they received.

Most of the discussions related above pertained to the AFDC and the food-stamp program. Fewer problems and less negative attitudes were manifested concerning supplemental services, such as family planning, provided by welfare offices.

CONCLUDING OBSERVATIONS

Because of the federalization of the adult categorical welfare programs during the period of this study, no conclusions will be drawn, since the original programs no longer exist. It is hoped that the inconsistencies and lack of information disseminated on these former programs for the blind, the disabled, and the aged have been rectified by the establishment of the SSI program. Hence, comments are in order concerning only the operations of the AFDC and the food-stamp program.

With regard to AFDC, its current status can be assessed only in light of the process by which the program evolved. The original rationale for AFDC when it was created in the 1930s was to establish a minimum income floor for needy families that had lost a male breadwinner. In other words, it was largely conceived as being a "widow's program."[13] Over the years the vacuum created by the absence of a national income-support program based on participant need, rather than participant characteristics, led inevitably to AFDC's becoming a substitute income-maintenance program for a number of low-income families.[14] In the nation in general and in the South in particular, eligible AFDC families have been overwhelmingly female-headed ones.

AFDC benefits tend to be a substantial portion of the total income of the recipient families in the rural South. This is caused by the characteristics of the client group (that is, not only does the woman have dependent children, but she tends to be middle-aged; to have had little, if any, work experience; to have a low level of educational attainment; and often she is a person from a racial minority group that has endured economic, social, and political discrimination in the recent past in the region and that may still suffer vestiges of these practices and attitudes). Moreover, given the program requirements, even if the participant could find employment, the financial penalties are such that there is little incentive to seek work. In addition, the very low wage levels that characterize the Southern rural labor market would provide little work inducement, even if the aforementioned obstacles were overcome. This is especially true if consideration is given to the costs of working (for example, child care, transportation, and meals away from home). As a result, the AFDC program is more than simply an income-assistance program. It is the only program that provides direct income to most of the recipients; thereby it is, in effect, an antipoverty program. Those people associated with the administration of the program may not conceive of AFDC as such as an antipoverty program per se, but to the poor people who receive its benefits and, what is more, to most of the general public there is no distinction made between welfare and antipoverty efforts. They are perceived as being the same thing. Consequently, AFDC must be evaluated in terms of the function it assumes.

As for the food-stamp program, it is apparent that this is rapidly becoming the major income-supplement program available to low-income families in the rural South. Yet, despite its relatively higher participation rates, it is an important finding of this study that the number of eligible participants greatly exceeds the number of actual recipients. Here, too, greater outreach efforts are needed to inform eligible recipients of the availability of the program and to facilitate the purchase of food stamps by increasing the number of sales offices, extending the hours, providing mobile offices, and sensitizing the program administrators to the importance of the program to the people they serve. A preferred alternative to these reforms would be replace the food-stamp program with a direct cash-disbursement program associated with a comprehensive national minimum-income program.

The findings of this chapter are that the welfare system as it currently exists is simply not structured to handle the human problems of poverty in the rural South. The benefit levels do not begin to approach the federally stipulated poverty thresholds for rural households. Moreover, only about 70 percent of the female-headed households eligible for coverage are receiving it. Thus, the real problem is not the large number of people receiving AFDC in rural areas but, rather, the few people who are eligible for such assistance, compared to the many in need. Even if it were possible through aggressive outreach efforts to enlist all of the families eligible for such assistance, it would not mean that there would be much impact on the magnitude of Southern rural poverty. Most of the needy families of the rural South are not eligible for AFDC (for example, the male-headed household in which the male is unemployed; the male- or female-headed household in which the head is employed but is unable to earn an income sufficient to pull the family over the established poverty threshold; and the childless family with an employed head who is unable to earn an income above poverty levels). Thus, because benefit levels are grossly inadequate, because little effort is made to reach eligible families who are not actual participants, and because the program's own eligibility rules preclude participation by a substantial number of needy families, the AFDC program must be judged a failure in its service to the rural poor. It is apparent, therefore, that the current AFDC program must be federalized, as was the case in 1974 with the adult programs. The states of the South either cannot or will not raise their benefit levels and broaden their eligibility standards to provide sufficient and adequate coverage to the needy of the region. In Chapter 10 a detailed estimate is made of the potential impact on the rural South of a proposal made in 1972 to accomplish this very feat.

NOTES

1. Daniel P. Moynihan, "The Crises in Welfare," Public Interest (Winter 1968): 3-29.

2. See Daniel P. Moynihan, The Politics of a Guaranteed Income (New York: Vintage Books, 1973); Vincent J. Burke and Vee Burke, Nixon's Good Deed: Welfare Reform (New York: Columbia University Press, 1974).

3. Moynihan, "The Crises in Welfare," p. 22 (emphasis is in the original).

4. Burke and Burke, Nixon's Good Deed, p. 197.

5. In December 1973 the national average monthly payment per recipient was $76.16 for OAA, $112 for AB, $109 for APTD, and $56 for AFDC. No Southern state had an average payment that exceeded the national figures, except for OAA. Mississippi was lowest in all categories: $53.82 for OAA, $65.19 for AB, $64.72 for APTD, and $14.39 for AFDC. Florida had the highest average OAA payment ($83.33); the highest AB, APTD, or AFDC payments were in Virginia ($103.48, $102.37, and $50.93, respectively). The inadequacy of payments in the rural South is obvious when contrasted to these figures. Data were obtained from U.S. Department of Health, Education and Welfare, Social Security Bulletin 37 (June 1974).

6. Much confusion arises from this because many people argue that the food-stamp program was never designed to eradicate poverty. See, for example, Malcolm Galatin, "A Comparison of the Benefits of the Food Stamp Program, Free Food Stamps, and an Equivalent Cash Payment," Public Policy 21 (Spring 1973): 291-302.

7. Gene D. Sullivan, "Food Stamps: A Boost to the Southeastern Economy," Monthly Review 58 (June 1973): 86-91. The Southeast is defined as Tennessee, Georgia, Florida, Alabama, Mississippi, and Louisiana.

8. This section draws heavily on analysis found in a report by Brian Rungeling and Lewis H. Smith, Factors Affecting Food Stamp Nonparticipation in the Rural South, a Report to the Income Security Policy/Analysis Branch, Department of Health, Education and Welfare (University, Mississippi: Center for Manpower Studies, University of Mississippi, 1975).

9. For a detailed discussion of the problems such attitudes create, see Alfred Kadushin, Child Welfare Services (New York: MacMillan, 1967); John M. Remonyshin, Social Welfare (New York: Random House, 1971); Gilbert Steeree, The State of Welfare (Washington, D.C.: The Brookings Institution, 1971); Henry J. Aaron, Why Is Welfare So Hard to Reform? (Washington, D.C.: The Brookings Institution, 1973).

10. For a brief overview of the technical aspects of welfare administration, see John G. Turnbull et al., Economic and Social Security, 4th ed. (New York: The Ronald Press, 1973), pp. 519-67.

11. Clair Wilcox, *Toward Social Welfare* (Homewood, Ill.: Richard D. Irwin, 1969), p. 238.
12. See Kadushin, *Child Welfare Services*.
13. Moynihan, "The Crises in Welfare," p. 13.
14. Ibid., pp. 12-15.

CHAPTER 8

MANPOWER DEVELOPMENT AND TRAINING

The history of the United States is resplendent with examples of human-resource policies—for example open immigration, the land-grant colleges, the military draft, the creation of the public employment service, and the G.I. Bill.[1] But it is widely recognized that it was not until the 1960s that the nation embarked upon a conscious course to develop the employment potential of its human resources.[2] In fact, that decade has been touted as the era of the "manpower revolution" with respect to the emergence of public policy.[3] The revolution took the form of a series of legislative actions and administrative deeds. The overriding characteristic of the various policy endeavors was the underlying assumption that a variety of policy measures were needed to attack differing problems. Categories of programs were established for separate groups of needy individuals—for example, welfare recipients, unemployed youth, older workers, functional illiterates, and technologically displaced workers. The administration of these programs was, in general, centralized in Washington, D.C.

In the early 1970s most, but not all, of the categorical programs created in the 1960s were absorbed into the Comprehensive Employment and Training Act of 1973 (CETA). This act was intended to decategorize programs, and it embraced the concept of administrative decentralization in the form of special manpower-revenue sharing to state and local governmental bodies.

For the present purposes, however, the important matter is not the form but the substance of manpower policy. The factors that prompted the manpower revolution necessarily shaped the character of the programs themselves and determined the funding priorities. These factors were numerous and diverse. Among the major considerations were fears of technological displacement of workers due to automation; the wave of civil disorders that symbolized unrest among racial minority groups, especially among urban blacks; a rapid increase in the number of persons receiving welfare assistance, with the largest numbers occurring in urban areas; and a belief that skill shortages in selective labor markets triggered inflationary pressures during periods of low unemployment.[4] The unifying thread that ran through all of these prompting forces is that they were largely responses to urban stimuli. Although there was recognition of the rural origin of some of the contemporary urban population, the rural economy was not perceived as a crucial concern for manpower legislation.

The fact remains, the programs were not primarily designed to address any rural genesis. This is not to say there were no programs in rural areas but rather to underline the point that they were usually extensions of existing programs designed primarily to meet urban problems. The pattern clearly indicated that attention to rural manpower problems was largely an afterthought. Moreover, the rules, regulations, and guidelines associated with the programs that operated in the rural sector usually were identical to those required of urban program sponsors. Often these requirements were incongruent with the economic and political realities in rural settings.[5]

In addition to substantive and procedural difficulties, manpower programs in the rural South have another handicap: They are widely identified as endeavors specifically designed for racial minorities. The presumed designation has not helped the programs gain local acceptance or accomplish their placement goals.[6]

This study has convincingly demonstrated that the labor force of the rural South is woefully deficient in human-capital endowments. Thus, the irony of the situation is that the workers of the rural South have perhaps the greatest need of persons in any region of the nation for viable manpower programs, but prior to 1974 they scarcely had an opportunity to participate.

National data for federally funded manpower programs show that prior to the passage of CETA, FY 1972 was the peak year for enrollments (1.6 million); FY 1973 was the peak year for federal obligations ($2735.5 million).[7] Similar state data reveal that during FY 1974 the four states in which the field work for this study was conducted received 7.5 percent of the total expenditures ($200.3 million) for federally supported manpower-training programs. The principal amounts were allocated to Manpower Development and Training Act (MDTA) institutional training, Neighborhood Youth Corps (NYC), job opportunities in the business sector, and migrant programs. Among the four states, expenditures per capita were highest in Georgia and Texas, in part a reflection of their relatively large urban populations.

No published data were available in a form to permit an urban-rural analysis. Some rough estimates of program allocations were made by program and other administrators in the U.S. Department of Labor and its Atlanta regional office.[8] Their best "guesstimates" for the South were that program enrollments for FY 1974 exclusive of NYC were about 10 percent rural. If NYC is included, the proportion would be from 21 to 25 percent rural. Program allocations of funds exclusive of NYC were estimated at 10 to 12 percent rural; including NYC, the proportion was estimated at about 25 percent rural. When it is noted that 35 percent of the Southern population was "rural" by Census definition and that an even larger proportion of the population lived in counties that met the criteria for this study, distortion in favor of the urban areas is apparent, particularly for adult programs.

There are a number of training sources other than federal manpower programs in rural areas. One of the most significant sources of human-resource development activity other than that provided by the Department of Labor is vocational education, usually administered by the local public schools, with state and federal support.[9] Prior to 1963 the vocational education statutes provided federal matching aid almost exclusively for vocational training in agriculture, home economics, and commercial subjects. Since 1963 there has been some broadening of the array of course offerings in rural areas, although the historic pattern of vocational programs remains and those subjects are disproportionately represented in most rural curricula.

TRAINING-PROGRAM PARTICIPATION

The findings of this study indicate that there is little formal training activity in the rural South and that the number of participants in existing programs of all types is very small. The household survey identified 741 persons out of the total population 16 years and over (7,481) who had experienced some formal training in any type of training programs. There were 30 persons who were currently enrolled. Of the total (741), only 45 were participants in the manpower-training programs of the Department of Labor. A review of all types of training experiences, regardless of source, was necessary to discover and appraise the past effectiveness and current potential for job training in rural areas.

Recognizing that even in rural areas a considerable variety of training vehicles and institutions exist, the primary household survey

TABLE 8.1

Participation in Training Programs, 1974
(number)

	All Persons 16 and Over[a]	Heads of Households[b]
High school	41	11
Junior college	45	17
Trade and vocational school	198	118
Correspondence school	21	13
Military	134	126
Manpower programs	45	19
Formal apprenticeship	16	12
OJT	34	23
Other	206	128
Subtotal	740	467
No training	6741	2890
Total surveyed	7481	3357

[a]These numbers represent trained individuals, not training programs. The totals include 66 persons who participated in two programs and 8 persons who participated in three programs, but exclude 1 who did not state training source. In cases of multiple training sources, the first taken was used for classification purposes.

[b]Includes 18 persons who participated in two and 5 who participated in three programs (see note a).

instrument was designed to identify the training sources.* Participation in training programs by persons in the survey sample is shown in Table 8.1. Of the total adult population aged 16 years and over,

---

*All training program category titles are self-explanatory with three exceptions. First, "manpower programs" includes all of the U.S. Department of Labor's categorical program efforts; second, "on-the-job training" refers exclusively to private employer provided or financed job training; and "other," which is a residual, embraces a wide variety of training types, such as private professional school graduates, nurses aids, and so on, with fewer than ten participants in any one type. Although numerous in the aggregate, the "other" category is not particularly useful for analytical purposes because of the diversity of training experiences with only a few participants in any single category. Hence, it has been included in the analyses that follow only where its influence might affect results.

only 740 (9.9 percent) had any formal job training*; of household heads, only 467 (13.9 percent) had any formal job training. For all persons aged 16 and over, the most frequently reported type of job training (exclusive of the "other" category) was trade and vocational schools, with 198 participants. Second in frequency was military training, with 134 participants. Manpower programs accounted for only 45 people. Similar data for heads of households establish "other" as the most important single source, followed by military and trade and vocational schools. As measured by participation, the remaining categories are minor by comparison.

Despite a well-publicized attempt in recent years to develop a coordinated and comprehensive manpower policy, involvement in training programs of all types in rural areas was negligible. Considering that these data report lifetime and not single-year experience of the respondents, the small number of participants takes on even greater significance for policy purposes.

Table 8.2 shows the types of training classified by broad occupational categories. Approximately 32 percent of the individuals (237) took training related to manufacturing jobs. Next in importance was training for the professions (this latter category includes a variety of training types, and merging them may exaggerate individual significances). Training related to clerical-technical jobs was third in frequency (107) and might well have been second if the "professional category" were more strictly defined. Service ranked fourth in number with 97. Very little training was reported for jobs in the areas of agriculture, extractive industries, and the construction trades. When the type of training is viewed in conjunction with the source of training (Table 8.1) there is strong justification for believing that training for upgrading disadvantaged workers has been minimal. This feeling is reinforced by analysis of the characteristics of those who did participate in training programs.

Selected demographic characteristics of training program participants and nonparticipants are given in Table 8.3. The level of training-program participation by all adults 16 years and older varied by county, ranging from 17.1 percent in Natchitoches Parish to 5.2 percent in Sunflower County. The level of participation among household heads was greater than for all adults 16 years and older; however, the county participation patterns were similar.

Among participants 16 years and older, 270 (approximately 35 percent) were women. (If those trained by the military, who are primarily male, are excluded, the female proportion of the trained total is 45 percent.) The differentials in age, family circumstances,

---

*Actually, the number was 741: One person with training did not report the source.

TABLE 8.2

Type of Training Program Taken by All Adults

Type of Training	Number
Professional	129
Administration-management	31
Clerical-technical	107
Domestic service	3
Service workers	97
Farming (all types)	47
All manufacturing	237
Construction trades	42
Transport	7
Mining, logging, and extractive industries	1
Amusement-recreation	1
No answer	39
Total*	741

*Includes one who did not report training source. See Table 8.1, note a.

and cultural backgrounds serve to explain the lower participation by females than by males. This was particularly marked for Chicano women, with only 2.9 percent having received training, as compared with rates of 9 percent for Anglo women and 6.5 percent for black women. (Of the total, 8.5 percent had been living outside the county five years previously; however, 110 of those trained [14.8 percent] had been living outside the county five years previously. Data as to where training was obtained were not available. A comparison of the proportions, however, suggests that some, at least, was obtained outside the region.)

Among all adult participants, 165 (21.7 percent) were black; 135 (17.7 percent) were Chicano; and 460 (approximately 60.5 percent) were Anglos. (If military, which is 62 percent Anglo male, is excluded, the number is 364.) Both blacks and Chicanos participated less than proportionately to population and labor force when compared with Anglos.

The comparative age structures of participant and nonparticipant groups are as expected, with about 95 percent of those having training being between ages 16 and 65. The number of participants tends to decline as age rises.

TABLE 8.3

Adult Training-Program Participants and Nonparticipants, by Race, Sex, and County, 1974

	Participants	Nonparticipants
Race		
Anglo	58	41
Male	36	18
Female	22	23
Chicano	19	28
Male	15	12
Female	4	16
Black	24	31
Male	12	13
Female	12	18
County		
Dodge[a]	28	25
Male	17	11
Female	11	14
Natchitoches[b]	40	21
Male	22	9
Female	18	12
Starr[c]	20	28
Male	16	12
Female	4	16
Sunflower[c]	12	26
Male	7	11
Female	5	15
Total	100	100
Male	62	43
Female	38	57
Total number	741	7481

Note: One female and six male adults who reported "other" races are excluded.

[a]Includes nine who took two and three who took three training programs.

[b]Includes ten who took two and four who took three training programs.

[c]Includes seven who took two training programs in each of Starr and Sunflower counties.

TABLE 8.4

Regression Analyses for Adult Participation
in Any Training Program and Any Program
Exclusive of Military and "Other"

Dependent Variable: participation in any training program				
	Includes Military and Other		Excludes Military and Other	
Independent Variable	Regression Coefficient	Partial F Values	Regression Coefficient	Partial F Values
Race (Anglo)	0.05961	(5.558)*	-0.00282	(0.019)
Race (black)	0.00858	(0.108)	-0.01115	(0.279)
Sex	0.02338	(8.362)*	0.00808	(1.584)
County (Natchitoches)	0.06668	(6.761)*	0.08591	(17.051)*
County (Sunflower)	-0.04209	(2.643)	0.01076	(0.263)
County (Dodge)	-0.00778	(0.090)	0.03391	(2.590)
Age	-0.00206	(114.524)*	-0.00152	(99.326)*
Head of household	0.08865	(101.837)*	0.04027	(33.023)*
Education	0.00178	(8.923)*	0.00110	(5.493)*
Constant	0.08889		0.06427	
R square	0.06092		0.03580	
F	53.85680		29.41876	
Degree of freedom	9,7472		9,7132	

*Values are significant at the 0.05 level.

    The influence of sex, race, age, and certain other characteristics in determining participation in training programs may be assessed by regression analysis. The results of two regression equations are summarized in Table 8.4. The first is for all adults (age 16 years and over) who indicated ever having started a formal training program. The second is identical except that it excludes those persons who indicated the military and "other" as the sources of their training. The results of the two equations are similar for the most part.

    As can be seen from Table 8.4, the participation level varies significantly with location, age, education, and whether or not the participant is a head of household.* Race and sex are not significant variables except when the military participants are included.

---

    *The variables age, location, education, and whether or not a person is head of a household were measured as of the time of interview (1974). Theoretically, these should have been measured as at the time of starting training. These variables are being used, nonetheless, on the assumption that the relative status of each respondent was the same at the time of training as it was at the time of the interview.

The implication of the regression analysis may be summarized briefly. Natchitoches Parish residents (location) have a higher probability of participation in training than do those of Starr County, other things being equal, perhaps because of the existence of a state university in Natchitoches City. Age has a negative coefficient, indicating a lower probability of older persons having participated in any training program. However, as noted, the age recorded is that in 1974 and not that at the time of participation. Thus, this result may indicate that the programs were not as available in earlier as in recent years. Moreover, these data cannot reflect the responses of persons with training who migrated from the areas; thus, these data may be understated. Finally, education has a positive effect on participation, as expected. Many programs are administered by vocational or technical high schools or junior colleges and can be used basically only by those who stay in school. In addition, many skill-training programs, including those in the manpower-training category (prior to CETA), have required a minimum of eight years of education as a precondition to enrollment.

When the individuals trained by the military are excluded, neither sex nor race is a significant variable. This is because almost all of those with military training are men, and more than 60 percent are Anglos. Military training programs are unique in that in the past they have been largely involuntary and restricted substantially to certain age groups. Therefore, it was hypothesized that those reporting military training should not be merged with those participating in civilian programs. This premise was evaluated by comparing the results of two regression equations, one including all respondents and one in which the responses of those reporting the military as their training source were omitted (see Table 8.4). Because the results indicate that the premise is correct, those who participated in military training programs were subsequently included only where their influence might be valid—for example, in analysis of willingness to participate in training programs in the future.

The characteristics of participants in the three major types of training programs (trade and vocational schools, manpower programs, and OJT) also were analyzed to determine the variables that influenced participation. The findings were substantially as expected, based on the nature of the various programs. In the trade and vocational school programs, age, sex, and location were the significant variables. In the manpower programs, participation was related to race, sex, and age. Age had a negative coefficient, as expected. Minority group membership had a positive influence because minorities are target groups among the economically disadvantaged. Women also had a higher probability of participation in these programs, because many, particularly WIN, were designed primarily for women. For OJT, the only significant characteristic was education, other things being equal. This regression measures results after placement and thus gives no evidence of discrimination by sex or race—a fact that does not conflict with the findings of a considerable degree of employment discrimination in rural labor markets (see Chapters 4 and 5).

EFFECTS OF TRAINING ON PARTICIPANTS

Several factors may give an indication of the success of post-training efforts in rural areas in spite of the low level of participation. Among these are completion rates, relevance of training to jobs, and the impact of training on wage levels.

Table 8.5 summarizes the completion rates of training programs. On the average, the probability of a head of household completing the training program that he started is 78.4 percent; for all adults 16 years and older, 73.8 percent. The highest program drop-out rates reported are for junior colleges, followed by trade and vocational schools. Both represent a relatively insignificant proportion of the total trained, however.

Training-program completion rates also were analyzed using major programs and individual characteristics as explanatory variables. As one would expect, the military and OJT programs had statistically significantly greater completion rates than did the others. Age also was a significant factor in explaining completion rates.

Relevance of Training

All adults (16 years and older) were classified, respectively, as participants and nonparticipants in training programs by source of training taken and present occupation. In addition to the ranking of programs by frequency of use, the data indicate certain county differences. Manufacturing and professional, administrative, and managerial occupations were most frequently reported in Dodge County and Natchitoches Parish. Service and professional occupations were most frequently reported in Sunflower and Starr counties. Also notable is the considerable similarity between the distribution of occupations reported by both the participants and nonparticipants in training programs, a fact that suggests that industrial structure (and job opportunities), not training per se, largely determines the occupational distribution in rural areas. This finding further confirms that little upgrading of the disadvantaged through training has occurred.

The relevance of training programs is further revealed by the extent to which the training is actually useful in employment. To

TABLE 8.5

Frequency of Participation and Completion Rates, by Types of Training Programs, 1974

Type of Program	Head of Household[a]			All Persons[a] Above 16 Years of Age		
	Number Taking	Number Completed	Percent Completed[b]	Number Taking	Number Completed	Percent Completed[b]
High School	11	9	81.8	41	26	63.4
Junior College	17	6	35.3	45	20	44.4
Trade and vocational	118	76	64.4	198	121	61.1
Correspondence school	13	10	76.9	21	14	66.7
Military[c]	126	118	93.7	134	125	93.3
Manpower programs	19	14	73.7	45	30	66.7
Formal apprenticeship	12	9	75.0	16	13	75.0
OJT	23	18	78.3	34	27	79.4
Other[c]	128	96	75.0	206	146	70.9
Total	467	356	78.4	741	522	73.8

[a]Thirteen heads of households and 30 adults (16 and over) were still taking training.

[b]Those "still taking" training were included in computing these percentages.

[c]Excludes one who did not identify training type. Military and "other" both were included to show the numbers involved.

determine this, those who had participated in one or more training programs were asked whether they "ever used" their training and, if so, in what jobs. These data show that the training was thought to be useful in current employment by 69.4 percent. (Of the 491 adults, age 16 years and older, who answered that they "ever used" their training, 353 stated a current occupation; of these, 139, or 39 percent, were currently employed in the same occupation as that in which they used their training.) Use of training by all who had participated in and completed training programs was assessed by multiple regression analysis (see Table 8.6).

Use of training in jobs is significantly related to sex, age, and education. Among training sources, the only type significant except "other" was OJT. A relationship between type of training and occupation of user does exist. In rank order from low to high, established by beta weights, the occupations in which training was used are farming, clerical-technical, service, construction, and manufacturing.

TABLE 8.6

Regression Analysis of "Ever Used" Training
in Any Job for Those Who Completed Their
Training Programs

Dependent Variable: used training		
Independent Variable	Regression Coefficient	Partial F Values
Race (Anglo)	0.19477	(5.103)
Race (black)	0.12683	(1.959)
Sex	-0.15805	(12.894)[a]
County (Natchitoches)	-0.14126	(2.753)
County (Sunflower)	-0.11580	(1.614)
County (Dodge)	-0.05966	(0.473)
Age	0.00358	(12.520)[a]
Vocational and trade school training	0.03580	(0.649)
Military training[b]	0.02288	(0.230)
Manpower	-0.02574	(0.154)
OJT	0.21749	(10.414)[a]
Other training[b]	0.16854	(14.845)[a]
Head of household	-0.04536	(1.175)
Education	0.02595	(36.903)[a]
Service	0.49680	(122.735)[a]
Clerical/technical	0.48563	(118.324)[a]
Farm	0.59714	(101.480)[a]
Construction	0.71727	(108.493)[a]
Manufacturing	0.64792	(302.640)[a]
Other occupation	0.61457	(72.162)[a]
Constant	-0.01053	
R square	0.55908	
F	31.76272	
Degree of freedom	20,501	

[a]Values are significant at the 0.05 level.
[b]Military and other are included to permit training type comparisons.

Those in manufacturing have the highest use of training, as one would expect.

Chicanos used their training significantly less than did Anglos; the difference between blacks and Chicanos is not statistically significant in this respect. However, the data may indicate the effects of

MANPOWER DEVELOPMENT AND TRAINING

discrimination for Anglos. Men have a lower probability of having used their training than women. This may be explained by the facts that training for women may be more job specific than that for men, and there is a concentration of women in the sources of training for occupations for which there is greater demand.

The age relationship to training usage is significant, as would be expected. Education also has a positive influence on training use. In part, education correlates with placement because the training taken seems likely to be selected to fit the individuals' interests and career plans.

Despite the statistical relationships established, the relatively low use of training is significant. This may indicate that the types of skills offered in vocational training programs available in these areas do not correlate with the job openings. This interpretation, together with the relatively small numbers of participants, may have real importance to policy development in rural areas.

Wage Rates and Training

In order further to evaluate the success of human-resource development programs in the study, participants were compared with nonparticipants as to wage rates. As the data in Table 8.7 show,

TABLE 8.7

Wage Rates of Participants and Nonparticipants among Employed Heads of Households, 1974
(percent)

Wage Rates	Participants	Nonparticipants
No answer	7.9	10.6
Less than $1.20	2.6	5.8
1.20-1.59	4.0	12.6
1.60-1.99	10.2	15.3
2.00-2.39	10.2	12.4
2.40-2.99	11.6	10.0
3.00-3.49	12.5	9.1
3.50-3.99	8.7	5.7
4.00-4.49	7.6	3.4
4.50-4.99	4.4	3.3
5.00 or more	20.4	11.8
Total percent	100.0	100.0
Total number	344	1511

the wages of participants are greater than are those for nonparticipants. Only 16.8 percent of the participants receive wages below $2.00 an hour, whereas 33.7 percent of the nonparticipants have wages below the $2.00 mark. At the upper end of this distribution, 32.4 percent of the training program participants receive wages higher than $4.00 or more an hour; among the nonparticipants this percentage is only 18.5 percent.

Although these data suggest a relationship between wage rates and training, further analysis is required to establish such a relationship. The results of regression analysis shown in Table 8.8 indicate that training-program participation has a positive effect on wage rate, other things being equal.

Job Tenure

The tenure of household heads at present jobs also was investigated as a further measure of success of training. The mean tenure (8.5

TABLE 8.8

Regression Equation for Wage Rates of All
Persons 16 Years and Older, Military and
"Other" Trainees Excluded

Dependent Variable: hourly wage rate		
Independent Variable	Regression Coefficient	Partial F Values
Participation dummy variable	1.89606	(4.902)*
Race (Anglo)	1.51739	(0.714)
Race (black)	-6.98090	(14.092)*
Sex (male)	3.80512	(34.166)*
County (Natchitoches)	6.77374	(13.556)*
County (Sunflower)	5.41710	(8.868)*
County (Dodge)	6.56708	(12.786)*
Age	-0.01269	(0.430)
Head of household	5.47824	(62.959)*
Education	0.59856	(123.604)*
Constant	10.42185	
R square	0.21101	
F	67.98285	
Degree of freedom	10, 2542	

*Values are significant at the 0.05 level.

MANPOWER DEVELOPMENT AND TRAINING

years) for those who had participated in some kind of training and were then employed was shorter than was the average tenure (10.5 years) for those who had not participated and were then employed (see Table 8.9). Although the reasons for this difference are not determinable from the data, one possible explanation is that people without training are less likely to change jobs than are those with some kind of training. In addition, the numbers of weeks worked in 1973 were greater for those who received training.

In general, the results of the preceding analysis indicate that training is of benefit to those who receive it in terms of usefulness on the job and earnings. Unfortunately, analysis of the effect on earnings of manpower-training programs per se could not be undertaken. The small percentage of those trained who received training through manpower programs makes analysis of program success hazardous at best. Nor can the results support the recommendation that training will have beneficial results for future participants in the absence of expanded job opportunities.

ATTITUDES TOWARD TRAINING PROGRAMS

The success of training programs in any area is partially dependent on the attitudes that both potential participants and employers have toward the programs, as well as the attitudes of local officials and the population generally. The attitudes of these groups toward manpower training programs are particularly relevant for future policies and programs.

In all four counties the public school systems have a history of vocational training. Originally restricted to agriculture, home economics, and business, in some counties these programs have been expanded to include a wider occupational mix. The schools are also involved in Neighborhood Youth Corps programs and Work Study, both of which may include some on-the-job experience. The attitudes of local officials toward the newer federal programs are generally supportive but include a range from "they are a waste of money" to "if they are effectively managed, they can provide significant work experience and income to disadvantaged youth." In Dodge County and Natchitoches Parish the school officials indicated strongly that continuous counseling and work with employers and participants were essential if the experiences were to be meaningful. In both cases, the programs were criticized for not providing adequate resources to permit real supervision. In a number of cases there also was comment that the instructors of most target programs are poorly trained themselves and are unable to teach others.

TABLE 8.9

Job Tenure for Heads of Households Classified by Participation or Nonparticipation in Training Programs, as Reported in 1974

	Yes			No			Total	
	Number	Percent of Category	Percent of Total	Number	Percent of Category	Percent of Total	Total	
No answer	1.0	0.2	0.0	14.0	0.5	0.4	15.0	0.4
Under 6 months	31.0	6.6	0.9	145.0	5.0	0.9	176.0	5.2
6 months to 1 year	26.0	5.6	0.8	91.0	3.1	0.8	117.0	3.5
1 year	25.0	5.4	0.7	66.0	2.3	0.7	91.0	2.7
2 years	28.0	6.0	0.8	115.0	4.0	0.8	143.0	4.3
3 years	26.0	5.6	0.8	105.0	3.6	0.8	131.0	3.9
4 years	24.0	5.1	0.7	78.0	2.7	0.7	102.0	3.0
5 years	18.0	3.9	0.5	92.0	3.2	0.5	110.0	3.3
6 years	18.0	3.9	0.5	76.0	2.6	0.5	94.0	2.8
7 years	15.0	3.2	0.4	48.0	1.7	0.4	63.0	1.9
8 years	9.0	1.9	0.3	52.0	1.8	1.5	61.0	1.8
9 years	4.0	0.9	0.1	36.0	1.2	1.1	40.0	1.2
10 to 14 years	45.0	9.6	1.3	172.0	6.0	5.1	217.0	6.5
15 to 19 years	20.0	4.3	0.6	128.0	4.4	3.8	148.0	4.4
20 to 24 years	28.0	6.0	0.8	103.0	3.6	3.1	131.0	3.9
25 years or over	26.0	5.6	0.8	190.0	6.6	5.7	216.0	6.4
Not employed	123.0	26.3	3.7	1379.0	47.7	41.1	1502.0	44.7
Total	467.0	13.9		2890.0	86.1		3357.0	100.0

MANPOWER DEVELOPMENT AND TRAINING

Manufacturing industries, particularly those which had settled in the counties most recently, showed some interest in OJT programs, including wage subsidies. The experience was mixed with respect to performance, however, and the remark of one large employer probably typifies the attitudes in all four counties:

> More consideration must be given to the development of criteria and greater selectivity exercised in placement, if the program is to succeed. We run a business, not a welfare agency. Pretraining with respect to the need for regular hours and daily attendance, and, in a few cases, personal cleanliness and other habits, would be helpful.

On the whole, one can only surmise that the attitudes toward federally supported manpower training and OJT programs have been mixed, though the numbers of both programs and participants have been so small as to preclude conclusions.

The general comments of employers and local development officials with respect to federally funded training programs may be summarized briefly. First, employers and officials feel that the funding available is inadequate to meet the area need. In order to attract growth industries, significant numbers of skilled personnel will need training. This will require support of a larger order than is presently available for a longer period than is now contemplated. The present scale of operation of the programs relative to the number of people who need their services is so small that "the problems dwarf the resources."

Second, in the view of local officials, job-creation activities seem to be of greater significance than training. The local areas simply have too few jobs in the private sector for those who have been trained. Adequate training, if provided, may tend to promote out-migration to the detriment of the areas. There were frequent comments on the need for involvement of the community leaders in program activities and the development of a strong basis for attracting new firms.

LIMITATIONS OF PAST FEDERAL MANPOWER TRAINING EFFORTS

When all past training activities covered by the survey included, less than 10 percent of the population 16 years old and older has been directly involved. If consideration is restricted to those who have participated in manpower programs, less than 0.5 percent has been involved. Unfortunately, these data reflect lifetime training-program participation, making evaluation of manpower programs for a given time period impossible.

Some county data for federally funded training programs are available from the state and county governments and the community action agencies. However, for a number of reasons, the state and local offices were unwilling to cooperate effectively, and comparable quantitative information for the survey counties could not be obtained from these sources. Nevertheless, the striking fact that emerges from this study of the four counties is the comparatively small number of training programs instituted and the relatively few training opportunities provided. As has been noted elsewhere, this has been due in part to the limited funding available and the lack of available jobs for which to train, giving emphasis to the income maintenance forms of the programs (Neighborhood Youth Corps and Operation Mainstream, for example). Although precise information is not available, estimates for the four counties, based on discussions with relevant agency personnel, suggest the involvement in FY 1974 of less than 1000 people: 375 in programs with a training parameter and 550 in programs offering primarily employment or income assistance.* Clearly, given the population, labor force, and income information previously developed, the impact of these programs is insignificant. As noted, discussions with government and community leaders in these areas affirmed that conclusion, as did the findings from the household survey.

Second, the method of distributing funds within each of the states has varied considerably, but it seems apparent that in addition to numbers (urban problems seem to get primary recognition), there are political overtones involved in the distribution of funds. The programs are segmented for administrative purposes. When resources are distributed through several layers of government, amounts available and constraints imposed at each level serve to compound the problems. Coordination on the basis of national thrust, with local input, seems essential if the program is to succeed, yet a successful method for achieving this has not yet emerged.

---

*As was indicated, the household survey results produced 30 participants currently in training programs of all types at the time of the survey. Adjusting sample to total data suggests a participation of perhaps 200 in the four counties—a number that comes close to slots available, not to total annual participation, in the programs. The overrepresentation of older families in the study survey may help to account for this apparently low level of participation in manpower programs.

Designed to assist target populations of the disadvantaged as well as to assist in providing some geographic and job mobility, a variety of programs with specific training objectives was initiated at the national level. Limitations of objectives and problems of administrative origin restricted the impacts of these activities, but where training was coordinated with local development plans, as they were to some extent in Dodge County, results appear substantially improved.[10]

Third, the geographic areas in question are seriously in need of coordinated economic planning and development. Lack of training-program coordination with area-development activities, industrial development, and job requirements at the local level has foredoomed many of the training activities to failure. On the other hand, in areas where job opportunities exist, as in the paraprofessional health areas, and in cases where the trainee will move to another location to secure employment, the programs have been successful both in raising the incomes of the trainees and in providing a long-term outlook for improved job viability. The evidence suggests that where there are job opportunities these programs are working. Thus, attention should be given to strengthening developments of this type. Some experimentation in this direction has been tried in clerical skills in Dodge County and, to a lesser extent, in Starr County with some success. Such efforts should be expanded.

Use of training for any job requiring a high degree of skill now must presume out-migration. Provision of opportunity at the local level through developmental assistance and moving subsidies for those trained and eligible would seem to be primary prerequisites for successful manpower-training programs.

Fourth, the structure of some of the programs was poor for serving the needs of rural areas, institutional training centers were located at considerable distances from the persons to be served and there was inadequate development of employer interest in training. Moreover, some of the teachers are ineffective, with the result that no real change can be anticipated and further discouragement for those already disadvantaged must result.

The programs also are misunderstood by participants in many cases. For example, training-program participant heads of households in 82.2 percent of the cases report that they received no training from their employers. There is a basic difference between the answers of the respondents to this survey and the comments of employers interviewed. The latter group in a majority of the cases stated that some employee orientation and training were always provided, even if informally. Clearly the respondents to the primary survey perceived this as informal or simply job orientation, not as job training per se. One may note also the possibility that employer-financed training in some cases was not perceived as employer provided.

Fifth, a number of programs in Starr County have been designed explicitly for migrant workers. These programs—which have ranged from OJT to public service employment in the winter season, and include special education, health, and food programs—have created bitterness toward the migrant poor (who are eligible for these benefits) by the nonmigrant poor (who often are not). In addition, some migrant workers complain that the programs tie them to the migrant stream because, if they quit, they will lose their eligibility for these programs.

As has been noted, the employment service is not represented in two of the counties. Full-service offices are located in the other two. In the counties where the public employment service offices are located, employer attitudes generally vary with the types of services used.* On balance, it appears that the activity of the public employment service in these rural areas is not adequate to the need, a fact that may be partially explained by the means used to finance its programs.[11] The operation of programs in rural areas must be undertaken by agencies geared to perform the task. Funding must be commensurate with responsibilities. The present system of funding the employment service by a formula that is tied to placement activities and other operating functions is unsatisfactory for operations in rural areas, where substantial efforts must be devoted to development and other service functions. "Budget credits" must be provided for the work undertaken, not simply for specific placements, tests, or development visits. A positive program and budget must be accepted, based on performance measures other than those conventionally used. Counselling, training, out-migration support, and the like must be integrated into the support base.

POTENTIAL FOR MANPOWER PROGRAMS IN RURAL AREAS

It is clear that the number of persons in the rural South who have participated in manpower programs or, in fact, in any type of training program is extremely small. Further, the opportunities for participation have been and continue to be limited. To appreciate fully the significance of these facts it is necessary to view them in light of the number of persons who are eligible to participate in man-

---

*Comments such as "poor-quality applicants" and/or "disinterested applicants primarily interested in validating their compensation" were often heard. On the other hand, when special services were requested, as for example, a resurvey of the Dodge County labor market to establish unemployment, the attitude was one of acceptance.

power programs under existing legislative criteria or who could reasonably be expected to benefit from training.

Under Title I of CETA, those persons eligible for institutional training, OJT, or work experience include the unemployed, the underemployed, and the economically disadvantaged.[12] Among those 16 years of age and older surveyed for this study, approximately 3000 persons (40 percent of the total) fit into at least one of these categories. It is important to note that over 40 percent of all household heads were eligible. It can be reasonably argued that most of those persons over 65, although technically eligible under CETA, are not really in the labor market, nor do they desire to be. Further, they are less likely to have family responsibilities. Thus, the important figure that indicates the potential for manpower training programs in the rural South is the number of eligible persons between the ages of 16 and 64. There were approximately 2,300 such persons in the survey. Of those eligible, 830 were household heads. Thus, at the time of the survey one-third of the household heads under 65 years of age were eligible to participate in Title I programs. Clearly, the availability of programs is far surpassed by the availability of potential participants.

Manpower programs may be viewed as a method for providing employment opportunities to those currently without jobs. The method also may establish a mechanism by which the economically disadvantaged may obtain access to jobs superior to those to which they are presently restricted by lack of training, lack of labor market knowledge, or other factors. The form that manpower programs will in fact take is dictated in part by the characteristics of potential participants. A substantial portion would benefit from work experience under Title I or from public service employment as envisioned under Title II, but the number who could immediately benefit from skill training, whether under CETA or from some other source, is significantly less.

Table 8.10 contains information on selected criteria of household heads eligible for Title I programs. Factors, such as age, education level, physical disabilities, household responsibilities, and desire for training, all affect the true potential of an individual to participate in or benefit from skill training, whether institutional or OJT. Based on the assumption that those persons who could be involved beneficially in skill-training programs at the present time should possess at least an eighth-grade education, should be over 16 but under 55 years of age, and should have no physical disability that prevents work activity without special training, approximately 3650 persons (of which 1103 are household heads) could be considered "available" for skill training. However, less than 40 percent of these persons were eligible to participate in CETA programs. Although the number of persons in the rural South who are eligible under CETA and who could benefit

TABLE 8.10

Characteristics of Potential CETA Title I
Participants, Household Heads,
Ages 16 to 65, 1975

Characteristic	Percent
Age	
16-20	1.8
21-54	71.0
55-64	27.2
Employment status	
Employed	51.1
Unemployed	12.5
Out of labor force	36.4
Health problems	36.7
Participated in training program	45.4
Total number	830.0

from skill training is small relative to the total CETA eligible, in absolute terms the number is substantial. The major restrictions to skill training in the rural South would appear to come from such limitations as inadequate financial resources available to fund programs or the absence of job opportunities for someone completing a skill-training program, not from lack of eligible participants. In fact, lack of job opportunity might itself discourage participation particularly in institutional and skill-training programs, for training without a relatively clear job possibility is unlikely to be attractive. When such programs are coordinated with industrial development activities or are coupled with a mobility-assistance program, thereby offering real alternatives, individual attitudes toward training as well as the real potential benefits will be altered.

The above discussion should make it clear that the pressure on manpower agencies in the rural South will be toward programs, such as work experience, that place people immediately into jobs, or toward job-creation type programs. Not only do the numbers argue for such a course, but politically such programs will be locally more attractive because skill programs for the disadvantaged create the potential for worker displacement. There also is a strong basis for believing that basic education or work-orientation programs may still be valid and valuable uses of manpower funds in the rural South. Remedial education, providing for eighth-grade or superior equivalency, could assist 1019 (or about 20 percent) of all adults aged 16 to 54, 521 of whom are household heads. Significant numbers of the household heads, however, noted an unwillingness to obtain further education or to take training. An additional observation is perhaps germane: Although 1019 of the adult population indicated an education level of less than the eighth grade, among those between 18 and 35, only 302, or about 10 percent, reported less than this education level. To enhance eligibility for additional training-program efforts, as well as to increase the capability of the population for work, greater emphasis needs to be given to vocational and technical training, thereby increasing job skills while retaining students in school longer.[13]

The willingness of potentially eligible persons to accept training is obviously an important factor in determining program success. Of the total household heads between ages 16 and 64 interviewed (2,400), approximately 40 percent indicated a willingness to participate in training programs in the future. Most, however, favored some form of job-related training in the form of OJT.

If the manpower programs in the rural South are to become more than simply job-creation schemes, the need for the development of industry—that is, bringing jobs to the area and training the populace for them—becomes apparent. Other programs may have to be developed to provide training and to facilitate mobility, although in the last analysis it may be both cheaper and more effective to subsidize out-migration and provide training in the area of relocation.

Further, the data make it very clear that although a large proportion of the rural population is eligible for and might benefit from skill training, a large proportion of the rural population is not available for this type of training. For those who are aged 65 and over, clearly, skill training has little applicability. For those aged 55 to 64, job-creation- and income-assistance-type programs rather than skill-training programs would seem to provide a reasonable solution. Neither skill training nor area economic development will be of much assistance with either of these groups.

POTENTIAL FOR IMPROVEMENT UNDER CETA IN RURAL AREAS

The Comprehensive Employment and Training Act of 1973 sought to accomplish major changes in the administration (through decentralization) and effectiveness (through decategorization) of the federally sponsored manpower programs.

As for decentralization, the plain fact is that most rural governments are incapable of administering human-resource programs. The problem is more pervasive than simply lack of staff and expertise. Too often there is a vested interest in rural areas of the South that is hostile to change. Rural governments often are too concerned with maintaining the status quo. Despite claims that they seek industrial diversification and economic growth, an examination of the types of industries that are actively sought reveals little interest in enterprises that will alter the basic economic structure and power relations within the rural community.

With respect to program decategorization, there is very little reason to expect that the result is anything more than a cosmetic change. The emphasis of the federally sponsored manpower endeavors in rural areas before CETA was largely toward programs that did not provide a training component (for example, Neighborhood Youth Corps, Operation Mainstream, Emergency Employment Act). The pattern of program offerings was dominated by job creation endeavors that are fine for as long as they last. But, essentially, in terms of job preparation, the participant is little different after the experience than he or she was before it. As a high local government source in Starr County observed a few months before CETA became effective:

> I think the intentions are good but I question the effectiveness of the current manpower programs. If you go back a year or two later, after they are out of the programs, I doubt if you will see much difference in the lives of the participants. Many are back in the migrant stream, or unemployed, or doing what they were doing before.

Since CETA merely revived all of the old programs under a single act, there is no reason to believe that the post-CETA experience will differ significantly from the past.

Moreover, there is also a vested interest within local governments to use manpower slots for political purposes. Because of the lack of job opportunities in the private sector, the public sector tends to loom relatively large in rural areas. The absence of any public-sector unions, as well as the virtual nonexistence of any civil service or formal personnel systems, means that there are few safeguards to prevent political manipulations at the local level. Political loyalties are strong, and patronage is a method of strengthening such ties. As a result, all the pressures lead to job creation rather than to skill provision as the preferred policy objective. In this regard, CETA has contributed to this tendency by its increased reliance upon local decision making. In addition, many local government officials do not share the views of those who have written CETA with regard to the importance of serving racial minorities and the economically disadvantaged. The issue is less significant in counties like Starr, where the administrators and the recipients are of the same race, than it is where they are of different races. But as a general statement it is fair to say that the attitudes of many local government officials toward the potential for change of manpower programs is negative. Yet these are precisely the persons in whom CETA has vested the responsibility for its actions.

In no other geographic region of the nation are the incidence of poverty and the proportions of racial minorities so high as in the rural South. Yet the fundamental finding of this study with respect to manpower programs is not so much the type of program in which the participants were enrolled as it is the fact that so many people were either ineligible or not participating due to both the low level of program operations and the lack of interest in them among the county populations.

Part of the problem pertains to the CETA formula for the allocation of funds. The CETA allocations rely heavily upon the unemployment levels in the determination of the amounts of funding available to states. Such a formula discriminates against states that have large rural populations where official unemployment rates are low. In the rural South, as has been amply demonstrated in this study, high levels of subemployment and of discouraged workers are important explanations for the pervasive low-income patterns. The unemployment rates tend to be relatively low when compared with national figures. Hence, funds allocated to states with large rural areas under CETA are inadequate relative to their needs. It is unlikely that there is any single formula that can be used for both urban and rural areas simultaneously. One most plausible alternative would be to separate the legislation that applies to urban and rural manpower needs.

Lastly, CETA in many ways has worsened an already serious administrative problem with respect to the operation of manpower programs in rural areas. The applicable rules, regulations, and guidelines as well as the statutory provisions of the act itself are simply out of kilter with the rural reality. These requirements often are either ignored or cursorily acknowledged. They create more ill than good will because, if they were literally followed, there would be few if any programs (for example, see the 26 separate "assurances" specified in the act for public employment programs under Title II). The result is that rural program officials must try to fit their needs to the provisions of the legislation rather than the preferable reverse situation.

CONCLUDING OBSERVATIONS

Training and retraining are important aspects of improving the quality of the labor force and, hence, the welfare of a region or a nation. It is generally agreed that "manpower programs must play an important role either as a part of rural development strategy or as facilitators of rural to urban adjustments."[14]

Participation in all types of training, excluding military, is low in the rural South. There is no question that training programs have been advantageous to those who have participated and that many others could be expected to benefit from training. A significant proportion of the population could be benefited by training, but the numbers likely to participate are relatively small unless program changes and other developments are encouraged. Without coordinated development and migration programs, the number of participants, even with qualification adjustment, will continue to be low.

Because job opportunities in the area are limited to turnover in addition to those occasioned by growth, manpower policy must emphasize industrial growth and coordinate training programs with job opportunities. It also must consider training for opportunities that exist in other areas and encourage geographic mobility. Whether training should be provided locally or at the site of the opportunity is a separate question and not investigated in this study.

Future programs must be carefully evaluated. Data classified to permit evaluation of individual programs should be required of all administrative units to permit assessment of policies and programs.

NOTES

1. Eli Ginzberg, Manpower Agenda for America (New York: McGraw-Hill, 1968), pp. 11-22.

2. Garth L. Mangum, The Emergence of Manpower Policy (Holt, Rinehart, and Winston, 1969). Also see Vernon M. Briggs, Jr., "National Manpower Policy," The Encyclopedia of Education 6 (New York: Macmillan, 1971), pp. 60-64.

3. Garth L. Mangum, ed., The Manpower Revolution: Its Policy Consequences (Garden City, N.Y.: Doubleday, 1965).

4. See Charles C. Killingsworth, "Automation, Jobs, and Manpower: The Case for Structural Unemployment," in The Manpower Revolution: Its Policy Consequences, ed. Garth L. Mangum (New York: Doubleday, 1965), pp. 97-116; Kenneth B. Clark, Dark Ghetto (New York: Harper & Row, 1965); National Advisory Commission on Civil Disorders, Report (New York: Bantam Books, 1968), pp. 140-42; Daniel P. Moynihan, "The Crises in Welfare," The Public Interest (Winter 1968): 3-29; Charles C. Holt et al., The Unemployment Inflation Dilemma: A Manpower Solution (Washington, D.C.: The Urban Institute, 1971).

5. There is a shortage of case studies of the operation of manpower legislation and its related administrative requirements in rural

areas. One detailed study of the difficulties encountered with the requirements of the Emergency Employment Act of 1971 is available for the City of Laredo, Texas, and the four rural counties of South Texas of which it is the principal city. See Vernon M. Briggs, Jr., "The Public Employment Program in Texas," Case Studies of the Emergency Employment Act in Operation (Washington, D.C.: U.S. Government Printing Office, 1973), pp. 1126-34.

6. See Vernon M. Briggs, Jr., "Manpower Programs and Regional Development," Monthly Labor Review 91 (March 1968): 56-57.

7. See U.S. Department of Labor, Manpower Report of the President, 1974 (Washington, D.C.: U.S. Government Printing Office, 1975), Appendix F, Tables F1 and F2, p. 317ff. Joint program operations (HEW/Labor) altered the reporting of some programs with some impact on the data reported. Similarly, increased benefits, wages, and other costs being derived from the same appropriations will provide for fewer enrollments.

8. Letter dated May 20, 1976 from Howard Rosen, Director, Office of Research and Development, Employment and Training Administration, U.S. Department of Labor and oral discussion with Charles R. Benfield, confirmed by letter dated May 3, 1976.

9. Department of Labor, Manpower Report of the President, 1974, Table F14, p. 332.

10. Also see U.S. Congress, Subcommittee on Fiscal Policy, Joint Economic Committee, "The Effectiveness of Manpower Training Programs: A Review of the Research on the Impact on the Poor," Paper No. 3, Studies in Public Welfare, 92nd Cong. (Washington, D.C.: U.S. Government Printing Office, 1972.

11. For detail, see U.S. Department of Labor, Office of Employment Service Administration, United States Employment Service, Balanced Placement Formula for Measurement of Employment Service Performance and Allocation of Title III E.S. Funds to States, staff handbooks (Washington, D.C.: U.S. Government Printing Office, 1974).

12. U.S. Congress, "Comprehensive Employment and Training Act of 1973," U.S. Code Congressional and Administrative News, 93d Cong., 1st sess. (St. Paul, Minn.: West, 1973), Sect. V.

13. See, for example, U.S. Congress, Committee on Education and Labor, House, General Subcommittee on Education, Hearings on HR 15066 (National Advisory Council on Vocational Education), 90th Cong., 2nd sess., (1968).

14. Ray Marshall, Rural Workers in Rural Labor Markets (Salt Lake City, Utah: Olympus, 1974).

CHAPTER

9

ECONOMIC DEVELOPMENT

High rates of industrialization and economic growth are new to the South. Recent growth in employment in the South is significant by all counts. Regionally, over one-third of the employment growth in the United States between 1960 and 1970 took place in the South.[1] However, despite evidence of high aggregate growth rates since the end of World War II, by most economic indicators the South continues to trail the rest of the nation, as it has for more than a century.

Furthermore, most of the recent growth and expansion of employment opportunities in the South has been an urban phenomenon. Over 76 percent of the employment growth between 1960 and 1970 in the South took place in urban areas. Hence, not only has the South lagged behind the rest of the nation, but the rural South has lagged the urban South.

The previous analyses of income, poverty, and labor markets in this work have clearly established the need for economic improvement in the rural South. This chapter will focus on the labor-demand implications of economic development activities and policies. Moreover, because in the rural South the mechanization of agriculture has reached the stage where further economic development through this means is unlikely, the analysis assumes that significant economic development in the rural South means industrialization in the nonagricultural sector.

MEASURES OF ECONOMIC DEVELOPMENT

A variety of measures are currently used to indicate levels of economic development or of industrialization. Some emphasize the complexity of the economy, others the position of the economy in terms

ECONOMIC DEVELOPMENT

of output. Here, both human-resource and industry-based statistics will be used to infer levels of economic development. In this context, real per capita income, despite its limitations, is an important indication of the present level of as well as the need for economic development.

Industrial Measures

Industrial development of the study area is measured by three indexes: one is the primary data contained in Chapter 3; the other two are computed from secondary data. The rural study counties then are compared with their respective states and the United States. Table 9.1 provides data on value added by manufactures for establishments with 20 or more employees. This table shows that value added by manufactures is low for both the counties and the states of the study when compared with the United States.

The industrial index derived from the primary survey in Chapter 3 was inferior to that for the United States as a whole—that is, it had a value of less than 1. The index is lowest for Starr and Sunflower counties, reflecting the relative importance of agriculture, in the two counties. Table 9.2 shows this industrial index for 1973.

Based on the major industry groupings, this index contains a potential regional bias in the implicit assumption of homogeneous industries across regions. The relationship between the median wage in a given industry and the median across all industries may be different between a region and the United States. Typically, the industrial index would tend to overstate the case for rural Southern counties. More employment is found in low-wage industries in the survey counties than in the United States. An explanation for the value of this index in each county can be found in part by examining the proportion of employment in manufacturing, a relatively high-wage industry, and agriculture, a low-wage industry. This information is contained in Table 9.3.

Agriculture is an important source of employment in all four counties compared with the United States, a condition sometimes regarded as indicative of a low level of development and industrial diversification. At the same time, with the exception of Dodge County, the relative importance of manufacturing in terms of employment in the counties is below that of the United States.

Human-Resource Measures

Three types of human-resource measures are included as indicators of economic development. These relate to income, employment,

TABLE 9.1

Value Added by Manufacture and Number of Establishments Employing More than 20 Employees, Selected Areas, 1972

	Value Added by Manufacture (per input dollar)	Number of Establishments (per 1,000 population) Employing More than 20 Employees
Georgia		
State	1.56	0.56
Dodge County	0.76	0.56
Mississippi		
State	1.25	0.47
Sunflower County	0.94	0.27
Louisiana		
State	1.14	0.30
Natchitoches Parish	0.12	0.14
United States	1.70	0.50

Note: Data for Starr County, Texas, are not available due to disclosure problems associated with the small number of establishments in the county.

Sources: U.S. Department of Commerce, Bureau of the Census, United States Census of Manufactures 1972, subject series: General Summary, MC72(1)-1, Table 7; area series: Georgia, MC72(3)-19, Table 4; Louisiana, MC72(3)-19, Table 4; Mississippi, MC72(3)-25, Table 4. U.S., Department of Commerce, Bureau of the Census, Census of Population, 1970: General Social and Economic Characteristics, Final Report PC(1)-C1, United States Summary, Table 140; Georgia, Table 119; Louisiana, Table 119; Mississippi, Table 119.

TABLE 9.2

Industrial Index for the Study Counties, 1973

Dodge	Natchitoches	Starr	Sunflower
97	92	87	87

Source: For method of calculation, see Chapter 3.

TABLE 9.3

Employment in Agricultural and Manufacturing
Industries, by County and the United States, 1970
(percent)

	Dodge	Natchitoches	Starr	Sunflower	United States
Agriculture	11.2	7.7	24.6	20.7	3.5
Manufacturing	27.5	7.5	3.2	0.1	24.4

Source: U.S. Department of Commerce, Bureau of the Census, Census of Population, 1970: General Social and Economic Characteristics, Final Report PC(1)-C1, United States Summary. Also see "Labor Markets in the Rural South" prepared for the U.S. Department of Labor, Employment and Training Division, March 1977.

and education. Table 9.4 contains figures on real per capita income for the study counties and that portion of the United States outside the metropolitan counties making up SMSAs. According to the annual rates of change, all the study areas sustained growth in per capita income during the 1950-72 period, with the exception of Starr County, which had an annual rate of change of -0.2 percent during the period 1950-59. Generally, however, the rates of growth in real income in the survey counties compare favorably with the rates of growth experienced in the nonmetropolitan United States.

Comparison of rates may mask the true picture, since the base for rate computation varies across the areas. The absolute dollar difference between real per capita income in the counties and in the nonmetropolitan United States has generally increased from 1950 to 1972, even though the relative difference has declined. The exception is Sunflower County, which recorded a small decline in the absolute difference. As measured by real per capita income, the absolute level of economic well-being in the study counties is substantially below that of the nonmetropolitan area in the United States.

Another type of income measure used to indicate the level of economic development is median household or family income. Although a family and a household are not equivalent, they are considered here as roughly the same in order to facilitate the following county-national comparison. (Over 94 percent of the households in the primary survey contained only one family.) Table 9.5 shows the median income of households in the survey counties and in the United States outside metropolitan areas in 1973. Three of the survey counties had slightly more than one-third of the U.S. median non-

TABLE 9.4

Real per Capita Income by County and
Nonmetropolitan United States:
1950, 1959, 1969, 1972
(1967 dollars)

	Dodge	Natchi-toches	Starr	Sun-flower	United States
1950	893	976	750	960	1476
1959	1111	1125	735	1176	1747
1969	1920	1836	1337	1785	2565
1972	2188	2026	1426	2362	2862
Annual percentage rate of change					
1950-59	2.5	1.6	-0.2	2.3	1.9
1959-69	5.6	5.0	6.2	4.3	3.9
1969-72	4.4	3.3	2.2	9.8*	3.7

*The high rate of growth between 1969 and 1972 in Sunflower County is probably attributable to a relatively large increase in manufacturing jobs and the continued importance of the agricultural sector.

Source: U.S. Department of Commerce, Bureau of Economic Analysis, Business Conditions Digest, Series ES1, no. 74-6 (Washington, D.C.: Government Printing Office, June 1974); "Local Area Personal Income," Survey of Current Business, vol. 54, no. 5, pt. 2 (Washington, D.C.: Government Printing Office, May 1974); Adams et al., "Labor Markets in the Rural South," prepared for the U.S. Department of Labor, Employment and Training Division, March 1977.

metropolitan income for households; the other county, Dodge, had slightly more than one-half the U.S. median.

Since measures of central tendency sometimes obscure large distributional differences, one final income measure is provided. Table 9.6 contains the proportion of households with a total income of less than $3000, an arbitrary measure of acute poverty, for the rural counties and nonmetropolitan United States.

Table 9.5 shows the nonmetropolitan U.S. median household income as two to three times higher than those of the study counties. As is shown in Table 9.6, the proportion of households with incomes less than $3000 in the study counties is four to five times greater than in the United States. With the nonmetropolitan United States as

TABLE 9.5

Median Household Income, by County and for
Nonmetropolitan Areas of the United States, 1973
(dollars)

	Dodge	Natchitoches	Starr	Sunflower	United States, Nonmetropolitan
Median	5703	3928	3711	3816	10,366
Percent of United States	55.0	37.9	35.8	36.8	—

Sources: Data for United States from U.S. Department of Commerce, Bureau of the Census, "Money Income in 1973 of Families and Persons in the United States," Current Population Reports, series P-60, no. 98, Tables 57 and 58. County data contained in Adams et al., "Labor Markets in the Rural South," prepared for the U.S. Department of Labor, Employment and Training Division, March 1977.

TABLE 9.6

Households with Total Income Less than $3000,
by County and Nonmetropolitan Areas of the
United States, 1973

	Dodge	Natchitoches	Starr	Sunflower	United States Nonmetropolitan
Percent	30.0	41.0	39.4	40.7	8.4
Ratio of County to United States	3.6	4.9	4.7	4.8	—

Source: Data for United States from U.S. Department of Commerce, Bureau of the Census, "Money Income in 1973 of Families and Persons in the United States," Current Population Reports, series P-60, no. 98, Tables 57 and 58. County data contained in "Labor Markets in the Rural South," prepared for the U.S. Department of Labor, Employment and Training Division, March 1977.

a standard and income as a measure, the level of economic development in the rural South has been quite low.

Labor force measures of economic development usually include underemployment and subemployment, each reflecting underutilization of human resources in a region. As noted in Chapter 5, estimates of subemployment for household heads in the four rural counties were significant. Low levels of LFPRs also were observed. Table 9.7 contains LFPRs by age for the survey respondents and the United States. It is apparent from the table that labor force participation across age groups for the study counties is about 20 percent lower than rates for the United States. A number of explanations have been provided earlier to account for the low LFPRs, not the least of which is that rural workers typically face a smaller quantity and diversity of jobs. Of relevance to economic development, the low LFPRs reflect to a certain degree underemployment of the working-age population.

The educational level of the working-age population, as shown in Table 9.8, is low in the rural counties. These figures are typical for the rural South, and the lack of industrial development is reflected in the low levels of education. For example, Ray Marshall notes that "except for resource-oriented activities like mining and pulp and paper mills, rural nonfarm employment has been dominated by marginal, labor-intensive, dead-end jobs."[2] Many of these jobs are found in nondurable manufacturing plants, which do not require very high educational levels of the labor pool.

TABLE 9.7

Labor Force Participation Rates, by Age for Survey Respondents and the United States, 1973 (percent)

Age	Survey Respondents	United States
16–24	34.6	69.0
25–34	63.6	80.0
35–44	62.5	80.5
45–54	57.2	77.9
55–64	42.1	64.6
65+	8.4	17.9
Total	42.3	66.3

Source: U.S. Department of Labor, Bureau of Statistics, Handbook of Labor Statistics, 1974 (Washington, D.C.: Government Printing Office), Table 2.

TABLE 9.8

Percentage Distribution of the Adult Population,
by Years of School Completed of Survey
Respondents and Persons in the
United States, 1973

Years of School	Survey Respondents	United States
Less than 8	35.2	10.2
8-11	31.5	25.5
12-15	27.8	52.1
16 or more	5.5	12.2

Note: Survey respondents are 16 years of age and over; U.S. persons are 18 years of age and over.

Source: Chapter 4. U.S. figures computed from U.S. Department of Commerce, Bureau of the Census, "Money Income in 1973 of Families and Persons in the United States," Current Population Reports, series P-60, no. 97, Tables 57 and 58.

These industrial and human-resource measures have two separate interpretations in terms of economic development in the four counties. In one sense they reflect the constraints under which development must take place; in another sense they reflect the result of previous activities and attitudes toward development. These general characteristics of the counties tend to be representative of the rural South as a whole, and they explain the previous development of marginal, labor-intensive industries in much of the rural South. The constraints of low educational levels combined with underemployment and subemployment make prime labor market conditions for certain types of industries. These low-wage industries have helped to perpetuate low educational levels because of low work-entry levels and the need in the rural South to supplement family incomes.

A substantial industrial development in agriculture may be recognized by a sharply rising capital-labor ratio. Industrial development of the rural South through industrial diversification, however, has not kept pace with the changes in agriculture. The slow pace of industrial diversification is partially a result of inactivity in many parts of the rural South in providing an attractive environment for investment. In addition, many community leaders often possess unfavorable attitudes towards industrial diversification.

THE ECONOMIC DEVELOPMENT PROCESS

One possible approach to an economic study of the rural South is based on a theory of development stages.[3] The first stage of development is characterized by a heavy reliance on primary activities like agriculture. As per capita income grows, there is a decline in the proportion of the working force engaged in agriculture. Increased emphasis on manufacturing indicates a later stage of development. The "final" stage of development is characterized by the growth of service industries.[4]

The stage, or sector, theory has been criticized on a number of accounts.[5] Critics claim that the primary-secondary-tertiary sequence is too rigid to describe economic well-being. Furthermore, it does not provide sufficient insight into the process of economic growth, nor does it account for external factors influencing internal growth. In spite of these deficiencies, the sector theory is still utilized by many to examine the relationship between the industrial structure and economic well-being of regions and nations. Even though sector analysis is not precise, it does allow generalization concerning major changes that are occurring throughout an economy.

Based on empirical studies, a different view of the process of economic development has emerged. One such study, although not specific to Southern rural industrialization, found that nonmetropolitan areas had experienced significant industrialization during the 1960s.[6]

Another study that did pertain specifically to the rural South found that counties more than 50 miles from an SMSA had increases in manufacturing employment that exceeded or were equal to that of the SMSAs.[7]

A 1973 study by Brian Berry of nonmetropolitan growth areas throughout the nation noted the "filtering" of manufacturing industries into small towns within and just beyond the metropolitan growth zone.[8] Berry also noted that the filtering in the South was racially selective inasmuch as areas with high proportions of blacks were bypassed.[9]

As a consequence of such research, a controversy has emerged over the concept of growth centers in rural areas. The finding that some rural areas grow and that others do not has led to the policy decision that development efforts should be concentrated at the small SMSA or small urban level.[10]

Other researchers, however, doubt the viability of the entire growth center strategy insofar as the smaller metropolitan areas are concerned. For example, linkages with the growth-center hinterlands have been found to be lacking for the smaller areas. One particular study concluded: "So far as growth center policy for regional development is concerned it is premature until strong linkages have been established with [the] hinterlands making such a policy productive."[11]

Regardless of development policy approaches, it is obvious that parts of the South have moved into the second stage of the development process. Since 1960 industrialization has proceeded at a faster rate in the South than in the United States as a whole, and manufacturing employment has increased rapidly. A good share of this type of development has been in labor-intensive low-wage industries. In fact, the rural South's share of low-wage and labor-intensive industry in the 1960s was greater than that of either the metro-South or the United States. Although Thomas Till's study found that the low-wage labor-intensive industries had the largest employment net gains in the 1960s, the second and third largest net gains were in the higher-wage-paying industries of electrical machinery and transportation equipment. The study hypothesized that it is possible that Southern rural industrialization goes through two stages, "in which the low wage, labor intensive firms of the first stage prepare a factory trained labor force which then attracts the relatively higher-wage, more capital intensive firms of the second stage."[12] It is obvious that areas of the rural South differ as to the stage of industrialization into which they fall. Some counties, such as Dodge and Natchitoches, experienced some growth and development. It also is evident that many other counties in the rural South, such as Starr and Sunflower, still have not been able to enter into the first stage of industrial development and continue to rely heavily on agriculture as a source of income and employment. Few Southern rural counties have entered into the final stage dominated by service industries.

IMPEDIMENTS TO ECONOMIC DEVELOPMENT

Impediments to economic development, such as racial discrimination and low educational and skill attainment, have been discussed in earlier chapters. The present discussion therefore will center on institutional barriers to development.

Industrial development in the rural South has usually been controlled by formal or informal elite groups. Although such power groups are often difficult to identify, they tend to influence whether industries will be attracted to or allowed to locate in a given community. Such groups are reluctant to upset present wage structures or to cause labor shortages for established industries. Therefore, many times when firms are sought for location in a community, the primary goal will be to find a specific type of firm requiring a specific type of labor. Rarely will firms that are competitive in the local labor market be sought.

A society that has long been dominated by agriculture distrusts change, diversity, and development. Cultural changes and improvements for certain population subgroups may be consciously or subconsciously feared. New jobs mean additional wage opportunities, higher incomes, more political acumen, and the possibility of unions. Any or all of these threaten the status quo that the local power structure often seeks to preserve. It may not be able to stop change, but attempts to control the pace and the nature of the change may occur. As an example, one elected official in Starr County candidly stated:

> The obvious question is that with all of the economic advantages we have [that is, an available labor supply, a good climate, a low cost of living, and the proximity to the retail market of buyers from Mexico], why don't we have more economic development? I believe it must be the human factor—that is, politics. A lot of people don't want to see us grow and diversify. Change brings about too much uncertainty for some.

Furthermore, as matters now stand in many rural Southern counties, the rules governing the operation of the workplace are minimal. Federal laws are usually all that prevail and, when they are enforced, simply set minimum standards. Unions are bitterly resisted, and at the present time only a few are located in the four study counties. Such unions are usually associated with companies that have a nationwide contract or at least an outside collective-bargaining contract. No union has located in any of these counties as a result of an indigenous movement, even though unsuccessful attempts have been made in Starr County.

EFFORTS TO ATTRACT INDUSTRY

In each of the four survey counties, some degree of effort has been expended to entice enterprises to locate within their respective counties. In Dodge and Natchitoches, the efforts have met with limited success. In Starr and Sunflower, they have not.

In Dodge County, the need to diversify the local economy was recognized in the early 1960s by local bank and business leaders who joined county and city governments to form the Industrial Development Council. Since 1960, the council's full-time director has been engaged in the development of materials to promote the attraction of industry. Banking leaders have been participants in development activities, and supportive financing for development has been provided locally. Local government efforts have also been undertaken to secure maximum federal funding and assistance in the development of tertiary sewerage and water plants. An industrial park has been established, and several

ECONOMIC DEVELOPMENT   245

firms have been attracted to the county. There remains, however, a local demand for unskilled agricultural workers. In fact, there are certain employers and service enterprises in the community that are interested in maintaining a supply of unskilled labor to serve agriculture during certain periods of the year.

The Chamber of Commerce and the Industrial Development Council have conducted "available labor" surveys and established certain training facilities through the local educational system, including OJT. Development has not been restricted to particular types of industry, but light manufacturing is the principal industrial prospect. Distance from major product or factor markets is a detractor for manufacturers of heavy goods. Generally, industrial and community leaders emphasize the need for greater employment of both men and women and encourage industrial development that would utilize all those available to work under existing market conditions. There appears to be some desire to minimize the growth of unions in the county, but representatives of present industry and county government recognize that growth will necessitate higher wages and more favorable working conditions.

Similarly, in Natchitoches the Parish Police Jury, the governing body of the parish, has become active in industrial development. The parish is a contributing member of a multiparish industrial development organization. The policy jury has a modest financial commitment for economic development and promotion of the parish. One of its grants contributes to the support of a private organization in the parish, the Natchitoches Area Action Association. The policy jury also has established the Parish Planning Commission and has investigated the feasibility of a port on the Red River. As for the municipalities in the parish, all are active in community development, particularly with respect to utilities, drinking water, natural gas, sewerage, and drainage.

Another organization involved in industrial development is Natchitoches Industries, Inc., which was created for the sole purpose of development. Natchitoches Industries has no staff, and all functions are accomplished through time contributed by businessmen who are members. Although the organization does not make the initial contacts, many attribute the location of several light manufacturers to the salesmanship of the organization. Natchitoches Industries owns some acreage and has constructed at least one general-purpose building to lease or sell to any industrial prospect.

Industrial loans are not an important source of loan activity for the local banks in Natchitoches, although all the banks express a willingness to provide such loans. Their ability to do so, however, is questionable, even though they have normal correspondent banks in larger cities that can provide an extended line of credit.

In contrast to Natchitoches County's experiences, Starr County has had little success in attracting outside industries to their locality. The governing body of the county, known as the Commissioner's Court, is headed by the county judge. In addition to providing public services to the county, the Commissioners' Court has provided the public services necessary in the county's largest city, Rio Grande City, since it became insolvent in the 1930s. Financial support of any magnitude for economic development from the county government is not possible. In fact, the feuding political environment is such that many businessmen feel it has produced a retarding effect upon the prospects for economic development.

There is only one financial institution in the county. The local bank specializes in short-term consumer loans and is reluctant to make more speculative long-term capital loans. In essence, there is no financial support within the county for new firms that might require moderate amounts of start-up capital.

Some nonfinancial support for industrial development exists, however, in the form of the Starr County Industrial Foundation. This private nonprofit organization was established in 1974 for the purpose of providing information services to prospective new firms. It has no paid staff. It is most interested in obtaining labor-intensive manufacturing plants to take advantage of the large pool of unskilled labor. Among the special problems that the foundation faces in promoting the county is the problem of unclear land titles in part of the county that stems from Spanish land claims, an acute shortage of water, and the fact that about one-third of the county's population is made up of migrant farm workers and their dependents, for whom it is likely a considerable effort will be needed to retrain and to reorient to work in nonagricultural enterprise.

There is strong antiunion sentiment among the business and government sectors of the county. The local power structure would like to keep it this way, even if it means that economic development is precluded.

Likewise, in Sunflower County the leadership of the community is divided itself over the merits of industrial expansion and diversification. A small but relatively influential number of businessmen are strongly interested in seeing the county industrialize without restrictions. A second faction is interested in seeing new industry move into the county, but only if it is considered clean with respect to air and water pollution and will utilize the surplus labor available, predominantly made up of black women. These businessmen also feel that growth should be controlled to avoid disrupting the labor market. New industry should not compete with existing firms for the male labor force. The third group consists of those closely associated with agriculture and the "old-time" politicians in the county.

ECONOMIC DEVELOPMENT

This group is not openly hostile to development, but neither does it actively support industrial development.

Despite the factions, a modern industrial park has been established. At present, those who wish a controlled industrial growth are most influential in determining what industries will be courted for this facility. Controlled growth in this view means one new industry every five years in order that existing wage structure and employment patterns will not be dramatically affected.

Industrial development throughout the county is undertaken primarily by the individual communities. There is no overall industrial development program for the county. This, in part, reflects the strong agricultural influence. There are several development agencies operating on a regional basis, and it is through such groups that those committed to industrialization find that they must work to be effective.

The state of Mississippi has a program called Balance Agriculture With Industry (BAWI), which has a mixed effect on current efforts to industrialize Sunflower County. This law permits political subdivisions to issue full-faith and credit bonds. The funds raised may be used to acquire a manufacturing plant and rent same to an industry with rentals sufficient to amortize principal and interest of the bonds for up to 25 years.

A second program is the Industrial Revenue Bond Program. Revenue bonds are unlike BAWI bonds in that they are backed solely by the rentals of the projects and can be issued in an amount up to $5 million. For the industry the effect is essentially a property-tax exemption for the terms of the bond issue in both cases.

These programs represent a substantial inducement as they provide both a source of long-term capital financing and an effective tax exemption. However, in those communities in Sunflower where this program has been utilized there is strong opposition to issuance of additional bonds because of a conservative "pay one at a time" attitude.

Most firms presently located in Sunflower County are low- to medium-wage industries, and many stated that plentiful low-cost labor was a major consideration in their decision to locate in Sunflower County. They also stated that they oppose the entrance into the labor market of new firms that might raise wage levels, a view shared by those in agriculture.

FEDERAL LEGISLATIVE EFFORTS TO ENCOURAGE REGIONAL ECONOMIC DEVELOPMENT

Historically, most of the development efforts in rural areas have been concerned with farmers and their problems. Beginning in 1937 with the establishment of the Farm Security Administration, the federal government acknowledged that some farmers were poorer than others. Programs concerned with the planning of state and local land use were investigated during this time period. However, it was not until the 1950s that a Rural Development Program was initiated and interagency activities were first implemented.[13]

Numerous programs have been administered on an agency basis involving the Farmers Home Administration, Rural Electrification Administration, Federal Interior Service, Farmer Cooperation Service, Soil Conservation Service, and the Forestry Service. Although such programs and agencies indirectly affect and help all of the rural population, their primary objective is to help the farmer. It has been observed that "federal policies with respect to development of a national growth policy continue to emphasize small towns and rural areas."[14] Although this appears to be true, it is important to recognize that even these policies have not been extensive and they have not affected all residents of all rural areas. Moreover, the role that the federal government, especially the Department of Agriculture, has played in fostering technological displacement of rural workers has been a significant one. Much of the rapid introduction of farm mechanization and the application of new production techniques has been made possible through federal financial support of agricultural research. In this regard, one rural labor market expert testified before Congress in 1970:

> I am simply saying that probably 95 percent of all the research moneys in the U.S. Department of Agriculture and its land-grant affiliates is technologically oriented, and therefore, oriented toward the displacement of people.[15]

The Area Redevelopment Act (ARA) of 1961 was the first federal legislation to examine the problems of rural areas other than those of agriculture. The act had the stated goal of implementing an effective program to alleviate conditions of substantial and persistent unemployment and underemployment in certain economically distressed areas.[16] The ARA provided low-interest loans for new firms and expansions of existing facilities, financial aid to improve public facilities, technical assistance, and training programs to distressed areas. The program could be considered experimental because of the duration of the act (1961-65) and the relatively modest amounts of funding authorized.

In contrast to urban areas, for which unemployment rates were used, the criteria for designating an area as "depressed" recognized the difficulty of using such an indicator in rural areas as a measure

ECONOMIC DEVELOPMENT

of conditions of labor supply. A successful effort by some legislators was made to have the criteria sufficiently lax to include areas in their districts. In any case, one would expect to find that in rural areas the communities with the lowest levels of economic activity should have received the greatest amount of assistance. However, during the period 1961-65, A. B. Johnson found no significant correlation between per capita income and per capita aid among the rural areas receiving aid during that period: "[The] evidence suggests that the allocation of loans and grants was influenced more by noneconomic factors (one of which could be political) than by those of need or the criteria specified in the legislation."[17] In part, this explanation needs to be considered in the face of the often made criticism of the program that it "overextended its limited resources."[18]

Over one-third of the counties in the United States were eligible to receive assistance under the provisions of the ARA. These counties accounted for nearly 40 million persons in the United States. The act also limited the effectiveness of the industrial loans by providing that only businesses that could not get credit at a reasonable rate of interest in the open market could qualify. Loans were limited, therefore, to marginal or new enterprises.

By and large, although the program was viewed as experimental, it was in support of the goals of the Employment Act of 1946. In addition to the problems noted above, the ambitious undertaking was plagued by a number of other problems: the political realities of public works programs, poor administration, and problems in the national economy that affected regional development.[19]

Beset with these and other troubles, the Area Redevelopment Administration was sacrificed for reasons of political expediency. Accepting the goal of the ARA that economically lagging areas could be stimulated through such tools as public works and technical assistance, the Public Works and Economic Development Act of 1965 was enacted. This act differed from the ARA in a number of ways. Whereas the ARA accepted that rural areas had the basic infrastructure for development, the new legislation was designed primarily to provide such infrastructure. A concerted emphasis on planning stressed improvement in the quality of planning and planners. As opposed to using the county as a planning unit, the multicounty district was to be used. Reflecting the European influence as well as a search for alternatives to urban migration, the legislation included the capability to designate certain areas as growth centers. Specifically, five target goals were developed as measures of program success:

1. Reduction of the incidence of substantial and persistent unemployment characteristics of certain designated and qualified regions, counties, Indian reservations, and communities to a level commensurate with the levels prevailing in the national economy.

2. Improvement of the economic development planning, coordinating, and implementing capabilities at all levels—federal, state, substate, district, and local

3. Provision of a basis for improved coordination of and continuity for federal, state, and local activities relating to regional economic development, and for more efficient utilization of all resources (federal, state, local, and private) available for regional and local economic development

4. Provision of a basis for rapid, effective, and efficient expansion of federal, state, and local expenditures to promote economic development if and when such expansion is determined to be desirable and necessary (for example, required by changes in the national economy or because of allocation of certain federal funds to states) and is found to be in the national interest

5. Development of alternatives to present patterns of migration of the unemployed and underemployed—now directed to larger urban areas—by expanding economic opportunities in more suitable locations.[20]

The development process as advocated by the Economic Development Administration (EDA) which was created under the act of 1965 is based on the following principles: The initiative and the requests for assistance must originate locally; full cooperation between the public sector and private enterprise is essential; maximum coordination of all federal, state, and local programs is required; emphasis is given to the planning process. These principles tend to be idealistic, and difficulties in implementing them have presented various degrees of problems in the various districts. Lack of local initiative, intercounty squabbling, interagency coordination problems, and poor planning all have produced mixed results of EDA programs.[21]

EDA also suffers from a problem of the earlier Area Redevelopment Administration in that it has not had adequate funds to provide significant economic development in many areas. Although EDA subscribed to the growth-center approach, many of those areas identified for assistance did not have a high potential for growth. A final criticism is that "greater attention to investment in health, education, and training of the labor forces in lagging areas probably would be more effective than investing in sewer and water lines."[22] This nonhuman resource-development orientation, administered through a regional system of economic development districts having no regional government toward which to relate, has not proved effective for rural areas. The urban areas within the districts have the most influential voices, due to the relatively larger constituencies involved. In terms of rural development, the ARA and the Public Works and Economic Development Act have had very limited impact.

ECONOMIC DEVELOPMENT

The Rural Development Act of 1972 also is an investment-oriented piece of legislation designed to provide for improving the economy and living conditions in the rural United States.[23] The act authorized grants of up to $482 million annually for such diverse measures as water and waste-disposal construction and planning, development planning, industrial-pollution abatement, industrial park facilities, rural-community fire protection, and rural development research and education. In 1974, $163 million was appropriated, representing about 34 percent of the total authorization.

Actual expenditures under the act have been even lower. Authorized expenditures for FY 1973-75 were $397 million; however, only 33.5 percent ($133 million) of the authorization was expended. More specifically, in 1974 less than 9 percent ($34 million) of the total three-year authorization was expended.[24]

There are those who would argue that the Rural Development Act of 1972 does not represent an effective means of encouraging development in rural areas. The act is "farm"-oriented, and the term "rural" includes many institutions and activities that are far from being exclusively "farm." The act is a U.S. Department of Agriculture (USDA) statute by virtue of the fact that the USDA is the agency responsible for administering the act, as well as by the fact that many of the provisions of the act are extensions of existing USDA programs or are modelled after existing programs.[25] The act does not provide for the development of human resources as an integral part of the development process. It does not "contain an adequate conceptual framework for a rural development policy."[26] As stated earlier, it is an investment-oriented piece of legislation reflecting the attitude that if money and facilities are poured into rural areas, development will take care of itself.

THE RURAL SOUTH: POTENTIAL FOR DEVELOPMENT

The process of economic development, particularly as it pertains to efforts to increase the demand for labor in quantitative terms and to alter the composition of labor demand in qualitative terms, clearly raises a number of policy questions for the rural South. In the survey counties and throughout most of the rural South, economic development is viewed as a panacea to current problems. In the past in selective areas large financial disbursements by various governmental agencies had had an important impact on the development of the South. Special regional programs, such as the Tennessee Valley Authority and Tennessee-Tombigbee have had, and will continue to have, significant impacts on certain Southern areas. Growth has also occurred in some rural areas adjacent or close to metropolitan areas. The nature and type of growth are sometimes questioned but, in general, rural residents should benefit from an influx of income.

It also is evident from the data generated in this study that there are differential possibilities for growth in many Southern rural counties. Counties like Dodge and Natchitoches have much more potential, relatively, than do Starr and Sunflower, because of less isolation and more resources (human, physical, and financial). Despite all of this, the evolving literature of regional economics stresses the reality that in many rural communities significant private economic development is not practical, given the potential for return on investment. It is doubtful that a sufficient number of businesses and industries willing to locate in all of the counties in the rural South exists for the foreseeable future.

It is not surprising that the survey data of this study would show clearly that the available labor supply in the rural South lacks the education and training to meet the skill requirements of many average or above-average wage industries. These, of course, are precisely the industries envisioned as the types required if economic development is to be increased. Low-wage industries need little additional encouragement to come to the rural South, although there may be active competition between individual communities to land a particular low-wage enterprise. These industries do provide employment opportunities and an additional source of income, but communities are unlikely to become significantly better-off.

The issue is even more complex; it is not simply one of job creation. This study shows a limited pool of persons who could at present benefit from extensive skill training or retraining. In addition, there are those who are poor, undereducated, and sick and who, even if jobs were available, probably would not get them. Hence, a serious dilemma of economic development in the rural South is exposed. Should public policy attempt to attract industries whose occupational requirements exceed the skill levels of the local labor supply? The result would be that the new enterprises would import many skilled workers and skim off the best of the local labor force for the remainder. Or should public policy advocate training local people for jobs currently not available—and jobs that, in some instances, will not materialize in the near future for the many underdeveloped rural communities? More concisely, the problem is that human-resource policies will not help the rural South (as a region) if there are no jobs, and jobs do not help if there is no human-resource development. Human-resource policies have helped to increase the alternatives available to residents of the rural South (out-migration), but they have had only limited success in terms of linkages to economic development. Hence, those persons remaining behind in the rural South have received limited benefits from such policies.

ECONOMIC DEVELOPMENT

In the past, skill training has primarily provided to persons an escape route by making out-migration an alternative to "staying behind." Such an alternative should continue to be provided; however, it should be noted that continued out-migration inhibits the emergence of a skilled pool of labor as a possible attraction for industry. Hence, for those remaining, government transfer payments have become a major source of income. Most who convert a training "potential" into a skill or vocation leave, and the rural area they have left is condemned for providing a second-rate existence. With the best people gone, those who remain are not an attraction to private industry.

Limited prospects for private-sector development and a large dependent population have resulted in the continued economic lag in many parts of the rural South. Significant increases in government spending and government public works programs would certainly improve the well-being of the residents and the depressed areas of the rural South. However, limited resources and political considerations offset the feasibility of such action, and, furthermore, rural Southern interests (with the exception of agriculture) have few champions of their cause.

Given limited resources, the strategy of focusing developmental activities into designated growth centers has been posited as one way of solving the problem. That is to say, funds for both economic and human resource development would be concentrated on designated intermediate-sized cities and their present and potential labor supply to the exclusion of all other rural communities. The explicit assumption is that the lack of good job opportunities in many rural communities may induce people to migrate to those growth centers where the jobs and matching training will be available. The analogue of this approach is that little would probably be done in the vast rural areas that do not have rural growth centers to prevent this migration from occurring. Ideally, relocation allowances would be available to cushion the financial costs of moving and to assist in the settlement of a designated area. Similar to the views towards out-migration, this strategy argues that rural people are not the same as rural areas and that public policy should elect to serve the needs of people when a choice must be made.

From a regional view, the growth-center strategy has much appeal, but from a local community or county perspective, it has little to offer for many rural areas except the prospect of population atrophy and community decline. There is small likelihood, for instance, that the four survey counties would be designated as growth centers if objective economic criteria were used and political manipulation were not involved in the decision-making process. It is precisely because of the political considerations that it is unlikely that a growth center strategy will become the only accepted development policy of this nation. The absence of relocation allowances from the available array of publicly supported labor market policies adopted to date in this nation is no accident. Politicians are loath to support policy proposals that encourage the exodus from established political districts of populations that are in fact the basis for the existing political jurisdictions. Accordingly, it is hardly conceivable that governmental bodies at any level will ever embrace a policy that simply writes off the future of the rural population, no matter how logical the objective case for doing so may be in some cases.

As the recent problems of urban areas have revealed, there is little to be gained, from a social standpoint, by a strategy of encouraging large numbers of poorly trained and inadequately educated rural persons to gravitate to growth centers. The lifestyle changes for those rural persons who would have to adjust to an urban orientation of life may not be desirable. Further, given the poor preparation of many rural workers, there is little assurance that receiving communities in the South would be supportive of such relocation efforts.

As for the economic factors, a real problem of growth-center strategy is that it can be successful only if it assumes a systems approach. To date, most of the concern of growth-center policy has dealt with physical infrastructure projects. Little attention seems to be paid to the need to integrate the strategy of encouraging the gravitation of people to these regions with the necessity of preparing the receiving communities to accommodate these new immigrants. More than job creation is involved. Housing arrangements, transportation facilities, health services, and educational needs are only some of the major concerns that must be addressed before much support can be given to the concept. Unfortunately, most of the rationale for the growth-center strategy is restricted to its industrialization potential. By the same token, the growth-center strategy offers nothing for the people who do not move.

In an effort to cope with reality and at the same time search for an acceptable policy alternative, this study questions the value of the growth-center strategy. For many rural communities significant economic development simply will not occur. Some low-wage industries seeking to escape the high costs of production in urban areas may settle at least temporarily in some Southern rural communities, but they are not likely to offer broader job opportunities or higher income.

Federal policy, in attempting to stimulate development, could play a pragmatic role. Where exceptional cases arise in which either state or local efforts are successful in enticing above-average wage-paying enterprises to locate in the rural South, federal funds should be available to cover the full cost of adapting the local labor to the needed skill requirements. And should a local enterprise consider expansion, federal funds to cover the costs of institutional and on-the-

job training of local workers should be immediately available. An
expanded role for the Small Business Administration (SBA) is essential.
The SBA is currently restricted from making loans to assist expansion
of existing businesses. OJT for small businesses, either those that
are expanding or those that are newly created, should be available at
all times. In addition, special attention should be given to small
minority business enterprises. The role of EDA (or some similar
type of governmental body) in rural areas should be focused on a
supportive mission. When a community has succeeded in attracting
an employer to its locality, EDA should provide housing assistance,
transportation development, and aid for the development of public
services.

As matters now stand in the rural South, efforts to diversify local
economies from their historic domination by agriculture have fallen
into the purview of local business and government officials. Economic
development in some rural Southern areas is favored by these people
as an abstract concept as long as it can be controlled. These local
groups usually do not wish to see prevailing power relationships altered
between individuals and groups. They fear unions. They only wish
to see certain industries that are interested in absorbing available
labor surpluses (for example, minority-group women who come into
the community). Therefore, it makes little sense to vest responsibility for change in the hands of those who are opposed to it.

Alternative proposals to the problem can only be conjectured.
One possibility rests with the establishment of community development
corporations (CDCs). Some experimentation with this concept is being
carried out in a 15-county area of the Mississippi Delta. Such activities should be carefully and objectively monitored. These corporations enable local people to achieve ownership and control over
business enterprises that they create or can attract. This approach
escapes the domination of the local power structure, which favors
only controlled industrialization. By transcending political boundaries
in their membership and operations, the development corporations
avoid the parochialism of a single municipality or county. In the
rural South, CDCs also have the advantage of drawing upon the increasing feelings of racial pride among Blacks and Chicanos. Because of
the unique nature of its diverse racial population, the rural South is
in a position to tap the strength and solidarity that is a part of a growing racial awareness among groups who have long been suppressed.

On the other hand, this study indicates that the CDC approach
has conceptual drawbacks which may limit its effectiveness. The
most obvious problem (especially if the scale is enlarged to include
any sizable portion of the rural South) is the source of funds. It is
unlikely that a poor population can raise sufficient funds to engage in
any large enterprises that would represent a step toward real economic

development. It also is unrealistic to believe that strongly established vested interests are likely to do nothing if a CDC should begin to compete actively for local labor or local markets. Given the severe capital restraints, a CDC would have difficulty entering into a national market. This means that it is likely to be dependent entirely upon local demand, which, by definition, is likely to be limited in size and purchasing power. Therefore, the CDC approach may be limited as a general approach to economic development. The strength of CDCs appears to be more one of community involvement than community development. It is hoped, however, that CDCs as well as rural cooperatives will be tried. In some localities, their success may lead to other steps forward.

The economic development of the rural South may well have to wait until the nation itself decides upon a firm policy toward broad scale rural development. There are limits to the extent of urbanization that are desirable for a nation. Eventually, attention must turn to the importance of striking a balance between urban and rural life. Until then, it is likely that the thrust of federal policy should be to assist in a purely supportive manner the local and state efforts to attract industries. In a larger context, it may be necessary to rely upon income-maintenance and job-creation measures to help "those left behind," until such time as a national rural development policy is enunciated.

NOTES

1. U.S., Department of Agriculture, Economic Research Service, Social and Economic Characteristics of the Population in Metro and Nonmetro Counties, 1970, Report no. 72 (Washington, D.C.: U.S. Government Printing Office, March 1975), p. 34.

2. Ray Marshall, "Program and Research Issues in Rural Development," The Southern Economic Journal 41 (April 1975): 562.

3. Colin Clark, The Conditions of Economic Progress (London: Macmillan, 1940); A. G. B. Fisher, "Capital and Growth of Knowledge," Economic Journal 43 (September 1933): 379-89; A. G. B. Fisher, "Production Primary, Secondary, and Tertiary," Economic Record 15 (June 1939): 24-38.

4. Fisher, "Production Primary, Secondary, and Tertiary," p. 33.

5. For a synopsis of these criticisms, refinements, and expansions of sector theory, see Stuart J. Greenfield, Poverty and Industrial Structure (Austin, Tex.: Bureau of Business and Economic Research, The University of Texas, September 1975).

6. Claude Haren, "Rural Industrial Growth in the 1960s," *American Journal of Agricultural Economics* 12 (August 1970): 431.
7. Thomas E. Till, "Two Models of Nonmetropolitan Industrial Development and Poverty Impact in the South," *Labor Law Journal* 24 (August 1974): 473.
8. Brian J. J. Berry, *Growth Centers in the American Urban System* (Cambridge, Mass.: Ballinger, 1973), p. 151.
9. Ibid.
10. Niles M. Hansen, *Population Turnaround in Nonmetropolitan Regions: Its Implications for Manpower and Regional Policies* (Austin, Tex.: University of Texas at Austin, n.d.).
11. Charles T. Steward and Virginia T. Benson, *Linkages between Small Metropolitan Areas and Their Hinterlands, with Implications for Regional Development Policies* (Washington, D.C.: George Washington University, May 1973), p. 84.
12. Thomas E. Till, "Changes in Industries Located in the Nonmetropolitan South, 1959-1969," *American Journal of Agricultural Economics* 56 (May 1974): 308.
13. Varden Fuller, "Rural Poverty and Rural Areas Development," in *Poverty in America*, ed. Margaret S. Gordon (San Francisco: Chandler, 1965), p. 392.
14. Hansen, *Population Turnaround in Nonmetropolitan Regions*.
15. U.S. Congress, Senate, Committee on Labor and Public Welfare, Subcommittee on Migratory Labor. Hearing: Testimony of Daniel Sturt, Director of the Rural Manpower Center, Michigan *State University*, 91st Cong., 1st and 2d sess., part 7-B (April 14, 1970), p. 4550.
16. Raymond H. Millikan et al., *Alleviating Economic Distress* (Lexington, Mass.: D. C. Heath, 1972), pp. 3-10.
17. A. Bruce Johnson, "Federal Aid and Area Redevelopment," *The Journal of Law and Economics* 14 (April 1971): 277.
18. J. M. Becker, William Haber, and Sar A. Levitan, *Programs to Aid the Unemployed in the 1960s* (Kalamazoo, Mich.: W. E. Upjohn Institute for Employment Research, 1965), p. 22.
19. Ibid.
20. Gregg Chappell, "The Economic Development Administration's Experience with Economic Development and Manpower Planning in Rural Areas," in *Manpower Planning for Jobs in Rural Areas*, ed. Collette Moser (East Lansing, Mich.: Michigan State University, 1972), pp. 93-95.
21. Ibid.
22. Sar A. Levitan, Garth L. Mangum, and Ray Marshall, *Human Resources and Labor Markets* (New York: Harper & Row, 1972), p. 538.

23. Information obtained from U.S. Congress, <u>1975 Revised Guide to the Rural Development Act of 1972</u>, a Committee print, no. 41-664. 93d Cong., 2d sess., January 1, 1975 (Washington, D.C.: U.S. Government Printing Office, 1975).

24. U.S., Congress, House, Committee on Agriculture, <u>Rural Development Act of 1972–Administration and Expenditures: Hearing</u>, 94th Cong., 1st sess. (1975), p. 188.

25. George A. Rold, "The Rural Development Act," in U.S. Congress, <u>Proceedings of a National Conference on Rural Development</u>, a Committee print, no. 25-237, 93d Cong., 1st sess., January 2, 1974 (Washington, D.C.: U.S. Government Printing Office, 1974), p. 87.

26. Ray Marshall, <u>Rural Workers in Rural Labor Markets</u> (Salt Lake City, Utah: Olympus, 1974), p. 84.

CHAPTER

10

SPECIAL ISSUES

In addition to the general analysis of the preceding chapters, there remain two topics that deserve special consideration. One pertains to the unique factors that surround the rural Chicano labor force, with its high incidence of migratory farm workers. The second issue involves the secular decline of employment opportunities in agriculture—which has been historically the major industry of the rural South.

CHICANOS: MIGRANTS AND NONMIGRANTS

The inclusion of Texas into the analysis of Southern rural labor markets introduces a second major racial minority in addition to blacks: the Mexican Americans. This group, increasingly referred to as Chicanos, represented 14.9 percent of the population of Texas in 1970. The actual proportion undoubtedly is higher than these official figures, due to acknowledged problems of statistical undercount that have plagued Census counts of groups with inordinately large numbers of low-income individuals and families.[1]

Because of the shortage of water over vast stretches of land, it is often the case that rural workers in Texas (and throughout the Southwest) live in urban areas but work in rural areas for some portion of the year. In Texas, for instance, 39 percent of the Chicanos over age 16 who were employed in agriculture in 1970 resided in urban areas. Part of the explanation of this inordinately high percentage, which is a unique characteristic of the Chicano work force, is the fact that many migratory farm workers use an urban area as their home address. It is to this home base that they return during off-season winter months. Another contributing factor is that in

Texas, historically, farm ownership (or farm tenancy) by Chicanos has been very low. In 1970 only 19 percent of the Chicano labor force over age 16 that was employed in agriculture actually resided on farms (the comparable figure for Anglos was 48 percent).

Starr County, Texas, was included in this study of the rural South to portray the rural labor market experience of Chicanos and to represent a segment of the South. With a Chicano population in excess of 98 percent, the Starr County experience can serve to illustrate both the similarities and the differences of Chicano rural experience from that of other racial groups in the rural South. There are some important, unique factors that affect Chicano economic opportunity in rural areas, such as migrant farm workers and the proximity of the Mexican border.

The Rural Labor Market of South Texas

The distinguishing characteristic of the rural labor market of South Texas is the presence of a sizable number of migratory workers. Much has been written about migratory workers while they are "on-the-road" away from their home base. It undoubtedly is true that the higher national visibility of migrant farm workers (who compose only about 5 percent of the nation's agricultural labor force) relative to that of nonmigrant farm workers has contributed to the disproportionately greater amount of public policy attention paid to the migrants. A special feature of this research has been the opportunity to study the economic activity and characteristics of migrant workers in their home base as well as to separate the characteristics of the migrant and nonmigrant population for the purpose of comparisons.

Of the 810 household heads interviewed in Starr County, 461 (56.9 percent) were reported in the labor force at the time of the survey. For the purpose of analysis, the household heads can be divided into three distinctly separate groups:

1. Household heads of migrant families currently in the labor force: This category comprised 17 percent of the total survey households during the off-season winter months while they were in Starr County.

2. Household heads of nonmigrant families who were in the Starr County labor force year-round: This category comprised 48 percent of the total survey households.

3. Household heads who were not in the labor force: This category comprised 34 percent of the total survey households.

As might be expected, the household heads not in the labor force were considerably older than the other two sectors, which had the

TABLE 10.1

Age Distribution of Household Heads, by
Major Segments, 1974
(percent)

Years of Age of Household Head	Migrant Household Heads	Nonmigrant Household Heads in Labor Force	Nonmigrant Household Heads Not in Labor Force
13-18	0	0.3	0
19-24	8.5	5.4	0.7
25-44	39.7	46.4	11.1
45-64	47.5	42.6	23.7
65-99	4.3	5.4	64.6
Mean Age (years)	44	44	64

identical mean age and approximately the same age distribution (see Table 10.1). The fact that the category of household heads who were not in the labor force accounted for 34 percent of the total households indicates a large dependent population of older adults in the rural economy.

Of the 141 household heads who reported that they had been migrant workers in the past year, 63 percent were in the labor force of Starr County during their off-season. For purposes of comparative analysis, the labor force of Starr County is divided in Table 10.2 between those workers who had been migrants in the past year and those who had not. Clearly, the migrant household heads were far less likely to find a job than were the nonmigrant household heads. The unemployment rate of migrant job seekers was over seven times that of nonmigrant job seekers. In fact, unemployed migrant household heads accounted for 60 percent of the unemployed in the county.

The proportion of female heads of households was approximately the same for migrant household heads (8.5 percent female-headed) and nonmigrant household heads in the labor force (10.3 percent female-headed). The percentage of female-headed households who were in the "not in the labor force" category was 47 percent. The incidence of marriage among migrant and nonmigrant households in the labor force was virtually identical.

With respect to the labor market activity of spouses, the survey data for Starr County show a very low rate of labor force participation for all household divisions. The figures are consistent with other findings that Chicano women have the lowest rate of labor force

TABLE 10.2

Employment Status of Starr County Labor
Force, by Migrant and Nonmigrant
Household Heads, 1974
(percent)

Labor Market Sector	Migrant Household Heads	Nonmigrant Household Heads in Labor Force
Employed	70.8	95.9
Unemployed	29.2	4.1

participation of any major racial or ethnic group in the U.S. labor force.[2] The low participation rate of spouses in the labor market magnifies the importance of data on household heads as the most consequential describer of economic behavior and welfare for the Chicano family.

The only remaining category of possible labor force participants includes those over age 16 who are neither household heads nor spouses. These could be either unrelated or related family members. Of the former, only 12 families reported anyone other than a family member living with them. Of the people over 16 years of age who were neither household heads nor spouses, 24.7 percent were in the labor force. Of those, 19 percent were unemployed. Presumably, most of these persons were older children still living at home.

Population Stability

A significant proportion of each of the three population segments has resided in Starr County for over 50 years (see Table 10.3). Despite the fact that long-time residency is a major population characteristic, it is also true that the population of Starr County has increased steadily since the end of World War II. The major cause for this growth has been the infusion of immigrants from Mexico. This immigration presents a number of unique problems to public policy makers that make solutions to rural poverty in Starr County more complex than elsewhere.

Wages and Income

In all of the rural counties surveyed, wages were virtually the sole source of earned income. But there was considerable variation

SPECIAL ISSUES

among the four rural counties in the mean hourly wage received by household heads. Starr and Sunflower counties had identical mean wage rates ($2.65 per hour) that were considerably below those of both Dodge and Natchitoches ($3.46 and $3.33, respectively). In Starr County there was a considerable difference between the mean wage rate received by nonmigrants ($2.78) and migrants ($1.89) who were working in the off-season in Starr County. The migrants pulled down the overall mean wages workers in the county—still, the mean rate for nonmigrant workers in Starr County was well below the mean rate for all the counties combined ($3.02 per hour). Yet when wage rates for Chicanos in Starr County are compared with those for blacks in each of the other three counties (see earlier findings in Chapter 4), the mean wage rates for Chicanos were higher than those of blacks in each instance. Although the wage levels are low for both racial minorities, the finding that Chicanos fare somewhat better than blacks is consistent with other research findings.[3] The mean wage rate of the migrant household heads who were working in Starr County, however, was below the mean wage of male blacks in all of the three counties.

TABLE 10.3

Years of Residency in Starr County by Major Labor Market Segments, 1973
(percent)

Years in County	Migrant Heads of Households	Nonmigrant Household Heads in Labor Force	Nonmigrant Household Heads Not in Labor Force
1 or less	1.4	4.9	0.7
2	2.1	2.8	0.7
3	1.5	0.7	2.8
4	2.8	1.3	1.4
5	1.4	1.8	1.1
6-10	11.3	3.6	4.0
11-15	8.5	2.8	1.4
16-20	4.3	3.1	3.2
21-25	5.7	7.7	2.2
26-30	7.1	10.1	7.2
31-35	7.8	8.2	0.7
36-40	5.7	9.3	4.3
41-45	9.2	9.0	3.6
46-50	11.3	9.0	4.3
50 or more	19.9	24.7	62.4

TABLE 10.4

Distribution of Hourly Wage Rates for
Employed Migrant and Nonmigrant
Workers in Starr County, 1974
(percent)

Hourly Wage Rates (dollars)	Employed Migrant Household Heads	Employed Nonmigrant Household Heads	Both Groups
Below 1.19	1.7	6.8	6.1
1.20 to 1.39	13.3	4.2	5.6
1.40 to 1.59	16.7	10.7	11.6
1.60 to 1.79	33.3	16.4	18.9
1.80 to 1.99	3.3	3.3	3.3
2.00 to 2.19	10.0	8.9	9.1
2.20 to 2.39	5.0	4.5	4.5
2.40 to 2.59	5.0	5.4	5.3
2.60 to 2.79	0	2.1	1.8
2.80 to 2.99	0	2.4	2.0
3.00 to 3.49	8.3	8.3	8.3
3.50 to 3.99	1.7	6.5	5.8
4.00 to 4.49	0	4.8	4.0
4.50 to 4.99	0	3.0	2.5
5.00 to 7.49	1.7	9.8	8.6
7.50 to 9.99	0	1.8	1.5
Over 10.00	0	1.2	1.0

Table 10.4 presents a distribution of hourly wage rates in Starr County, with a separate breakdown for employed household heads, migrants or nonmigrants, in Starr County. It is important to recall that the federal minimum wage at the time of the field survey was $1.30 an hour for covered agricultural workers and $1.60 for covered nonagricultural workers. The Texas minimum wage at that time was $1.40, and it applied mostly to local public employees who at that time were not covered by the federal statute. The highlights of the table are that 32 percent of the employed migrant household heads and 22 percent of the employed nonmigrant household heads earned less than $1.60 an hour. In total, 23.3 percent of the employed household heads earned below that figure. The largest percentage of both groups was in the interval that contained the prevailing federal minimum wage (that is, 33.3 percent of the migrant household heads and 16.4 percent of the nonmigrant heads or, when combined, 18.9

percent of all employed household heads were in the wage interval of $1.60 to $1.79). Of the migrants 68 percent were earning less than $2.00 an hour; 41 percent of the nonmigrants were earning below that figure. In total, 45.5 percent of the employed households were earning below $2.00 an hour less than two months before the federal minimum wage was raised to that level.

Starr County had the lowest mean levels of income of the four counties (see Table 5.1). Yet, as shown in Table 10.5, the aggregate mean income in all four counties distort the fact that the means for minority groups are considerably lower than the average figures. The comparison by counties by race does show that, although both Chicanos and blacks are considerably below the income level of Anglos, rural Chicanos have higher income levels than do rural blacks.

Within Starr County, however, there also is a wide variation in income levels between the major segments of the county's population (see Table 10.6). In this case, it is clear that the income levels of household heads who are migrant workers approximate the income figures presented in Table 10.5 for blacks in the other rural counties.

Table 10.7 shows the total family income levels for the three major segments of the Starr County population. Again the migrant-worker families are well below the levels of the nonmigrant families who are in the labor force. But perhaps the most significant item contained in Table 10.7 is the indication of the extremely low levels of income for those families whose household head is not in the labor force (and that are not headed by a person who had been a migrant worker in the past year). Of this group, which comprised 34 percent of all households in the county, 44 percent had a total family income of below $2000 a year, and 72 percent were below $3000. The income figures for the migrant households are a combination of their income

TABLE 10.5

Mean Incomes of Household Heads, by Counties and by Race, 1973
(dollars)

	Anglo	Black	Chicano	All Groups
Dodge	6986	3268	—*	6209
Natchitoches	6133	2855	—*	4821
Sunflower	7724	2698	—*	4268
Starr	9867	—*	3861	4126

*Dashes indicate no such households in county.

TABLE 10.6

Income of Household Head for Major Labor Market Segments in Starr County, 1974
(percent)

Income Class (dollars)	Migrant Household Heads	Nonmigrant Household Heads in Labor Force	Nonmigrant Household Heads Not in Labor Force
0-999	10.2	5.7	15.3
1000-1999	21.9	10.6	51.6
2000-2999	24.1	11.4	20.2
3000-3999	23.4	16.4	5.2
4000-4999	10.9	9.1	3.2
5000-5999	5.1	10.4	1.2
6000-6999	0.7	6.8	0.8
7000-7999	1.5	4.9	1.6
8000-8999	0.7	6.8	0.4
9000-9000	0	4.9	0
10,000-14,999	0.7	7.8	0.4
15,000-24,999	0.7	4.2	0
25,000-99,999	0	1.3	0
Mean Value	$2188	$5920	$1718

Combined mean value of all groups: $4126

experience "on the road" as migrant farm workers and any work experience while in residence during the winter months in South Texas. In total, therefore, the migrant household heads were able to earn in 1973 a mean income of only $2188, with total migrant family income averaging $4288. The magnitude of the number of migrant household heads with annual incomes of below $4000 was 80 percent. In addition, 55 percent of the migrant families had a total family income below $4000. Members of the year-round labor force working in Starr County do receive relatively higher income levels than do either of the aforementioned groups. But the relatively higher mean values for this group are clearly distorted by a few high incomes. The fact remains that 44 percent of the household heads of nonmigrant families who worked year-round in Starr County had an annual income level of below $4000, and 35 percent of the families had a total annual income below $4000. Thus, by this basic barometer of economic welfare, it is clear that for all three groups the rewards for working are not substantial.

SPECIAL ISSUES

To find explanations for the pervasive patterns of low income that characterize the rural economy of South Texas, it is necessary to examine a number of factors. Moreover, it is the combination of all of those considerations that will make for understanding the forces that cause and perpetuate these conditions.

Lack of Year-Round Employment

Of that in the four survey counties, the labor force in Starr County was the most dependent upon agricultural employment. Agricultural employment is notorious for its irregular employment requirements. Large numbers of workers are needed at times of planting and harvesting; fewer are needed between these times. In Chapter 5 it was shown that household heads in Starr County worked fewer weeks per year than did workers in any of the survey counties. Migrant workers worked considerably fewer weeks a year (35.9 weeks) than did nonmigrants (40.4 weeks) in Starr County. It should be recalled that

TABLE 10.7

Total Family Income, by Major Labor Market Segments for Starr County, 1974
(percent)

Income Class (dollars)	Migrant Household Heads	Nonmigrant Household Heads in Labor Force	Nonmigrant Household Heads Not in Labor Force
0-999	5.0	3.4	8.4
1000-1999	10.1	7.8	35.5
2000-2999	17.3	8.6	28.2
3000-3999	23.0	15.3	9.9
4000-4999	9.4	9.1	5.7
5000-5999	15.8	6.5	4.6
6000-6999	7.2	7.5	3.1
7000-7999	3.6	4.2	2.3
8000-8999	3.6	7.5	0.8
9000-9999	1.4	6.2	0.4
10,000-14,999	2.9	13.8	1.1
15,000-24,999	0.7	8.3	0
25,000-99,999	0	1.8	0
Mean Values	$4288	$7475	$2531

Combined Mean of all Groups: $5409

the figures for migrants include both their work on the road and in their home base. The figures would suggest a high incidence of discouraged workers among household heads in Starr County for at least part of the year.

Lack of Human-Capital Endowment

The paucity of human-capital endowment remains a significant characteristic of the Chicano rural labor force. This characteristic not only limits the type of industries and occupations that can employ local workers, but it also restricts the outward mobility of those people who wish to move away from the limited opportunities available in the rural economy.

Starr County, with a mean educational attainment of its population of only 6.1 years (5.8 years for Chicanos), was the lowest of the four survey counties. Of the three racial groups that comprise the population of these counties, however, the educational difference between rural Chicanos and rural blacks (6.5 years) is not much. Both of these groups suffer from very low levels of formal schooling.

Within Starr County there is also a wide difference in the educational attainment levels of the three household divisions of the county's population. Table 10.8 shows that all three groups contain a significant number of household heads who have had absolutely no formal education. The nonmigrant not in the labor force group obviously is the least educated. Thus, it is not only true that 64 percent of this group is over age 65 but also that 66 percent of the household heads not in the labor force have an educational attainment of under five years.

The educational attainment levels of migrant workers also are exceptionally low: 54 percent had less than five years of educational attainment. The educational attainment levels of the migrants are considerably below those of the nonmigrant labor force. The difference confirms the general impression that many persons with very low levels of educational attainment really have little choice but to enter the migrant stream. Yet it is apparent that a significant number of the nonmigrant labor force also have extremely low levels of educational attainment, which locks them into unskilled and low-wage jobs in the rural economy.

A further indication of the low state of human-capital development in rural South Texas is the lack of job-training opportunities for almost all the labor force participants. The survey found that 83.1 percent of the household heads in Starr County have never had any formal job training. The percentage was slightly higher for migrant household heads (90.1 percent) than for nonmigrant household heads in the labor force (87.7 percent), but the difference is too small

TABLE 10.8

Educational-Attainment Distribution of
Household Heads, by Major Segments
in Starr County, 1974
(percent)

Years of Educational Attainment	Migrant Household Heads	Nonmigrant Household Heads in Labor Force	Nonmigrant Household Heads Not in Labor Force
0	15.6	9.3	31.7
1-4	38.3	19.4	34.5
5-7	20.6	14.5	18.3
8	9.2	6.5	5.0
9-11	8.5	14.0	5.8
12	7.1	18.6	2.9
13-15	0.7	7.5	1.4
16-20	0	10.3	0.4
Mean	4.8 years	8.2 years	3.6 years

to be of consequence. Of the 11.9 percent of the household heads who reported any form of occupational training, the largest single source of training was the military (36.5 percent). As was the case in all the survey counties, very little formal occupational preparation is available.

Poor Health

Another critical factor affecting the state of human capital is the health of the population. A significant number of the household heads, both migrant (31.2 percent) and nonmigrant (26.8 percent) stated that they had health problems. Of those household heads with health problems, 86 percent were currently under a doctor's care. Of those, 86 percent believed their problems would last more than six months. Information received from medical sources in Starr County confirms the existence of extensive illness.

Although high illness rates are not uncommon in rural areas, the types of illnesses in rural South Texas are significantly different from those normally encountered.[4] Among these are high incidences of infectious and parasitic diseases such as tuberculosis, dysentery, leprosy, hepatitis, polio, tetanus, encephalitis, and venereal diseases. In addition, the long-term stability of the relatively small population of the county has led to extensive intermarrying, which has led to widespread cases of diabetes and glandular imbalances. Poor nutrition and inadequate diets also were cited by health authorities as a cause of anemia and orthopedic problems. Many of the community health problems stem from substandard housing, lack of pure drinking water, improper garbage and sewage disposal, and inadequate rodent and insect control. Many of these illnesses not only cause interruptions in the ability to work and to gain regular income but also restrict the types of work possible and the opportunities for training.

Lack of Opportunities for Second Jobs

One factor that explains the low family-income level in rural areas is the almost total absence of opportunities for second jobs. In Starr County only 6.4 percent of the household heads held a second job. This was the lowest percentage in all four counties. No doubt it is the dominance of agriculture that explains the low number of dual job holders. The normal workweek for agricultural workers in Starr County is six days. Agricultural employment is not covered by the overtime premium pay requirements of the Fair Labor Standards Act. Hence, the income levels for many persons in Starr County need to be interpreted in light of the fact that household heads often must work longer hours, as a condition of employment, than is the case elsewhere. Starr County had the highest percentage of household heads who were employed 35 hours or more a week (61.5 percent) of the four survey counties, but it had the lowest level of income for household heads.

Proximity of Mexican Border

A sizable portion of the geographic border of Starr County is also the international boundary between Mexico and the United States. It was therefore not surprising that 94.1 percent of the households interviewed stated that they spoke Spanish. The most consequential effect of the border is its influence on the labor market of South Texas. The flow of immigrants, both legal and illegal, as well as the daily commuting of workers is overwhelmingly one-way in direction: toward jobs in the United States. With its three legal crossing points, in addition to miles of essentially unguarded riverside, it is logical that Starr County would be affected by the mass migration of human beings that is occurring all along the border.[5]

The special labor market problems associated with border and immigration policies, however, transcend the Starr County experience. The issues raised—especially those pertaining to labor market influences—affect the entire South Texas area, regardless of proximity to the border itself. Moreover, it is increasingly being recognized that border and immigration policies affect large portions of the rural labor market of the entire Southwest, and increasingly the urban labor markets of the Southwest and elsewhere as well.[6]

Of the 810 households interviewed in Starr County, 19.5 percent of the heads of households reported that they were born outside the United States. Immigration, therefore, is of significant consequence to the population growth of rural Starr County, and therefore to the labor market. It was not possible to estimate how many of these immigrants were illegal entrants. It is widely known that illegal aliens represent "a shadow labor force" whose presence and magnitude is often discernible but seldom verifiable.[7]

In addition to legal and illegal immigration, there is another group of people that influences the local labor markets in Texas and the Southwest: namely, the group known as resident aliens (or more commonly "green carders"). In the survey, 2.2 percent of the Starr County household heads reported themselves to be resident aliens.

The importance of green carders, however, rests not with the resident aliens who reside in the United States on a year-round basis. Rather, it is the green carder who actually lives in Mexico but who commutes on a daily or seasonal basis to the United States who causes inequities to exist. These persons work for low wages and minimum fringe benefits because they receive a substantial real income advantage over fellow workers who must live full-time in the United States. By living in Mexico on a permanent or seasonal basis, their cost of living is significantly lower than that confronting a worker who lives permanently in the United States. The legality of the status of green carders who reside outside the United States on a permanent basis is a matter of debate.[8] It has been acknowledged by the courts that it is "amiable fiction" that many green carders actually reside in the United States, despite the seeming legislative mandate that they must. Everyone familiar with the Southern border knows differently. One study has aptly observed that "the commuter is this generation's bracero."[9]

Another category of border crossers is the "white carder," or legal visitor category. As the name implies, these are foreigners (Mexicans in this case) who obtain a pass (I-186 card) that enables them to cross into the United States to shop, visit, or tour within a 25-mile radius of the border for up to 72 hours. The white card, however, is not dated, so there is not real way of determining how long the bearer has been in the United States. Supposedly, a white carder is forbidden from being employed while visiting in the United States, but this, too, is often not the case.[10] Many are employed full time.

The survey of households conducted as part of this study cannot capture the true dimension of commuting green carders or white carders to the economy of Starr County. For the most part, these people reside permanently in Mexican border towns but work on a daily or seasonal basis in the United States. Their importance can be obtained only from secondary sources, personal interviews, or personal experience. Drawing upon all three, it can be reliably stated that the impact of Mexican workers is substantial throughout the labor market of all South Texas. The largest agricultural enterprise in Starr County (and second only to the county's school system in terms of the number of employees on its payroll) runs a daily round-trip bus from the international crossing at Roma to its fields near Rio Grande City. Workers from Mexico were instrumental in the defeat of efforts in 1966, 1967, and 1975 to establish a union for agricultural workers in Starr County.

But the most important impact of commuters and illegal aliens is the depressive effect that their collective numbers exert on the prevailing wages on the area. For most employers the supply of labor appears to be infinitely elastic at any given wage rate. The prevailing rate is usually the rate set by the federal minimum wage for nonagricultural workers and for agricultural workers. Any increase in this wage level that is actually enforced becomes a major factor in efforts to increase family income in South Texas.

On the other hand, the border does have some positive effects on employment opportunities in Starr County: Local businessmen in the retail and wholesale trades depend extensively upon Mexican citizens to spend a sizable portion of their income in the United States. Officials of the local bank and the local Chamber of Commerce estimate that about 35 percent of all retail and wholesale sales are made to Mexicans. The 1970 Census reported 17.6 percent of the Starr County labor force to be employed in the trade sector. The household survey conducted during this study found that 16.2 percent of all employed persons were at work in the trade sector. Excluding the government and agricultural sectors, the trade sector was by far the largest employment sector in Starr County. Local merchants are especially dependent upon Mexican consumers because of two unique factors. First, the large number of migrants who reside in the county are absent for up to half the year, which greatly reduces the purchasing power of the local population. Even when they return, it is obvious from their income levels that they do not bring a substantial sum of income earned outside the county, even if collectively totaled. Second, because of the low wages that characterize the entire rural labor market of Starr County, even in the aggregate there is not very much personal disposable income available to be spent. In fact, on several occasions local businessmen complained during interviews about the local wage structure. As one candidly observed, "people cannot buy anything at these wages."

Migrant Farm Workers

One of the most important aspects of the labor market of South Texas is the high incidence of migrant farm work. Although precise regional figures on the number of migrants are unavailable, reliable estimates are that about 40 percent of the nation's migratory labor force comes from the South Texas areas.[11] In 1973, a house-to-house count by the local community action agency of Starr County places the number of out-migrants during the year at 5731.[12] This figure, which is a total family figure of all men, women, and children, represents about one-third of the county's entire population. For the same year, the Texas Employment Commission (TEC) reported that the number of registered migrant workers (as required under the Crew Leader Registration Act of 1963) for Starr County was 409 families, of which 1602 were workers over age 16, with an additional 689 dependent children or aged adults who accompanied the workers.[13] The TEC figures do not include the "freewheelers," who migrate as individuals rather than as members of organized work crews. Nor do they count the work crews or crew leaders who simply do not register. The crew leader is essentially a "middle man" between the migrants and the out-of-state growers, whose function is to supply workers to harvest crops at prescribed times.

The general proposition that no one becomes a migrant farm worker if there are any other possible employment alternatives has been often documented.[14] The highest elected official in Starr County observed: "About 30 percent of our population are migrant workers. These people, however, are not nomadic by nature but rather by necessity. The proof of their stability is the fact that they always return here where their roots are." The explanations for the lack of employment alternatives in the South Texas area, however, often receive less research attention than the work and living conditions of the migrants while they are on the road. Low educational attainment, lack of job training, and poor health have already been cited as characteristics of the migrant labor force. The survey data also reveal that a disproportionately high percentage of the household heads of migrant families were born in Mexico (29.1 percent). It is well known that many of the migrants from Mexico (both legal and illegal) come from rural agricultural backgrounds. It is not surprising, therefore, that many of these immigrants become migrant farm workers or seek employment in the local agricultural economy of South Texas. Immigrants from Mexico have long influenced the labor market of South Texas by constantly adding to the pool of surplus labor.15 But no doubt the major factor prompting migrancy is the stagnant state of economic development of the rural economy of South Texas. As indicated earlier, 63 percent of the migrant household heads in the survey were in the labor force of Starr County during the off-season. Of those in the labor force, 29 percent were unemployed at the time of the survey. Of the migrant household heads who were employed, 46 percent were employed in local agriculture. The next largest sector was government, in which 22 percent of the migrant household heads were employed—usually in unskilled-laborer occupations. The remainder of the employed migrant household heads were scattered across the array of industries that compose the local economy. Thus, it is apparent that with 37 percent of the migrant heads not even in the local labor market, with 29 percent of those in the local labor force unemployed, and most of those who are employed during the winter being in agriculture, the limited economic opportunities preclude the attainment of income sufficient to pull most families out of poverty.

Water and Land-Ownership Restrictions

Among the special factors that limit economic development prospects in Starr County are disputed land titles and the scarcity of water. Both of these issues represent capstones to any immediate prospect for industrial diversification or economic development. To the degree that this is true, of course, opportunities to alter prevailing income and employment patterns are forestalled.

In substance, the problem of a shortage of water has always existed in the area. From the time of the early Spanish settlements in the Starr County region in the eighteenth century the land was parceled out so as to give landowners direct access to the water of the river now known as the Rio Grande River. The land grants divided the land into long but thin slivers called a porción. For most landowners, there was direct access to water. Because over the centuries the river bed had worn itself down below the level of the land and because the Spanish settlement process began in an area before the availability of machine pumps, irrigation was not deemed possible in this particular region during the settlement era. So, in sharp contrast to the Spanish waterlaw that was so prevalent throughout the Southwest, a riparian water system was established in the Starr County area. Landowners were given the right to unlimited use of the water that touched their porción. After the area became part of the State of Texas, a system of state-regulated water-use rights was adopted. Starr County landowners felt that their system of unregulated

SPECIAL ISSUES

water rights took precedence over the newer apportionment system, and few formal claims were filed. The issue came to a head following an international treaty between the United States and Mexico in 1945 and the subsequent construction of a system of dams along the Rio Grande. The river ceased to be "free flowing" and all water was subject to a strict allocation system. Following a long series of unsuccessful court challenges, Starr County residents lost their claims and their historic usage of the water. Except for "pueblo rights" that entitle towns to draw water for domestic uses only, Starr County residents and enterprises cannot use the water that flowed through their county for use further downstream to irrigate crops. Consequently, without water, a wide range of industrial enterprises are precluded from locating in the area despite the availability of a surplus labor force.

There remain a number of porciones in which the land title is unclear. Over the centuries the number of heirs who have legal claims to a piece of the land originally given to one family, has multiplied in some instances to numbers almost beyond comprehension. It takes decades usually to partition a porción among legitimate claimants. Because of the uncertainty of land titles of those porciones, economic development is discouraged. Large areas of the county have yet to be geologically surveyed because businessmen cannot obtain clear title to the land. Efforts of some business firms to locate in these same land areas also are precluded because of the inability of the interested parties to purchase the land needed to build their plants. The financially poorest school district in Starr County reports that it is unable to collect property taxes on over 60,000 acres of land within its boundaries because of the inability to determine the rightful landowners. Although some efforts are in progress to untangle this legal jungle, it will be years, if ever, before it will be completed.

The Dilemma of Public Policy in South Texas

The causes of the massive poverty of the rural South in general and of South Texas in particular are obviously complex. As was true of all the other survey counties, a disproportionately high number of household heads living in poverty are not in the labor force, nor could they be considered even potential labor force participants. Most of those in the labor force are at least nominally employed, although year-round employment opportunities are scarce. Nonetheless, unemployment per se does not surface as a major concern. Rather, the situation is one in which working people are largely unable to earn sufficient income to raise themselves and their dependents above poverty thresholds. The major problems stem from a surplus labor pool, a low level of human capital endowment, and a low state of economic development. But despite the similarities of problems throughout the rural South, it is apparent that some of the causes of the problems differ between South Texas and the remainder of the rural South.

A review of these causes for the pervasive low-income patterns of South Texas leads to the policy dilemma that is raised by the human problems of this rural area: Those factors that are unique causes for the widespread impoverishment of the region involve issues that are largely beyond remedial correction by local or state governmental agencies, even if those agencies were inclined to seek solutions. To a significant degree they involve issues that fall within the sole province of the federal government. If it elects not to address these issues, the social and economic problems of the region fester and multiply. The fact that they have now reached such massive proportions is due directly to inattention by policy makers at all levels of government over the years. A recognition, however, of the primacy of federal obligations to initiate remedial policies is the first step toward any plan for altering the prevailing situation.

Mexican Immigration

The migration of citizens of Mexico into the United States—both legally and illegally—has been a fact of life as long as a political border has separated the two nations. During the latter half of the nineteenth century the movement was only a small trickle. By the 1970s, however, it had reached tidal-wave proportions. One congressional inquiry in 1970 into the economic conditions along the Southwest border succinctly characterized the situation as "a massive hemorrhage."[16]

When viewed from the national level, it does not seem difficult to absorb the 70,000 or more legal immigrants who now come from Mexico each year. But because research shows that a very high proportion of the Mexican legal immigrants remain in the Southwest in general and in the border area in particular, legal immigration does contribute to the general labor surplus throughout the region.[17] The same research shows that legal Mexican immigrants are quite unlike legal immigrants from most other nations in that a disproportionately high number of Mexican immigrants are craftsmen, household workers, nonfarm laborers, and farm laborers.[18] These are precisely the occupational groups already in surplus in the region.

Legal immigration from Mexico, however, is only the tip of the Mexican immigration iceberg. The overwhelming characteristic of the Mexican immigration movement is illegal in nature.[19] In 1975, for instance, 680,392 illegal Mexican aliens were apprehended in the United States. They represented 89 percent of the total number of alien apprehensions by the Immigration and Naturalization Service during the year. Moreover, the figures represent only those apprehended. It is estimated that for every one apprehension, there are five or six illegal aliens who enter the nation undetected.[20] Typically, the illegal alien from Mexico is male, single, younger than 30 years old, unskilled, from a rural area, poorly educated if at all, speaks little English, and is likely to be employed at least some time in the rural economy of the United States.[21] In South Texas, the incidence of rural employment by illegal aliens is substantial.[22]

The Immigration and Nationality Act of 1952 expressly states that it is national policy to reserve available jobs for the domestic labor force. Referring to this act, the California Court of Appeals ruled in 1973 that the number of illegal aliens in the Southwest "represents an abject failure of national policy." Moreover, the court observed that the lack of meaningful corrective action "must be ascribed to self-imposed impotence of our national government."[23] Illegal entry from Mexico is still widely considered to be only a "regional problem"; hence the topic has not been very high on the list of national priorities. If the federal government decides not to act, little can be done.

Migrant Workers

It is no accident that almost half the remaining seasonally migrant agricultural workers in the United States are Chicanos who come from the South Texas region that borders on Mexico. Many Chicanos of this region are forced to become migrant laborers because the local labor market is overrun by illegal Mexican aliens and border commuters.

Although numerous public policy efforts by the federal government have sought to improve the economic status of migrant workers by preparing them for nonmigrant vocations, all attempts have failed. One basic reason is that the programs have never been able to handle the basic problem that causes internal seasonal migrancy: Too few job opportunities that offer wages at a level permitting a decent standard of life are available in the workers' home-base communities. The influx of illegal Mexican immigrants and of border commuters has set in motion a process whereby poor Mexicans make poor Chicanos poorer.[24]

In addition to the failure to address the problem of the "push" factors that contribute to migrancy, the fact that most migrants cross state boundaries means that their well-being can be only safeguarded if the federal government will assume full responsibility for their welfare. A comprehensive study of one large-scale effort that was federally financed involved an interstate program to assist Chicano migrant workers to settle out of the migrant stream. This study revealed widespread discrimination against Chicanos by the respective state agencies charged with administering the programs.[25] These state agencies (usually the respective state employment services) and the local employer and community groups from whom assistance was sought were more than willing to have Chicanos in their states as workers but wanted no part of "Texas Mexicans" as permanent residents.

As matters now stand, the federal government has intervened in a number of piecemeal ways, attempting to help migrant workers. In most instances they have been singularly unsuccessful. For instance, efforts to correct abuses by crew leaders led to the Crew Leader Registration Act, but most crew leaders do not register. The requirements for minimum housing standards for migrants while they are on the road have resulted largely in employers not complying and no longer using state employment services for employment referral purposes. Rather, employees contract directly with unregistered crew leaders for farm workers.[26] This means that fewer employers or employees now have contact with the employment service. The special health, food, and education programs that are federally financed have benefited many recipients, but they also have created much bitterness between the migrant poor (who are eligible for these benefits) and the nonmigrant poor (who are not eligible) in the home-base communities. On the other hand, some migrants complain that these special programs tie them to the migrant stream because they would lose all of the benefits for themselves and their families if they should quit being migrants. The absence of a national income maintenance program clearly contributes to this classic double-bind situation with respect to federal assistance to migrants.

For a variety of reasons most manpower programs addressed to migrants have been singularly unsuccessful. During the course of this study an effort was made to learn why. A common complaint was that the educational-attainment requirements for participation in most programs were too high. In most instances, an eighth-grade education was the minimal norm. The mean years of education for migrant household heads in Starr County was a scant 4.8 years, and 74.5 percent of the migrant households had 7 or fewer years of education. Thus, most migrants have been ineligible for most manpower programs—especially for those that contain a training component. Relatedly, the fact that the Adult Basic Education program, which could help some Chicanos to qualify for training programs, does not provide stipends means it is very difficult for adults to participate in any of these endeavors. Such program requirements and characteristics confirm the general impression held by many Chicanos that most manpower programs were not designed to meet their needs.[27]

Moreover, during many of the formative years of manpower policy, no explicit recognition of the cultural distinctiveness of Chicanos was given to the program design.[28] The most crucial factor pertains to the retention and use of the Spanish language. There also are other considerations with respect to heritage, family ties, and machismo that affect participation.[29]

With specific reference to migrants, interviews with program officials reiterated the primacy of the issue of timing. Programs to help migrants that start after late fall are not of help to migrants. Although participants may enroll, they are not the hard-core migrant population.

A number of present and past officials of manpower programs were critical of the quality of local program operations. The fact that most programs could serve only the economically disadvantaged was seen as a limitation to widening the range of experience of the participants. Also, it was felt that there were a number of participants who did not really want to benefit from the program but who did want the stipends. The inability to drop these people in order to make room for others who could benefit was blamed on a combination of factors. In some instances it was the unwillingness or indifference of the program officials to address the issue. In other instances, it was rationalized that to drop these people in light of the absence of jobs or any available form of income maintenance would be an unjust act. As one program administrator candidly stated: "Many people go into training programs simply to avoid starvation." The view was widespread that many of the programs were serving an income-maintenance function.

The poor quality of the instructors was also cited by some as another indication of the shattered expectations that some participants have experienced. The official added: "Because the programs often lack professional staffs, well-intentioned programs are often poorly implemented."

There also were a number of complaints voiced that the local manpower programs were heavily saturated with local politics. Who was accepted as a participant as well as who was employed on the program staffs, it was alleged, had little to do with ability to benefit or qualifications to serve, but rather the criterion was whom they supported during political elections. Politics in Starr County has been described as a "profession." There is a long history of family control and bitter feuds that transcends the passage of time. Patronage and political loyalty have been a way of life. It probably is not an unexpected development that, in a situation in which the primary alternative is to stop work in agriculture, the public sector should assume prominence. It is not surprising, therefore, that manpower training slots would be used to reward political friends and to punish political enemies. Yet it is doubtful that the best interests of the programs themselves are being served by placing so much of the responsibility for program operations in the hands of local officials. The local people often have no choice but to act as they do, but federal officials should recognize the folly of continuing such a delegation of authority. If anything, the decentralized character of CETA has served to exacerbate this problem from what it was when the field work for this project was conducted.

Experience has demonstrated that the problems of migrant farm workers cannot be handled by individual states due to the interstate aspects of migrants' travels.[30] Over the years the federal government has sought to introduce a number of ad hoc programs for migrants, but despite its good intentions, the programs have lacked a comprehensive approach. It is likely that the federal government's role must be expanded to include total responsibility for employment, transportation, housing, health, and education of children of migrant workers. The present hodgepodge of laws and programs at both the federal and state level seem to be of marginal influence to the economic welfare of migrants. What has been done has been accomplished largely due to the presence of the federal government; what remains to be done must wait for the federal government to act further.

Water Rights and Landownership Claims

There currently is no available answer to the dilemma posed by the legacy of legal decisions that have created the water shortage and multiple landownership claims that bedevil local economic development in the Starr County area. Because much of the water problem stems directly from the dams constructed by the federal government along the Rio Grande River, which is an international boundary line in this area, it would seem that there is a federal responsibility to seek a solution or to formulate a comprehensive relocation plan for any people who might voluntarily wish to leave but cannot afford the expense. In a like vein, the landownership problem stems back to the time that the area was annexed by the United States in the aftermath of the Mexican War of 1846-48. Hence, it would seem that federal legal assistance should be made available to expedite the effort to untangle this legal thicket.

Concluding Observations

The general profile of economic disadvantagement of Chicano rural population is quite similar to that of other racial groups in the South. Yet, with respect to the causative factors, the rural Chicano population is confronted not only with all of the same problems that foster and perpetuate massive impoverishment to others in the rural South but also with a host of additional factors. Thus, although the symptoms of economic illness are similar, correction of the problems endured by rural Chicanos will require policy measures that extend beyond those needed by other groups in the rural South.

AGRICULTURAL WORKERS IN THE RURAL SOUTH

The decline in importance of the agricultural sector as a source of employment in the South has been well documented. The counties surveyed for this work reflect the changing position of agriculture, and analyses of their economies help to highlight the continuing problems of agricultural workers.

Census data for 1950 showed that agricultural occupations accounted for 52 percent of total employment in the four survey counties. By 1970 their share had declined to 13 percent. Data in Table 10.9 reveal that the decline was large in all counties, with Sunflower having by far the greatest numerical decline, although Natchitoches had the largest percentage decline. In Dodge and Sunflower counties, the reduction in agricultural employment resulted from a significant reduction in the total labor force, as well as from reduced jobs in agriculture. In Starr County, it is the inordinately high number of migrant farm workers that keeps the county's labor force the most dependent of all those of the survey counties on agriculture.

In addition to declining agricultural employment there has been a dramatic reduction in the number of farms and in the percentage of agricultural workers who run their own farms. This is particularly evident in Sunflower, Dodge and Natchitoches. Blacks have tended to lose the most, both in terms of employment and farm ownership. At the same time, the average farm size has been increasing.

It would be a mistake to assume that agriculture is no longer important to the rural South. As the four study counties illustrate, agriculture still accounts for an important share of total employment (see Table 10.9). The value of farm output remains substantial and in Natchitoches Parish actually doubled from 1950 to 1970. The number of acres of land in the four counties as a whole used for agricultural purposes increased from 1950 to 1970 in spite of the tremendous employment declines in agriculture.

Although the changes in agriculture have been significant in the past several decades, agricultural workers still find themselves in an economically disadvantageous position relative to the average

TABLE 10.9

Agricultural Employment for Four Survey Counties, 1950 and 1970

	Number, 1950	Percent of Total Employment	Number, 1970	Percent of Total Employment	Percent Change (1950-70)
Dodge	2454	39	488	8	-80
Natchitoches	3984	39	606	6	-84
Starr	1358	43	955	23	-29
Sunflower	10,944	65	1853	18	-83
Total	18,740	52	3902	13	-79

Sources: U.S. Department of Commerce, Bureau of the Census, Census of Population: 1950, General Social and Economic Characteristics, Final Reports PC(1)-C24 Mississippi; PC(1)-C11 Georgia; PC(1)-C20 Louisiana; PC(1)-C45 Texas. U.S. Department of Commerce, Bureau of the Census, Census of Population: 1970, General Social and Economic Characteristics, Final Reports PC(1)-11 Georgia; PC(1)-C20 Louisiana; PC(1)-C24 Mississippi; PC(1)-C45 Texas.

nonagricultural worker. The household survey conducted as part of this study helps to illustrate the nature and dimensions of problems faced by agricultural workers.

Characteristics of Agricultural Workers

Of the survey respondents, 457 persons were in agricultural occupations at the time of the survey. They represented 14 percent of the total labor force. The majority of these workers were located in Sunflower and Starr counties. Figures in Table 10.10 show that agricultural workers were more likely to be men than was true for the entire work force. There also was a tendency for agricultural workers to be older than the average for all workers.

It is significant, as an example of the changes that have occurred in agriculture in the rural South, that only 18.6 percent of the agricultural workers surveyed actually lived on a farm; 80 percent did live outside an incorporated area.

There were 319 household heads (10 percent of the total) employed in agricultural professions in the study sample. An additional 111 household heads did farm work some time during the 12 months prior to the survey date. Table 10.11 contains selected characteristics for household heads who did farm work. The differences in race, sex, and age between household heads who were farm workers and those who were not are similar to those previously discussed for all agricultural workers. From the standpoint of income needs, the large family size of many farm families reflected by the data in Table 10.11 is significant. However, the level of education and training of farm workers indicated by the data is a strong basis for suspecting that the income position of farm workers is inferior relative to that of nonfarm workers. These characteristics are similar to what has been found by previous studies of farm workers.[31]

The characteristics just discussed, when examined carefully, strongly justify the position that farm workers could be expected to have lower income and earnings than nonfarm workers. The results of this study bear out this presumption. Table 10.12 contains income data for households headed by a farm worker and those headed by a nonfarm worker. The distribution of income is obviously skewed in favor of nonfarm workers, with almost 70 percent (67.9) of all farm

TABLE 10.10

Selected Characteristics of Agricultural and All Workers 16 Years of Age and Older
(percent)

	Agricultural Workers	All Workers
Race		
Anglo	33.0	47.0
Chicano	34.6	24.0
Black	32.4	29.0
Sex		
Men	91.7	63.6
Women	8.3	36.4
Age		
16-24	17.9	19.6
25-34	21.0	22.8
35-44	15.8	20.1
45-54	18.2	19.6
55-64	19.9	14.3
65 and over	7.2	3.6
Total number	457	3164

TABLE 10.11

Selected Characteristics of Household Heads
Employed During 1973, by Farm Work and
No Farm Work
(percent)

	Farm Work	No Farm Work
Race		
Anglo	17.7	55.2
Black	38.7	19.1
Chicano	43.5	25.7
Sex		
Men	6.7	17.9
Women	93.3	82.1
Age		
16-24	8.5	7.9
25-34	21.2	20.9
35-44	23.5	20.9
45-54	20.7	23.6
55-64	18.0	19.7
65 and over	8.1	7.0
Family size		
1-2	22.9	37.7
3-4	27.8	37.0
5-6	23.8	17.5
7-8	14.3	5.0
8 or more	11.2	2.8
Years of education		
0-8	74.0	34.9
9-12	20.9	45.4
13 or more	5.1	19.7
Job Training		
Received	9.4	20.2
Did not receive	90.6	79.8
Total number	434	1706

households having incomes below $5000, compared to 31.5 percent of nonfarm households. The average income was $5364 for farm households and $8823 for nonfarm.

A variety of factors, including hourly earnings and weeks worked, help explain these results. The average hourly earnings of household heads employed in agriculture was $2.13, compared with an average of $3.20 for all other occupations. Almost 50 percent (46.4) of the

SPECIAL ISSUES   285

household heads employed in agriculture earned less than $1.60;
another 35 percent earned between $1.60 and $2.00. The comparative
figures for other occupations were 11.7 percent and 12.8 percent,
respectively. Most farm workers whose earnings exceed $5.00 per
hour were among the 13 percent of the total employed in agriculture
who own their farm. In other words, 87 percent did agricultural
work for someone else.

In addition to earning less per hour, agricultural workers had
a high probability of working less during the year than other workers.
Table 10.13 shows the distribution of weeks worked for farm and
nonfarm workers. Obviously, the seasonal nature of farm work had
an adverse affect on the yearly work time of agricultural workers.
Over 40 percent (42.3) worked less than 36 weeks in 1973. Although
many did not seek employment outside agriculture, in spite of the
large amount of lost work time, nearly 50 percent of all agricultural
workers worked at least one week during 1973 in some other type of
job.

Several other factors provide additional insight into the economic
problems of agricultural households. Few (3.9 percent) were able
to supplement their earnings by a second job, although those in other
occupations also had difficulty in this respect (5.6 percent had a

TABLE 10.12

Household Income in 1973 for Farm and
Nonfarm Workers
(percent)

Income (dollars)	Farm	Nonfarm
0-999	6.4	2.2
1000-1999	16.0	6.5
2000-2999	17.6	6.7
3000-3999	19.8	8.7
4000-4999	8.1	7.4
5000-5999	8.3	8.7
6000-6999	5.2	8.0
7000-7999	4.3	6.4
8000-8999	2.4	6.4
9000-9999	2.6	5.8
10,000-14,999	4.8	20.2
15,000-24,999	1.9	10.6
25,000 and over	2.6	2.5
Total number	420	1630

TABLE 10.13

Weeks Worked in 1973 for Farm and
Nonfarm Workers
(percent)

Weeks Worked	Farm	Nonfarm
1-8	7.2	2.6
9-16	9.2	3.3
17-24	9.2	2.8
25-34	17.6	5.6
35-44	9.0	7.1
45-48	9.8	5.9
49-52	38.3	72.7
Total number	430	1704

second job). There also was less likelihood of additional income from spouse's earnings. In only 9.2 percent of the households headed by a farm worker was the spouse employed, compared to 30.4 percent of other households.

In general, the inferior economic position of households headed by an agricultural worker can be explained relatively easily. Unfortunately, the prospects for relative improvement are not bright.

Opportunities for Unionization

One of the specific factors that distinguishes agricultural workers from all other workers is their exclusion from federal protection of the right to bargain collectively. The exclusion has been an obstacle to the establishment of unions for farm workers. Although the issue is applicable to all of the survey counties, it has surfaced only in Starr County, where efforts to establish a union of farm workers have been made on an intermittent basis since the mid-1960s. Each time, the effort has been rebuffed. Often these encounters have been characterized by the use of strikebreakers, intimidation, and violence.[32]

The main reason that agricultural workers were excluded from coverage of the National Labor Relations Act (NLRA) when it was enacted in 1935 was "political expediency and the powerlessness of farmworkers."[33] Such considerations hardly warrant a continuation of this exclusion. Coverage by NLRA will not guarantee that collective bargaining systems are established or will succeed. In fact, Caesar Chavez, head of the United Farm Workers, AFL-CIO, has some serious reservations to a blanket extension of coverage to include farm workers.[34] But there is no question that the current void of federal law has created a situation in which it is difficult for agricultural workers to organize collectively. There is no protection against recrimination for union activity, no way to conduct impartial elections to see whether workers wish to bargain as a group, and no way to protect either employees or employers from unfair labor practices. It is conceivable, of course, that the individual states could pass laws similar to the legislation enacted in California in 1975 to legitimize the voting procedures for bargaining agents in agriculture. But it is unlikely that any state in the South is prepared to pass such legislation. If it is to happen, it must be the federal responsibility to make it a reality.

But even if federal coverage were extended or if a similar state statute were adopted, this does not mean that unionism would come to agricultural workers. Farm workers tend to be dispersed over vast geographical areas. As a result, organizational costs would be high and farm workers' incomes are low. Raising sufficient dues to establish and maintain an effective union would be difficult. Moreover, in South Texas the problem of pools of available strikebreakers remains in the form of illegal aliens, "green carders," and other unemployed indigenous rural workers. The presence of migratory agricultural workers adds to the organizational difficulties.

Prospects for Improvement

Farm workers suffer from lack of education and lack of skills, from a lack of job opportunities, and from low wages. In other words, their major problems generally are the same as those of all workers in the rural South, only more intensive. There have been recommendations that more training is needed in farm related occupations and that increased access of "small farmers" to land ownership is desirable.[35] Certainly, the results of this study are in agreement with such recommendations. However, neither course will prove to be a major avenue for improvement among farm workers. The depressed wages in agriculture, the continuing decline in farm ownership, as well as the 35-percent greater average size of farm families, all indicate that alternatives to agricultural employment are needed. Although the extension of the $2.30 per hour minimum wage, if enforced more rigorously than appears to have been true in the past, will bring some improvement, it will not alone solve the problems. Nor will skill upgrading solve that for agricultural jobs that are not there. In short, although it may be possible to improve the general situation in the agricultural sector or the rural South, there will continue to be an outflow of people from this sector for many years to come. Clearly, the agricultural sector cannot be looked upon as a major area for general improvement in the rural South.

NOTES

1. For example, the U.S. Bureau of the Census revised upwards in 1974 its 1970 estimate of the Mexican-origin population by 40 percent: from 4.5 million persons to 6.3 million persons. The revision represented an estimate of the undercount in the 1970 figures. There was no revision in the state breakdowns, only of the aggregate estimate for the nation. See U.S. Department of Commerce, Bureau of the Census, "Persons of Spanish Origin in the United States: March, 1973," Current Population Reports, series P-20, no. 259 (January 1974).

2. U.S. Department of Labor, "Spanish Speaking Americans: Their Manpower Problems and Opportunities," Manpower Report of the President, 1973 (Washington, D.C.: U.S. Government Printing Office, 1973), p. 97.

3. For example, see Walter Fogel, "The Effects of Low Educational Attainment on Incomes: A Comparative Study of Selected Ethnic Groups," The Journal of Human Resources 1 (Fall 1966): 22–40. Also see Vernon M. Briggs, Jr., Negro Employment in the South: The Houston Labor Market (Washington, D.C.: U.S. Government Printing Office, 1971), Ch. 2, which compares black and Chicano income and employment statistics. The figures for Chicanos were consistently more favorable than those for blacks, despite the fact that the black educational attainment median was three years higher than that of Chicanos.

4. Starr County Migrant Health Project, "Report of the Starr County Migrant Health Project, 1973," Progress Report to the U.S. Department of Health, Education, and Welfare and Texas State Department of Health (Rio Grande City, Tex.: September 1973), p. 18.

5. Vernon M. Briggs, Jr., The Mexico-United States Border: Public Policy and Chicano Economic Welfare (Austin: Bureau of Business Research, University of Texas, 1974).

6. Vernon M. Briggs, Jr., "Mexican Workers in the United States Labor Market: A Contemporary Dilemma," International Labor Review 112 (November 1975): 351-68.

7. Vernon M. Briggs, Jr., Mexican Migration and the United States Labor Market (Austin: Bureau of Business Research, University of Texas, 1975), Ch. 5.

8. Sheldon L. Greene, "Public Agency Distortion of Congressional Will: Federal Policy toward Non-Resident Alien Labor," George Washington Law Review 40 (March 1972): 440-63.

9. David North, The Border Crossers—People Who Live in Mexico and Work in the United States (Washington, D.C.: Trans-Century Corporation, 1970), p. 72.

10. Briggs, The Mexico—United States Border, pp. 16-18.

11. U.S. Congress, Senate, Committee on Labor and Public Welfare, Subcommittee on Migratory Labor, The Migratory Farm Labor Problem in the United States (Washington, D.C.: U.S. Government Printing Office, 1969), pp. 126-27.

12. Community Action Council of South Texas, "Annual Progress Report of Starr County Migrant Health Project," mimeographed (September 30, 1973), p. 1.

13. Texas Employment Commission, "Migrant Crews and Workers by Local Office Area and County of Crew Leader Residence," mimeographed (1973), p. 3.

14. For example, see Senate Subcommittee on Migratory Labor, "The Migratory Farm Labor Problem"; Vernon M. Briggs, Jr., Chicanos and Rural Poverty (Baltimore: The Johns Hopkins University Press, 1973); Paul Sultan and Enos Darryl, Farming and Farm Labor: A Study in California (Claremont, Calif.: Center for Urban and Regional Studies, 1974).

15. Briggs, Mexican Migration and the United States Labor Market.

16. Statement by Senator Walter F. Mondale in U.S. Congress, Senate Committee on Labor and Public Welfare, Subcommittee on Migratory Labor, "Manpower and Economic Problems," Hearings on Migrant and Seasonal Farmworkers Powerlessness, pt. 7-B (Washington, D.C.: U.S. Government Printing Office, 1970), p. 4548.

17. David S. North and William G. Weissert, Immigrants and the American Labor Market, monograph no. 31 (Washington, D.C.: U.S. Department of Labor, 1974), pp. 17-18.

18. David S. North and William G. Weissert, Immigrants and the American Labor Market (Washington, D.C.: Trans-Century Corporation, 1973), pp. 47-48.

19. Briggs, Mexican Migration and the United States Labor Market, Chs. 3, 4.

20. Lawrence Meyer, "Aliens Hard to Count," Washington Post, February 2, 1975, pp. A-1, A-12.

21. Julia Samora, Los Mojados: The Wetback Story (Notre Dame, Ind.: Notre Dame Press, 1971), Ch. 2.

22. See James Webb et al., The Citrus Labor Market of the Lower Rio Grande Valley of Texas: A Study of Labor Utilization Problems (Austin: Center for Study of Human Resources, 1975).

23. Diaz v. Kay-Dix Ranch (1970), as reprinted in U.S. Congress, House, Hearings on Illegal Aliens, pt. 1 (Washington, D.C.: U.S. Government Printing Office, June 21, 1971), p. 179.

24. Briggs, The Mexico-United States Border, pp. 10-21.

25. ABT Associates, An Assessment of the Experimental and Demonstration Interstate Program for South Texas Migrants: Final Report (Cambridge, Mass.: ABT Associates, 1971).

26. Texas Good Neighbor Commission, Texas Migrant Labor: Annual Report 1972 (Austin: The Commission, 1973), pp. 6-14, 6-15.

27. See, for example, U.S. Department of Labor, Manpower Administration, "A Piece of Action," Manpower, September 1971, pp. 10-13. This is a printed dialogue between four Spanish-speaking Americans who discuss the manpower needs of their people.

28. For a more complete discussion of the issue of cultural distinctiveness of Chicanos and its relationship to manpower programs, see Vernon M. Briggs, Jr., "Implications and Noninstitutional Considerations upon the Effectiveness of Manpower Programs for Chicanos" (Austin: Center for the Study of Human Resources, 1973).

29. Paul Bullock, "Employment Problems of the Mexican-Americans," in Mexican Americans in the United States, ed. John Burma (Cambridge, Mass.: Schenkman, 1970), p. 149.

30. Texas Good Neighbor Commission, Texas Migrant Labor: Annual Report 1973 (Austin: The Commission, 1974), p. 20.

31. See, for example, C. E. Bishop, Farm Labor in the United States (New York: Columbia University Press, 1967); Ray Marshall, Rural Workers in Rural Labor Markets (Salt Lake City, Utah: Olympus, 1974).

32. For example, see the discussion in the U.S. Supreme Court decision, A. Y. Allee et al. v. Francisco Medrano et al., 42 L.W. 4736 (1974).

33. Ray Marshall, Policy and Program Issues in Rural Manpower Development (Austin: Center for the Study of Human Resources, 1973), p. 54.

34. Briggs, Chicanos and Rural Poverty, p. 57.

35. Marshall, Rural Labor Markets.

CHAPTER 11

WELFARE REFORM IN THE RURAL SOUTH: A SPECULATIVE VIEW

In the early 1970s, after a long series of welfare-related proposals extending back into the mid-1960s, a comprehensive reform of the nation's welfare system appeared imminent.[1] Indeed, several significant portions of the proposed welfare reform package were ultimately enacted. For example, a uniform federal income guarantee for the aged, blind, and disabled became effective January 1, 1974. The program, SSI, represents the first national cash-income guarantee program.

SSI was one portion of an omnibus piece of legislation that was officially known as the "Social Security Amendments of 1971" or, more commonly, as "H.R. 1" of the 92d Congress. H.R. 1 passed the House of Representatives on June 22, 1971. President Nixon stated that he supported the bill in the form that it passed the House. In the Senate, however, the bill became involved in a protracted series of political maneuvers in which some forces sought to liberalize its provisions, some sought to restrict its provisions, and some sought to kill it in its entirety. The most controversial portion of H.R. 1 was the section that would have replaced the federal-state supported program, AFDC. This portion of H.R. 1, known as Title IV, would have established a federally guaranteed system of uniform benefits for poor families. It would have replaced the prevailing quilt-work pattern of contradictory eligibility and unequal benefits that existed among the 54 different political jurisdictions responsible for welfare administration in the nation. It would have based eligibility solely on the need for income. The working poor—working fathers and nonwelfare mothers—would have been included in coverage. In many states, unemployed fathers also would have been eligible for the first time for a cash supplement to support their families.

The details of the fight for Title IV of H.R. 1 are discussed elsewhere.2 The upshot of the legislative debate was that Title IV was deleted by the Senate from the final version of H.R. 1 that was ultimately signed into law on October 17, 1972. As the South in general and the rural South in particular would have been among the chief beneficiaries of this extensive welfare reform effort, it is appropriate to speculate briefly on the impact that Title IV would have had in the four counties that were intensely surveyed during this study. Such speculation is even more interesting given the social injustice and administrative inadequacies of the welfare system detailed earlier in Chapter 6.

RELEVANT SECTIONS OF H.R. 1

Under terms of Title IV of H.R. 1 as it passed the House of Representatives in 1972, the bill would have abolished federal aid for state welfare payments and also food-stamp eligibility for cash recipients. In their place, a federal income floor that would provide uniform cash payments was to be established on a nationwide basis.

Eligible low-income families would have been divided into two groups: those with an employable adult (including families in which the father was working full time for low wages) and those without an employable adult. Those with an employable adult would have been enrolled in a program called Opportunities for Families (OFF); the remaining families would have been enrolled in the Family Assistance Plan (FAP). Exact rules were set to determine who would enroll in which program. In 1973 it was estimated that 2.6 million families would be enrolled in OFF, and 1.4 million families in FAP.3

Putting aside the lengthy technical issues involved in classifying eligibility, it is useful to focus on the provisions of these programs. For those families enrolled in OFF, provisions were made for child care and the use of supportive services to enhance the prospects for adult employability. Among the extensive list of supportive services to be provided were to be counselling, testing, coaching, job orientation, classroom occupational instruction, OJT, job development, job placement, work experience, skill upgrading, relocation assistance, and follow-up services to those people placed in jobs. Special efforts were to have been made to place enrollees into jobs in the private sector. But if such placement efforts were unsuccessful, a public-service employment program was to have been created to provide socially useful work at a wage level at least equal to the prevailing federal minimum wage.

Under OFF and FAP a guaranteed income floor would have been established. Each family with children under 18 (or 22 if regularly attending school) would have been eligible for coverage if its income was below a set minimum. Each eligible family could have received annually as much as $800 for each of the first two members of the family; $400 for each of the next three members; $300 for each of the next two members; and $200 for the next one member. A family of four, therefore, would have been eligible for a maximum benefit of $2400. The highest minimum benefit (for a family of eight or larger) would have been $3600.

The novelty of the OFF program was that it did provide some incentive for working. The first $720 a year of earned income would not result in a reduced support level (that is, the offset) as this sum was assumed to be associated with the cost of working (transportation, lunches, clothes, and tools). Of any additional income earned, the family would retain one-third, while two-thirds would be used to offset benefits. Thus, a family would always be better off if an adult member was working. For example, a family of four in which no one worked would receive $2400; if the adult earned $720 a year, the family's income would be $3120; if the earnings were $1680 a year, the family would receive $3440; and the family would continue to receive a wage supplement until its income exceeded $4140. For the family of eight (the maximum size for which payments would be made), the wage supplement would continue up to a level of $5940.*

ESTIMATED IMPACT OF H.R. 1
ON THE SOUTH

By all estimates, the passage of H.R. 1 would have represented a major transfer of income from the non-South to the South.[4] The reform would have been felt in terms of the aggregate amount of dollars, the number of individuals eligible for benefits, the increase in the level of benefits available to eligible families, and the specific subgroups of the Southern population who would have been affected the most.

Using the U.S. Census definition of the South, Table 11.1 indicates the estimates of coverage for H.R. 1 for the Southern region. Among other things, it shows that the gross transfer of funds to the South for FY 1973 would have been $2.3 billion. In terms of total people covered, 45.5 percent of all eligible persons would

---

*The computation of the benefits is done by reducing total earnings by the size of the "disregard" (that is, $720) and then applying two-thirds of the remainder to reduce the assistance payment for the specified family size. No payment would be made of less than $120 a year (or $10 a month).

TABLE 11.1

Estimates of Coverage of H.R. 1 in the South, FY 1973

1. Number of eligible families in the South	1,625,000
Percentage of covered families in the South relative to all covered families in the nation	42.6
2. Gross payment to families in the South	$2,346,000,000
Percentage of gross payment to families in the South relative to all payments in the nation	40.4
3. Total number of persons in covered families in the South	8,114,000
Percentage of covered persons in the South relative to total number of covered persons in the nation	45.5
4. Average payment per family in the South to eligible families	$1,455
5. Average family size in the South for eligible families	4.99 persons

Source: U.S. Congress, "Social Security Amendments of 1971," Report of the Committee on Ways and Means on H.R. 1, 92d Cong., 1st sess. (Washington, D.C.: U.S. Government Printing Office, 1971), p. 229.

have been Southerners. Had H.R. 1 passed, the estimated increase in the number of persons covered over those presently receiving AFDC would have exceeded 140 percent. Moreover, the effect within some of the separate states that compose the South would have been even more startling. The number eligible under prevailing law would have more than doubled in Georgia, Mississippi, South Carolina, Tennessee, Texas, and Virginia and more than tripled in North Carolina and Arkansas. As for payment levels, Table 11.1 shows that average payment to the 1.6 million eligible families in the South would have been $1455. With the exceptions of Virginia and the District of Columbia, all of the remaining 15 southern states would have had a higher absolute benefit level for a family of four with no income under H.R. 1 than the level of benefits in existence at the time under prevailing AFDC programs.[5] With respect to the effect on subgroups, Table 11.2 shows that 22.1 percent of all the eligible families for H.R. 1 coverage in the South would have been headed by a black man (or 39.5 percent of all male-headed eligible families in the South. Table 11.2 also shows that 25.6 percent of all eligible families in the South would have been headed by a black woman (or 58 percent of all eligible female-headed families in the South). In total, 47.7 percent of the families eligible for H.R. 1 coverage would have been black families. Drawing upon the total number of families in the South as reported in the 1970 Census (see Table 11.3), it is possible to approximate the impact that H.R. 1 would have had on the total number of black and white families in the South. Combining the information presented in Tables 11.2 and 11.3, therefore, it can be estimated that 4 percent of white male-headed families would have received some income supplementation, whereas 16.6 percent of all black male-headed families would have been eligible. Of all

TABLE 11.2

Estimates of Racial and Sex Characteristics of Family Heads in the South Eligible for Coverage under H.R. 1, FY 1973

	Number	Percent
Total number of eligible families in the South	1,625,000	100.0
Number of white male-headed families	549,000	33.8
Number of nonwhite male-headed families	359,000	22.1
Subtotal for males	908,000	55.9
Number of white female-headed families	301,000	18.5
Number of nonwhite female-headed families	416,000	25.6
Subtotal for females	717,000	44.1

Source: U.S. Congress, "Social Security Amendments of 1971," Report of the Committee on Ways and Means on H.R. 1, 92d Cong., 1st sess. (Washington, D.C.: Government Printing Office, 1971), p. 229.

TABLE 11.3

Total Number of Families in the South, 1970

	Number	Percent
Total number of families in the South	15,907,699	100.0
Number of white male-headed families	12,155,689	76.4
Number of nonwhite male-headed families	1,905,151	12.0
Subtotal for males	14,060,840	88.4
Number of white female-headed families	1,180,157	7.4
Number of nonwhite female-headed families	666,702	4.2
Subtotal for females	1,846,859	11.6

Source: U.S. Department of Commerce, Bureau of the Census, United States Census of Population: 1970, General Social and Economic Characteristics, Final Report PC(1)-C, United States Summary, pp. 1-449.

white female-headed households, 27.2 percent would have been eligible for income supplementation; 66.7 percent of all black female-headed households would have been eligible for such assistance. It is to be recalled that H.R. 1 did not apply to households in which there was not at least one child under 18 years of age (or 22 if regularly attending school). Hence, if allowance is made for childless families and for families in which children have grown past the school-age years, the impact percentages of H.R. 1 upon only those families with children would have been considerably higher than those presented in this paragraph.

The effect of a federal program like H.R. 1 on a region in which approximately one-half of the nation's total number of impoverished families reside could be expected to be substantial. The economic effect, however, is much greater than simply the increase in the incomes of the recipient families in the South. Because the level of Southern income is substantially below the levels of the non-South regions of the nation, the federal taxes used to finance the program would be disproportionately raised from taxpayers outside of the South. Thus, one study concluded that H.R. 1 "should have a multiplier effect, thereby increasing both aggregate southern income and the incomes of even those southern residents who do not receive direct payments. . . ."[6] This study estimated that slightly over

$4 billion would have been pumped into the South if the bill had been enacted. Of this sum, it was estimated that about $768 million of this increase would have been paid by Southern taxpayers in the form of higher taxes. Accordingly, the net additional interregional transfer of funds would have been $1.3 billion to the South. Using an estimate of the regional multiplier of 2.5 (a figure computed from a study of the impact of defense expenditures in the South), the study concluded that H.R. 1 would have increased Southern regional income by $3.4 billion during its first year.[7] The initial impact in rural areas of the South—where incomes are the lowest—would have been considerably higher, since this is where the infusion of funds would have been the greatest. It also is possible that the multiplier effect would be higher in rural areas, because the propensity to save at such low levels of income should be much lower than at the higher levels of income in urban areas. However, the nature of the rural economy is such that considerable leakage of funds would occur, making the actual multiplier effect difficult to estimate.

Mention also should be made of the fact that the federalization of AFDC would have freed millions of dollars of local and state tax dollars for other public uses.

PRIMARY IMPACT IN SAMPLE COUNTIES

Analysis of primary survey data reveals that the potential impact in the rural South should be greater than that in the total South.[8] The percentage of Anglo households in the sample affected by H.R. 1 is 5 percent, approximately the same as for the entire South. The percentage of non-Anglo households that would have been eligible is almost 33 percent, several percentage points greater than that for the total South. There also is a difference in the average payment that would have been made. For eligible families the average payment under H.R. 1 in the rural South would have been $1525 (as estimated by this study), compared with $1455 for the entire South (see Table 11.1).

As the sample data indicate, the effect of H.R. 1 would not have been evenly distributed among the various components of the population in the rural South (see Table 11.4). Not only is the percentage of total families affected greater for non-Anglos than for Anglos, but the number of non-Anglo families eligible for family assistance exceeds the number of Anglo families in absolute terms. The differences in the number of eligible families by race, in conjunction with the general differences in racial composition of the four sample counties, account for the variation in numbers of eligible families across counties.

TABLE 11.4

Potential Impact of H.R. 1 on Various
Population Groups in the Four
Sample Counties

Population Characteristic	Percent of Sample Families Affected	Percent of Eligible Families
Sex of head		
Male	19.0	69.9
Female	22.2	30.1
Race		
Anglo	5.1	11.6
Black	32.4	49.0
Chicano	32.5	39.4
County of residence		
Dodge	9.7	12.4
Natchitoches	15.2	19.8
Sunflower	23.2	28.4
Starr	32.1	39.4
Number of families	3158	628

One of the major provisions of family assistance involved the inclusion of male-headed families, which in 1973 were not eligible for any cash-assistance programs. The importance of this is seen by the fact that 60 percent of the sample families eligible under family assistance received no cash benefits from any program in 1973. Over 90 percent of the female-headed families received AFDC payments during that year (see Table 11.5). Thus, most of the eligible families who received no benefits in 1973 were headed by a man.

Although the absolute number of eligible families headed by a male is substantially greater than the number of female-headed families, in terms of the relative proportions the eligibility is greater among families with a female head—19 percent, compared with 22.2 percent. Since a major provision of welfare reform was to replace AFDC, such a result is not unexpected. In fact, the relative percentages are closer than anticipated. The results are significantly affected by the inclusion in the sample of a relatively large Chicano population with comparatively few female-headed households.

The mean age of potential recipient family heads under welfare reform was 44 years and did not vary significantly by race or sex. The mean is higher than would be expected a priori, but the findings regarding AFDC in Chapter 6, and discussed at that point, are consistent with this result. The most surprising finding regarding age was that in 13.4 percent of the cases the family heads were between 55 and 64 years of age, and in 10.7 percent they were 65 years of age or older. The latter fact is particularly relevant because of the prohibition against receiving both SSI and family assistance and because Social Security payments are treated as income subject to 100 percent tax. This could have a significant effect on the decision to participate under family assistance.

Another characteristic that is important in determining the extent and nature of the impact of family assistance is family size. The average family size for the eligible population was 5.2 persons. The difference between male- and female-headed families was one person (5.6 versus 4.5), indicating that the number of children was basically the same regardless of sex of head. The average family size was 4.2 persons for Anglos and 5.3 for non-Anglos, indicating that in absolute terms the impact of family assistance should be greatest on non-Anglo families, other things being equal.

Employment and Income of Eligible Families

If family assistance had been introduced, there should have been a substantial impact on the working poor. Eligible families represent approximately half of all poor families in the primary sample, but they include 80 percent of the working poor. At the time of the survey, over half (56.9 percent) of the families eligible for family assistance were employed.

More importantly, from the standpoint of potential impact, 72.6 percent of the heads of eligible families worked sometime during 1973; more than 30 percent worked over 40 weeks. Table 11.6 contains data showing weeks worked in 1973 by current employment status. With over 50 percent of the family heads employed more than half

TABLE 11.5

1973 Income for Eligible Families, Selected Sources

Income Source	Percent of Families Receiving
OAA	5.7
ABD	5.6
AFDC	28.7
Social Security	15.3
Current earnings	73.1

TABLE 11.6

Weeks Worked in 1973: Eligible Families, by
Current Employment Status of Household Head
(percent)

Weeks Worked	Total	Current Employment Status		
		Employed	Unemployed	Out of Labor Force
0	27.4	.6	13.2	75.0
1–8	5.6	1.6	16.9	9.2
9–16	6.4	5.8	11.3	6.0
17–24	7.0	8.9	9.4	3.2
25–32	12.6	16.8	24.5	2.8
33–40	9.4	12.6	18.9	1.8
41–48	6.4	9.8	3.7	1.0
49–52	25.2	43.9	2.1	1.0
Number of families	627	357	53	217

the year and with 61.7 percent of the eligible families receiving over three-quarters of their yearly income from earnings, it is reasonable to assume that the number of working poor families affected would have been significant.

Two sources of income, OAA and AB or APTD (now combined into the SSI program), could present a problem for some families eligible under family assistance. Under H.R. 1, no family could receive benefits from family assistance and from another program, such as OAA, at the same time. Thus, for 11 percent of the eligible families, a choice would have to be made. Based on a comparison of 1973 income with the estimated income under family assistance, 34 percent (24) of the families receiving OAA or ABD would be worse off, in terms of total income, under the provisions of H.R. 1. However, most of the families that would have their income reduced were receiving payments under AFDC as well as from OAA or ABD. If it is assumed there is no AFDC income (as would have been true under H.R. 1), only 13 percent of the families receiving OAA or ABD would lose under H.R. 1, and in all cases the loss would be marginal (less than $100 a year).

A similar problem is encountered by eligible families who received Social Security payments in 1973. Almost a third of the eligible families who received Social Security payments would have had a net income loss, assuming they had participated in the family-assistance program. All but 2 of these 30 families received payments in 1973 not only from Social Security but also from AFDC, OAA, or ABD, or some combination of the three. Of the families involved, 19 received AFDC payments, 17 received payments under OAA or ABD, and 8 received payments under more than one of the programs.

In all cases where AFDC was involved, the amount of AFDC payment exceeded the difference between H.R. 1 income and actual 1973 income, making it reasonable to assume that these families would participate in family assistance. In the remaining cases, however, the combination of Social Security, OAA, or ABD, and other income sources would have left families in a superior position if they did not participate in the family-assistance program. The fact that such a large proportion of eligibles receiving Social Security or assistance under a categorical program would actually have been hurt by the introduction of H.R. 1 intimates that this was an area that was carefully investigated, perhaps because it was assumed that few families with a head over 65 years of age would qualify. (Over 70 percent of the families receiving Social Security Income did so under the retirement provisions.)

Income Effect of Welfare Reform

The mean 1973 income reported by families that would have been eligible under family assistance was $2776 (see Table 11.7). The income differences revealed in Table 11.7 by race, sex, and employment status are basically what would be expected based on the analysis in Chapter 4.

Under family assistance, the average family income would have increased by 35 percent ($980) over the 1973 level. As the data in Table 11.7 show, black families would have received the largest average increase and the Anglo families the smallest. Surprisingly, the increase in dollar terms for male-headed households would have exceeded that for female-headed households, although in percentage terms the two were identical. The difference in dollar terms may be a reflection of the difference in family size.

A similar conclusion relating to family size also may be reached regarding differences in H.R. 1 total income between those families in which the head was in the labor force and those in which the head was not in the labor force at the time of the survey. The mean family size for the former group of families was 5.4, while that for the latter was 4.8. The difference in income also may reflect the work incentive built into the benefit structure.

Not all families eligible for payments under H.R. 1 would have benefited from the family-assistance program. In all 77 families, 12.3 percent of those eligible would have lost income with the intro-

TABLE 11.7

Mean Income of Eligible Families, by Selected
Characteristics, 1973 Income and H.R. 1 Income
(dollars)

Family Characteristics	H.R. 1 Mean Income	1973 Mean Income
Total Eligible	3759	2776
Sex of family head		
Male	4051	2992
Female	3074	2275
Race		
Anglo	3590	2941
Black	4006	2628
Chicano	3600	2911
Labor force status		
Employed	4207	3084
Unemployed	3741	2492
Out of labor force	3025	2341

duction of welfare reform. Of those who would have lost income, 70 percent were families discussed in the previous section. In all cases the families were receiving assistance under a categorical welfare program in 1973 or were receiving Social Security. Many cases involved supplemental earnings raising the distinct possibility that the 100-percent tax on Social Security or the prohibition on receiving payment under a program other than family assistance was the reason for the negative effects of family assistance.

The average income that would have been received under FAP does not reveal the actual amount of payment. In fact, the mean payment of $1525 would be considerably greater than the average increase in income of $980. As would be expected with AFDC being replaced totally, the mean payment would be greater to families headed by a woman ($1809) than to those headed by a man ($1402). There would be substantial differences in payments by race (for Anglos $1202, for blacks $1652, for Chicanos $1460). However, the percentage difference in payment would have been substantially less than the relative impact on total income (see Table 11.7). The mean payment in fact would have been greater if some families adversely affected had opted not to participate.

WELFARE REFORM

IMPACT ON ENTIRE RURAL SOUTH

An estimate of the direct impact that family assistance would have on the entire rural South may be obtained by using a combination of Census data for total families and sample data for income effects. (It is necessary to assume that the number of families in the rural South in 1973 was the same as in 1970 and that the racial distribution of families was the same as that of the total population.) Table 11.8 contains data pertaining to the number of families in the rural South as well as the number affected by H.R. 1. The proportion of total families eligible under H.R. 1 is almost identical to the previous estimates of the proportion of all families in the affected South.

Using data in Table 11.8 and the figures in Table 11.7 relating to income of eligibles, an estimate of total impact in dollar terms can be obtained. The figure derived for the first year of program operation, assuming all eligible families participated, is $900,198,350, with over two-thirds of the amount going to non-Anglo families. Given the existing income structure in the rural South, it is reasonable to assume that this could result in limited income redistribution. Although no comparable data are available for urban areas of the South, it is reasonable to assume that some redistribution of income from urban to rural areas would have occurred.[9]

Multiplier Effects

It is not unreasonable to assume that the inflow of family-assistance income would have resulted in the generation of additional income through a multiplier effect. The exact amount of this secondary income is impossible to obtain. First, no accurate estimate of a multiplier for the rural South exists. Second, the extent of the total impact depends on what portion of the increased income to the

TABLE 11.8

Total Number of Families and Total Number of Eligible Families in the Rural South, 1973

Characteristic	Total	Eligible
Anglo	4,593,445	229,672
Black	1,004,281	325,387
Chicano	108,417	35,235
Total	5,706,143	590,294

rural South is paid for by taxes on residents of the rural South. It is possible to estimate both figures. One multiplier, derived to determine the impact of defense expenditures, concluded that $2.50 is generated for each additional dollar of income brought into the South.[10] A separate study placed the proportion of family-assistance expenditures in the South paid for by taxes on personal and business incomes in the South at 38.4 percent.[11]

If the figures discussed above are applied to the figures derived in this study for the rural South, the estimated dollar amount of new income is $554,522,183. Applying a multiplier value of 2.5, the total amount of income generated in the rural South by family assistance would be $1.38 billion.

Normally, it is assumed that in general the lower the mean per capita income level, the higher the ultimate multiplier value. On this basis it would be concluded that a multiplier for the rural South should be higher than the one estimated for the South as a whole. Such a conclusion does not consider how much of the increased consumption will take place in the area itself or what proportion of the goods consumed are produced outside of the rural South relative to the total South. Although no good estimates are available, it is probable that the two factors mentioned above will reduce the value of the multiplier relative to the total South and, therefore, reduce the total impact previously derived. Informal estimates place the multiplier for rural areas close to one.

Effects of Family Assistance on Work Incentives

In addition to the income effects of welfare reform discussed in the preceding section, there are other areas where the potential impact is significant. One such area is work incentives. Analysis in this study, based on the cross-sectional data, provides little insight into the work-incentive question. Although previous evidence is scant, the consensus supports the conclusions that persons in low-income families desire to work as much as do other income groups and that welfare reform of the type proposed in H.R. 1 will not have a major effect on labor force participation or on hours worked.[12]

In the rural South several factors could significantly influence work incentives, all resulting in decreased work effort. First, for many women workers with a family to support, the welfare levels have never been sufficient in the rural South to challenge even the low wages paid to domestic servants—as low as $30 a week. Family assistance would change that, and, given the alternative, some labor force withdrawal could be expected.

A second factor to consider is the case of adjustment in work time for many rural workers. As Table 11.6 revealed, almost 50 percent of the eligible family heads worked at some time, but less than 40 weeks, during 1973. This makes the adjustment of earnings to meet built-in disincentives relatively easy without running afoul of work provisions such as those in H.R. 1.

A third factor to consider, particularly for many farm workers and migrant farm workers, is the low income level they currently receive and the unpleasantness of their work environment. These factors could well persuade such workers to withdraw from the labor force and be satisfied with income received under family assistance.

WELFARE REFORM AND FOOD STAMPS

One factor that has not been included in the analysis to this point is the effect of food stamps on participation or on the actual increase in real income received under H.R. 1. FAP as proposed would have prohibited participants from receiving food stamps. It is unlikely that the prohibition would have altered the participation in family assistance, but it would have had a significant effect on the real benefits of the program.

If it is assumed that all persons in the family-assistance subsample purchased the full allotment of food stamps to which they were entitled, and did so every month during 1973, then 64 percent of the subsample (400) would have experienced a decline in income under family assistance. (All 628 persons in the H.R. 1 subsample were eligible to receive food stamps.) The average amount of income loss is estimated to be between $350 and $400.

Several qualifications must be considered before any conclusions can be reached. First, only 65 percent of the subsample actually received food stamps during 1973. It is unlikely that participation would ever be 100 percent (see Chapter 7 for a discussion of the reasons for such a conclusion). Second, all households did not receive food stamps every month during the year. Some were not eligible all 12 months; others may have chosen not to purchase stamps in some months. Finally, many households do not purchase the full allotment of stamps each month.

All three factors mentioned support the conclusion that the impact of food stamps on income is less than the estimate stated above. However, even when such qualifications are considered, it is apparent that the provision that would eliminate families receiving payments under family assistance from participation in the food-stamp program would substantially reduce the effect of a family-assistance-type program on the individual families and on the entire rural South.

CONCLUDING OBSERVATIONS

A few general observations can be derived from the discussion of welfare reform in the rural South. First, although a substantial number of Anglo families would be affected, the impact in relative and absolute terms would be greatest on low-income minority families. This could have an effect on the political as well as on the economic structure of the rural South. In fact, the limited economic freedom provided low-income families under welfare reform could, in the long run, have a major impact on local politics. The extent and nature are, of course, purely speculative.

Although family assistance would alter the dimensions of poverty in the rural South, it would by no means eliminate it. In fact, only a small percentage of the eligible families would be above the poverty level after welfare reform. Further, a substantial proportion of poor families would be unaffected. Given the problems of the rural South's economy, discussed in Chapters 7 and 8, it is unlikely that it would be possible to devise a welfare-reform program, politically or economically, that would substantially reduce the total number in poverty.

Finally, considerable discussion was generated by H.R. 1 concerning the impact on Southern migration patterns. It is impossible, of course, to calculate the actual impact of welfare reform on migration. However, it is possible to use logical inference to discuss the likely effect. In the case of the rural South, it should be small. In general, out-migration occurs among younger population groups, those least likely to be affected by welfare reform. To the extent that the "pull" to migrate is employment-oriented, family assistance, even with the associated multiplier effect, is likely to have minor impact at best.

As often mentioned, though seldom written, one potential impact of welfare reform is the return to the South of previous out-migrants, who because they exist on welfare elsewhere, could have a higher real income in the South and under such conditions would return. The magnitude of this, if true, is impossible to determine. Regardless of the extent, given the present manpower and development problems of the rural South, such a result could hardly be considered advantageous, either to the rural South or to the nation.

NOTES

1. For a review of the rationale and history of the events leading to the emerging of the welfare legislation of the 1970s, see Daniel P. Moynihan, The Politics of Guaranteed Income (New York: Vintage

Books, 1973); Vincent J. Burke and Vee Burke, Nixon's Good Deed: Welfare Reform (New York: Columbia University Press, 1974).

2. Ibid.

3. U.S., Congress, "Social Security Amendments of 1971," Report of the Committee on Ways and Means on H.R. 1, 92d Cong., 1st sess. (Washington, D.C.: U.S. Government Printing Office, 1971), p. 229.

4. For example, see Richard Armstrong, "The Looming Money Revolution down South," Fortune, June 1970, pp. 66-69, 151-58.

5. U.S. Congress, "Social Security Amendments of 1971," p. 174. Because of the reliance upon secondary information sources, it is necessary to use the racial references of black and white in this chapter. This means that when "white" is used, the Chicano figures are included in that term.

6. John F. Kain and Robert Schafer, Regional Impacts of the Family Assistance Plan, discussion paper no. 195 (Cambridge, Mass.: Harvard Institute of Economic Research, 1971), p. 28.

7. Ibid., pp. 33-35. The estimates in this study understate the financial impact as they were based on a formulation in which a family of four would receive $1600, whereas H.R. 1 provided $2400 for such a family.

8. The estimated number of families eligible for H.R. 1 in this study sample probably has a conservative bias. First, asset information was not sufficiently detailed to allow calculation of the $1500 cutoff. Therefore, all families with property, other than that on which they lived, and all families with financial assets other than demand deposits were considered ineligible. Second, certain income exclusions, such as earnings of students regularly attending school, could not be removed from total family earnings. In all cases in which it was necessary to make an estimate for eligibility calculations, the decision was made to use the method which was not restrictive in terms of eligibility. Calculations were made according to U.S. Congress, "Social Security Amendments of 1971," pp. 30-33.

9. Comparison of sample results with impact estimates for the total South supports this hypothesis; see Kain and Schafer, Regional Impacts.

10. Roger Dalton, Defense Purchases and Regional Growth (Washington, D.C.: The Brookings Institution, 1966).

11. Kain and Schafer, Regional Impacts. The percentage was derived using figures relating to the South's share of family assistance and the portion of total U.S. corporate and personal income taxes paid by the South.

12. For a discussion of the effects of welfare payments on work incentive, see Christopher Green, Negative Taxes and the Poverty Problems (Washington, D.C.: The Brookings Institution, 1967),

Ch. 8; Leonard Goodwin, Do the Poor Want to Work? (Washington, D.C.: The Brookings Institution, 1972); Leonard Haussman, "The Impact of Welfare on the Work Effort of AFDC Mothers," in President's Commission on Income Maintenance Programs: Technical Studies (Washington, D.C.: U.S. Government Printing Office, 1972), pp. 83-100; Edward Kalachek and Frederick Raines, "Labor Supply of Low Income Workers," in President's Commission on Income Maintenance Program: Technical Studies (Washington, D.C.: U.S. Government Printing Office, 1970), pp. 159-86 (this study finds a very large disincentive effect); Glen Cain and Harold Watts, eds., Income Maintenance and Labor Supply (New York: Academic Press, 1973); Sar Levitan, Martin Rein, and David Marwick, Work and Welfare Go Together (Baltimore: The Johns Hopkins University Press, 1972).

CHAPTER

12

CONCLUSIONS AND POLICY IMPLICATIONS

The preceding chapters have described the seriousness of the prevailing employment and income conditions in the rural South. Despite the contemporary publicity given to the economic boom in "the new South," the fact remains that the popularly discussed phenomenon is occurring largely in urban areas or in rural counties that are adjacent to expanding urban markets. The rural South remains, with certain exceptions, relatively untouched by this economic development.

The findings of this work indicate that areas of the rural South remain economically depressed. There is little likelihood of their being able independently to provide the volume of employment needed to provide "adequate" incomes. In general, from the findings of this work the economy of the rural South can be characterized as one with an excess of labor, deficient in human-resource development, hindered in its operation by institutional constraints, and encompassing a relatively narrow variety of job opportunities. Although not all local labor markets are the same or have identical problems, in general the differences between labor markets in the rural South are more of degree than of structure of operation.

The possibility that the major exodus of population from the South has abated, coupled with the increasing financial difficulties of large urban areas in the North, may well divert attention from the problems of the rural South. There may even be a tendency to believe that the problems of cities are no longer accentuated by the inflow of rural migrants and that, if left alone, the population of the rural South will "adjust." The findings of this work portend that such is not the case. Out-migration from the rural South, probably at a reduced level, will continue. Although an increasing proportion of those who leave the rural South will migrate to the expanding urban areas of the South, nevertheless a significant portion will follow the traditional migration patterns to the North. Those who leave in the future are likely to be as unprepared as has been the case in the past. Nor are most areas of the rural South likely to be able (unaided) to solve the problems of the remaining population.

In stressing the magnitude of these problems, the goal is to stimulate concern rather than to generate hopelessness. The interrelationships of many of the social and economic problems of both rural and urban United States in the twentieth century have been well documented elsewhere. In the past, urban areas have actively sought the exodus of surplus rural workers to meet expanding urban labor market shortages of unskilled workers. The rural South, in turn, was often glad to be rid of the excess labor supply from its declining agricultural sector. The short-run advantages, however, have given way to the long-run realities. The urban areas of the North and South could not indefinitely absorb the flow of relatively unskilled and poorly educated workers (as well as their dependents) from the rural South. Not only has technological change drastically reduced the demand for such workers, but the availability of housing, health, welfare, and education funds and facilities that are needed to accommodate these persons has largely evaporated. In the same context, if the rural South is ever to reverse its secular decline, it can ill-afford indefinitely to lose its young, ambitious workers. Nor can it increasingly accumulate a large dependent population of old and infirm persons. Therefore, both the urban and the rural United States should have a common interest in solutions to the problems of the rural South.

In this quest for answers, this study focused upon the operations of the Southern rural labor markets in terms of the opportunities they provide and the income they generate: what they do and, equally important, what they cannot do.

The primary function of labor markets, whether in the rural South or elsewhere, is to provide employment for the available supply of labor within the confines of the existing industrial structure and human capital endowment of the workforce. Ideally, the labor market, through employment, will provide workers with adequate income to maintain a humanely tolerable living standard. Over the long run, the labor market must also adjust to structural changes that alter the skill requirements of the workforce. In so doing, it should provide the necessary incentives to encourage skill development in the young. Through this method, short-run occupational imbalances are overcome and the average earning capacities of workers are increased. As more skilled workers emerge, the need for increased human capital as one of the foundations for economic growth is provided.

Traditional measures that are used to evaluate labor market operations yield a conflicting and somewhat confusing picture of rural

Southern labor markets when compared with the findings of this study. The explanation for the apparent contradictions that occur at times derives from the fact that conventional criteria for interpretation of labor market behavior and performances are drawn either from research studies that are exclusively urban-based or from national studies that are heavily biased by urban data. As this study was based largely on primary source data for four rural counties, the findings that conflict with the conventional wisdom are not necessarily abnormal.

FINDINGS AND CONCLUSIONS

Inability to Obtain an Adequate Level of Income

The primary finding of this study is that the foundation for many of the problems faced by the people of the rural South is an inability to obtain an adequate level of income through work. A major reason for the difficulty is a deficiency in both the quantity and quality of job opportunities provided by the rural economies of the South. The support for this finding is derived from the following considerations.

Inadequate Demand for Workers

The level of demand for workers is inadequate to provide jobs for all who desire them. The Southern rural economy has been severely affected by the secular decline in agricultural employment due to the mechanization that has occurred primarily since the end of World War II. All the survey counties continue to give evidence of this displacement and the related decline of the businesses that once served the agriculture industry.

The nonagricultural private sector, dominated by small business firms, has been unable to grow sufficiently to offset the loss of job opportunities in the agricultural sector. Despite the continuation of outmigration of many of the young, as attested by interviews with school officials, there remains a considerable surplus pool of labor—people who are either unemployed, are working part-time involuntarily, or are discouraged from actively seeking employment.

This study found the labor force participation in the study counties to be a mere 42.3 percent. The significant difference between this rate and the national average (61 percent), however, does not indicate a difference in the behavior of the people of the rural South from those elsewhere. Rather, the low level of labor force participation is reason to believe that the typical rural labor market in the South is unable to provide employment opportunities for a substantial portion of the population.

Unemployment rates, among the most widely used labor market indicators, are poor measures of worker availability in rural areas. When allowances are made for those persons who are involuntarily among the part-time employed, for discouraged workers, and for employed household heads whose adjusted family income is below established poverty lines, as well as for those who are unemployed, a better measure of employment problems (that is, a subemployment index) can be computed. In the case of the rural county sample, the subemployment index was 41 percent in 1974. This rate can be compared with a similar 1972 index of 11.5 percent computed for the entire economy. Clearly, such an index is a much better descriptor of the rural South than are those presently computed and published.

Workers are sometimes forced into the migrant stream by the shortage of local jobs. In Starr County, for example, this is the primary explanation for the fact that one-third of the population annually must leave the county as migratory farm workers. When these migrants returned during the winter months, 37 percent of the migrant household heads did not even try to find jobs. Of those who did try, 29.2 percent were unemployed.

Even where local leaders are committed to efforts to expand job opportunities, they usually lack the knowledge and experience to be successful in their efforts, and they do not have the financial means to obtain the necessary expertise. This absence of enthusiasm in some instances and of knowledge in others too often has meant that impetus for economic growth had to be generated outside the local power structure and often outside the rural South itself.

Another impediment at the local level has been the lack of capital for economic development. Small businessmen have been unable to acquire needed capital due to restrictive eligibility criteria for existing federal programs, as well as to a deficiency of local funding sources. Large capital requirements are not capable of being supplied locally. The result often is total outside ownership of new companies locating in rural areas.

Although there have been efforts—sometimes substantial ones—to promote economic development in rural areas, they have suffered from the lack of a purposeful and consistent national policy toward rural areas, and toward rural development, particularly. Rural development policy at the national level suffers from lack of coordination among existing government agencies. Rural development today is a hodgepodge activity that takes place in a piecemeal fashion, often solely on the basis of which community is the most aggressive and the best able to articulate its needs. Many agencies—the Appalachian Regional Commission, Tennessee Valley Authority, Economic Development Administration, U.S. Department of Housing and Urban Development, and the U.S. Department of Agriculture—all are engaged in aspects of rural development with little visible coordination.

CONCLUSIONS AND POLICY IMPLICATIONS

Poor Quality of Jobs

Despite its continuing secular decline, agriculture has remained the largest private industry of employed persons in three of the four counties (and it was very high in the fourth). Agricultural employment is noted for its low wages, irregular employment patterns, and lack of unionization. Furthermore, in the rural South the nonagricultural sector reflects these same characteristics.

The mean level of earnings in 1974 for the four counties was $6002 for all household heads, which compares with a national mean of $7330 for all workers in 1973. For Anglos, the mean earnings were higher, $8244, but for blacks they were only $3403, and for Chicanos only $4587. For female heads of households mean earnings were a scant $3049. Over 34 percent of the poverty households in the study were headed by a person employed full-time. For 25 percent of the families, the presence of two or more wage earners was insufficient to pull the family above minimum poverty levels. The mean hourly wage rate for all employed heads of households was only $3.02; that for all employed persons was $2.68, with considerable variation again being noted by race and sex. The national average for all persons employed in the private sector in 1973 was $4.22 per hour.

With respect to the working poor, 36 percent were receiving wages equal or close to the federal minimum wage ($1.60 for nonagricultural employment at the time of the survey). In addition, 22 percent of the working poor were receiving wages below the agricultural minimum wage ($1.30 at the time). Aside from documenting the low financial rewards provided to many rural workers, this finding suggests that there is a significant incidence of violation of the minimum wage provisions of the Fair Labor Standards Act.

In addition, there are virtually no fringe benefits provided by either agricultural or nonagricultural private employers. Although public-sector employment often provides "choice" jobs, the situation with respect to fringe benefits is much the same as in the private sector. Fringe benefits are few, local civil service systems virtually nonexistent, and formal (written) personnel systems scant. In the interviews, local leaders frequently stated that public-sector jobs are used as a power base to reward political allies and supporters. As the public sector accounted for 25 percent of the employed persons in the four survey counties, the character of employment conditions in this sector is of major consequence.

For the 55 percent of the household heads employed (82 percent were male household heads and 18 percent were female household heads), the low wage structure forces many to work long weekly hours. Of the men, 24 percent reported working 49 hours a week or more, as did 10 percent of the females. Thus, 22 percent of the household heads surveyed, as compared with 10 percent of all workers nationally, were working 49 hours or more a week. Only 10 percent of the total number of surveyed employed household heads, however, reported receiving an overtime premium. This compares with a national figure (May 1974) of 40 percent. Agricultural employment is among those industries in which long weekly hours are common (a six-day week being usual), but industries that do not require overtime premium pay. Moreover, at the time of this study, agricultural workers were subject to a federal minimum wage which was 23 percent lower than the nonagricultural minimum wage.

Agricultural workers often do not seek or are prevented from securing regular employment in other occupations. However, many nonagricultural employers in the study indicated that some of their best workers left seasonally to work the fields during peak-season periods. Because the pay was often less, due to lower minimum wages, such behavior is difficult to explain logically. In some cases, however, the pressure appeared to stem from past financial obligations to the agricultural entrepreneur.

The low wage structure and long hours help to explain the extensive problems with labor turnover cited by employers, despite the evidence of labor surplus. This finding was especially the case in the manufacturing sector, even though its wage rates were among the highest in these communities. Since most of these jobs required low-skill workers, employers were able to replace these workers easily. Apparently the wages, which were relatively higher than those elsewhere in the rural economy, were not high enough to hold employees.

It also is of consequence that the rural South is almost devoid of labor organizations. This means that certain possible constraints on the labor market activities of both employers and employees are not present; it also means that workers must depend totally on governmental legislation for protection. There are indications that such protection, including enforcement of minimum-wage legislation and access to unemployment payments, is inadequate. Further, lack of unionization means that one possible avenue to improving earnings, fringe benefits, and job stability is unavailable.

Limitations of the Industrial Structure

Jobs in the public sector are highly prized for their relative security and, in sharp contrast to the private sector, there is relatively little turnover. These public-sector jobs are frequently controlled by local political forces. As electoral turnover is infrequent in Southern politics, persons in these jobs have little fear of

CONCLUSIONS AND POLICY IMPLICATIONS 315

losing them. Many of the public sector jobs are blue-collar jobs associated with maintenance and repair work. There are, of course, a fair number of white-collar jobs. Some of these are low-paying clerical jobs, but others are administrative and teaching positions that are relatively better. But the fact that there is very little voluntary turnover means that there are few opportunities for others to enter these occupations, although this is the largest employment sector.

The next largest private-sector industries are agriculture and retail trade. In Sunflower and Starr counties, agriculture jobs exceeded retail jobs. In total, these two industries accounted for almost one-third of all employed persons in the four counties. Both of these industries are noted for their low wages, minimal job benefits, and the absence of promotion possibilities.

When retail trade and agriculture are combined with the public sector, they account for about 60 percent of the total number of employed persons in the survey counties. The remaining workers are scattered across the array of industrial categories. Most are employed by small firms. Of all the firms in the survey counties, 91.2 percent employed fewer than 20 employees; 74 percent employed fewer than 7 employees. Not only are these enterprises small in size, but they are few in numbers. Most of these industries simply draw from the surplus labor pool for their workers without appreciably affecting the local wage structure.

The limitations of the industrial structure portend particularly serious problems for rural youth. The narrow choice of industries in the rural South offers young rural workers little opportunity for exposure to the spectrum of occupations that are needed if new industries are to be enticed to these communities. Moreover, if these young people out-migrate, they do so with little or no urban job preparation.

Leadership's Opposition to Job Expansion

One of the greatest obstacles to economic development in the rural South is the attitude of local leadership toward economic and social change. It is extremely difficult to foster development in the rural South if the local leaders are not committed to that end. The rural leadership in the past has tended to be self-serving and to lack recognition of and the need for purposeful growth as well as the need for institutional and social change. In interviews with local businessmen and elected public officials, repeated mention was made of the importance and necessity of economic development and industrial diversification. But it was readily apparent from these interviews and from an examination of the results of earlier efforts to attract industry that some of those in power place sharp restrictions on the types of new industries that are welcome.

The distribution of wealth in rural areas is highly skewed, a distortion that has led to a power structure that in many respects is independent from the general population of the rural South. Many of the individuals identified with the power structure have substantial interests in agriculture or agriculture-related businesses. Attempts to protect vested interests often have directly and indirectly retarded industrial development. For example, any active development organization existing in a rural community is usually dominated by the local power structure, and potential new industries are carefully screened to assure that they are the "correct" type.

Agriculture interests are not supportive of efforts to attract industries that might bring more attractive jobs with high wages that would compete for their existing work force. Many local business people are equally resistant to new enterprises that will disturb the prevailing wage structure. Enterprises that are unionized or are likely to become so are often not welcomed. The only firms that are sought are those that can be specifically targeted to the absorption of obvious surplus labor pools. In particular, the most sought-after businesses are those that will hire black or Chicano women in low-skilled occupations. Moreover, some of those enterprises that are attracted to the rural South are drawn there by the lack of employee organizations. They are looking for low-skilled workers to whom they can pay low wages and offer few fringe benefits. They have no incentive to upgrade their workforces.

These restrictive conditions form one barrier to the attraction of a sufficient number of firms to absorb the available labor pool. When new firms do locate in the rural South, those who are employed are better off then they would otherwise have been. However, the financial rewards are seldom substantial and, given the high turnover rates, they are frequently of short duration to the employees.

Education or training, no matter in what occupation, has little relevance or value if the only existing employment opportunities are jobs requiring little or no skill. Inability of the rural South to grow economically continues to be a major factor in the efforts to upgrade the labor force.

In one sense it is unfair to argue that the labor markets in the rural South have operated inadequately. Encouragement of the development of a large number of highly skilled workers would not by itself have solved any of the problems discussed above. The demand has been for unskilled workers. Similarly, it is unrealistic to expect local rural labor markets to have exerted the necessary pressure for occupational upgrading of those who migrated to urban areas or to expect that skill needs of urban areas would be felt in

CONCLUSIONS AND POLICY IMPLICATIONS 317

rural labor markets. However, it remains true that the encouragement of skill development has not been generated by the labor market either for the current labor force or for the youth in the rural South.

Availability of Job Information

There is a relatively free flow of reliable job information concerning wage rates, job openings, and hiring plans. The relative ineffectiveness of the public employment service (ES) in the rural South is at least partially a result of this word-of-mouth information network. The results of the household survey show that the majority of actual and potential labor force participants rely upon informal word-of-mouth channels to learn of job opening and prevailing wage rates. The data also show that the ES in rural areas often is called upon to place only those who have the greatest difficulty in finding employment (that is, members of minority groups with little training or education) or those who register for placement only because they are required to do so by law. The general awareness of the scarcity of job opportunities and the prevailing low wage structure is certainly a factor influencing low labor force participation.

There is no evidence that lack of job information is a major deterrent to labor force participation or to employment in rural Southern labor markets. In fact, good knowledge of job opportunities would appear to be one of the factors influencing low labor force participation.

Although it is difficult to establish actual motivations, the evidence is that there is no less desire to work on the part of the rural population than is generally true elsewhere in the United States. Only a very small percentage of the rural population have the access to unearned income that would allow any "reasonable" standard of living without working. Several findings of this study make it clear that despite the low rates of labor force participation, many of those outside the labor force desire to work. Both the percentage of involuntary part-time employment and the incidence of labor force withdrawal due to discouragement exceed national figures. In fact, the presence of "discouraged workers" was found to be over four times greater in the rural South than for the nation as a whole.

Until economic development is well under way in the rural South, neither expanded private employment nor public employment will be able to create enough employment opportunities to prevent outmigration, nor should they try to do so. The major need is not to thwart all migration from rural areas but to prevent what occurs from having an adverse effect on urban areas. Although efforts to improve information about local labor markets are unwarranted at present, information concerning employment opportunities in urban areas available to potential migrants is poor, as is attested by the current patterns of rural southern migration. Existing patterns cannot be altered without better information.

Poor Health and Educational Deficiencies

The second and equally important conclusion of this study is that efforts to increase income for workers in the rural South are severely hampered by the very low levels of educational attainment, the absence of formal training, a shortage of work experience, and work-inhibiting health problems.

<u>Educational and Job-Training Deficiencies</u>

A substantial portion of the labor force of the rural South is untrained and poorly educated. To this degree, the earning capacity of much of the rural labor force is severely constrained. In the survey counties, 25 percent of the labor force had less than an eighth-grade education; 54 percent had less than a high school education. For blacks and Chicanos these figures were considerably higher.

Perhaps even more distressing than the educational deficiencies was the low level of job training of any sort. Less than 10 percent of the labor force had ever participated in any kind of formal training. Moreover, of those few who had job training, the largest single source of that training was the military, with vocational education a distant second. Less than 1 percent of the labor force claimed ever to have been in an apprenticeship program or to have participated in any form of OJT program. Less than 1 percent of the labor force had ever been in a federally sponsored manpower program. Most of those who were in manpower programs were in those that contained no skill-training component (for example, Neighborhood Youth Corps, Operation Mainstream, or Public Service Employment). The training deficiency is even more severe than these findings indicate as 60 percent of the small number who had any training at all were persons with a high school education or better.

It is possible to gain job experience without formal training programs, but the survey evidence indicates that this experience, too, is notably absent in the rural South. Of those in the labor force, 27 percent had been in their current jobs for less than a year, 57 percent less than five years. Of those with long job tenure, most were in farming, professional, or administrative occupations.

One reason for the inability of rural labor to adapt to economic changes over time stems from the apparent lack of skill development in the rural labor force. Based on the results of these surveys, the most visible reason is lack of necessary programs and facilities. As mentioned previously, little incentive for employer-sponsored training exists. Consequently, few formal OJT programs are found in the study counties. Even where the job requires a sufficient degree of skill to make training beneficial, the employers display little interest in formal programs.

Although there are exceptions, state and local training facilities in the four counties do not provide the needed alternative to employer training. Facilities are often inadequate, qualified instructors are in short supply, and curricula are almost always limited in scope and often misdirected, given the local and even regional job opportunities and industrial structure.

This study found high school vocational training particularly deficient. Emphasis continues to be on curricula oriented toward preparation for college. In areas where the development of a private and parochial school system has had an impact on student enrollment, vocational facilities and curricula in public schools are notably deficient.

Reluctance to Move

Although out-migration continues in the survey counties, a strong reluctance to move was expressed by members of the households surveyed. Over 75 percent of the persons over age 16 were born in the county in which they now live. Over 85 percent of those over 16 were living in the county five years prior to the time of the interview. When asked whether they could conceive of a circumstance that would make them move from their present county, 85 percent of the household heads responded, "no." The most common explanation was the noneconomic consideration that "this is my home." Only 8 percent indicated that job attachment was what kept them where they were.

Nonparticipation in Skill-Training Programs

The number of persons who could benefit from skill training in the rural South greatly exceeds the number presently being served. In determining the potential clientele for manpower programs, it is calculated that 40 percent of the actual or potential labor force in the survey counties are eligible for training under current legislation (CETA). At the time of the study, less than 1 percent of that group was being served. The number who could presently benefit from skill-training programs was less than one-half of the total eligible for CETA programs. However, most could benefit from public-service employment programs or work-experience programs.

Obviously, many working poor and unemployed persons could benefit from such programs rather than rely on the limited opportunities currently available for them in the private sector.

To be of maximum benefit, however, training programs must be a part of a broad coordinated plan of economic development to expand job opportunities. Such developmental activities should include skill training, work-experience programs, and improved delivery systems.

A major problem of current manpower programs and the delivery system (CETA) results from a strong urban bias. Programs do not assume the tremendous employment problems of the rural South. Further, the concept of a single prime sponsor for all rural areas within a given state (that is, "balance of state" category) places an unreasonable burden on a single office in most Southern states. It also places rural areas at a disadvantage relative to medium-size cities.

Bias also is found in the funding of manpower programs. In part, this results from the distribution of funds based on formulas that incorporate statistics that are not as reflective of labor market conditions in rural areas as they are of urban areas.

Lack of necessary expertise to implement manpower policy and programs continues to be a problem for most of the rural South. Knowledge of the unique problems of rural areas in establishing effective manpower programs is generally absent at the state level and to some extent at the national level. In many respects, however, the absence of persons with the knowledge to organize and conduct efficient and effective programs at the local level is the greatest handicap to manpower policy in the rural South.

Health Problems

Throughout the household survey, health problems (defined as work-impairing physical ills under medical care) consistently appeared as important explanations for low wages, inadequate income, low labor force participation, inability to be trained, and irregular work patterns. Of all household heads, 23 percent indicated having health problems. The incidence was higher among black and Chicano workers than among Anglos. It was considerably higher among female than among male heads of households. In all groups, half of the individuals reporting a health problem had had it for over five years.

Interviews with county health officials and doctors indicate that many illnesses in the rural South are no longer common in urban areas. Instances of polio, tuberculosis, leprosy, tetanus, encephalitis, and dysentery were reported. Many health problems are clearly preventable as they stem from poor nutrition and inadequate diets.

CONCLUSIONS AND POLICY IMPLICATIONS

Some of these problems derive from lack of information. But these health problems are caused primarily by low incomes that do not allow opportunities to buy adequate quantities of wholesome food or to live in above-standard housing. Other problems are the outgrowth of impoverished communities: These are lack of pure drinking water, improper garbage and sewage disposal, and inadequate rodent and insect control. The high incidence of health problems and the disproportionately large numbers of elderly and young in rural areas justify the need for improved health care. As indicated by the four-county study, the rural South probably suffers from a deficiency in health care professionals, particularly medical specialists and dentists. Poor transportation and an inadequate delivery system limit the ability of rural residents, particularly the elderly, to utilize available facilities. There also is a strong presumption that the quality of health facilities and care is low.

Despite the lack of adequate delivery systems, personnel, and facilities, the inaccessibility of health care due to low income is the most serious problem. Few low-income families can afford the luxury of private health and disability insurance. Many are forced to depend on the limited care provided under Medicaid, Medicare, or other public health programs.

The Need for Welfare Reform

A third significant finding of the study is that neither employment nor available income-transfer programs have been able to eliminate the massive poverty that continues to be the dominant characteristic of the Southern rural economy. Welfare reform (such as that proposed that originally gave rise to this study) would have a significant beneficial impact on many low-income families and the overall economy of the rural South.

The Nature of Rural Poverty

Using the federal income guidelines at the time of the study, 41.3 percent of the households in the survey fell below the poverty threshold. Unlike the situation in most of the nation, poverty in the South is more a rural than an urban characteristic. The poverty rate for the rural South is almost twice that for the entire South and three times that for the nation. The absolutes of poverty are usually more severe in the rural South than in urban areas, and large portions of the Southern rural poverty population survive at bare existence levels.

One dimension of rural poverty as evidenced by the results of this study is that many are permanently outside the labor force.

Those who are poor by virtue of inability to participate in the labor market include the elderly, those sick or disabled, and those whose family responsibilities require their presence at home. A disproportionate percentage of the poor were found to have health and disability problems. Some of the working-age population (especially those in the 55-to-64 age group) suffer from health problems that probably eliminate them permanently from the labor market.

The incidence of poverty among the aged in rural areas of the South is critical. Over 40 percent of the poor in the study counties are 65 years of age or over. This group remains mired in poverty despite recent increases in coverage and benefits of Social Security, SSI, Medicare, and Medicaid. As there are virtually no employment opportunities for older persons in rural areas, many of the aged who are in poverty are totally dependent on federal income for their existence. Most Social Security and SSI recipients have only the income received from these programs to live on. Voluntary out-migration of this group is unlikely, and there is nothing to be gained by forcing the elderly to migrate from rural areas. Given the extremely small probability of development of jobs for the elderly who can work, improvement in the income position of the elderly rural poor will require changes in welfare programs.

This study also found a large number of persons of labor force age without disabilities who were outside the labor force. Some were restricted in the ability to participate by artificial impediments such as discrimination. Discrimination was found to be a factor limiting the employment opportunities of blacks and Chicanos. It was also a factor for women of all races. Although sex discrimination may place limits on labor force participation of all females, it is a more critical problem when the female is the household head with dependents to support. The probability of a household head being in poverty in rural areas is substantially increased if the head is a woman.

Although every single poverty case could be analyzed to discover some type of employment handicap, the limited size of the labor market remains a major cause of poverty. The high subemployment rates calculated in this research attest to the extent of the limitation. Depending on the speed of economic development, this means that the public sector must provide support if the rural poor are to improve their living standards.

Yet even if there is full-time employment, income above the poverty level is not assured. Though employment of a secondary family worker—usually the spouse—was a factor in preventing poverty, the low level of labor force participation by married women appears to be a major limitation in raising family income. For about a quarter of the families the existence of more than one wage earner did not

CONCLUSIONS AND POLICY IMPLICATIONS   323

push total family income above the poverty level even though it raised overall family income. Thus, it must be concluded that labor markets in the rural South fail to provide many families with a level of income that society in general has deemed "necessary."

Ineffectiveness of Antipoverty Programs

The various aspects of public antipoverty policy—Community Action Programs, AFDC, and Food Stamps—have not been effective in changing the relative income status of many poverty groups or individuals. AFDC and food stamps suffer from lack of adequate funding (benefits) or eligibility restrictions. At the same time, there are large segments of the rural poverty population eligible but not participating in these programs. Almost half (44.6 percent) of the eligible households were not participating in the food-stamp program. In addition to the relatively low participation rate (67.3 percent) of the eligible AFDC recipients, the low benefit levels in these counties have left recipient families well below poverty thresholds.

The multiplicity of administrative structures for welfare and related programs adversely affects the costs and efficiency of these efforts. This study found the attitudes of many program officials interviewed to be lackadaisical in regard to potential program eligibles. Prejudices and the poor training of many of the welfare-agency interviewers (persons who screen for eligibility) allow ineligibles to participate and often prevent eligibles from participating. Red tape, including complex eligibility requirements, discourages program participation and permits program abuses.

Current welfare policy omits certain poverty groups and, therefore, arbitrarily ignores the extent and depth of poverty. For example, unemployed heads of households and the working poor in most states are not covered by existing programs. Childless couples under 76 years of age with no labor force participant are eligible only for food stamps. There also are a large number of "near poor," as defined by the arbitrary federal poverty guidelines. That is to say, if households living within 125 percent of the poverty threshold are included, the poverty population in the survey counties would increase by 23 percent. In other words, if this group were included, 50.8 percent of the households could be classified as poverty stricken. Thus, a small change in the definition would increase substantially the number of persons in poverty in the rural South.

It is an inescapable conclusion that the public sector will have to bear a major share of the burden in any effort to solve poverty problems in the rural South. Given the limited financial capacities of local and state governments in the rural South, as well as the administrative problems that exist, major financing and guidance must come from the federal level.

Welfare-Reform Proposal of 1971

The welfare-reform proposal put forth in 1971, if it had been enacted, would have had a major impact on the people and the economy of the rural South. Under the proposed reform, the average family income of those covered would have been increased by 35 percent ($980) over the actual income average in 1973. Black families would have had the greatest increase in their incomes; Anglos would have had the least. Yet, although it would have altered the dimensions of poverty in the rural South, the reform measure by no means would have eliminated it.

Not all eligible families would have benefited from the change. Many families participating in other transfer programs—primarily Social Security—would have lost income under the proposed program, because such income would have been offset against benefits. In addition, due to the fact that food stamps would have been discontinued under the proposed reform, as much as 50 percent of those eligible for coverage under the welfare-reform proposal potentially would have faced a reduction in real incomes. Furthermore, a substantial portion of the poverty population of the rural South—families without children and single-member households—would not have been eligible for coverage.

In terms of overall impact, it was estimated that in excess of $800 million would have been distributed to poor families in the rural South. Conservative multiplier estimates place the total income that could have been generated at a net income addition to the rural South of $1.2 billion.

Discrimination by Race and Sex

A fourth major finding of the study is that employment discrimination by race and sex remains a major cause of low income in the rural South.

Patterns of Employment Discrimination

Pervasive patterns of employment discrimination in terms of restricted employment opportunities and of differential wage rates persist in the rural South. The county studies show that racial discrimination restricts minority workers to lower paying occupations. In addition, there still exists substantial discrimination in earnings between Anglos and blacks for the same occupations. The extent to which racial discrimination actually limits access to the labor market is impossible to determine. With the overall labor force participation rate almost 6-percent lower for blacks than for Anglos in these counties, it is reasonable to assume that there is a discouragement effect.

The patterns of occupational segregation must dampen the motivation that would otherwise lead minority workers to engage in training and education. More importantly, the lack of observable adult models for minority youth in the more desirable occupations serves to diminish significantly the enthusiasm of minority youth for education, as the high school-dropout rate attests.

Sex Discrimination

Women have difficulty in securing entry into the same occupations as men—for example, the higher-skilled positions in manufacturing and in administrative positions. Moreover, in those cases where women and men were in the same occupations, wage differentials were prevalent and sizable.

Lack of Antidiscriminatory Action

A major impediment to improved earnings and job access for racial minorities and women in the rural South is the absence of an effective enforcement agency to investigate equal employment opportunity cases. The rural Anglo power structure has shown little concern for minority problems, and most Southern states have not established equal employment opportunity agencies. The U.S. Equal Employment Opportunity Commission has shown little interest in rural areas. Yet it should be clear that, given the limited number of jobs and the large number of minorities and women, major employment displacement effects can be expected from a reduction in discrimination. Anglo men would be the chief losers, and women would be the chief beneficiaries.

POLICY AND PROGRAM NEEDS IN THE RURAL SOUTH

The policy discussions throughout this book have emphasized that the issues confronting the rural South became dilemmas because of insufficient resources to attack the problems comprehensively. To overcome the dilemmas, it is necessary not only to alter perspectives but also to change the parameters. The prevailing situation in the rural South will require a conscientious decision that it is in the national interest to arrest the continuing economic atrophy. If so acknowledged it would follow that a comprehensive series of coordinated steps could be taken that are designed to benefit the entire population of the rural South. An option to out-migration would be created. The resulting programs would reduce the disparity between life in the rural and the urban United States.

National Rural Policy

The unique problems of rural areas argue for adoption of a national rural policy. If adopted, this policy should be in harmony with the goals of the urban economy insofar as there are common problems. However, it should recognize that specific programs for rural areas will have to be implemented. The policy should encourage private-sector initiatives but recognize that much of the responsibility will for some decades be that of the federal government. The implementation of such policy will call for cooperation among agencies primarily of the departments of Labor, Agriculture, and HEW. Further, within the Department of Agriculture a major policy reorientation must occur, shifting attention from what are largely farm matters to all rural problems.

The policy should address the need for economic growth in rural areas as well as incorporate the specific objectives of elevating the standard of living and quality of life in rural areas. All communities within the rural South do not possess equal development potential at the present time; thus, development policy should include planning for areas where development will occur independently.

An additional component of a national rural policy should be a concerted effort to increase social overhead capital in rural areas and to create the type of employment opportunities that will allow residents OJT in skilled occupations. An expanded program of job creation and public works should be initiated where feasible. Public works projects, such as the Tennessee Valley Authority of the 1930s and the Tennessee Tombigbee Project of the 1970s, are highly labor-intensive and can be directed toward improvement of the rural infrastructure projects that are supportive of private industrial development.

Although contracting out the administration of specific programs to state governments should be allowed, state administration should not be the only method of implementation in rural areas. Responsibility should be retained at the federal level for representing rural areas in national policy matters, for developing new programs for rural areas, and for compiling the needed statistics to make visible the true problems of the rural United States. There should be coordination of the distribution of funds to support economic development, manpower training, public-service employment, and work-experience programs. A state or local community sponsor should be able to obtain a total development package, including funds for such items as

CONCLUSIONS AND POLICY IMPLICATIONS 327

industrial-park development, planning assistance, and start-up training programs for local workers.

Income-Maintenance System

A nationwide comprehensive income-maintenance system that is federally administered and financed should be enacted. The system should establish an income floor below which families and individuals could not fall. It should include coverage for those who work and those who cannot. Eligibility should be premised exclusively upon income and not on the personal characteristics of the poverty population. The program should cover all persons and should not be limited by marital status, family composition, or any other factor except for need. It is implicit that the current AFDC program be terminated and that the SSI program and the food-stamp program become an integral part of the overall program. Social Security payments should be treated the same as earned income and should not be subjected to a 100-percent benefit offset, as would have been the case under the welfare reform proposals in 1972. A strong work incentive should be included as well as major financial penalties for refusal to work by those able to seek or accept employment. Public-service employment and public-works components should be implemented when and where needed to provide jobs to rural workers when jobs are unavailable in the private sector.

National Health Care System

A national health care system should be established, including three components: (a) a national health insurance system guaranteeing all persons the ability to obtain adequate medical and dental care, (b) preventive health care for all persons, and (c) adequate facilities and personnel to assure ability to deliver needed care throughout the nation. An important part of the third component is the assurance that such facilities and personnel are readily accessible to all persons regardless of their location.

Mobility Programs

Not all migration from rural areas should be thwarted, but migration that occurs must be prevented from adversely affecting urban areas. Movement can also be rural to rural or rural South to urban South. Better preparation for the urban environment and improved labor market information are needed. Specifically, mobility programs should include (a) relocation allowances, (b) reorientation of migrants to urban life, (c) accurate job information for directing mobility, and (d) assistance in obtaining employment. In addition, in order to meet the shortages of a few skilled workers and professional persons, a relocation policy should include assistance to communities to "import" these persons if such persons cannot be found in or trained from the local labor pool.

National Youth-Employment Program

A national youth employment program should be instituted. This program should be designed to provide jobs in the public sector for long-term unemployed youth (ages 16 to 21). Not only would such a program increase the job orientation and job experience of youth, but it would allow rural youth the option of remaining longer in rural areas, thereby increasing the probability that they could be absorbed into the local labor market.

CURRENT PROGRAM PRIORITIES FOR RURAL AREAS

In the absence of consensus with respect to a comprehensive national rural policy, existing programs must be better oriented toward the needs of rural areas, or responsive new programs must be designed and implemented. The severity of poverty and underemployment in the rural South requires that such action should not wait for the achievement of a consensus. Such programs should be implemented with a view toward ultimate integration into a comprehensive national policy. The following recommendations flow from this study.

Amendment of AFDC and Food Stamps

The AFDC program should be federalized, as was done with the former programs for the blind, the disabled, and the aged in 1974, and should be extended to households with male heads. This move would at least standardize nationally the eligibility, benefit levels, and administrative practices for those families whose heads are outside the labor force. This would greatly reduce the inequities and inherent unfairness of the existing system. It also would free local and state funds for use in other areas of broader public need.

In addition, the food-stamp program should be amended so that participants receive stamps in an amount equal to the calculated bonus without purchase requirement. The results of this study indicate that the purchase requirement was a major factor in non-participation by eligible households. As an illustration, families

CONCLUSIONS AND POLICY IMPLICATIONS

eligible to purchase $200 in food stamps for $50 were often unable to obtain the necessary cash. The program would better serve the needs of those eligible if in this case $150 in stamps was given without purchase requirement.

Improvements in Manpower Programs

Manpower efforts in rural areas should be reoriented to recognize the difference in needs between those persons with a high probability of remaining in the rural South and those with a high probability of leaving (that is, primarily younger persons). Work experience and OJT should constitute the emphasis for persons likely to remain. Institutional training, not necessarily oriented to the local occupational structure, with supportive counseling services should be the focal point of manpower programs for potential migrants.

Institutional training should be available in situations in which the training can be related to specific job placements, such as start-up training for new or expanding industries. Efforts also should be made to enlist a wider participation of small business firms in OJT programs.

Funding levels under Title II of the Comprehensive Employment and Training Act (noncyclical public service employment) should be significantly increased for prime sponsors with major rural responsibilities. Employment as an alternative to welfare will require the establishment of a substantial number of public-service jobs.

Effective manpower programs will require improved quality in the administration of programs at the local level. Increased efforts should be made to upgrade the quality of manpower personnel. Utilizing expertise at regional colleges and universities, upgrading programs could combine an extension component to educate local officials and a component to furnish intensive training of program administrators and planners.

In the area of educational improvements, pre-skill-training programs of a basic educational nature should be established for rural workers. The programs should be comprehensive and geared to providing general skills. Such a program might reveal unknown interests and could be a motivational device. These programs should provide stipends for participants. An adult basic educational program should be undertaken stressing improvement in the quality of life for rural residents. In addition to literacy components, the program should include areas of consumer education, nutrition, health, and family planning.

Extensive study of rural primary and secondary education needs should be instituted. This should include identification of special needs of minority groups, examination of alternative methods of funding education, instigation of incentive programs to encourage high school completion, and a general assessment of the quality of rural general and vocational education with designation of major areas of deficiencies.

Improvement in Health Care Delivery

An overall health-resources plan should be developed that provides funds necessary to provide quality facilities, adequate health manpower, and an effective delivery system for rural areas. Efforts should be directed toward the development of effective health delivery systems, such as comprehensive health care centers that utilize paraprofessionals as well as professionals.

Emphasis should be placed on the development of outreach programs to meet the needs of the chronically ill and the elderly. Utilization of the public school system to identify and assist in correcting health deficiencies among youth in rural areas could be valuable. This program should include an adult education phase to make parents aware of the health needs of their children.

Major efforts are needed to find new ways of attracting health professionals to the rural South and of maintaining them. A system of financial aids for medical students who are willing to practice in rural areas should be established with preference given to students from rural areas. Special training should be incorporated in medical curricula that prepares health professionals for the unique problems of the rural population and a rural practice.

Additional study of the extent and nature of health problems in the rural South is required. More information related to health conditions, attitudes toward health care, and special health problems of minorities is needed, with emphasis on the limitations that discrimination places on access to health care.

Economic Development

The problem of development is hindered by lack of private capital as well as lack of skill training. Increased private-sector job opportunities will require new methods of establishing business firms. Continued encouragement should be given to experimentation and research involving alternative economic-development strategies through such organizations as rural cooperatives and CDCs. Although quantitatively, their impact would seem to be quite small, their potential as a method of promoting rural development still should be carefully and impartially evaluated.

In addition, through a system of low-cost, long-term loans, the federal government should make it possible for local business operations to be funded. The SBA in rural areas should be able to guarantee loans for industrial capital purposes for new business enterprises (not just for expanding old enterprises, as is now the case). Federal support should be given to educational programs for local leadership in the area of economic development.

In areas where the infrastructure exists and past efforts in private development have not succeeded, the federal government could itself initiate action to establish industries in rural areas with a long-term plan for private sector acquisition of the firms from the federal government. Such a system not only would create private-sector jobs in the long-run but also would help establish the type of jobs that allow skill upgrading of rural workers. Upgrading and reorienting rural leadership in the area of economic development must occur. An educational program for local leadership is recommended. Further, a corps of development experts should be established, experts who can be assigned to various areas on request without local cost.

Programs designed to ease the transition of those who migrate from the rural South to urban areas should be established. In those urban areas that are major receivers of rural migrants a special office within the ES should be established. This office should provide aid to migrants through counseling and through housing location, as well as in job placement. In rural areas a continuing educational program to make potential migrants aware that such services are available should be conducted.

Equal Employment Opportunity Program

To address the pervasive racial and sex discrimination in the labor market of the rural South, a special program within the U.S. Equal Employment Opportunity Commission should be created to address the problems of discrimination in rural areas. Several rural areas in the South should be randomly selected for immediate intensive investigation of hiring, firing, and promotion policies in both the private and public sectors. States should be held responsible for establishing equal employment opportunity in public jobs for all political subdivisions of the state.

Unionization

Impediments to unionization of rural workers should be removed. Development of the rural South will ultimately require the interest and cooperation of many groups not only in providing funds and leadership, but also in orienting the population to development. Worker organizations could play a major role in these efforts. Coverage of the National Labor Relations Act should be extended to include agricultural workers. Furthermore, Section 14(b) of the Taft-Hartley Act, which has allowed almost every state in the South to adopt so-called right-to-work laws, should be repealed.

Emphasis on Rural Chicanos

Special problems arise for rural Chicano workers because many are recent immigrants from Mexico, lacking labor market knowledge, a command of English, or relevant job skills. To orient new workers, a special program should be instituted that contains provisions to deal with each of these issues. Additional problems arise because of the inflow of illegal immigrants and border commuters. With respect to the border commuters, persons who work in the United States should be required to live in the United States. The act of employing illegal aliens should be made an illegal act with heavy civil penalties imposed upon employers, and illegal aliens should be identified and vigorously prosecuted. Solution of this problem can be achieved only at the national level with federal direction. The budget and manpower of the Immigration and Naturalization Service should be increased to a level commensurate with its duties. With regard to migrant farm workers, the federal government should assume total responsibility for the administration, coordination, and conduct of all programs involving their welfare.

BIBLIOGRAPHY

Aaron, Henry J. Why Is Welfare So Hard to Reform? Washington, D.C.: The Brookings Institution, 1973.

Abt Associates. An Assessment of the Experimental and Demonstration Interstate Program for South Texas Migrants: Final Report. Cambridge, Mass.: ABT Associates, 1971.

Adams et al. Labor Markets in the Rural South. Report prepared for U.S. Department of Labor, Employment and Training Administration: March 1977.

Alchian, Armen A. "Information Costs, Pricing, and Resource Unemployment." In Edmund S. Phelps et al. Microeconomic Foundations of Employment and Inflation Theory, New York: Horton, 1970.

American Statistical Association Conference on Surveys of Human Populations. "Report on the ASA Conference on Surveys of Human Populations." American Statistician 28 (February 1974): 30-34.

Armstrong, Richard. "The Looming Money Revolution down South." Fortune, June 1970, pp. 66-69, 151-58.

Ashenfelter, Orly, and Albert Rees, editors. Discrimination in Labor Markets. Princeton, N.J.: Princeton University Press, 1973.

A. Y. Allee v. Francisco Medrano, 42 L.W. 4736, 1974.

Back, W. B. "Economic Growth and Rural Poverty: Discussion." American Journal of Agricultural Economics 54 (1972): 355-56.

Baldwin, R. E., and Burton Weisbrod. "Disease and Labor Productivity." Economic Development and Cultural Change 22 (April 1974): 414-35.

Barth, Peter S. "Unemployment and Labor Force Participation." Southern Economic Journal 34 (1968): 375-82.

Batchelder, Alan B. The Economics of Poverty. New York: Wiley, 1973.

Becker, J. M., William Haber, and Sar A. Levitan. Programs to Aid the Unemployed in the 1960s. Kalamazoo, Mich.: W. E. Upjohn Institute for Employment Research, 1965.

Berkowitz, Monroe, and William Johnson. "Health and Labor Force Participation." Journal of Human Resources 9 (1974): 117-28.

Berry, Brian J. J. Growth Centers in the American Urban System. Cambridge, Mass.: Ballinger, 1973.

Bishop, C. E. Farm Labor in the United States. New York: Columbia University Press, 1967.

Bobo, J. R., and D. A. Dudley. Statistical Abstracts of Louisiana, 1971. New Orleans, La.: Business and Economic Research, LSUNO, 1972.

Bonnen, J. T. "Rural Labor Markets and Poverty." Michigan Farm Economics, no. 353. Michigan State University, 1972.

Bowen, W. B., and T. A. Finegan. "Labor Force Participation and Unemployment." In Employment Policies in the Labor Market, edited by Arthur M. Ross. Berkeley: University of California Press, 1965.

Bowen, W. G., and T. A. Finegan. The Economics of Labor Force Participation. Princeton, N.J.: Princeton University Press, 1969.

Bradshaw, Benjamin S., and Dudley L. Poston. "Texas Population in 1970: Trends, 1950-1970." Texas Business Review 45 (1971): 97-109.

Bradshaw, Thomas F. "Job Seeking Methods Used by Unemployed Workers." Monthly Labor Review 96 (February 1973): 35-40.

Brannan, Jack. "Job Absenteeism Rated 9 Days." Commercial Appeal, February 3, 1974.

Bretzfelder, R. B. "Geographic Trends in Personal Income." Survey of Current Business 50 (1970): 14-32.

Briggs, Vernon M., Jr. Chicanos and Rural Poverty. Baltimore: The Johns Hopkins University Press, 1973.

_____. "Implications of Noninstitutional Considerations upon the Effectiveness of Manpower Programs for Chicanos." Austin: Center for the Study of Human Resources, 1973.

_____. Mexican Migration and the United States Labor Market. Austin: Bureau of Business Research, University of Texas, 1975.

_____. Negro Employment in the South: The Houston Labor Market. Washington, D.C.: U.S. Government Printing Office, 1971.

_____. "Texas." Case Studies of the Emergency Employment Act in Operation. Washington, D.C.: U.S. Government Printing Office, 1973.

_____. The Mexico-United States Border: Public Policy and Chicano Economic Welfare. Austin: Bureau of Business Research, University of Texas, 1974.

_____. "The Public Employment Program in Texas." Case Studies of the Emergency Employment Act in Operation. Washington, D.C.: U.S. Government Printing Office, 1973.

_____. "Manpower Programs and Regional Development." Monthly Labor Review 91 (March 1968): 56-57.

_____. "Mexican Workers in the United States Labor Market: A Contemporary Dilemma." International Labour Review 112 (November 1975): 351-68.

_____. "National Manpower Policy." The Encyclopedia of Education, vol. 6. 10 vols. New York: Macmillan, 1971.

Brinkman, G., editor. The Development of Rural America. Lawrence, Kansas: University Press of Kansas, 1974.

Bromley, D. "Use of Discriminant Analysis of Selecting Rural Development Strategies." American Journal of Agricultural Economics 53 (May 1971): 319-22.

Bullock, Paul. "Employment Problems of the Mexican-Americans." In Mexican Americans in the United States, edited by John Burma. Cambridge, Mass.: Schenkman, 1970.

Bureau of Business and Economic Research. "Migration Estimates 1960-1970." Mimeographed. University, Mississippi: Bureau of Business and Economic Research, University of Mississippi, 1974.

Burke, Vincent J., and Vee Burke. Nixon's Good Deed: Welfare Reform. New York: Columbia University Press, 1974.

Cain, Glen G. Married Women in the Labor Force. Chicago: The University of Chicago Press, 1966.

_____, and Harold Watts, eds. Income Maintenance and Labor Supply. Chicago: Rand-McNally, 1973.

_____. Income Maintenance and Labor Supply. New York: Academic Press, 1973.

_____. "Toward a Summary and Synthesis of the Evidence." Income Maintenance and Labor Supply. Chicago: Rand-McNally, 1973.

Cardenas, Gilberto. "Patterns of Employment: The Mexican American Experience in Five Texas Cities." Mimeographed. Austin: Center for the Study of Human Resources, University of Texas, 1973.

Chappell, Gregg. "The Economic Development Administration's Experience with Economic Development and Manpower Planning in Rural Areas." In Manpower Planning for Jobs in Rural Areas, edited by Collette Moser. East Lansing, Mich.: Michigan State University, 1972: 93-103.

Clark, Colin. The Conditions of Economic Progress. London: Macmillan, 1940.

Clark, Kenneth B. Dark Ghetto. New York: Harper & Row, 1965.

Cline, W. R. "Agricultural Strategy and Rural Income Distribution." Food Research Institute Report 12 (1973).

Cohen, Malcolm S. "Sex Differences in Compensation." Journal of Human Resources 6 (1971): 434-47.

College of Business and Industry. Mississippi Statistical Abstract. 1973. Mississippi State University: Division of Research.

BIBLIOGRAPHY

Collins, T., R. C. Yoeman, and H. Stoevener. "Impact of Major Economic Changes on a Rural Economy." Oregon Agriculture Experiment Station Bulletin 614. Corvallis, Oregon, 1973.

Community Action Council of South Texas. "Annual Progress Report of Starr County Migrant Health Project." Mimeographed, September 30, 1973.

Copp, James H. "Poverty and Social Order: Implications and Reservations." American Journal of Agricultural Economics 52 (December 1973): 743.

Corty, F. "Impact of Land Clearing Development in Louisiana." Louisiana Agriculture Experiment Station. 1972.

Dalton, Roger. Defense Purchases and Regional Growth. Washington, D.C.: The Brookings Institution, 1966.

Davis, Joseph M. "Impact of Health on Earnings and Labor Market Activity." Monthly Labor Review 95 (October 1972): 46-49.

Denison, Edward P. The Source of Economic Growth in the United States and the Alternative before Us. Supplementary Paper No. 13. New York: Committee for Economic Development, 1962.

Department of Public Welfare, State of Mississippi, Division of Food Assistance. Food Assistance Manual. Food Stamp Section, Food Stamp Program Revisions for vol. 12.

Dodge County Planning and Development Committee. Dodge County Overall Economic Development Program. 1970.

Donald, Sherry Mills. "A History of Sunflower County, Mississippi." Mimeographed. University of Mississippi, 1968.

Douglas, Paul H. The Theory of Wages. New York: Macmillan, 1934.

Duncan, Otis Dudly. "A Socioeconomic Index for all Occupations." In Occupations and Social Status, edited by Albert J. Reiss. New York: Free Press, 1961: 109-38.

Dyer, Lee D. "Managerial Job Seeking: Methods and Techniques." Monthly Labor Review 95 (December 1972): 29-30.

Eldridge, E. "Community Resources and Human Development." *American Journal of Agricultural Economic Research* 53 (December 1971): 828-34.

FDIC. *Summary of Accounts and Deposits in All Commercial Banks, June 31, 1971.*

"Federal Judge Rules against J. C. Guerra, School Officials." *The South Texas Reporter*. 1974.

Feldstein, Martin S. "Estimating the Supply Curve of Working Hours." *Oxford Economic Paper* 20 (March 1968): 74-80.

Finegan, T. A. "Hours of Work in the U.S.: A Cross Sectional Analysis." *Journal of Political Economy* 70 (October 1962): 452-70.

Fisher, A. G. B. "Capital and Growth of Knowledge." *Economic Journal* 43 (September 1933): 379-89.

_____. "Production Primary, Secondary, and Tertiary." *Economic Record* 15 (June 1939): 24-38.

Fleisher, Belton. "The Economics of Labor Force Participation: A Review Article." *Journal of Human Resources* 6 (Spring 1971): 139-48.

Fogel, Walter. "The Effects of Low Educational Attainment on Incomes: A Comparative Study of Selected Ethnic Groups." *The Journal of Human Resources* 1 (Fall 1966): 22-40.

Foster, M. I. "Is the South Still a Backward Region?" *American Economic Review* 62 (May 1972): 195-203.

Freeman, Richard B. "Changes in the Labor Market for Black Americans, 1948-72." *Brookings Papers on Economic Activity 1973*, No. 1, edited by Arthur K. Okun and George L. Perry. Washington, D.C.: Brookings Institution, 1973, pp. 67-120.

Friedman, Rose. *Poverty: Definition and Perspective*. Washington, D.C.: American Enterprise Institute for Public Policy Research, 1965.

Fuchs, Victor R. "Hourly Earnings Differentials by Region and Size of City." *Monthly Labor Review* 90 (January 1967): 22-26.

BIBLIOGRAPHY

Fuller, Varden. "Rural Poverty and Rural Areas Development." In Poverty in America, edited by Margaret S. Gordon. San Francisco: Chandler, 1965.

Galatin, Malcolm. "A Comparison of the Benefits of the Food Stamp Program, Free Food Stamps, and an Equivalent Cash Payment." Public Policy 21 (Spring 1973): 291-302.

Galloway, Lowell E. Poverty in America. Columbus, Ohio: Grid, Inc., 1973.

_____. "The Impact of New Industry: An Application of Economic Base Multiplier to Small Rural Areas." Land Economics 48 (1972).

_____. "Measuring the Income of Rural Families." Department of Economic Research, North Carolina State University, 1972.

Georgia Bank Commissioners. "Published Statement of the Banks' Assets and Liabilities." Atlanta: The Commissioners.

Georgia Department of Family and Children's Services. Annual Report, July 1, 1970-June 30, 1971. 1971.

Ginzberg, Eli. Manpower Agenda for America. New York: McGraw-Hill, 1968.

Good Neighbor Commission. Annual Report for 1974 on Texas Migrant Labor. Austin: The Commission, 1975.

Goodwin, Leonard. Do the Poor Want to Work? Washington, D.C.: The Brookings Institution, 1972.

Gordon, David M. Theories of Poverty and Underemployment. New York: Heath, 1972.

Gramm, Wendy L. "The Labor Force Decision of Married Female Teachers: A Discriminant Analysis Approach." Review of Economics and Statistics 55 (August 1973): 341-48.

Grebler, Leo. The Mexican-American People. New York: Free Press, 1973.

Green, Christopher. Negative Taxes and the Poverty Problems. Washington, D.C.: The Brookings Institution, 1967.

Greene, Sheldon L. "Public Agency Distortion of Congressional Will: Federal Policy toward Non-Resident Alien Labor." George Washington Law Review 40 (March 1972): 440-63.

Greenfield, Stuart J. Poverty and Industrial Structure. Austin, Tex.: Bureau of Business and Economic Research, The University of Texas, September 1975.

Greenwood, Michael J. "Research on Internal Migration in the United States: A Survey." The Journal of Economic Literature 13 (June 1975): 397.

Grossman, Michael. "On the Concept of Health Capital and Demand for Health." Journal of Political Economy 80 (March-April 1972): 224.

Gunderson, Morley. "Impact of Government Training Subsidies." Industrial Relations 13 (October 1974): 319-24.

_____. "Statistical Models for Dichotomous Dependent Variables." Mimeographed. Toronto: University of Toronto, 1972.

_____. "Training Subsidies and a Disadvantaged Worker: Regression with a Limited Dependent Variable." The Canadian Journal of Economics 7 (November 1974): 611-24.

Gwartney, James. "Discrimination and Income Differentials." American Economic Review 63 (June 1973): 396-408.

_____, and Richard Stroup. "Measurement of Employment Discrimination According to Sex." Southern Economic Journal 39 (April 1973): 575-87.

Hansen, Niles M. Population Turnaround in Nonmetropolitan Regions: Its Implications for Manpower and Regional Policies. Austin: University of Texas at Austin, n.d.

Haren, Claude. "Rural Industrial Growth in the 1960s." American Journal of Agricultural Economics 12 (August 1970): 431.

Harrington, Michael. The Other America: Poverty in the U.S. New York: Macmillan, 1962.

Hathaway, D. "Technical Change and Distribution of Income in Rural Areas." Labor Market Information in Rural Areas, edited by C. Moser. East Lansing, Mich.: University of Michigan, 1972.

BIBLIOGRAPHY

Haussman, Leonard. "The Impact of Welfare on the Work Effort of AFDC Mothers." In President's Commission on Income Maintenance Programs: Technical Studies, pp. 83-100. Washington, D.C.: U.S. Government Printing Office, 1972.

Hilaski, Harvey J. "How Poverty Area Residents Look for Work." Monthly Labor Review 94 (March 1971): 41-45.

Hill, C. Russell. "The Determinants of Labor Supply for the Urban Working Poor." In Income Maintenance and Labor Supply, edited by Glen Cain and Harold Watts, pp. 182-204. Chicago: Rand McNally, 1973.

Holt, Charles C. et al. "How Can the Phillips Curve Be Moved to Reduce Both Inflation and Unemployment?" Microeconomic Foundations of Employment and Inflation Theory, edited by Edmund S. Phelps. New York: Horton, 1970.

____, and Martin H. David. "The Concept of Job Variances in a Dynamic Theory of the Labor Market." The Measurement and Interpretation of Job Vacancies. New York: National Bureau of Economic Research, 1966.

____ et al. The Unemployment Inflation Dilemma: A Manpower Solution. Washington, D.C.: The Urban Institute, 1971.

Horgan, Paul. Great River: The Rio Grande in North American History, vol. 1. New York: Minerva Press, 1954.

Houser, Robert, and David Featherman. "White-Non White Differentials in Occupational Mobility among Men in the United States, 1962-1972." Demography 11 (May 1974): 247-66.

Jeffrey, D., E. Casetti, and L. King. "Economic Fluctuations in a Multi-regional Setting: A Bi-factor Analytic Approach." Journal of Regional Science 9 (December 1969): 397-404.

Johnson, Bruce A. "Federal Aid and Area Redevelopment." The Journal of Law and Economics 14 (April 1971): 277.

Johnson, Florence Scott. Historical Heritage of the Lower Rio Grande. Rio Grande City: La Retama Press, 1965.

Kadushin, Alfred. Child Welfare Services. New York: Macmillan, 1967.

Kain, John F., and Robert Schafer. Regional Impacts of the Family Assistance Plan, discussion paper no. 195. Cambridge, Mass.: Harvard Institute of Economic Research, 1971.

Kalachek, Edward, and Frederick Raines. "Labor Supply of Low Income Workers." In President's Commission on Income Maintenance Programs: Technical Studies, pp. 159-86. Washington, D.C.: U.S. Government Printing Office, 1970.

Kaldor, Donald R., and Donald G. Zytowski. "A Maximizing Model of Occupational Decision-Making." Personnel Guidance Journal 47 (April 1969): 781-88.

Kelly, Terence F. "Factors Affecting Poverty: A Gross Flow Analysis." In The President's Commission on Income Maintenance Programs—Technical Studies. Washington, D.C.: U.S. Government Printing Office, 1970.

Killingsworth, Charles C. "Automation, Jobs, and Manpower: The Case for Structural Unemployment." In The Manpower Revolution: Its Policy Consequences, edited by Garth L. Mangum, pp. 97-116. New York: Doubleday, 1965.

Koziara, Edward C., Karen S. Koziara, and Andrew G. Verzilli. "Racial Differences in Migration and Job Search: A Case Study." Southern Economic Journal 37 (July 1970): 97-99.

Kreps, Juanita M., editor. Employment, Income and Retirement Problems of the Aged. Durham, N.C.: Duke University Press, 1963.

Lee, Everett S., Martin R. L. Levin, William Pendleton, and Patricia D. Postma. Demographic Profiles of the United States. Oak Ridge National Laboratory-U.S. Department of Housing and Urban Development Joint Publication No. 24, volume 5.

Lefcowitz, Myron J. Poverty and Health. Madison, Wisc.: Institute for Research on Poverty, The University of Wisconsin, 1970.

Lester, Richard A. "Shortcomings of Marginal Analysis for Wage-Employment Problems." American Economic Review 36 (March 1946): 63-82.

Levitan, Sar A., Garth L. Mangum, and Ray Marshall. Human Resources and Labor Markets. New York: Harper & Row, 1972.

Levitan, Sar A., Martin Rein, and David Marwick. Work and Welfare Go Together. Baltimore: The Johns Hopkins University Press, 1972.

Levitan, Sar A., and Robert Taggart. "Employment and Earnings Inadequacy: A Measure of Worker Welfare." Monthly Labor Review 96 (October 1973): 19-27.

Lloyd, Cynthia, editor. Sex, Discrimination, and the Division of Labor. New York: Columbia University Press, 1975.

Long, Clarence D. The Labor Force under Changing Income and Employment. Princeton, N.J.: Princeton University Press, 1958.

Long, James E. "Public-Private Sector Differences in Employment Discrimination." Southern Economic Journal 42 (October 1975): 89-96.

Louisiana Agricultural Experiment Station. Louisiana Crop Statistics by Parish, through 1970. D.A.E. Research Report no. 436. The Station, Louisiana State University, 1972.

Louisiana Almanac, 1973-1974. Baton Rouge, La.: Pelican Press, 1973.

Louisiana Health and Social Rehabilitation Services Administration. Division of Family Services Statistics, January, February, and March, 1974.

Louisiana State Department of Education. Louisiana State Directory. 1971-72.

Louisiana State Department of Education. One-Hundred Twenty-Fourth Annual Report for the Session 1972-73, no. 1239.

Louisiana State Department of Health. Statistical Report of Bureau of Vital Statistics, 1960-1970.

Louisiana State Department of Public Welfare. Activity Report, July 1, 1971-June 30, 1972.

LSUNO. Statistical Abstracts of Louisiana, 1971. New Orleans: Business and Economic Research, LSUNO.

Luft, Harold S. "The Impact of Poor Health on Earnings." Review of Economics and Statistics 57 (February 1975): 43-57.

Lurie, Melvin, and Elton Rayack. "Racial Differences in Migration and Job Search: A Case Study." Southern Economic Journal 23 (July 1966): 81-95.

Maddison, A. Economic Progress and Policy. New York: Norton, 1970.

Maddox, James G. The Advancing South. New York: The Twentieth Century Fund, 1967.

Mangum, Garth L. The Emergence of Manpower Policy. Holt, Rinehart, and Winston, 1969.

_____, editor. The Manpower Revolution: Its Policy Consequences. Garden City, N.J.: Doubleday, 1965.

_____, and John Walsh. A Decade of Manpower Development and Training. Salt Lake City, Utah: Olympus, 1973.

Marshall, Ray. Labor in the South. Cambridge, Mass.: Harvard University Press, 1967.

_____. Policy and Program Issues in Rural Manpower Development. Austin: Center for the Study of Human Resources, 1973.

_____. "Program and Research Issues in Rural Development." The Southern Economic Journal 41 (April 1975): 562.

_____. Rural Workers in Rural Labor Markets. Salt Lake City, Utah: Olympus, 1974.

_____. "The Economics of Racial Discrimination: A Survey." Journal of Economic Literature 12 (September 1974): 849-72.

Masters, Stanley. "The Effect of Educational Differences and Labor Market Discrimination on the Relative Earnings of Black Males." Journal of Human Resources 9 (Summer 1974): 342-60.

McCall, J. J. "Economics of Information and Job Search." Quarterly Journal of Economics 84 (February 1970): 113-26.

McGuire, Joseph W., and Joseph A. Pichler. Inequality: The Poor and Rich in America. Belmont, Calif.: Wadsworth, 1969.

McWilliams, Carey. North from Mexico. New York: Greenwood Press, 1968.

Meyer, Lawrence. "Aliens Hard to Count." Washington Post, February 2, 1975, pp. A-1, A-12.

Miller, Herman P. Income Distribution in the United States. Washington, D.C.: U.S. Government Printing Office, 1966.

_____. "Measuring Subemployment in Poverty Areas of Large U.S. Cities." Monthly Labor Review 96 (October 1973): 11.

Millikan, Raymond H. et al. Alleviating Economic Distress. Lexington, Mass.: D. C. Heath, 1972.

Mincer, Jacob. "The Distribution of Labor Incomes: A Survey with Special References to Human Capital Approach." Journal of Economic Literature 8 (March 1970): 1-26.

Morgan, James W. et al. Income and Welfare in the United States. New York: McGraw-Hill, 1962.

Mortensen, Dale T. "Job Search, the Duration of Unemployment, and the Phillips Curve." American Economic Review 60 (December 1970): 847-61.

Moses, Leon. "Income, Leisure, and Wage Pressure." Economic Journal 72 (June 1962): 320-34.

Moynihan, Daniel P. "The Crises in Welfare." Public Interest (Winter 1968): 3-29.

_____. The Politics of a Guaranteed Income. New York: Vintage Books, 1973.

Mushkin, Selma J. "Health as an Investment." Journal of Political Economy (Supplement) 70 (October 1962): 129-57.

National Advisory Commission on Civil Disorders. Report. New York: Bantam Books, 1968.

Nevin, David. The Texans: What They Are—and Why. New York: Bonanza Books, 1968.

North, David S. The Border Crossers—People Who Live in Mexico and Work in the United States. Washington, D.C.: Trans-Century Corporation, 1970.

_____, and William G. Weissert. <u>Immigrants and the American Labor Market</u>. Washington, D.C.: Trans-Century Corporation, 1973.

_____. <u>Immigrants and the American Labor Market</u>. Washington, D.C.: U.S. Department of Labor, 1974.

Ornati, Oscar. <u>Poverty amid Affluence</u>. New York: The Twentieth Century Fund, 1966.

Orshansky, Mollie. "Counting the Poor: Another Look at the Poverty Profile." <u>Social Security Bulletin</u> 28 (January 1965).

_____. "Who's Who among the Poor: A Demographic View of Poverty." <u>Social Security Bulletin</u> 28 (July 1965).

Parnes, Herbert S. "Labor Force and Labor Market." In <u>A Review of Industrial Relations Research</u>, vol. 1. In Woodrow L. Ginsburg et al. Industrial Relations Research Association, 1970.

Perlman, Richard. "Observations on Overtime and Moonlighting." <u>Southern Economic Journal</u> 33 (October 1966): 237-44.

Perrella, Vera C. "Moonlighters: Their Motivations and Characteristics." <u>Monthly Labor Review</u> 93 (August 1970): 62.

Popkin, E. M. "Economic Benefits from the Elimination of Hunger in America." <u>Public Policy</u> 20 (Winter 1972): 133-53.

President's National Advisory Commission on Rural Poverty. <u>The People Left Behind</u>. Washington, D.C.: U.S. Government Printing Office, 1967.

Projector, Dorothy S., G. S. Weis, and E. T. Thoresen. "Composition of Income as Shown by the Survey of Financial Characteristics of Consumers." In <u>Papers on the Size Distribution of Wealth and Income</u>, edited by Lee Scanlon. New York: National Bureau of Economic Research, 1969.

Public Affairs Research Council. <u>Statistical Profile of Natchitoches</u>. Baton Rouge, La.: The Council, 1973.

_____. <u>Statistical Profile of Natchitoches</u>. Baton Rouge, La.: The Council, 1974.

Rayner, A. C. "On the Identification of the Supply Curve of Working Hours." <u>Oxford Economic Papers</u> 21 (1969): 293-98.

Rees, Albert. "Information Networks in Labor Markets." American Economic Review 56 (May 1966): 559-66.

_____, and George D. Shultz. Workers and Wages in an Urban Labor Market. Chicago: The University of Chicago Press, 1970.

Remonyshin, John M. Social Welfare. New York: Random House, 1971.

Ribich, Thomas I. Education and Poverty. Washington, D.C.: The Brookings Institution, 1968.

Rocha, Joseph R., Jr. "The Differential Impact of an Urban Labor Market upon the Mobility of White and Negro Potentially Skilled Workers." Ph.D. dissertation, MIT, August 1967.

Rold, George A. "The Rural Development Act." In U.S. Congress, Proceedings of a National Conference on Rural Development, a Committee print, no. 25-237, 93d Cong., 1st sess., January 2, 1974, p. 87. Washington, D.C.: U.S. Government Printing Office, 1974.

Rosen, Sherwin. "On the Interindustry Wage and Hours Structure." Journal of Political Economy 77 (March-April 1969): 249-73.

Rosenfeld, Carl. "Job Seeking Methods Used by American Workers." Monthly Labor Review 98 (August 1975): 39-42.

Rostow, W. W. The Stages of Economic Growth. Cambridge, Mass.: Cambridge University Press, 1960.

Rungeling, Brian, and Lewis H. Smith. Factors Affecting Food Stamp Nonparticipation in the Rural South. Report to the Income Security Policy/Analysis Branch, Department of Health, Education and Welfare. University, Mississippi: Center for Manpower Studies, University of Mississippi, 1975.

_____. Rural White Poverty in the Mid-South. Report to OEO, December 1973.

Rungeling, Brian, Lewis M. Smith, and Loren C. Scott. "Job Search in Rural Labor Markets," from Proceedings of the 28th Annual Winter Meeting (February 1976): 120-28.

Ryscavage, Paul M. "Measuring Union-Nonunion Earnings Differences." Monthly Labor Review 97 (December 1974): 3-9.

Samora, Julia. Los Mojados: The Wetback Story. Notre Dame, Ind.: Notre Dame Press, 1971.

Sawhill, Isabel V. "The Economics of Discrimination against Women: Some New Evidence." Journal of Human Resources 8 (1973): 383-95.

Schiller, Bradley R. The Economics of Poverty and Discrimination. Englewood Cliffs, N.J.: Prentice-Hall, 1973.

Schweitzer, Stuart O., and Ralph E. Smith. "The Persistence of the Discouraged Worker Effect." Industrial and Labor Relation Review 27 (1974): 249-60.

Scott, Loren C., Lewis H. Smith and Brian Rungeling. "Labor Force Participation in Southern Rural Labor Markets," Amer. J. Agr. Econ. 27 (1974): 249-60.

Sheppard, H. L., and A. H. Belitsky. The Job Hunt. Baltimore: The Johns Hopkins University Press, 1966.

Sobin, Dennis P. The Working Poor. Port Washington, N.Y.: Kennikat Press, 1973.

South Texas Development Council. Regional Historic Sites Surveys and Development Plan. Laredo: The Council, 1973.

Spencer, Byron G. "Determinants of the Labor Force Participation of Married Women: A Micro-Study of Toronto Households." Canadian Journal of Economics 6 (May 1973): 222-38.

Starr County Migrant Health Project. "Report of the Starr County Migrant Health Project, 1973." Progress Report to the U.S. Department of Health, Education, and Welfare and Texas State Department of Health. Rio Grande City, Tex.: September 1973.

State of Texas v. Starley. 413 S.W. 2d 451.

Steeree, Gilbert. The State of Welfare. Washington, D.C.: The Brookings Institution, 1971.

Stern, James L., Kenneth A. Root, and Stephen M. Hills. "The Influence of Social-Psychological Traits and Job Search Patterns of Workers Affected by a Plant Closure." Industrial and Labor Relations Review 28 (October 1974): 103-21.

Stevens, David W. "Racial Differences in Migration and Job Search: A Case Study—Comment." Southern Economic Journal 33 (1967): 574-76.

Steward, Charles T., and Virginia T. Benson. Linkages between Small Metropolitan Areas and Their Hinterlands, with Implications for Regional Development Policies. Washington, D.C.: George Washington University, May 1973.

Stigler, George. "Information in the Labor Market." Journal of Political Economy (Supplement) 70 (October 1962): 95-105.

Strand, Kenneth, and Thomas Dernberg. "Cyclical Variation in Civilian Labor Force Participation." Review of Economics and Statistics 46 (November 1964): 378-91.

_____. "Hidden Unemployment 1953-62: A Quantitative Analysis by Age and Sex." American Economic Review 56 (March 1966): 71-95.

Struyke, Raymond J. "Explaining Variations in Hourly Wage Rates of Urban Minority Group Females." Journal of Human Resources 8 (Summer 1973): 349-64.

Sullivan, Gene D. "Food Stamps: A Boost to the Southeastern Economy." Monthly Review 58 (June 1973): 86-91.

Sultan, Paul, and Enos Darryl. Farming and Farm Labor: A Study in California. Claremont, Calif.: Center for Urban and Regional Studies, 1974.

Sweet, James A. The Employment of Wives and the Inequality of Family Income, discussion paper. Institute for Research on Poverty, Madison, Wisconsin, 1971.

Texas Employment Commission. "Migrant Crews and Workers by Local Office Area and County of Crew Leader Residence." Mimeographed, 1973.

Texas Good Neighbor Commission. Texas Migrant Labor: Annual Report 1972. Austin: The Commission, 1973.

_____. Texas Migrant Labor: Annual Report 1973. Austin: The Commission, 1974.

Texas Office of Economic Opportunity. *Poverty in Texas*. Austin: The Office, 1971.

Thomas, George. "Regional Migration Patterns and Poverty among the Aged in the South." *Journal of Human Resources* 8 (Winter 1973): 78-79.

Thurow, Lester C. *Poverty and Discrimination*. Washington, D.C.: The Brookings Institution, 1969.

Till, Thomas E. "Changes in Industries Located in the Nonmetropolitan South, 1959-1969." *American Journal of Agricultural Economics* 56 (May 1974): 308.

_____. "Two Models of Nonmetropolitan Industrial Development and of Poverty Impact in the South." *Labor Law Journal* 24 (August 1974): 473.

Turnbull, John G. et al. Economic and Social Security. 4th ed. New York: The Ronald Press, 1973.

U.S. Congress. "Comprehensive Employment and Training Act of 1973," *U.S. Code Congressional and Administrative News*, 93d Cong., 1st sess. St. Paul, Minn.: West, 1973.

_____. *1975 Revised Guide to the Rural Development Act of 1972*, a Committee print, 1975, no. 41-664, 93d Cong., 2nd sess. Washington, D.C.: U.S. Government Printing Office, 1975.

_____. Senate. Committee on Labor and Public Welfare, Subcommittee on Migratory Labor, *Hearings on Migrant and Seasonal Farm Workers' Powerlessness*, pt. 7-B (Washington, D.C.: U.S. Government Printing Office, 1970).

_____. "Social Security Amendments of 1971." *Report of the Committee on Ways and Means on H.R. 1*, 92d Cong., 1st sess. Washington, D.C.: U.S. Government Printing Office, 1971.

_____. House. Committee on Agriculture. *Rural Development Act of 1972—Administration and Expenditures: Hearing*, 94th Cong., 1st sess., 1975.

_____. House. Committee on Education and Labor, General Subcommittee on Education. *Hearings on HR 15066*, 90th Cong., 2d sess., 1968.

BIBLIOGRAPHY   351

_____. Joint Economic Committee, Subcommittee on Fiscal Policy.
"The Effectiveness of Manpower Training Programs: A Review
of the Research on the Impact on the Poor," Paper No. 3,
Studies in Public Welfare. 92d Cong. Washington, D.C.: U.S.
Government Printing Office, 1972.

_____. Senate. Committee on Labor and Public Welfare, Subcommittee on Migratory Labor. The Migratory Farm Labor Problem in the United States. Washington, D.C.: U.S. Government Printing Office, 1969.

_____. "Manpower and Economic Problems." Hearings on Migrant and Seasonal Farmworkers Powerlessness, 91st Cong., 1st and 2d sess., pt. 7-B, 1970, p. 4548.

_____. Testimony of Daniel Sturt, Director of the Rural Manpower Center, Michigan State University: Hearings, 91st Cong., 1st and 2d sess., pt. 7-B, 1970, p. 4550.

U.S. Department of Agriculture, Economic Research Service. Social and Economic Characteristics of the Population in Metro and Nonmetro Counties, 1970, Report no. 72. Washington, D.C.: U.S. Government Printing Office, March 1975.

U.S. Department of Commerce, Bureau of Economic Analysis. Business Conditions Digest, Series ESI, no. 74-6. Washington, D.C.: U.S. Government Printing Office, 1974.

_____. Census of Business, 1967 Louisiana. Washington, D.C.: U.S. Government Printing Office, 1969.

_____. Census of Business, 1967 Mississippi. Washington, D.C.: U.S. Government Printing Office, 1969.

_____. County Business Patterns: Louisiana. Washington, D.C.: U.S. Government Printing Office, 1972.

_____. Georgia County Business Patterns. Washington, D.C.: U.S. Government Printing Office, 1972.

_____. "Money Income in 1973 of Families and Persons in the United States." Current Population Reports, series P-60, no. 97, Tables 57 and 58.

_____. "Money Income in 1973 of Families and Persons in the United States." Current Population Reports, series P-60, no. 98, Tables 57 and 58.

_____. "Persons of Spanish Origin in the United States: March, 1973." Current Population Reports, series P-20, no. 259, January 1974.

_____. "Revision in Poverty Statistics." Current Population Reports, series P-23, no. 28. Washington, D.C.: U.S. Government Printing Office.

_____. United States Census of Agriculture: 1950 Counties and State Economic Areas. Washington, D.C.: U.S. Government Printing Office, 1952.

_____. United States Census of Agriculture: 1959 Counties. Washington, D.C.: U.S. Government Printing Office, 1961.

_____. United States Census of Agriculture: 1969 County Data. Washington, D.C.: U.S. Government Printing Office, 1972.

_____. United States Census of Housing: 1950 General Characteristics. Washington, D.C.: U.S. Government Printing Office.

_____. United States Census of Housing: 1960. Washington, D.C.: U.S. Government Printing Office, 1961.

_____. United States Census of Housing: 1960 States and Small Areas. Washington, D.C.: U.S. Government Printing Office.

_____. United States Census of Housing: 1970 Characteristics for States, Cities, and Counties. Washington, D.C.: U.S. Government Printing Office, 1972.

_____. United States Census of Housing: 1970 General Housing Characteristics. Washington, D.C.: U.S. Government Printing Office.

_____. United States Census of Manufactures 1972. Washington, D.C.: U.S. Government Printing Office.

_____. United States Census of Population: 1950 Characteristics of the Population. Washington, D.C.: U.S. Government Printing Office, 1952.

BIBLIOGRAPHY 353

____. United States Census of Population: 1960 Characteristics of the Population. Washington, D.C.: U.S. Government Printing Office, 1963.

____. United States Census of Population: 1970 Characteristics of the Population. Washington, D.C.: U.S. Government Printing Office, 1972.

____. United States Census of Population: 1950 General Social and Economic Characteristics. Washington, D.C.: U.S. Government Printing Office, 1952.

____. United States Census of Population: 1960 General Social and Economic Characteristics. Washington, D.C.: U.S. Government Printing Office, 1961.

____. United States Census of Population: 1970, General Social and Economic Characteristics. Washington, D.C.: U.S. Government Printing Office, 1972.

____. "Local Area Personal Income." Survey of Current Business, vol. 54, no. 5, pt. 2. Washington, D.C.: U.S. Government Printing Office, 1974.

U.S. Department of Commerce, General Economic Statistics Administration. County Business Patterns—1970 Texas, CBP 70-45. Washington, D.C.: U.S. Government Printing Office, 1972.

____. County Business Patterns—1972 Mississippi, CBP 72-26. Washington, D.C.: U.S. Government Printing Office, 1973

____. County Business Patterns, 1973. Washington, D.C.: U.S. Government Printing Office, 1974.

U.S. Department of Health, Education and Welfare, Recipients of Public Assistance Money Payments by Program, State, and County. Washington, D.C.: U.S. Government Printing Office, 1973 and 1974.

____. Social Security Bulletin 37 (June 1974).

____. Social and Rehabilitation Service. National Center for Social Statistics, 1970, 1971, 1973.

U.S. Department of Labor. <u>Manpower Report of the President, 1968.</u> Washington, D.C.: U.S. Government Printing Office, 1968.

———. <u>Manpower Report of the President, 1972.</u> Washington, D.C.: U.S. Government Printing Office, April 1972.

———. <u>Manpower Report of the President, 1974.</u> Washington, D.C.: U.S. Government Printing Office, 1975.

———. <u>Manpower Report of the President, 1975.</u> Washington, D.C.: U.S. Government Printing Office.

———. "Spanish Speaking Americans: Their Manpower Problems and Opportunities." <u>Manpower Report of the President, 1973.</u> Washington, D.C.: U.S. Government Printing Office, 1973.

———, Bureau of Statistics. <u>Handbook of Labor Statistics, 1974.</u> Washington, D.C.: U.S. Government Printing Office.

———, Manpower Administration. "A Piece of the Action," <u>Manpower</u> vol. 3 (September 1971): 10-13.

———, Office of Employment Service Administration, United States Employment Service. <u>Balanced Placement Formula for Measurement of Employment Service Performance and Allocation of Title III E.S. Funds to States</u>, staff handbooks. Washington, D.C.: U.S. Government Printing Office, 1974.

U.S. Office of Economic Opportunity. <u>Federal Outlays in Texas—1973.</u> Washington, D.C.: U.S. Office of Economic Opportunity, 1974.

Vietorisz, T., R. Mier, and J. Giblin. "Subemployment: Exclusion and Inadequacy Indexes." <u>Monthly Labor Review</u> 96 (May 1973): 3-12.

Wachta, Michael. "A Labor Supply Model for Secondary Workers." <u>Review of Economics and Statistics</u> 54 (May 1972): 141-51.

Wachtel, Howard M., and Charles Betsey. "Employment at Low Wages." <u>Review of Economics and Statistics</u> 54 (May 1972): 121-29.

Waldmen, Elizabeth, and Robert Whitmore. "Children of Working Mothers, March 1973." <u>Special Labor Force Report</u> 165. Washington, D.C.: U.S. Department of Labor, 1974.

Walker, James L. *Economic Growth, Poverty and Race in the Nonmetropolitan South*. Austin: The University of Texas at Austin, 1973.

Webb, James et al. *The Citrus Labor Market of the Lower Rio Grande Valley of Texas: A Study of Labor Utilization Problems*. Austin: Center for the Study of Human Resources, 1975.

White, Rudolph A. "Measuring Unemployment and Subemployment in the Mississippi Delta." *Monthly Labor Review* 92 (April 1969): 21.

Wilcox, Clair. *Toward Social Welfare*. Homewood, Ill.: Richard D. Irwin, 1969.

Works Progress Administration. "Source material for Mississippi History."

ABOUT THE AUTHORS

JOHN F. ADAMS is Professor of Insurance and Director of the Center for Insurance Research, the Georgia State University College of Business Administration. Formerly the Executive Director of the Pennsylvania Bureau of Employment Security and Assistant Vice President for Research at Temple University in Philadelphia, his publications include unemployment insurance studies for several states, the Mid-Atlantic Region Older Worker Study, and experience rating and labor market studies for Pennsylvania. He has served as a consultant to the United States Departments of Labor, Defense, and Health, Education and Welfare, a number of state agencies and Canadian provincial governments, mainly in social insurance program procedures and costs development.

VERNON M. BRIGGS, Jr. is Professor of Economics at the University of Texas at Austin where he has taught since 1964. He holds M.A. and Ph.D. degrees from Michigan State University and a B.S. degree from the University of Maryland. He is the author or co-author of The Negro and Apprenticeship (Baltimore: Johns Hopkins Press, 1967); Chicanos and Rural Poverty (Baltimore: Johns Hopkins Press, 1973); and The Chicano Worker (Austin: The University of Texas Press, 1977). In addition he has authored articles on collective bargaining, apprenticeship training, manpower policy, public service employment, equal employment opportunity policy and immigration policy.

BRIAN RUNGELING is Associate Professor of Economics and Director of the Center for Manpower Studies at the University of Mississippi. He received his Ph.D. from the University of Kentucky. A recent book is entitled The Role of Unions in the American Economy (with Ray Marshall). He has presented papers at a number of professional meetings as well as having published articles in the American Journal of Agricultural Economics, Journal of Business, Growth and Change and the Monthly Labor Review. Dr. Rungeling is continuing his research on rural labor markets, welfare reform and unions.

LEWIS H. SMITH is Associate Professor of Economics at the University of Mississippi. In addition to presenting papers at numerous professional meetings, he is the author of several articles dealing with various aspects of labor force behavior which have appeared in Industrial Relations, American Journal of Agricultural Economics, Monthly Labor Review and Growth and Change. Dr. Smith holds a Ph.D. in Economics from the University of Tennessee.

RELATED TITLES
Published by
Praeger Special Studies

*COMMUNITY AND REGIONAL PLANNING: Issues
in Public Policy, Third Edition
      Melvin R. Levin

COMPREHENSIVE SERVICES TO RURAL POOR
FAMILIES: An Evaluation of the Arizona Job
Colleges Program
      Keith Baker, Myfanway Glasso,
      Don Goyette, C. Freemont Sprague

INCOME INEQUALITY IN THE UNITED STATES:
Public Attitudes Towards Distributional Justice
      Richard T. Curtin

INDUSTRIAL INVASION OF NONMETROPOLITAN
AMERICA: A Quarter Century of Experience
      Gene F. Summers, Sharon D. Evans,
      Frank Clemente, E. M. Beck,
      Jon Minkoff

THE LABOR SUPPLY FOR LOWER-LEVEL
OCCUPATIONS
      Harold Wool, assisted by
      Bruce Dana Phillips

POLITICIZING THE POOR: The Legacy of the War
on Poverty in a Mexican-American Community
      Biliana C. S. Ambrecht

QUALITY OF LIFE INDICATORS IN U.S. METROPOLITAN
AREAS: A Statistical Analysis
      Ben Chieh Liu

SOUTHERN NEWCOMERS TO NORTHERN CITIES:
Work and Social Adjustment in Cleveland
      Gene B. Petersen, Laure M. Sharp,
      Thomas F. Drury

*Also available in paperback as a PSS Student Edition.

LIBRARY OF DAVIDSON COLLEGE

Books on regular loan may be checked out for **two weeks**. Books must be presented at the Circulation Desk in order to be renewed.

A fine is charged after date due.

Special books are subject to special regulations at the discretion of library staff.

SEP 20 1978
FEB. 13 1979
FEB -8 1984

JAN 1 3 1993